# Plagiarism and Originality

Books by Alexander Lindey
with Morris L. Ernst

HOLD YOUR TONGUE
THE CENSOR MARCHES ON

Legal Books by Alexander Lindey

SEPARATION AGREEMENTS

MOTION PICTURE AGREEMENTS ANNOTATED

# Plagiarism
# and
# Originality

by

ALEXANDER LINDEY

Harper & Brothers Publishers
New York

TO ELLA

# Contents

# Foreword

PLAGIARISM enters into our daily lives more than we realize. It impinges on the things we say and do, the books and magazines we read, the plays and movies we go to, the works of art we see, the radio and television shows that flow into our homes.

The literature of plagiarism is considerable. Some idea of its extent may be gained from the partial bibliography I've appended. Most of the studies are specialized; some are excellent; a good many represent the findings of parallel-sleuths "keen to pursue to its authentic lair the last clue to a problem of authorship." None of them, as far as I know, presumes to view plagiarism in the round. This book is an attempt to treat the subject as an organic whole: to examine its various aspects, historical, aesthetic, psychological, ethical, social, legal and practical; to interpret and correlate these aspects; to trace the growth of property rights in the articulation of ideas from antiquity to the present; to make clear the distinction between borrowing and theft in the various media of expression, books and magazines, plays and motion pictures, art and music; and to survey the rôle that plagiarism plays in the current scene.

I've tried to do all this in a manner readily comprehensible to the lay reader. Since any discussion of plagiarism is, from a realistic standpoint, meaningless without reference to the legal consequences, I've devoted quite a bit of space to court cases. My purpose has been not to convert laymen into amateur lawyers, but to make them—if they ever imagine themselves victims of piracy or if they're accused of the offense—knowledgeable and tractable clients.

Conscious of the magnitude of the task, I've aimed at achieving a general picture rather than an all-inclusive one. I haven't set down all the historical facts; they'd fill a library. I haven't collected all the anecdotes; they run into the hundreds. I haven't told the story of all the court cases; they'd furnish a record of staggering dimensions and even more staggering repetitiousness. I've concentrated on the representative, the provocative, the significant. I doubt that a truly definitive appraisal of plagiarism will ever be made. Man is a protean creature, and nowhere is this more strikingly apparent than in the incredible diversity of his handiwork. In estimates of art, as in views on life, there's no finality; there can be no final conclusions with respect to plagiarism.

By the same token, the man who seeks a mechanical definition of infringement, who wants to know precisely how many lines of a copyrighted story or how many musical notes of a copyrighted song he may use without violating the law, is pursuing a will-o'-the-wisp. Plagiarism is not reducible to a science. The most lucid exposition of all the applicable legal rules will not answer every question. The rules themselves are in a state of flux and development; they are meaningful only when applied to the facts of a particular case, and no two cases are alike. But a grasp of the principles will enable us, in a given instance, to make an intelligent guess as to the outcome if the matter goes to litigation.

It will be noted that I've let men of letters and judges speak for themselves a good deal in the text. Writers have long pondered such topics as influence, tradition and literary theft; and where they've expressed themselves incisively on these matters, I've seen no reason to paraphrase them. As for the judges, they are the ultimate arbiters of infringement; in a real sense their accumulated opinions make up the law. Their utterances being, so to speak, revelation at the source, we must heed them even if at times they fall short of ideal illumination.

No man writes in a void drained of all personal conviction. I doubt that even the Olympians were Olympians in this respect. My objective has been to render a reasonably detached and balanced account of a complex subject, and yet to escape the blight of anemic neutrality. Having dealt with a great many plagiarism problems in the course of twenty-five years of active practice, I have naturally developed certain prepossessions. The reader will have no trouble in spotting them, nor in judging whether they are justified.

On the score of documentation I've borne in mind Professor Rodell's derisive dictum that every legal writer is supposed to be a liar until he proves himself otherwise with a flock of footnotes. All references, non-legal as well as legal, will be found at the back of the book, arranged chapter by chapter. The non-legal ones are linked to numbers in the text. The legal ones are not; their sequence parallels the order of discussion in the text. As to the former, I haven't felt it necessary or appropriate to document each fact or quotation; in the main I've limited the sources cited to those likely to prove rewarding to the reader for purposes of further investigation. As to the latter, I've been heedful of the fact that this is not a legal treatise. However, while the annotations do not include every single plagiarism case that was ever decided, they contain all the important ones, and attorneys will, I think, find them of substantial help.

I have not hesitated to draw freely on the literature of plagiarism. For anecdotes of recent years I'm indebted to Leonard Lyons, Sidney Skolsky, Walter Winchell, Earl Wilson and Bennett Cerf; for helpful data, to John Crosby, Lewis Gannett, John K. Hutchens and Orville Prescott. My thanks are also due to my good friend Barrett H. Clark for making available to me his personal files on the *Strange Interlude* case and the *Death Takes a Holiday* case; to George Brett, head of Macmillan's, for information regarding the *Gone with the Wind* case; and to William Brody for help with the galleys.

I cannot adequately express my indebtedness to my wife Ella Lindey for assistance in every stage of the preparation of this book. She did the factual research, contributed ideas, made many valuable suggestions, checked references, prepared the index and bibliography, corrected proof—all with skill and patience, enthusiasm and devotion. I salute her with gratitude and love.

The study of derivation and plagiarism is not an esoteric, dry-as-dust exercise for scholars and attorneys. It is an adventure full of color and excitement and drama. I hope I've succeeded in conveying this in the pages that follow.

ALEXANDER LINDEY

*New York, New York*
*October, 1951*

# Plagiarism and Originality

# 1

## Charting the Maze

Ideas, it has always been admitted, are free as air. If you happen to have
any, you fling them into the common stock, and ought to be well content
to see your poorer brethren thriving upon them.

—Augustine Birrell: Copyright in Books

---

DOROTHY PARKER has been the subject of two full-length
plays, *Here Today* by George Oppenheimer and *Over Twenty-
One* by Ruth Gordon. "If I ever wrote a play about myself," she has
said, "I suppose I'd be sued for plagiarism."

A pair of song writers undertook a particularly onerous assignment:
they had to turn out three new songs a week. "This job," a friend
told them, "will take a lot out of you." They shrugged their shoulders.
"That's so," they said, "but it'll take more out of Bach, Beethoven
and Brahms."

Frank Harris, who was never too scrupulous about his literary
borrowings, once recounted a story to a group which included Oscar
Wilde. He told it as though it were his own. Wilde recognized it as
having been lifted from Anatole France. "You know, Frank," he said
blandly, "Anatole France would have spoiled that story."

At the close of a preview in Hollywood, a friend said to the
author of the screenplay: "It's terrific. But isn't it a bit reminiscent?"
"Yes," replied the author, "it's reminiscent of the next picture you're
going to write."

"If our enemies commit a coincidence," says one commentator,
"it is plagiarism; when our friends pilfer, it is adaptation, version,

1

study in style, or some other euphemism." Another says: "If we steal thoughts from the moderns, it will be cried down as plagiarism; if from the ancients, it will be cried up as erudition." Still another: "Copying one book is plagiarism; copying several is research."

Behind stories and aphorisms like these lies the realm of plagiarism. It is a region vast and baffling, its landscape kaleidoscopic, its roadways labyrinthine, its soil rich in anecdote, its valleys full of echoes. In the market places of its towns one hears many outland tongues, and one sees wares from all points of the earth. It is a place of ancient origin. Its history is the history of man's striving for expression.

Many persons—critics, essayists, lawyers, scholars, parallel-hunters —have explored this realm, and have rendered accounts of what they've found. It is impossible to understand and evaluate these accounts or to make fresh explorations without a knowledge of the fundamental principles involved. Some of these principles are technical. I'll discuss them as briefly as possible.

## What Is Plagiarism?

Plagiarism is literary—or artistic or musical—theft. It is the false assumption of authorship: the wrongful act of taking the product of another person's mind, and presenting it as one's own. Copying someone else's story or play or song, intact or with inconsequential changes, and adding one's name to the result constitute a simple illustration of plagiarism.

Copyright infringement is the copying of all or a material or substantial part of copyrighted and copyrightable matter.

Plagiarism and infringement are not the same thing, though they overlap. Plagiarism covers a wider field; infringement involves more serious consequences. For purposes of plagiarism, the material stolen need not be in copyright; for infringement, it must be. There can be no plagiarism without the thief's posing as originator; infringement may occur even though proper authorship credit is given. The essence of the wrong in either case is the appropriation of the fruits of another person's mental labor and skill.

The vast bulk of our cultural heritage lies outside the bounds of copyright. Countless books, plays, pictures, statues and songs are in the public domain because they were never copyrighted or because their copyrights have expired. The copyright law does not prevent the publication of Catullus's poems or the public performance of a Beethoven symphony, any more than it stands in the way of presenting *Macbeth* on the stage or making reproductions of a Brueghel painting for profit, without license or royalty. Whatever is in the public domain is common property, free for anyone to avail himself of. But if matter in copyright is used without permission, the user commits infringement. And if someone were to take Elizabeth Barrett Browning's sonnets, affix his name and sell them, he would be heading for trouble too. The copyright law wouldn't stand in his way, but the law of fraud would.

The distinction between a pirate and a plagiarist is that a pirate makes no attempt to falsify authorship, while the plagiarist compounds the offense by posing as the originator.

Aretino, the Italian poet, dramatist and adventurer, discovered a manuscript chronicle of the Goths written in Greek by Procopius, the Byzantine historian. Believing it to be the only copy extant, he translated it, published it over his signature, and destroyed the original. It was only in 1444 when a second manuscript of Procopius was found that the theft came to light. Before James Joyce's *Ulysses* was judicially cleared of the charge of obscenity, a magazine publisher printed, without Joyce's permission but under Joyce's name, sizeable portions of the book in his periodical. Aretino was a plagiarist. The publisher was a pirate.

The terms "literary theft," "literary larceny" and "literary piracy" recur constantly in discussions of plagiarism. They have no precise legal signification. Sometimes they are applied to denote an act—any act—of plagiarism or infringement, regardless of wrongful intent; at others, an act of willful and deliberate stealing, as distinguished from unconscious taking; at others still, the publication and sale of a copyrighted literary work under the original author's name, but without his permission. Yet these terms have become so firmly imbedded in texts and court decisions—perhaps because it is more picturesque to speak of a pirate than of an infringer—that we shall meet them at every turn.

### What Copyright Protects

If a man writes an account of the methods of taxidermy used by the head-hunting Jivaros or of the amatory habits of the Piltdown man or of the symbolic significance of the hieratic winged bulls in ancient Assyrian art, he does not—even if he is a pioneer in the field —acquire the sole and exclusive right to deal with those subjects. By the same token, if a dramatist builds a play on the theme of the silver cord, if a painter depicts St. Anthony tormented by fiends, if a photographer takes a picture of jungle-choked Angkor-Vat, if a sculptor captures in marble the epic contest between Antaeus and Hercules, they do not, like so many gold prospectors, stake out claims on which none may trespass. And it makes no difference whether or not they copyright their handiwork. For the copyright law does not protect ideas, themes, subject matter as such, only the creator's particular treatment of them—his own "original" version. If it were possible for an author, by virtue of mere priority, to gain a monopoly—even a monopoly measured in years—over a theme, all creative effort would be disastrously impeded. Nor does the law safeguard words in the dictionary, isolated sounds or colors or elementary shapes, though an individual combination and arrangement of any of these is protectible.

For a copyright is not like a patent. The man who first invents a device and patents it gets the exclusive right to make, use and sell it for a number of years. If someone else independently stumbles on the same discovery, that someone is out of luck. He can't exploit it. The field has been pre-empted.

Not so with copyright. The same idea may serve innumerable masters. Each version is entitled to copyright as long as it is the result of the author's own craftsmanship, effort and judgment. Priority erects no KEEP OFF sign. No copyright owner can complain of a later work dealing with the same subject—even though it is very much like his own—unless he can show that it was *copied* from his.

But it would be idle to believe that once we've said that copyright protects the *form*, not the theme, of a creative product, we've solved the problem of diagnosing infringement. For it is not always a simple matter to distinguish between an idea and the form in which it is cast. More than any other class of cases, Justice Story remarked a century ago, copyrights approach "what may be called the metaphysics of the law, where distinctions are, or at least may be, very subtle and refined, and sometimes almost evanescent."

News, facts, historical or scientific data; material which was originally dedicated to the public; material on which the copyright has expired; material which is obscene, seditious or fraudulent—all these cannot be secured by copyright, even though the statutory requirements are complied with. You can't lift a ballad from the public domain and get a copyright on it that will stand up. The Copyright Office may, in the ordinary course, issue a registration certificate to you; but if someone else decides to take the ballad and sell copies of it or perform it in public for profit and you sue him for infringement, you will lose if he proves in court the source of your composition.

However, where you select existing materials from sources open to everybody, and arrange and combine them in a new form, exercising study and discrimination in the process, and producing something new, you will be entitled to copyright protection on what you've created. You won't be able to prevent others from seeking out the same sources that you did. A fresh and different use of those sources will not be an infringement; indeed, an independent new work will be as fully copyrightable as yours. There is one essential rule, though, that your followers will have to observe in order to preserve their immunity. They'll have to go to the original sources. If they take a short cut via your book, they'll infringe; and it won't do them any good to argue that *if* they had done the necessary spadework, the results would have been the same.

### Titles

Copyright covers only the *contents* of a copyrighted book or picture or song, not its name. In a proper situation a name will be protected under the theory of unfair competition.

In applying this doctrine, the courts seek to achieve three things: to secure to the honest creator that which fairly belongs to him; to prevent the dishonest opportunist from cashing in on the creator's popularity; and to shield the public from deception.

The doctrine comes into play when a name has acquired a "secondary significance." This occurs when a word or a phrase has become so closely associated with, say, a story that whenever the title is mentioned, the man-in-the-street will be led to assume it refers to the particular story. Before the triumph of Rodgers and Hammerstein's musical version of *Liliom*, the term "carrousel" was a generic one denoting a merry-go-round. After the production of the show, the term acquired a secondary meaning. Had anyone attempted, from then on, to appropriate *Carrousel* as the title for a play or a movie, he could and doubtless would have been enjoined.

Whether a name has became sufficiently linked with a work to warrant the law's intervention in its behalf, is a question of fact, depending in the main on the prosperity the work has enjoyed. Smith writes a historical romance; it sells twenty thousand copies, and is still going strong. If the movies try to filch the name, Smith can stop it. But let's assume Jones penned a drama twenty years ago; it was produced on Broadway and folded after three days; it has been dead and forgotten since. If a film now appears bearing the same title, Jones will be hard put to it to show that he'll be injured, or the public misled.

## Infringement

It is significant that the Copyright Act contains no definition of infringement. The definition must be extracted from precedents; that is to say, the opinions of judges in past cases. The general judicial definition is the one I've already given: infringement consists of the copying of all or a material or substantial part of a copyrighted and copyrightable work. Thus every charge of infringement raises five basic questions:

1. Is there any similarity between the earlier work and the later one?
2. Is the similarity (assuming it exists) the result of copying?
3. Has a material or substantial part of the original been copied?
4. Was the original duly copyrighted?
5. Was the portion which has been appropriated copyrightable?

If any one of these questions is answered in the negative, the claim falls.

Similarity—even close similarity—is not enough. To constitute infringement (and plagiarism), there must be copying, willful or unintentional, made possible by access.[1] The simplest and most flagrant example of copying is literal reproduction of a copyrighted work without the owner's consent. But copying "by evasion" is infringement too. The borrower cannot escape liability by resorting to paraphrasing, superficial changes or additions or omissions. It was said in a famous case that "a copy is that which comes so near to the original as to give every person seeing it the idea created by the original." The trouble is—as Judge Learned Hand indicated in the plagiarism battle over *Abie's Irish Rose*—that the moment we proceed from a case of word-for-word appropriation to one of theft by approximation, the legal inquiry is beset with difficulties; and prior court decisions, no matter how lucidly they enunciate the law, cannot help much in a new case. (In the chapters that follow, we shall frequently meet Judge Learned Hand. Recently retired from the Federal appeals bench after long and brilliant service, he is generally considered the most distinguished living jurist in the United States. The opinions in many important plagiarism cases have come from his pen. He has been chiefly responsible for expounding and crystallizing the law pertaining to literary theft during the last few decades.)

Copying must, of course, be proved. Direct evidence is rare. Just as in a divorce case the erring spouse is scarcely likely to invite friends in to witness the adultery, so when a man turns to literary larceny, he is careful not to get caught *in flagrante delicto*. The plundered author is thus compelled to rely on circumstantial evidence, i.e., access and similarity. The purpose of access is to show that the defendant had an opportunity to copy. The purpose of similarity is to show that he did not waste the opportunity. The two together may raise an inference of copying. The impact of the inference will depend on the strength of the proof. Where there is strong evidence of access, less proof of similarity will suffice. Conversely, where the evidence of access is weak, strong proof of similarity will be required.

But copying, in and of itself, is not enough. There must be *illicit* copying: the taking of a substantial or material part. The words "substantial" and "material" are not synonymous. One has to do with quantity, the other with quality. It is infringement to copy the major portion of a copyrighted work. It is also infringement to extract the essence of it, even though the essence, when measured quantitatively, does not bulk large. If what the borrower has appropriated sensibly diminishes the value of the original, he is liable.

In any event, the similarities must be the kind which the ordinary reader or observer will recognize, not the kind that necessitates dissection, elaborate explication or tortuous argument.

Wrongful intent is not essential to infringement. Here literary larceny differs from other kinds of theft. If you absent-mindedly take another man's overcoat in a restaurant, thinking it your own, you don't commit a crime. But if you hear a copyrighted melody and it becomes buried in your memory and you later set it down as your original composition in good faith, the law will not spare you. Unconscious plagiarism is infringement, and honesty of motive is no defense, either for the author or his publisher.[2]

Standing by themselves, definitions and rules are colorless, inert things. It is only when they are applied to concrete situations that they gain cogency and meaning. In Chapters 9 to 15 inclusive, we shall see how the principles outlined in this chapter actually operate in court cases involving fiction and non-fiction, the stage, the screen, art, music, radio and television.

## The Media of Infringement

As a rule, we think of infringement in connection with books, songs, plays and movies. Actually, it may involve any medium of expression recognized by the Copyright Act, including works of art, lectures, photographs and the like. And while the two works—the original and the wrongful copy—may both be in the same medium, they need not be.

It is infringement, of course, to incorporate in a new novel, without permission, substantial portions of a previous novel written and copyrighted by someone else. The public may buy the new for the old, to the earlier author's loss. Moreover, since under the Copyright Act the earlier author owns not only the book rights in his novel but also the right to dramatize it, it is infringement as well to transplant his novel into a play or a movie without license from him. Here the damage is presumed to be twofold: the original author may find it impossible to sell his dramatic and movie rights, and his book sales may suffer. By the same token, one can't steal a play or a movie and make it over into a novel.

There are other things that may not be done without authorization, such as expanding someone else's short story into a book; squeezing someone else's novel into a short story; merchandizing a doll or a toy based on someone else's animated-cartoon character; selling copies of the lyrics of someone else's song or photographs of someone else's work of art.

In all the examples above given we have assumed that the original is copyrighted *and* copyrightable. If a part of it is not copyrightable—as where it includes matter in the public domain—the protection extends only to the copyrightable portion. The copyright owner has no legal grievance if unprotected material is taken.

There is a point, however, where the legality of the process of transplantation from one medium into another becomes an intriguing puzzle. Botticelli based his "Primavera" and "Birth of Venus" on Poliziano's famous panegyric *Stanze*. Fielding used several figures from Hogarth's prints as models for characters in *Joseph Andrews* and *Tom Jones*. What if a character or a scene in a copyrighted book catches the fancy of an artist and he proceeds to give it graphic form in a painting? What if a writer describes a copyrighted picture in great detail in prose or poetry? Any infringement? Hardly. The likelihood of competition between the two media is too remote. As one judge has said, the historian who describes the charge of the cuirassiers at Friedland will scarcely expect to be sued by the owner of the copyright covering Meissonier's painting "1807." And so the presentation of a copyrighted picture as a *tableau vivant* has been legally condoned.

### The Price of Plunder

The consequences of the infringer's act may be serious. He may be enjoined, and he may have to pay damages and disgorge his profits. He may have to surrender the infringing material, to be impounded while the litigation is pending. If the case goes against him, he may be required to deliver up for destruction all plates and other means for making infringing copies.

"Infringer" includes not only the pirate or plagiarist but anyone else who, innocently or otherwise, collaborates with him in the manufacture and sale of the infringing material. In the case of a purloined magazine story, the publisher of the magazine is liable; in the case of a play, the producer; in the case of a movie, the movie company.

The remedies above indicated are civil ones. The Copyright Act prescribes criminal penalties as well, although these are not frequently resorted to. Willful plagiarism for profit is a misdemeanor punishable by imprisonment for not more than a year or a fine of not less than a hundred dollars nor more than one thousand dollars, or both.

## Fair Use

The monopoly of the copyright owner is not absolute. The fact that a work is covered by copyright does not mean that it may not be touched at all by others. A limited use of it is permitted without the owner's permission. This is known as "fair use."

To define fair use—as is often done—as the appropriation of less than a substantial or material part of a copyrighted composition, is to beg the question. Nor is it any more illuminating to say that fair use is a use which does not "sensibly" diminish the value of the original. The plain fact is that fair use can no more be precisely defined than plagiarism itself.

If I may offer a word of my own, as abstract as the foregoing but perhaps more meaningful in the social sense, fair use is the palliative that takes the curse off the monopoly aspect of copyright. "The sole interest of the United States," the Supreme Court has said, "and the primary object in conferring the monopoly lie in the general benefits derived by the public from the labors of authors." The purpose of copyright is to promote science and the useful arts; but it's obvious enough that unless the findings of science and the fruits of creative expression are permitted to circulate widely, the purpose is not achieved. It's clear, too, that unhampered dissemination on the one hand and monopoly on the other are antithetical. Fair use is a compromise between the two.[3]

The principles of fair use come into play in numerous and varied contexts. The chief among these are cases

(a)  Where, in the course of research, copyrighted source material is lifted and put into a new work, usually without credit;

(b)  Where copyrighted material is summarized for news purposes;

(c)  Where such material is subjected to critical scrutiny, and the critic either quotes or paraphrases extensively;

(d)  Where such material is lampooned, or its rendition mimicked;

(e)  Where the words of a copyrighted song are quoted in fiction or non-fiction to fix the period or set the mood and atmosphere.

Categories (b) and (c) rarely give rise to trouble; in any event, they involve no question of plagiarism. On the other hand, if fair use is exceeded in category (a), plagiarism results, and infringement as well if the original is in copyright. The risk of infringement inheres in categories (d) and (e) too.

It is difficult indeed to say just where and how the line can be drawn between fair use, which the law sanctions, and unfair use, which the law prohibits. The legal test is whether the amount of the borrowing is such as will materially reduce the demand for the original. If that happens, fair use is exceeded. The courts have laid down certain criteria for determining the probability of competitive damage. The criteria include the scope and purpose of the two works; the quantity borrowed in relation to the total of the original; the quantity borrowed in relation to the total of the borrower's work; the extent to which the borrower may be presumed to have consulted independent sources; the nature and value of the material taken; the intent of the taker; and the effect of the taking.

Obviously, the likelihood of competition is less where the two works are different in kind and make bids for different markets. A novelist may make more generous use of a book of history than a historian. A piece of fiction is not likely to supplant a historical study; another such study may. It's no piracy for the compiler of a cookbook to cull recipes from biographies or histories or travel accounts.

Criticism enjoys the widest latitude. When a critic discusses a novel —whether he does so in a newspaper review or a full-scale critical study—the intent is obviously not to have the appraisal supplant the book. No matter how fully the critic summarizes it, no matter how lavishly he quotes from it, there can be neither plagiarism (there is no false assumption of authorship) nor infringement. Humorous appraisal is no less privileged in this respect than serious comment. Nor does fair use become unfair merely because the criticism is harsh and the reader may be dissuaded from buying the thing criticized.

Unfair use is not made fair by the fact that the borrower acknowledges his source. While giving authorship credit to the originator eliminates plagiarism, it doesn't dispose of infringement. If you poach on private property, you can't purge yourself of trespass by tipping your hat to the property owner.

There are two flagrant misconceptions about fair use which should have been exploded long ago, but which persist with a tenacity that defies comprehension.

One is that there is a specific quantitative rule—twenty lines or two hundred words in literature, six bars in music—as to permissible borrowing. *There is no such rule.* Infringement is not a matter of so-and-so-many inches or so-and-so-many musical notes. A dozen paragraphs taken from a long book may be fair use; four lines from a six-line poem may be an infringement. The question is whether or not the borrower has unreasonably taken advantage of the creative effort of his predecessor.

The other wrongheaded notion is that none of the lyrics of a copyrighted popular song may be quoted in fiction or non-fiction without authorization, even though the mention may be casual and incidental. Thus there has grown up the obnoxious practice of requesting consents from copyright owners and cluttering up texts with copyright streamers and absurd by-permission-of salaams. *There is no legal warrant for all this.* I shall deal with the situation at some length in Chapter 9.

Since the privilege of fair use is in effect part of the consideration which society exacts from a creator for giving him a statutory monopoly, and since common law copyright exists independently of statute, it follows that no such privilege exists with respect to material in common law copyright.

## Most of Us

When "How to Guess Your Age," Corey Ford's wry commentary on applied geriatrics, appeared in *Collier's*, it struck a responsive chord in a multitude of no-longer-young hearts. Thousands of readers transcribed it and conveyed it to their friends, omitting Ford's name and thus implying that the gem was of their own creation.

In a non-legal sense, most of us plagiarize at one time or another. As young children we parrot the phrases of adults and are embraced for our precocity. We imitate our playmates in speech and behavior. In school we sometimes copy one another's homework. In college some of us make too-liberal use of reference texts in preparing our term papers, and a few of us are not above cribbing at examinations. Grown up, we glean political views from newspaper editorials and radio commentators, and put them blandly forward as our own. We utter vintage bon mots with an air of spontaneous invention. We repeat stock anecdotes as personal experiences. And those of us who have a touch of malice save up all the jibes we hear, and unleash them with a show of improvisation when the occasion arises.

Appropriations of this kind are, for the most part, innocuous enough. The point worth noting is that here, as in other areas of human conduct, the legal wrong—plagiarism—is a distant cousin, not a complete stranger, to a phase of our everyday behavior.

## 2

# Concerning Originality

So few are our originals, that if all other books were burnt, the lettered world would resemble some metropolis in flames, where a few incombustible buildings—a fortress, a temple, a tower—lift their heads in melancholy grandeur, amid the mighty ruin.

—Edward Young: Conjectures on Original Composition

THREE things should be said at the outset. First, there is no such thing as absolute, quintessential originality. Second, plagiarism and originality are not polar opposites, but the obverse and reverse of the same medal. Third, originality—as commonly understood— is not necessarily the hallmark of talent or the badge of genius.

### The Old and the New

There are few platitudes as trite as the one about there being nothing new under the sun. There are few as comprehensively true.

The present is the living sum total of all our yesterdays. In literature, art, music and architecture, as in customs, philosophy, law, religion and science, we unceasingly reiterate the past. Our most daring innovations, when closely scrutinized, turn out to be no more than variations on old themes. The debt to the past is incalculably great; no one escapes it. "The originals," says Emerson, "are not original. There is imitation, model and suggestion, to the very archangels, if we knew their history. The first book tyrannizes over the second. Read Tasso, and you think of Virgil; read Virgil, and you think of Homer; and Milton forces you to reflect how narrow are

14

the limits of human invention. *Paradise Lost* has never existed but for its precursors; and if we find in India or Arabia a book out of our horizon of thought and tradition, we are soon taught by new researches in its native country to discover its foregoers and its latent but real connection with our Bibles."[1]

When we salute Plato, we honor quotations from Solon, Sophron and Philolaus. Plato in turn has enriched the utterances of a host of latter-day philosophers. Many of the ideas and images in the *Divine Comedy* seem apocalyptic when first encountered; they appear less so when traced back to Boethius and Cassiodorus and Aquinas. La Bruyère is often credited with having blazed a trail with his *Les Caractères*; actually his literary portraits stem from Theophrastus' epigrammatic pieces. Pluck from Ben Jonson the plumes of Horace, Lucan, Petronius and Seneca, and you have a strangely altered bird. James Joyce's *Finnegan's Wake* has been hailed as an unparalleled attempt to expand the frontiers of language; yet as far back as the sixth century there were scholars in England and Ireland who played ducks and drakes with words, composing texts in a grotesque style, engrafting on their own tongue abstruse and bizarre phrases from abroad.

The Parthenon dominates many of our public buildings, as does the Colosseum our sport stadia, and the cathedrals of the Age of Faith our churches.

"The revolutionary's Utopia," says Arthur Koestler, "which in appearance represents a complete break with the past, is always modeled on some image of the lost Paradise, of a legendary Golden Age. . . . All Utopias are fed from the sources of mythology; the social engineer's blueprints are merely revised editions of the ancient text."

Modern European legal systems rest on the Code of Justinian. Our own Bill of Rights goes back to the Magna Carta. We think of vigilantes in connection with frontier justice; they originated in the Middle Ages.

Scientific ventilation is generally regarded as a twentieth-century development; recent discoveries indicate that the Pyramids of Egypt were expertly ventilated. There is evidence to show that the spinning machine, introduced in Europe five hundred years ago, had been invented two millennia before. Pliny the Elder says Nero had a ring with a gem in it. He looked through the gem as he watched the sword-play of the gladiators, and saw the scene more clearly than with the naked eye. Mauritius the Italian stood on the crest of his island and scanned the sea all the way to Africa with his nauscopite. So Nero had an opera glass, and Mauritius a telescope.[2]

Ancient Heraclitus speaks across the ages to Darwin, Hippias of Keos to John Stuart Mill, Empedocles to Freud, Lucretius and Democritus of Abdera to the modern atomic physicist. Freud himself has said that when a "new" idea is propounded in science, objective research usually soon proves that the discovery was made some time before and suffered obscurity.

Sainte-Beuve declares that everything has been said: there have been men—and thinking men—on the earth for more than seven thousand years. "One does but glean after the ancients," he insists. The ironic fact is that the ancients themselves repeatedly voice the same sentiment. Horace laments the fact that a poet is hard put to it to find an original theme. "Cursed be those," cries Donatus, "who said our things before us."

One of George Meredith's characters, echoing the perennial plaint, longs for those "youthful days of intellectual coxcombry, when ideas come to us affecting the embraces of virgins and swear to us they are ours alone and no one else have they ever visited: and we believe them."

All this mourning about the exhaustion of ideas is, of course, non-sense. However old general notions may be, new people are constantly coming into the world, and each generation, each epoch, looks about with different eyes, and speaks its heart and mind with fresh accents. The final word has not been uttered on anything, nor ever will be so long as mortals continue to walk the earth.

## Toward a Definition

Originality is an involved and baffling subject. We can, in small compass, do no more than briefly touch upon its chameleon attributes, its contradictions, and its mysteries.

The principal difficulty is that originality is bound up with the process of creativity, which is an arcanum in itself. Too, the very word has a number of different meanings; and people who use it don't as a rule bother to specify the particular sense they have in mind—if indeed they know.

The dictionary ascribes five meanings to the adjective "original": (1) Pertaining to the origin or beginning; initial; primal; first in order; (2) pertaining to or characteristic of the first or earliest stage of anything; primitive; pristine; (3) having the power to initiate or suggest new thoughts or combinations of thought; creative; (4) produced directly by an artist; not copied, imitated, translated or transcribed; and (5) fresh, novel, new, striking; never before thought of or used.

It will be seen from this that the term is sometimes used to denote a faculty that resides in the creative artist, and sometimes to describe a quality inherent in his work. The two don't, of course, necessarily go together. An original talent may falter and generate something unoriginal, and an unoriginal hack may, in a rare lucky moment, turn out something original.

The situation is further complicated by the fact that the layman takes one view of originality, aesthetics takes another, and the law a third.

### The Lay Concept

To the average individual, originality is apt to signify a talent for the fabrication of the novel, the strange and the extravagant. Since that which seems at first sight unprecedented may well turn out to be a copy of some obscure and ancient model, the lay concept is vulnerable on its own terms. Yet all too frequently does the prestidigitator, the charlatan, the seven days' wonder, win public accolade for originality.

Actually, originality resembles a one-way chemical equation: something original may be ingenious and startling, but something ingenious and startling may not be original in the true sense. Genuine originality extends beyond novelty, beyond the ability to conjure up the extraordinary theme, the unexpected plot, the singular character, the unfamiliar situation. It transcends eccentricity of style. Imagination is compounded of numerous ingredients. Inventiveness is only one of them, and by no means indispensable; its importance dwindles when the other—and more needful—components are present in full measure.

There have always been trail blazers in the arts. They strike out into the unknown, open up continents. Yet they are rarely the builders, the world-shakers. They seem to exhaust themselves in pioneering; they usually fail to exploit to the full the possibilities of what they discover. It is their followers who seize upon the gains, consolidate them, and reach the peaks of achievement. Men of the first rank, in turn, refuse to squander their energies in mere invention. Taking their plots, their images, their melodies where they find them, they concentrate the full force of their genius on intensifying and reinterpreting them, and giving them personal expression.

Donne was a greater innovator than Shakespeare, but a lesser poet. Picasso once said that pupils see farther than their masters. "In art," wrote Shaw, "the highest success is to be the last of your race, not the first. Anybody, almost, can make a beginning: the difficulty is to make an end—to do what cannot be bettered."[3]

## The Artist Defines

If the layman has failed to grasp the essence of originality, those better informed than he have evinced scant disposition to set him straight. For while men of letters have been intrigued by the subject since the earliest days, their pronouncements on it have been anything but precise.

To Voltaire, originality is nothing but judicious imitation; to Lamb, "that individualizing property which should keep the subject distinct in feature from every other subject, however similar, and to common apprehensions almost identical"; to Poe, the ability to bring out "the half-formed, the reluctant, or the unexpressed fancies of mankind"; to James Russell Lowell, "the indefinable supplement" that makes a thought fresh again; to Emerson, the extent to which one steals from Plato; to Faulkner, the capacity "to create out of the materials of the human spirit that which did not exist before"; to C. E. M. Joad, little more than skill in concealing origins.

"What we call originality," says Lowell, "seems not so much anything odd, but that quality in a man which touches human nature at most points of its circumference, which reinvigorates the consciousness of our own powers by recalling and confirming our own unvalued sensations and perceptions, gives classic shape to our own amorphous imaginings, and adequate utterance to our own stammering conceptions or emotions."

While some of these remarks are playful, some rapt, and some gnomic, you wouldn't say that they are shining examples of plain speaking. Actually, writers and critics have been unequivocal only in one respect. They have consistently and emphatically minimized the value of mere ingenuity.

"There is not less wit nor less invention," says the rationalist philosopher Pierre Bayle, "in applying rightly a thought one finds in a book, than in being the first author of that thought." "There is nothing original," observes Balzac; "all is reflected light." "The most original modern authors," says Goethe, "are not so because they advance what is new, but simply because they know how to put what they have to say as if it had never been said before."

Commentators take at least three different paths in endeavoring to track down the elusive firedrake of originality.

One approach focuses on the immemorial conflict between the traditional and the modern. Here values are fixed and judgments rendered according to the arbiter's own coloration. To the champion of academicism, tradition is the wellspring of originality, and modernism an inept, capricious and regrettable manifestation. To the standard-bearer of the *avant-garde*, the modern artist is original, and his convention-ridden confrere hackneyed and sterile. "What is valuable is not new," thunders the one, "and what is new is not valuable." "Tradition is all very well," jeers the other, "but what counts is creating a tradition, not living on one."

Absurd as it is to suppose that the past and the present can be summarily severed from each other, one thing is clear. During the last hundred and fifty years we have come to place an ever-increasing premium on novelty, virtuosity, flamboyance.

Ours is an age of self-assertion. To quote Professor Babbitt, in the days of Pope a man made his bid for fame by polishing a commonplace; nowadays he does so by launching a paradox. Where yesterday a person of real originality stood in danger of being accounted freakish, today many a freak passes for original.

There are reasons, some of them provocative, for this rise of the cult of the unorthodox. We need not inquire into causes here; it's the end product that claims our attention. As we ponder the phenomenon, one conclusion becomes inescapable. Every work of art is, in the final analysis, a compromise between tradition and revolt. It cannot be otherwise. For a composition that is wholly devoid of newness is dead; one that is wholly unconventional is incomprehensible. The make-up of the creator, his background, his temperament, his particular daemon, determine the kind of adjustment he makes. Whether he yields more to the one pull than to the other will affect the complexion of his work but not necessarily its excellence. For mediocrity is no less mediocre—nor more original—for speaking in a hitherto untried tongue, and the excellent no less original for using familiar accents.

"Significant originality," says Theodore Meyer Greene, "is an Aristotelian mean between sheer order or convention and sheer novelty or emergent difference. It is not merely an arithmetical mean between these extremes. Yet it is indubitably a function of both factors. The vitality of art depends, in part at least, upon how much order is combined with how much novelty. The greater the originality of the artist *within* the framework of convention, and the more articulated and precise the order through which his originality has expressed itself, the more vital and dynamic (other conditions being satisfied) is the resultant composition. The great artists in each of the major media are great partly because they have been able so successfully to combine tradition and inventiveness, orthodoxy and heterodoxy, order and novelty."[4]

The second approach concentrates on genius. It equates originality with superlative achievement. It hails Homer and Virgil, Dante and Molière and Shakespeare, Praxiteles and Leonardo, Bach and Beethoven as great "originals," and dismisses most of the other toilers in the arts as imitative and derivative.

This view hardly helps us. If anything, it adds to our perplexity. For the plain fact is that the titans who have, since the birth of civilization, given us the best in literature, the arts and music have been indefatigable borrowers.

The third approach comes closest to the mark. It is adumbrated in Brander Matthews' observation about the artist's being a person with a special pair of spectacles. Originality is individuality. It is the artist's gift of viewing life through the prism of his sensibility, his own way of reacting to experience, his own way of expressing his reactions.

It is the vital force which inheres in his personality and constitutes his uniqueness. It is, so to speak, his thumbprint, his aesthetic signature, so distinctive as to be instantly recognized. "It is not so much what the writer tells us that makes literature," says John Burroughs in *Style and the Man,* "as the way he tells it; or rather, it is the degree in which he imparts to it some rare personal quality or charm that is the gift of his own spirit, something which cannot be detached from the work itself, and which is as inherent as the sheen of a bird's plumage, as the texture of a flower's petal." When we go into a room with a Rubens or a Goya, a Renoir or a Van Gogh, a Chirico or a Dali, a Pippin or a Grandma Moses on its walls, we don't have to peer at name plates to identify the paintings.

Originality may be powerful or feeble, depending on the artist's gifts. Its force ordains the quality of the contribution. But its essential nature—personal vision—remains the same for a Michelangelo and for a humble, anonymous primitive.

### The Legal View

As we have seen, copyright resides in *form*: the particular treatment which an author gives to the idea he has chosen to deal with.

The law protects "original" works. For purposes of copyright, a work is original if its author has created it by his own efforts, without copying someone else's.

In a historic copyright case that arose more than a hundred years ago, the illustrious Justice Story pointed out that no man who put pen to paper labored unaided and uninstructed. No man, he said, created a new language for himself. Every writer borrowed and had to borrow; his thoughts were a combination of what others had thought and expressed before him, modified or exalted by his own genius. If a book which lacked strictly original elements were to be denied copyright, there could be no ground for copyright in modern times; indeed, we would be hard put to it to find, even in antiquity, a work entitled to such eminence.

Justice Story's dictum still holds. The law pays no heed to similarities or differences except to determine whether there has been any copying. If two authors independently take up the same subject and treat it the same way, or if they resort to common materials for the same purpose, there will be a natural and inevitable resemblance between their brain children. The one first in point of time will gain no advantage over the other. Both will be entitled to copyright.

I indicated in Chapter 1 the distinction between a copyright and a patent on the score of priority. There is a further difference. To secure a patent, the applicant must show that he has *invented* something: that he has devised a new art or found a new way of applying an old one. To justify the issuance of a patent, an invention must serve the ends of science; it must push back the frontiers of chemistry, physics and the like; it must make a distinctive contribution; it must represent a leap of the imagination. A book, on the other hand, need not be new and unprecedented to qualify for copyright. It can deal with ideas older than Methuselah; so long as it embodies the author's conception in his own idiom, the law will recognize his property rights in it, and will restrain and punish an infringer.

Nor does a story or a picture or a song have to possess artistic merit to be entitled to copyright protection. The law postulates no aesthetic standards, no code of criticism. It would be on perilous ground if it did. It safeguards alike "the humblest efforts at instruction or amusement, the dull productions of plodding mediocrity and the most original and imposing displays of intellectual power." All it requires is that the creator expend sufficient effort to impart to the result some characteristics that the raw materials did not possess, some quality that lifts it above absolute insignificance and worthlessness.

Thus the legal criterion of originality is more lenient than that of art or of popular belief.

### The Touchstone

Originality may reside in style or content or both. Art and the law concern themselves with style: the flesh that clothes the skeleton of an idea. When an artist tackles a theme, he can't worry about its family tree. If he did, he'd probably lose whatever spontaneity he had.

In weighing a man's originality, the fundamental question is not whether he has borrowed, but what he has done with the material he has taken. For the measure of an artist is not only his magical gift of spreading a new landscape before our eyes. It is also his capacity to make us see the old landscape in a new light—to select a long familiar symbol, infuse fresh life into it, and give it immediacy and urgency of meaning.

Let it not be thought, however, that borrowing must be touched with genius to be justifiable. The arts have many practitioners and few masters. A new work may fail to enhance the old one it derives from; yet so long as it's honest in its execution, it cannot be rightfully charged with plagiarism.

# 3

# Similarity

Heroes and heroines, as well as villains of both sexes, have for a time whereof the memory of the theatre-goer runneth not to the contrary, been precipitated into conventional ponds, lakes, rivers and seas; and the representation of such an incident on the stage is not sufficiently original to be subject to copyright.

—Serrana v. Jefferson, 33 Fed. 347 (1888)

---

JOHN SMITH is an unknown. He writes a play. He puts into it all he has of brains and heart. When it's finished, he has a tough time placing it. Somehow he gets hold of a theatrical producer who promises, unenthusiastically, to read it.

Smith waits. He waits for weeks, months. He writes to the producer, at first politely, then firmly, and at last angrily. Still no response. He finally calls for his play, which has been gathering dust on a shelf all the time, forgotten and unread.[1]

Smith is bitter, as he has reason to be. Not bitter enough, though, to abandon hope. He has heard about the trials of neophytes. He'll lick the game yet. He casts about for another producer.

The first producer then puts on a play which bears some resemblance to Smith's. Smith is incensed. He does not know that his script was never looked at, and nothing in the world can convince him that it wasn't. The producer, he clamors, could have read it, could have copied it, could have shown it to the other playwright. And so out of indignation and frustration, another plagiarism claim is born.

It may take years of litigation to convince Smith—if indeed he can ever be convinced—that such a claim cannot be sustained unless

24

substantial copying is proved, and that access, even when coupled with similarity, is not conclusive evidence of copying.

The predisposition of the average man to cry "Thief!" on the basis of similarity alone has been responsible for many plagiarism suits.

## The Causes of Similarity

Similarity between two plays—or any two works of art—may spring from any one or more of a number of causes that have nothing whatever to do with copying. The possible causes include:

1. The use, in both, of the same or similar theme;
2. The fact that commonplace themes carry commonplace accessories;
3. The use, in both works, of stereotypes or stock characters;
4. The fact that both employ the same well-weathered plot;
5. The limited number of plots generally;
6. The presence, in both, of hackneyed ingredients: episodes, devices, symbols and language;
7. The fact that both authors have drawn on the world's cultural heritage, or have cast their works in the same tradition;
8. The imperatives of orthodoxy and convention;
9. The impact of influence and imitation;
10. The process of evolution;
11. The dictates of vogue and fashion;
12. The fact that both authors have stolen from the same predecessor;
13. The fact that both have made legitimate use of the same news item, historical event or other source material;
14. The intervention of coincidence.

The demarcation between these causes is not sharp; the categories overlap. Tradition and influence merge; influence is one of the means by which tradition is transmitted and preserved. Vogues stem from imitation. Too, the degree of resemblance-generating force varies with each cause. The kinship between two pieces of decoration exhibiting the common omission of forbidden elements (as in Oriental and Hebraic art) may be slight. But if two novelists hit upon the same threadbare plot and the same standard dramatis personae, their books will be quite alike.

Let us see how these causes operate.

## Subject Matter

How may stories have we had about love requited and unrequited? About the eternal triangle, sin and retribution, the torments of adolescence, the duality of man's nature, high life and low morals, the rise and fall of a family? About the conflict between the young and the old, man against the earth, the dream betrayed, rags-to-riches, riches-to-rags, appearance versus reality, the disintegration of a personality? How many plays have we seen dealing with lust, greed, envy, mendacity, thirst for power, and all the other manifestations of human frailty and folly? How often have dramatists given us prince (princess) and commoner, life-after-death, the inexorable march of tragedy once the seeds of destruction are sown? How many movies have celebrated cops-and-robbers, Cinderella, boy-meets-girl, boy-loses-girl, boy-wins-girl?

Since every realistic pictorial treatment of the legend of Pygmalion and Galatea will presumably show an awe-struck sculptor facing a marble image of a young girl coming to life, it follows that each version will bear a family resemblance to the others, even though the creator of the latest version may never have seen the earlier ones.[2]

As we have noted, there can be no exclusive property rights in themes as such. Ideas remain in the public domain no matter who uses them or how. If an author could pre-empt a subject by the simple expedient of copyrighting his interpretation of it, the issuance of each copyright would progressively narrow the field of thought open for development. Literature, art and science would be stifled.

## Themes and Their Accessories

Rarely does the man who complains of plagiarism predicate his grievance solely on the theft of his theme. He will point to other "telltale" elements in both works.

The presence of these elements may betoken piracy. But not necessarily. Certain themes suggest a certain approach or treatment; they carry, so to speak, their own trappings. Whenever the themes are handled in routine fashion, the trappings are bound to appear.

Whoever tackles a subject will find, no matter how sincerely he strives to be original, unexpected and dismaying similarities between his work and those of others dealing with the same matter. There is an accustomed line of development, a stock of images, an aggregation of known devices and incidents which—given a topic—automatically recommend themselves and which authors adopt without a second thought. Many things permit of only slight variation. All definitions of the same thing must be nearly the same. Descriptions must always have in some degree that resemblance to each other which they all have to their object.

What I've just said is particularly true of formula material. Consider the components of the staple story about the South in the days of the Civil War—the proud family, the choleric Colonel who rules it, the eye-catching and tempestuous young daughter, the rival suitors (one of them a Yankee), the stately mansion, the age-old trees dripping with moss, faithful Negro retainers, moonlight and magnolias, battle scenes, conflagration and disaster. Consider, too, the paraphernalia of the standard boots-and-saddle epic: the fast-shooting, hard-riding hero, the heroine of devastating virtue, the wide open spaces, the photogenic horses and cattle, the frontier saloon with its villainous proprietor and bedizened ladies, the stage-coach, gunfights and hand-to-hand brawls and hot pursuit. Is there a run-of-the-mill costume film complete without a handsome young scapegrace, a beauteous spitfire, carousing, duels, hairbreadth escapes, seductions, betrayals, and general derring-do? Or a conventional gangster drama without the reptilian boss, the assorted henchmen, the night club, the harshly lit rendezvous before the big job, the getaway, the tracking down and the retribution?

An earlier writer cannot prevent a later one from taking the same idea and decking it out with the same clichés. By a sort of poetic justice, banality entails a penalty: it makes it that much harder to sustain a plagiarism claim.

### Stock Characters

Since time immemorial, literature has abounded in certain types. It has been an ever-growing gallery. Each age has added its own portraits. The Greeks and the Romans gave us the warrior, the adventurer, the siren, the victim of the Fates, the courtesan, the epicure, the philosopher, the voluptuary, the patrician, the satyr, the nymph. The Middle Ages contributed the knight, the lady unobtainable, the mendicant friar, the troubadour, the jester, the hunchback, the magician, the rotund, tippling monk, the wily courtier, the wicked cardinal. The early Italian and French farces supplied the bumbling cuckold, the adulterous wife, the bourgeois, the miser, the quack. The Restoration came along with the rakehell, the perfumed coxcomb, the promiscuous light-o'-love, the sharp-tongued bawd, the conniving servant.

The advent of the novel swelled the roster immensely. Melodrama furnished its quota. From vaudeville emerged the cartoon Englishman, Frenchman, Scot and Italian, the low-comedy Irishman, Negro and Jew. The screen produced the cowboy, the tenderfoot, the murderous Indian, the shifty-eyed Mexican, the vamp, the underworld czar, the love-goddess, and even such particularized types as the idealistic and not-too-bright young man who manages with his shy charm and in his blundering fashion to confound and destroy the forces of evil arrayed against him. Radio has yielded not only a new kind of wife (wise, capable, tolerant, she's ready for any emergency; without her, the household would fall apart), not only a new kind of husband (a likeable enough chap, decent and well-meaning, fond of his family, harmlessly boastful, and a little simple-minded; he leans on his spouse more than he realizes or likes to admit; she gets him out of all sorts of scrapes), but also a copious assortment of soap-opera figures.

Some stock characters are pure stereotypes: the old maid, the bluenose, the absent-minded professor, the temperamental diva, the brutal sea captain, the lovable old scalawag, the life-of-the-party, the endearing young nitwit. Others are not only stereotypes but race libels as well: the shiftless and illiterate Negro, the superstitious, drunken Irishman, the wily Jew, the criminal Italian.[3]

There are other types which are cardboard cutouts too, but with a little more embossing: the alcoholic old trouper trying to stage a comeback; the femme fatale ("sweet as sin, devastating as a Micky Finn, safe as a baby cobra"); the jaunty, raffish newshawk addicted to wisecracking, guzzling and flippant love-making; the dewy-eyed, petal-cheeked, sweet-voiced young thing who turns out to be a bitch; the private eye whose extraordinary capacity for absorbing punishment is matched by the combustibility of the sylphs he meets; the neat, efficient secretary who cherishes an unuttered and hopeless passion for her employer; the old lady in the wheel chair who is supposed to be paralyzed but who gets up in the middle of the night to commit the murder that baffles everybody; the mysterious catalytic stranger who appears out of nowhere, pops into a group where everyone has some kind of trouble, solves all the problems, and then quietly fades out of the picture; the Woman of Growing Awareness;[4] the enemy of society with a heart of gold.

Some types persist; others come and go. We still encounter the braggart, the cheat, the hoyden, the rebel, the scold, the black sheep, the star-crossed lover. Gone are Beau Brummel, the soldier of fortune, the gentleman cracksman, the sheik, the It-girl, the gigolo, the flapper. Now we have the huckster, the bobby-soxer, the chiseler, the yes man, the hepcat, the wolf.

Since stock characters are generalized, they exhibit standard physical traits and qualities. The low-comedy Irishman of the old days was barrel-chested and oak-limbed; he had a bald pate fringed with unruly red hair, and a boozy nose; his stance was belligerent and his brogue thick; he was ignorant, stubborn, irresponsible, and everlastingly thirsty. The low-comedy Jew had a hooked nose and a straggly mustache and whiskers; he was thin, hollow-chested and droop-kneed; he spoke with an accent; he was a symbol of cunning and greed.

Today's types, too, carry regulation equipment. The judge has silvery hair and sculptured features.[5] The hatchet man is thick-skulled, broken-nosed; he grunts Brooklynese. Mata Hari is dark, sultry and exotic, throaty of voice and feline of movement.

It goes without saying that the inclusion of the same stock character or characters in two novels or plays or movies will beget similarity. The inclusion may be pure accident. A writer need not be a larcenist to enrich his pages with a venal politician, a hussy, a wise guy, a go-getter. But even if the inclusion is due to copying, there is no basis for a plagiarism claim so long as the treatments differ.

### The Same Old Story

In 1906 Jack London wrote a short story called "Just Meat," and copyrighted it. Some time later Biograph produced a movie entitled *Love of Gold*. London sued for infringement.

The story and the play were strikingly similar. In both two thieves commit a burglary that nets them a sizeable haul. They return to their room and discuss, with a notable absence of harmony, the division of the booty. Each succeeds, unknown to the other, in putting poison into something the other is about to swallow.

London lost the case. Judge Lacombe adverted to the fact that the two works differed in composition and embellishment. "The plot," he said, "is highly dramatic and calculated to appeal powerfully to reader or spectactor. But it is an old one; it appears in Chaucer's 'Pardoner's Tale.' In the works of Chaucer . . . earlier versions of the story are given and it is traced back to the East. Sometimes there is one robber, sometimes more; sometimes one is killed by violence and the other by poison; but in all the criminals themselves are the avengers. . . . The plot is common property; no one by presenting it with modern incidents can appropriate it by copyrighting."

A plot is the plan or narrative progression of a composition, a connected series of incidents, as distinguished from a theme, which is merely general subject matter. In essence a plot is the development and elaboration of a theme.

Just as all formula stories exhibit the same staple ingredients, so they follow the same plot pattern. Take fistic melodrama on the screen. The prescription for it, as Otis L. Guernsey, Jr., has indicated, is rigid. "You take one golden boy, preferably a child of the gutter with ambitions and a mother and a girl. You introduce him to a manager who points the way to fame and fortune. You take him to the top of the prize-fighting heap in an atmosphere of gambling and hardening of the moral arteries. Nobody loves him at this point, not even his mother; and you bring him down in a resounding crash after one final, violent ring sequence."[6]

It should be remembered, however, that while a familiar plot is fair game for all, a fresh conception and an individual presentation of it will be protected by copyright. In ruling that the movie *Vendetta* infringed the novel *Mr. Barnes of New York,* Judge Goddard said: "Probably almost every conceivable plot has been the subject of many works. However, people will continue to write books, and the public continue to read them, because of the new characters and settings with which authors surround an old plot, and such of them as are independent productions may be copyrighted."

## Plots Are Few

A couple of years ago one of the popular magazines printed a story about a man who, having been captured by aborigines noted for their cruelty, devised a plan to escape torture. He told the chief of the savages that he could brew an elixir which would render him impervious to hurt. He proceeded to prepare his nostrum, applied it to his own neck, and invited the chief to put it to the test. The chief obliged; he swung his sword and struck off the man's head, as the latter had planned. New plot? Hardly. It goes back to Christopher Marlowe's *Tamburlaine the Great* (1587), and beyond that to Ariosto's *Orlando Furioso* (1516).

Dunlop, who made a comprehensive study of the European novel, came to the conclusion that there were, in all, about two hundred and fifty distinct stories, and that at least two hundred of them could be traced back thousands of years to the other side of the Black Sea. These figures are probably much too high. The estimates of most authorities run below fifty. Indeed, there are those who aver that in all romantic literature there are only two plots: Cinderella and Jack the Giant Killer.

Carlo Gozzi, the eighteenth-century Italian playwright, claimed that there were only thirty-six possible dramatic situations. Disagreeing with him, Schiller tried to prove that there were more; he wound up with less. Commenting on this, Goethe said: "It is almost impossible in the present day to find a situation which is thoroughly new. Only the manner of looking at it can be new, and the art of treating and representing it."

## Appurtenances

Trite ingredients—episodes, situations, devices, symbols, language —can no more be removed by use from the public domain than conventional story lines.

The chase, the escape, peril and rescue, mistaken identity, the last-minute reprieve, the big scene in which the worm turns or the sacrifice is made or the wrongdoer gets his deserts—these are common examples of episodes anyone can use. Less timeworn, perhaps, but still beyond the pale of protection are things like stowing away to escape pursuit; the unexpected discovery of the heroine in a place where she should not be; the use of a dummy as a decoy to cast a shadow on a window shade; the heroine held a prisoner in a Chinese opium den; injury to the bridegroom on his wedding day; the interruption of a stage performance by the supposed murder of a member of the audience. But a *new combination* of old materials is protectible by copyright.

Stock devices vary. There are structural ones, such as the story within a story (Conrad's *Youth*) and the play within a play (*Hamlet*, Molnar's *The Play's the Thing*, Maxwell Anderson's *Joan of Lorraine*); the linking together of a series of unrelated narratives by means of a day-to-day interlude (the *Arabian Nights*, Boccaccio's *Decameron*, Marguerite of Navarre's *Heptameron*, Chaucer's *Canterbury Tales*, Longfellow's *Tales of a Wayside Inn*, Virginia Stead's *Salzburg Tales*); the gathering in one place of an assortment of people whose lives rise to a climax (Vicki Baum's *Grand Hotel*, Thornton Wilder's *The Bridge of San Luis Rey*, Henry Morton Robinson's *Snow Bound*, John Steinbeck's *The Wayward Bus*). There are technical ones, such as the flash back, the close-up, the fade-out and the double exposure in the movies. There are miscellaneous ones, such as point counterpoint (love and hate, virtue and vice), the red herring in detective stories, the frame-up, the mistaken identity, the false confession, the double cross, the reverse twist, the happy ending.

Banal symbolism is probably best exemplified on the screen. Hollywood has standard cinematic euphemisms to suggest lovemaking—"a bee buzzing around the honeysuckle, the lily floating on the stream approaching an underground cavern, two tall poplars laced together during a violent rainstorm, or a bull gazing longingly at the signboard reproduction of Elsie the Cow."[7]

The clearest form of larceny is, of course, the word-for-word copying of an entire composition. Naturally it does not arise nearly so often as does the duplication of scattered clichés. Legally clichés are harmless enough, since they may burgeon independently; the trouble is that a claimant may pounce on them as internal evidence of copying if identical specimens appear in his opus and his adversary's. It seems hardly necessary to point out that no exclusive property rights can be successfully asserted in such inspired turns of expression as "sickening thud" or "sea of upturned faces" or "something snapped inside of him," nor in such scintillating bits of dialogue as "All right, if that's the way you want it" or "We can't go on like this" or "I'll never forget this as long as I live" or "You're very tired; you must get some rest now" or "I've stood just about enough; now *you* listen to me!"[8] And yet in the plagiarism case involving O'Neill's *Strange Interlude,* the lady who sued (and lost) pointed in all seriousness to the fact—among others—that in both plays someone was referred to as "an old fox," and that in her play a character said to a physician: "I count on your help," and in O'Neill's play a character said: "You've got to help me, doctor."

## The Setting

Some years ago an author wrote a novel about shanty-boat life in a particular part of the Louisiana bayous. It was a region which had previously been overlooked by writers. The book sold well. Within a year another novel appeared, by a different man, dealing with the same section of the country. It borrowed nothing from the first one except the locale. However, it was more warmly welcomed than the first. The pioneer was aroused and wanted to sue. "Why, I discovered the place," he cried, "and now someone else moves in and reaps the benefit!" He was amazed to learn that he could not, by being precursor, pre-empt a place or a region or a group of people for literary purposes.

Many years before, James Oliver Curwood had faced the same situation. Having popularized the Canadian Northwest in fiction, Curwood went to court to protect what he considered his private preserve. Judge Knox told him in explicit terms that he had not acquired and could not acquire any monopoly in the region or in the Royal Mounted Police. And it has been held in other cases that the choice of a theatrical boardinghouse, a reform school, a tropical island, the Hollywood Bowl, a convent, or Congressional circles in Washington as the milieu of a copyrighted work does not prevent others from resorting to the same setting.

The rule is the same whether the background is old or new. It holds good for imaginary places as well as actual ones. Any writer is free to roam in mythical kingdoms; he may visit Atlantis or Utopia; he may delve into the bowels of the earth or go voyaging in space. It does not matter that others have gone there before him and, returning, have copyrighted their accounts.

## The Fabulous Hoard

Whatever man has done since he first began to record his thoughts and feelings, whatever he has achieved by way of creative expression since the time he uttered his first chant, carved his first club, scrawled his first cave-wall image, makes up the aggregate of the world's cultural heritage. It is a prodigious accumulation. It includes the works of all the named and unnamed masters who have ever practiced art, literature or music.

This heritage has been likened to a noble structure to the raising of which each creative person has brought a stone; to a river which, fed by innumerable tributaries, affords life and verdancy to the shores it touches, only to receive new tributaries as it flows along; to a treasury from which anyone may borrow, since whatever he does with his prize is bound eventually to swell the store; to a miraculous garden that lends sustenance to every seed flung into it, and is fertilized by each new growth.

Myths and legends loom large among these riches. From Egypt, Chaldea, Assyria, Persia and Judea, from Greece and Rome, from the Scandinavian countries, tales of the exploits of gods and heroes have been handed down to us in various forms—epics and chronicles, inscriptions and wall paintings, mosaics and textiles, vase decorations and sculpture.

Mythology and folklore permeate the Babylonian *Gilgamesh* epic, the *Odyssey* and the *Iliad*, *The Aeneid,* the Hindu *Upanishads* and *Bhagavad-Gita,* the Mohammedan *Koran,* the *Eddas* of the North, the Old and New Testament, the *Tales of the Monks* (*Gesta Romanorum*), the *Song of Roland, Reynard the Fox,* the *Arabian Nights, Beowulf,* and *The Lusiads* of Luis de Camoëns. These works in turn have fired the imagination of poets and artists without number.[9]

Wherever we turn in literature and art, we encounter themes of pagan origin: the birth of the deities, the spinning of the Fates, Pandora's box, the touch of Midas, Echo's voice, the quest of the Golden Fleece, Niobe's grief, the labors of Hercules, the fall of Icarus—the list is endless. Prometheus defies Jupiter anew in Byron. Pan plays his syrinx for Leigh Hunt. Nymphs and fauns flit through the sunlit groves of Mallarmé's poetry. The sacred river Alpheus flows "through caverns measureless to man" in Coleridge's "Kubla

Khan." Glaucus and Scylla re-enact their tragic love in "Endymion."
Shelley gives us "Chorus from Hellas" and "Ode on a Grecian Urn";
Swinburne, "The Garden of Proserpine." The tale of Phaedra,
doomed by her criminal love for Hippolytus, pulses afresh in Euripides, Seneca, Racine and Pradon. Narcissus, Oedipus and Theseus
march across the pages of Gide. Horns and cloven feet and pointed
ears, though veiled from human gaze, wreak havoc in E. M.
Forster's *The Story of a Panic.* We meet Minerva in Phidias, Venus
in Botticelli, Zeus and Danaë in Titian, Achilles in Delacroix, and
a whole galaxy in Michelangelo.

The influence of the Bible has been profound beyond measure.
Itself an omnium-gatherum from every available source,[10] the Book
of Books has been a prodigal provider. The fall of man has had a
thousand tellings in every conceivable form, and so have the stories
of Cain and Abel, Joseph and his brethren, Joshua with his mighty
trumpet embattled before the walls of Jericho, Samson and Delilah,
David and Goliath, Solomon the wise, the prophet Elijah, Judith and
Holofernes, Ruth and Naomi. In the *Divine Comedy,* as in *Paradise
Lost* and *Paradise Regained,* religious lore is of the essence. The
Scriptures have provided Christian art—paintings, sculpture, architecture, crafts, music: a magnificent flowering—with an inexhaustible
supply of legends, parables, scenes, characters and images. The
Bible, says Emerson, is like an old Cremona; it has been played upon
by the devotion of thousands of years until every word and particle
of it is public and tunable.

Because they express man's primordial urges and have universal
meaning, myths and legends remain alive and lend themselves to
endless interpretation. The Tale of the Eaten Heart—a jealous husband feeds his faithless wife the heart of her murdered lover—occurs
successively in East Indian, Provençal, Italian, French and South
American literature. The story of the fourteenth-century Spanish
rake Don Giovanni—who, according to the modest estimate of his
valet, had twenty-five hundred mistresses throughout Europe—has
served many masters: Tellez, Molière, Shadwell, Byron, Balzac,
Rostand and Shaw. Malory and Tennyson and Edwin Arlington
Robinson give us, each in turn, a new King Arthur; George Bernard
Shaw, a new Pygmalion; Eugene O'Neill, a new Electra—for each

age views the past through its own eyes, and defines what it sees in its own terms.

Folklore too has been a copious wellspring. Robert Burns spoke of his imagination being fired by the words of an old woman who lived with his family when he was young. "She had," he said, "the largest collection in the country of tales and songs concerning devils, ghosts, fairies, brownies, witches, warlocks, spunkies, kelpies, elf-candles, dead-lights, wraiths, apparitions, cantrips, giants, enchanted towers, dragons and other trumpery. This cultivated the latent seeds of poetry in me." The interest in the folklore of his native land which was quickened in Pushkin by the stories of his nurse Arina Rodionovna, persisted throughout his life, and inspired some of his finest works. "Guess," he wrote to his brother, "what I am doing. All morning I work at my notebooks. Then, after a late dinner, I go for a gallop. In the evening I listen to folk tales, with which I eke out my wretched education. What a treasure these tales are: Every one of them is sheer poetry!" Hans Christian Andersen drew on folk material to construct the magical cosmos of his fairy tales.

Not all the legends go back thousands of years. The Faust fable originated during the Renaissance. There *was* a Dr. Faustus; he lived in the time of Martin Luther. He made his deal with the devil —so the story runs—and was damned. He died in 1538. In 1587 the first account of his life appeared; in half a century he had become a legend. Christopher Marlowe's *Doctor Faustus* (1604) and Goethe's *Faust* (1790-1833) are but two of the many treatments the story has received.

"Ordinarily," says Louis Untermeyer, "it takes hundreds of years to make a lasting legend, thousands to make a mythology. But here in America legends, like the country, grow fast. They increase with the range and vigor of these forty-eight varying but United States. The Northwest country is the home of some of our wildest folk-tales. Tall stories grow naturally among tall timber. The Best is never good enough, and even the Biggest lifts itself by its bootstraps to be higher. So with the folk-tale. It begins with an incident and becomes a legend; it starts with a person and becomes the property of the people. It travels about. It grows in the telling. American soil and American spirit have created Paul Bunyan. His forerunners are heroes who fed on fable and thrived on exaggeration: Hercules and Gargantua and Gulliver." There are other towering figures in American folk history to keep Paul Bunyan company: Captain Stormalong, Mike Fink, Jonathan Slick, Pecos Bill, Mose the Fireman, Joe Magarac, Davy Crockett. And new folk tales are constantly in the making, induced by unexplained phenomena, extraordinary achievement, upheaval, war.

Our cultural heritage is a repository of many traditions; classical architecture, Gothic sculpture, Shakespearean drama, eighteenth-century prose, Negro spirituals and Victorian *décor* are but a few examples. Adherence to tradition is apt to yield resemblance not only between the new work and the source but also between any two new works inspired by the same source. All pastorals bear the sights and scents and sounds of the country; all Persian miniatures look like Persian miniatures; all neoclassic edifices recall the Acropolis, the Pantheon, the Arch of Titus. If two synagogues present the same countenance, it is more likely that they do so because both architects let their gaze dwell overlong on the face of Byzantium than because one of them plagiarized the other.

4

# Similarity (Continued)

> Men who think for themselves should not be discouraged to find occa-
> sionally that some of their best ideas have been anticipated by former
> writers; they will neither anathemize others nor despair themselves. They
> will rather go on discovering things previously discovered, until they are
> rewarded with a land hitherto unknown, an empire indisputably their own,
> both by right of conquest and discovery.
>
> —Charles Caleb Colton: Lacon

## Orthodoxy and Convention

THE men who designed the pylon temples of ancient Egypt could
not give free rein to their fancy. They were bound by religious
imperatives. The plan of the temples—pylon, court, hypostyle hall,
sanctuary, girdle wall—was prescribed by rigid ritualistic requirements. By the same token, the artists of Islam and Judea were compelled to turn to geometry and plant forms for decorative subject
matter because orthodoxy forbade the representation of human
figures.

Strictly speaking, orthodoxy is adherence in belief and practice
to Christian doctrine as formulated by ecclesiastical authority. In a
broader sense it signifies obedience to the dogma dictated by any
religious hierarchy.

Orthodoxy in Christian art goes back a long way. As early as the
eighth century the Church, displeased with trends in iconography,
sought to regulate the choice of themes and the manner of treatment.
In 787, the Ecumenical Council issued an edict on this. "The composition of religious subjects," the Council said, "may not be left

38

to the initiative of the artists; it depends upon those principles which have been laid down by the Church, and upon sacred tradition. . . . The execution alone belongs to the painter, the arrangement and the disposition are determined by the Fathers."

Even the most devout artists—and many of them were less than that—found it difficult to keep within the narrow confines prescribed by canon. The Church regarded art as an adjunct to worship. If a painting inspired piety and devotion, it was compatible with Christian doctrine. If, however, it made the holy figures too human, or introduced homely details or bits of genre, or—worse than these —stressed elements of purely sensuous appeal, then it might quicken worldly thoughts and unspiritual desires, and was not to be tolerated.

The Spanish Inquisition went further. It banished all secular representation, and forbade "the making or exposing of any immodest paintings or sculptures on pain of excommunication, a fine of fifteen hundred ducats, and a year's exile." A Cordovan artist was flung into a dungeon for incorporating in a Crucifixion a delineation of St. John in trunk hose and of the Virgin in an embroidered petticoat.

In 1545 the Council of Trent barred from churches "any image inspired by false doctrine that might mislead the simple. . . . To eliminate all lures of impurity and lasciviousness, images must not be decked in shameless beauty." A decade later Veronese was lectured by the Holy Office for including extraneous and unworthy objects in one of his pictures. Several churches rejected, for the same reason, paintings they had ordered from Caravaggio. Titian's "Madonna with a Rabbit" was censured for its discursive elements, one of which was the rabbit.

To this day the Roman Index—which is composed of the *Index Librorum Prohibitorum* (books absolutely forbidden to Catholics) and the *Index Expurgatorius* (books which may be read if certain portions are expunged)—is an active instrument of orthodoxy.

Convention is folkways: social attitudes, customs and usages prevailing at a given time in a given place. Its chief means of expression is public opinion. It must be borne in mind, however, that what parades as public opinion on such matters as, say, sexual propriety is often nothing more than the prepossessions and prejudices of a highly articulate and aggressive minority.

The aim of orthodoxy is to promulgate and enforce a fixed pattern of thought and behavior. The effect of convention is the same, though to a lesser degree. If the compulsion is successful, the result is regimentation: the suppression of variation, experimentation, individuality.

Nowhere is this better illustrated than in the case of the censorship of the screen. Censorship is, of course, the big gun of both orthodoxy and convention. Although the Production Code of the film industry (ostensibly an implement of "self-regulation"), as well as the licensing laws of the states where movies must be approved by official censors before they are shown to the public, wear the outer garments of secularity, the odor of incense clings to them. Sex and religion are the censors' principal concerns. The point to be noted is that censorship of pictures has yielded a standardized product. On the screen virtue always triumphs, the criminal always gets his come uppance, decent men rarely make passes at girls, respectable women rarely feel the urge of the flesh, clergymen are pure in heart and dedicated, and the weak creature who strays even for a moment from the path of righteousness can never achieve happiness without first paying the price in bitterness and suffering.[1]

## Influence

"For my part," Henri Matisse once said to Guillaume Apollinaire, "I have never avoided the influence of others: I would have considered this a cowardice and a lack of sincerity toward myself."

Influence is the cement that binds together the bricks and stones of the monument that is our cultural heritage.

Elsewhere in this book, and particularly in Chapters 6 and 7, I shall discuss borrowing—the instrument of influence—in some detail. It may not be amiss, however, to cite a few examples here. The whole body of Western literature has been molded by Greek and Roman thought; a brilliant exposition of this may be found in Professor Highet's *The Classical Tradition*. St. Augustine's philosophy nourished Dante and Grotius, just as his theology fed Wyclif and Luther. Henry James had among his disciples such original writers as Joseph Conrad, Edith Wharton and Anne Douglas Sedgwick. Kierkegaard beckoned to Strindberg, and Strindberg to O'Neill. The voice of Walt Whitman rings in many of Thomas

Wolfe's impassioned passages. The impact of men like Proust, Joyce, Gide and Hemingway on authors everywhere has been incalculable.

"Either the spirit of Donatello lives in Michelangelo," says one scholar, "or that of Michelangelo already lived in Donatello." The seeds of El Greco's elongation of figures are in Tintoretto. Manet harks back to Ribera and Velasquez, the early Degas to Murillo and Manet, Despiau to archaic Greek sculpture, Barlach to German woodcutters, Miro to children's art and Indian picture writing and Egyptian wall paintings. When Delacroix chose in his "La Justice de Trajan" to paint a horse *pink*, he laid the basis for the use of arbitrary color in modern art. Allston's vision of night—see particularly his "Moonlit Landscape"—is mirrored in Ryder's haunted canvases of sea and sky.

The churches of the fourteenth and fifteenth centuries were the sovereign culmination of many shaping forces. They are perhaps the most impressive example of the fusion of a great variety of elements into a supreme whole.

Sometimes influence spans centuries, sometimes it operates by contact between master and pupil, or through groups and coteries. The members of Baldovinetti's workshop, who supplied the fire and vitality of the *quattrocento*, all worked in the same vein. So did Rembrandt's circle (Gooert Flinck, Jacob Backer, Nicolaes Maes), the Pre-Raphaelites and the Impressionists. Some of the cubist paintings of Braque and Picasso are so alike in conception and execution that on one occasion Picasso himself could not say with assurance whether a certain picture was Braque's or his. These men did not copy one another. Their works bore a family likeness because they shared a common aesthetic aim.

While an artist may come under the dominance of another to the point of turning plagiarist, influence ordinarily has to do with following the spirit, the approach, the aspirations (in other words, the intangible elements) of a source, not its specific lineaments. And so long as there is no appropriation of the *form* of expression, influence—however marked—is no token of larceny.

## The Sedulous Ape

Robert Louis Stevenson always kept two books in his pocket, one to read and one to write in. He made no secret of his purpose:

"Whenever I read a volume or passage that particularly pleased me, in which a thing was stated or a fact rendered with propriety, in which there was some conspicuous force or happy distinction in the style, I must sit down at once and set myself to ape that quality. I was unsuccessful and knew it. I tried again and was again unsuccessful, and always unsuccessful, but at least in these vain hours I got some practice in rhythm, in harmony, and construction and coordination of parts. I have thus played the sedulous ape to Hazlitt, to Lamb, to Wordsworth, to Sir Thomas Browne, to Defoe, to Hawthorne, to Montaigne, to Baudelaire and Oberman."

The ancients not only countenanced imitation but commended it as a salutary literary practice. No one accused Euripides of plagiarism for having imitated the second book of the *Iliad* in one of the choruses of *Iphigenia*; people regarded it as an homage rendered to Homer on the Athenian stage. Quintilian believed that a great portion of art consisted of imitation; he saw nothing wrong in this. Prime invention, he declared, held the first place of merit, yet it was of advantage to imitate what had been invented with success.

Marguerite of Navarre deliberately set out to imitate Boccaccio's *Decameron*. Sir Thomas More, like Erasmus, wrote imitations of Lucian. "In *Amadis of Gaul*," wrote Milton, "may be found the Zelmane of *Arcadia*, the Masque of Cupid of *The Faerie Queene*, and the Florizel of *The Winter's Tale*. Sidney, Spenser and Shakespeare imitated this book. Was ever a book honored by three such imitators?" Dr. Johnson penned his "Vanity of Human Wishes" in imitation of Juvenal's "Tenth Satire." Swinburne's "Atalanta in Calydon" has been called the truest and deepest imitation of Aeschylus in modern times. Out of Arnold Bennett's desire to repeat the pattern of Guy de Maupassant's *Une Vie, The Old Wives' Tale* was born.

Gounod once wrote to a friend: "Don't listen to those who tell you not to imitate the masters; that is not true. You must not imitate one, but all of them. You can become a master only on condition that you are akin to the best." "The imitation of other artists," says Lewis Mumford, "is one of the means by which a person enriches and finally establishes his own individuality, and on the whole such imitation is more promising than an icing of originality that hardens too quickly."

Whether imitation amounts to plagiarism depends on what is being imitated, and to what degree. The test is pretty much the same as in the case of influence. Emulation—an endeavor to approach, equal or excel a model via independent labor—is permissible. Reproduction is not. If a painter takes the elements of Chirico's evocative repertory—the cryptic arcaded buildings, the sexless mannikins, the statues, the plaster heads, the fruit no living tree ever bore, the incisive perspective, the shadows that do not conceal but vibrate with hallucinatory clarity—and recombines them in his own fashion, he stays within the law. If he copies a specific picture by the master, he becomes a plagiarist, and he does not escape the label by making inconsequential changes.

Parody is the imitation of the style or content of a work in a humorous or satirical manner. If feeble, it is parasitic. When handled with skill, it's not only a telling form of criticism but an achievement which has a validity of its own. (See Fielding's *Joseph Andrews*, which is a travesty on Richardson's *Pamela*.) In any case it is not infringement unless it is a transparent cover-up for stealing.

### "Natural Selection"

The passenger cars of the early trains looked like stagecoaches, the first automobiles looked like horse-drawn carriages, the first radios looked like phonographs. And though it may be a far cry from the old Winton of 1898 to the streamlined, chromium-and-enamel monarch of the road of today, we need only to glance at any illustrated chart of the growth of the automobile to realize that the process has been a gradual one. Each successive model has developed from the one before it, retaining many of the traits and components of its predecessor, and adding some new ones.

In art and literature and music, as in technics, we go from the old to the new: almost literally, the new rises out of the old. Styles and schools go through stages of birth, growth, maturity and decline. They are succeeded by others which stem from them but are re-invigorated by some new element. Transformation rarely occurs by chance or violence; it is usually the accumulation of countless slight changes in familiar forms. There is an organic continuity.

That this presents an analogy to biological phenomena has long been noted. Evolution is a gradual process of mutation: a permanent, hereditary, progressive movement away from type. Discussing the evolution of styles of ornament, Hamlin says: "Transmission by inheritance, persistence of type, occasional reversions toward the primitive type, exceptional forms analogous to the 'sports' that occur in Nature—all these are met with in the history of ornament, as well as the constant evolutionary progress from simple to complex, from the rudimentary to the highly organized."[2]

For example, it was inevitable that pre-Christian symbols should persist in the beginnings of Christian art. Christianity was born into a pagan world; it had a pagan inheritance. It carried over and adopted ancient forms and concepts. The early Christian sarcophagi were hardly distinguishable from their classical prototypes. Pagan mythology mingled with Biblical imagery in the decoration of liturgical vessels. The devil himself was not new: he grew out of the Talmudic Satan, who in turn traced his ancestry back to horned and cloven-footed Silenus of the Attic woodlands.

"*Le Cid*," says Professor Clark, discussing the genesis of Corneille's masterpiece, "does not mark a sharp break with tradition, a sudden spontaneous generation like the emergence of a rabbit from a conjurer's hat. It is a superb example of the universal process of creative evolution out of which all the great art forms arise. Beethoven's symphony springs from the dance suite, Michelangelo's frescoes from the primitive daubs in the Catacombs, the cathedral at Rheims from an experiment in rib-vaulting."[3]

## Vogue and Fashion

No one can say with any degree of certainty what makes a particular success a trend, a trend a vogue, a vogue a craze. Imitation, mob psychology, accident, commercialism—all these probably have something to do with it.

When Freud's theories made their first appearance in fiction and non-fiction, the public—for reasons which can be guessed—sat up and took notice. And soon we were deluged with Freudian novels, biography, criticism. We still are. No man between the covers of a book is a weakling or brute or misfit or reprobate, no woman a slut or a vixen, but because his or her father or mother was too loving or not loving enough.

Clarence Day's *Life with Father* precipitated a succession of family chronicles dominated by a single figure who is a tower of strength or a bundle of frailties, a homespun philosopher or an addlepate, a creature serene or explosive, a sterling character or a raffish one, but who is always picturesque and fundamentally endearing.

The first siren with rebellious breasts who graced the jacket of a novel must have appealed to the customers. She proved to be the forerunner of a whole army of well-exposed seductresses brightening the wrappers of historical romances.

Sidney Skolsky tells the story of a screen writer who gave a script to a producer to read. "It's great," said the producer; "it's gay and fresh and original." "Then you'll buy it?" asked the writer. "Oh, no," said the producer, "I couldn't. It's never been done before."

A movie comes along dealing with prison life; it hits the jackpot, and before you can say Georgia Chain Gang, a dozen other epics of the Big House flash across the screen. *Little Caesar* leaps to fame and fortune, and gangster melodramas come in droves. The moment some Hollywood super-genius discovers how to get around the sex taboo—you *can* have the male lead chase the female lead through six erotic reels for the avowed purpose of getting her to go to bed with him so long as you ring the marriage bells in the first reel—there is a flood of sly and titillating sex comedies. When the smirks begin to fade, we get a succession of other-world fantasies, cloak-and-dagger pageants, screwball farces, psychological thrillers, psychoanalytical "studies," prize-fight chronicles, race-prejudice documents, nostalgic musicals, science-fiction flights into interstellar space—each cycle initiated by an outstanding success or two.

Let people acclaim a radio or television show, let a song sweep the juke boxes, and opportunists will prick up their ears. They will seize upon the successful product, turn it this way and that, dissect it, and try to isolate the special quality, the magic ingredient that snares the crowds and the cash. Nine times out of ten they will come up with a formula and proceed to put it to work.

The band-wagon boys are a cagy lot. They don't steal. They just exploit the formula.

### Plagiarists Both

Gray composes a tune and copyrights it. Later on Black writes one that is virtually identical. Gray sues Black for infringement. Black's defense is that he took nothing from Gray; both of them, he says, copied from White. If he proves this, Gray can't win. And it makes no difference, as far as Gray's position is concerned, whether or not White's original is in copyright. If it isn't, Gray could not monopolize it by securing a phony copyright. If it is, Gray himself committed a wrong when he lifted it; he comes into court with "unclean hands," and will be thrown out. The equitable principle is that where both parties are equally at fault, the law will aid neither of them. Indeed, if Gray raises a fuss, it may all end up with White suing both Gray and Black.

In 1883, Charles Reade—whose frequent brushes with literary sleuths prompted him to fulminate on the subject of plagiarism on more than one occasion—published a story called "The Picture in My Uncle's Dining Room." A diligent bookworm, burrowing in the musty files of an ancient magazine, unearthed a tale entitled "The Old M'sieu's Secret." Another bookworm dug up an even earlier opus, "Where Shall I Find Her?" The three narratives were so alike as to rule out the possibility of coincidence. Tongues began to wag. Which story had Reade copied from? Then came the pay-off. A third investigator, with a longer reach than his colleagues', came forward with Mme. Raybaud's *Mlle. de Malepierre*, from which all the later stories had been stolen. Reade's elaborate theorizing about homogeneous and heterogeneous borrowing—homogeneous borrowing, he said, was cribbing from a *single* work, and hence plagiarism; but heterogeneous borrowing, being the utilization of a *number* of sources, was in the nature of research, and hence justifiable and proper—didn't help him to explain *that* little episode.

### Common Source

There are many instances, however, where two or more writers resort to a common source and make *legitimate* use of the material they find there. Such material includes current news, physical facts, past events and other data.

In covering a political convention, all the reporters will have access to the same agenda, the same publicity releases, the same advance copies of speeches to be delivered. It would be difficult indeed for their stories to be radically unlike.

Actual occurrences often serve as springboards for fiction. Few men spin yarns from their heads. A writer is no less a writer because he takes the stuff of reality and reshapes it.

*The Ring and the Book* was inspired by the Comparini murder case, recorded in a "yellowing square old book" that Browning picked up by accident in Florence; Dostoievsky's *The Possessed*, by the Nachaev affair; Melville's *Moby Dick*, by the story of the whaler *Essex*, sunk by a leviathan eighty-five feet long; his *Billy Budd*, by the Mackenzie case; Anatole France's *Crainquebille*, by the Dreyfus affair; Dreiser's *An American Tragedy*, by the Gillette case; Aldous Huxley's *The Gioconda Smile*, by the Greenwood poison-death mystery; Lillian Hellman's *The Children's Hour*, by a news item; John O'Hara's *Butterfield 8*, by the unlovely career of Starr Faithfull; Terence Rattigan's *The Winslow Boy*, by a *cause célèbre* that rocked England before World War I.

The Sacco-Vanzetti case alone has thus far given rise to a hundred and fifty poems, six plays, and a dozen novels. If a miscarriage of justice, a murder, an act of heroism, or any publicized oddity strikes one author as likely grist for the literary mill, it may strike others the same way. The man who first completes and copyrights his version (fictional or factual) can't stop those that follow from completing and copyrighting theirs. "It is to be expected," said Judge Mayer in *The Case of Becky* suit, "that two playwrights working independently from a common source will develop similarities in their plots and in their lines." But if someone copies a predecessor's *treatment* of an occurrence instead of composing his own version, he'll be liable.

### The Feeders

"The Archbishop of Canterbury," wrote Henry James, "repeated to me the few meagre elements of a gruesome spectral tale that someone had told him." The result was *The Turn of the Screw*.

Back in the days when he was a struggling writer, Sinclair Lewis sold a plot outline to Jack London for $7.50. London used it and got $1,200 for his handiwork.

"I wish," says Charles Jackson, author of *The Lost Weekend*, "I had a dollar for every time someone has told me or sent me a story that he thought I would be interested in and thus make use of, free, gratis, for nothing."

Charles Addams, the Edgar Allan Poe of *The New Yorker* cartoonists, gets an average of two hundred suggestions a week from people all over the country eager to stimulate his macabre fancy. H. T. Webster, whose genre is somewhat less spine-chilling, receives about forty ideas a month for his pictorial commentary on the exhilarations, frustrations and foibles of the human race in the New York *Herald Tribune*. The pungent fancy of the incomparable Peter Arno is quickened by idea-men.[4]

A dozen years ago a lady entertained J. B. Priestley and Channing Pollock at luncheon in London. She narrated an adventure she had had. Both literary guests saw possibilities in it, and tossed a coin for it. Pollock won and published the result in the *American Magazine* under the title of "Preview." The editor of *Harper's* later told him that he had received scores of letters pointing out that "Preview" had been stolen and used in another story in *Harper's*. The latter was the work of a well-known English contributor, and the editor wanted to know how Pollock felt about it. Displaying a magnanimity seldom encountered in similar situations, Pollock replied that the English writer had probably heard the tale as he and Priestley had done, and had an equal right to it. "Almost every professional," he said, "knows a dozen such stories that he refrains from writing because of the certainty that other authors know them too, and that one of them may beat him to the draw."[5]

The individual who corners a writer and insists on telling him of some dream or personal experience or anecdote which will be "perfectly wonderful" material for the writer, is a familiar figure. He is usually a nuisance. His "dream" or "personal experience" may turn out to be something already in print. And even in the rare case where he has a fresh idea, he's likely to cause embarrassment. For he's unable to stop talking. He will impart his idea to a dozen people, always with an air of fresh revelation. Two or more writers may thus be snared into elaborating the identical narrative.

Then there are the idea-merchants of Broadway and Hollywood— gag-men out of work, free-lance skit-fabricators, gimmick-coiners. They too pick up yarns, spin plots. They're no volunteers. They want money, and if they have anything of value to offer, they get it. Some of them are honest. Others don't hesitate to sell the same wares over and over again.

It may be argued that authors who lean on others for their ideas deserve to come to grief. That is beside the point. The point is that two writers may find themselves at loggerheads on the issue of plagiarism, and discover that instead of one of them being the victim of the other, they're both the victims of a third person.

## Coincidence

Newman Levy once wrote a piece of light verse about a golf player who became so exasperated with his wretched playing that he sold his soul to the devil for a bag of clubs with which he could invariably make a hole in one. He sent the poem to *The Saturday Evening Post*, only to learn that Bert Leston Taylor had hit on the same conceit years before, and had sold it to the *Post*.

While he was editor of *The Atlantic Monthly*, William Dean Howells received from a woman contributor a manuscript so closely paralleling a story of his own which he was about to publish that he felt it necessary to show her his proof sheets to convince her of his honesty.

Wagner set Heine's "Two Grenadiers" to music and inserted the "Marseillaise" at the finish. When he learned that Schumann had already composed a score for the poem and had also included the "Marseillaise," he became fearful he'd be accused of theft. He hastened to assure Schumann that he had written his piece the previous winter, before Schumann's version had been made available.

"Literature is full of coincidences," says Oliver Wendell Holmes, "which some love to believe are plagiarisms. There are thoughts always abroad in the air which it takes more wit to avoid than hit upon." When La Bruyère was told that something he had said had been uttered before by Horace and Boileau, he retorted: "I take your word for it, but I said it as my own. May I not have the same thoughts after them, as others may have after me?"

The seeds of common experience are many; the shoots they send up and the flowers they bear are of necessity often alike. A coincidence may easily occur without any communication. Human nature has changed but little since the birth of civilization. It is no more than natural that writers of all ages, contemplating the same virtues and vices, the same hopes and fears and passions of mankind, should have expressed similar sentiments.

The elements of folk tales are the same the world over. Since they cannot all be traced to a common source, and since isolation factors in many instances preclude the possibility of borrowing, the conclusion is inescapable that, given certain conditions, certain types of stories will spring up. Identical archetypes can be found in simple fables from the South Seas and in the sophisticated pages of Ovid's *Metamorphoses*. The *Arabian Nights* did not reach Europe until the eighteenth century; yet there are many intimations of it in Celtic and Scandinavian folklore.

The artifacts of almost all primitive cultures reveal certain common decorative motifs (the zigzag, the checker, the spiral, the scroll) and common forms. These flow from similarity of function, materials and tools, not from copying. For example, a strong kinship in design— but no discoverable link—exists between the decorated pottery of ancient Persia (going as far back as 3500 B.C.) and that of American Indians.

"My first painting in America," says Max Ernst, the surrealist, "was 'Napoleon in the Wilderness.' . . . About a month after completing it I happened to be in Washington and I came upon the Piero di Cosimo 'Allegory' in the Kress Collection at the National Gallery. I was amazed at the resemblance between the iconographic features of this picture I had never seen before and those I had employed in my painting—for instance the strange horse dancing, guarded by a female figure with wings, and the sea monster in front."

In 1938 Jacob Rabinow, chief of the Ordnance Mechanics Section of the National Bureau of Standards, invented a three-dimensional motion picture system. He was bitterly disappointed to find, on making a patent search, that someone had anticipated him by nearly thirty years. "If I had not seen the date 1910 on the patent describing my three-dimensional movies," he says, "I would have sworn on a stack of Bibles that the drawing was a copy of my ideas, and the man who submitted it a thief."

Nowhere is the logical fallacy of *post hoc, ergo propter hoc* more vividly illustrated than in connection with plagiarism claims. Let those who, encountering a parallel, feel impelled to impute piracy, pause and reflect that sequence in itself does not establish causation; that there can be no plagiarism without copying; and that many things besides copying may induce similarity.

# Parallel-Hunting

Onelie to point out, and nakedlie to joyne together [works and their models, in parallel columns], with no farder declaring the manner and way, how the one doth folow the other, were but a colde helpe to the encrease of learning.

—Roger Ascham: The Schoolmaster (1570)

---

A REVIEWER of Evelyn Waugh's *Scott-King's Modern Europe* praised the following excerpt as a "burst of stylish writing":

He [Scott-King] was older, it might have been written, than the rocks on which he sat; older, anyway, than his stall in chapel; he had died many times, had Scott-King, had dived deep, had trafficked for strange webs with Eastern merchants. And all this had been but the sound of lyres and flutes to him.

"Stylish, indeed!" cried a reader with a long memory. The passage, he said, was obviously a paraphrase of the celebrated description of La Gioconda in the chapter on Leonardo in Walter Pater's *The Renaissance*:

She is older than the rocks among which she sits . . . she has been dead many times, and learned the secrets of the grave; and has been a diver in deep seas . . . and trafficked for strange webs with Eastern merchants . . . and all this has been to her but as the sound of lyres and flutes.

John K. Hutchens, the book critic who published this intelligence, did not take it too seriously. It was the sort of thing, he felt, that could have happened to anybody. He was right.

The art of tracking down sources goes back thousands of years.

At first it was a limited activity: a literary exercise or a display of erudition or a projection of malice. With the invention of the printing press and the rise of the concept of literary property, it burgeoned into a distinct brand of criticism and research. And with the advent of mass-produced books, easy pictorial reproduction, the phonograph and the movies—all of which confer rich rewards on those whose efforts click—it became a formidable weapon in legal warfare.

### Crack Shots and Duffers

Parallel-hunters fall into several groups. Plagiarism claimants and litigants come first; then scholars and critics and commentators; then amateur sleuths and general readers.

The first category includes not only tyros who are ignorant of the rules of infringement, and who, seeing a passage or two of theirs duplicated, raise a hue and cry, but also knowledgeable people who honestly—and perhaps justifiably—feel they've been robbed. It comprises, too, sharks and schemers who know their claim is flimsy but who count on the cost of defense and the fear of publicity to force a settlement, and psychopaths who are obsessed with the notion that everyone they meet is plotting to despoil them of the fruits of their labor.

The second category, like the first, is a mixed lot. Able and perceptive scholars, who explore the genetics of the creative effort in order to illumine, not to demolish, stand beside others whose philosophy represents the polar opposite. The latter—"pedants without insight, intellectuals without love"—comb cows' tails to gather the seeds of weeds. Here, also, are frustrated writers who seek, consciously or unconsciously, to assuage their sense of personal failure by demonstrating that the great ones weren't so great after all.

In his *Essay on Criticism*, Pope poured scorn on pseudo scholars and similarity-chasers:

> The bookful blockhead, ignorantly read,
> With loads of learned lumber in his head. . . .
> All books he reads, and all he reads assails,
> From Dryden's Fables, down to D'Urfey's Tales.
> With him, most authors steal their works, or buy;
> Garth did not write his own Dispensary.

"There is, I fear," wrote Tennyson, "a prosaic set growing up among us—editors of booklets, bookworms, index-hunters, or men of great memories and no imagination, who *impute* themselves to the poet, and so believe that *he* too has no imagination, but is forever poking his nose between the pages of some old volume in order to see what he can appropriate. They will not allow one to say, 'Ring the bell' without finding that we have taken it from Sir P. Sidney, or even to use such a simple expression as the ocean 'roars' without finding out the precise verse in Homer or Horace from which we have plagiarized it."[1]

Speaking of the professors who evince a tendency to belittle the literary figures they've undertaken to study, Edmund Wilson suggests that they may do so because deep down they don't *like* their subjects as persons. The easiest way to undermine an author is to impugn his originality. This the professors contrive to do by prodigious reading, by concentrating on nonessentials, and by acrobatic reasoning. And while the resulting treatises may add nothing to our understanding of the men dealt with, they do create the impression of mountainous labor on the part of the scholars, and win them prestige in the hierarchy of academic society.

The third category runs the gamut from scrupulous investigators like Professor Wigmore (he's a professor of law, not of literature) to the casual member-of-the-public who has little interest in letters and no knowledge of the law, but who, having come across a similarity, sends a gleeful note to the papers about it. Professor Wigmore was struck, some years ago, by the marked resemblance between Poe's "The Murders in the Rue Morgue" and the files of an early French murder case. He did a superb job of sleuthing, and came to the conclusion that Poe had not plagiarized.[2]

### Parallel Lines Sometimes Meet

While each source-hunter does his digging his own way, the technique for the presentation of findings is fairly standard. It consists of comparison by conjunction, and the comparison is usually invidious. You take excerpts from the supposedly offending work, and corresponding ones from the alleged source, and you put them one below the other, or—more effective still—side by side. You see to it that both the selection and the arrangement underscore the resemblances. You make no mention of any differences unless you have to. Sometimes you add barbed comments; sometimes you let the presentation carry its own freight of censure.

The technique makes a weak case look strong, and a good case look devastating. It flourishes in court and out of court.[3] Here is a sample of the non-legal variety, culled from the Funny Coincidence Department of *The New Yorker:*

[From "King of the Cowboys," an article by Claude Stanush, in *Life*, May 13, 1946]

At this he insisted on unfastening his boot and showing me his leg, and when I told him it was the worst-looking leg I had ever seen he warmed up a bit.

Uncle Steve Crosby killed a "nester" (homesteader). . . . Crosby's father . . . won Crosby's mother in a drawpoker game.

To relieve monotony he lassoed young antelope, which he found he could run down with a fast horse. . . . On one occasion when a state tick inspector paid a visit, the Crosby boys roped and held 200 steers for him in a single day.

He loved to rope wild horses by their hind legs and send them crashing to the turf with a loud plop. Crosby defends his rough handling of horses, by pointing to the perfect manners and subservience of his mounts. "A hoss is like a woman," he says. "They'll mind yuh a little for love but a lot more for fear. Of course it's a heap easier to get a hoss afeard of yuh than a woman."

[From "Men's Tears," a story by Brenda Ueland, in *Collier's*, February 19, 1949]

Then he'd unfasten his boot and show you his leg. . . . When you told him it was the worst-looking leg you had ever seen he would warm up a bit.

His Uncle Bill had killed a nester, that is, a homesteader, he'd tell you, and his father won his mother in a drawpoker game.

As a little boy he would be alone on the range for days and to relieve the monotony he lassoed young antelope which he found he could run down with a fast horse. At twelve he roped a hundred steers in one day for an astonished state tick inspector.

Larry Brown, on the other hand, loved to rope horses by the two hind legs and send them crashing to the ground with such a loud plop that you would think they'd burst wide open. And he defended this by pointing to the mildness of his mounts. "A hoss is like a woman. They'll mind yuh a little for love but a lot more for fear. Of course it's a heap easier to git a hoss to be afeared of yuh than a woman."

"Ah always said if ever Ah found a lady Ah couldn't kiss, Ah was gonna marry her."

A few weeks later in Fort Worth, Crosby was waylaid by five cowboys. . . . "We locked horns," Crosby relates, "and rolled over the ground like tumbleweeds. This bull nurse thought he had his finger in muh eye. But he had it in muh mouth, and Ah bit off the end of it. 'Why don't you fight fair,' he yells. 'Ah didn't know there was any sech thing as fightin' fair,' Ah shout back. Ah then get loose and jump on him and stomp him with muh boot heels. Ah knowed Ah shouldna done it, 'cause those other four hands piled in on me. When they got through, muh nose was laid over to muh cheekbone. . . . When Ah got home, Ah had to interduce muhself to muh wife."

"I always said if ever I found a lady I couldn't kiss, I was gonna marry her."

"In Fort Worth me and five cowboys locked horns and rolled over the ground like tumbleweeds. This bull nurse thought he had his finger in my eye, but he had it in my mouth and I bit off the end of it. 'Why don't yuh fight fair?' he yells. 'I didn't know there was any sech thing as fightin' fair,' I shouts back. I then git loose and jump on him and stomp him with my boot heels. I knowed I shouldna done it because those other four hands piled in on me. When they got through my nose was laid over on my cheekbone and when I got home I had to interduce myself to my little brother Tom."

### In the Courts

Though the pursuit of parallels, as a form of literary research, is not the brisk industry it once was—back in Victorian days hardly an editor of a classic or a neoclassic deemed his job complete without digging out and annotating all the sources of his man—in litigation it flourishes with unquenchable vigor. For a plagiarism plaintiff never walks into court armed only with his book and his adversary's. He never trusts the judge to perceive, unassisted, the spoor of the raider. He brings along a double column "analysis." Designed presumably to highlight and summarize, this analysis is often more voluminous than the exhibits themselves.

The courts have long frowned on this practice. More than thirty years ago Judge Hough said that it illustrated the classic difficulty of not being able to see the forest for the trees. Infringement, he declared, was to be determined by comparative reading, not by dissection. In the *Abie's Irish Rose* case, Judge Learned Hand expressed himself to like effect. The proper approach, he said, had to be more ingenuous, more like that of a spectator who would rely upon the complex of his impressions.

In the *Strange Interlude* case, Miss Lewys charged that O'Neill had looted her *The Temple of Pallas-Athenae* [*sic*] for language, characters and plot. With respect to language alone, she cited *four hundred and fifty-five* items of alleged pilferage, including these:

| *Temple* | *Strange Interlude* |
| --- | --- |
| Pete . . . Peter, for God's sake. | For Pete's sake. |
| You ought to find consolation in your child. | My baby's happiness comes first with me. |
| Patricia Obermyer is a beautiful girl in her teens. | Madeline Arnold is a pretty girl of nineteen. |
| Dr. Cramwell has aged. | Dr. Darrell has aged. |
| I count on your help. | You've got to help me, Doctor. |

This exhausted the patience of Judge Woolsey, a notably unirritable man. "She has allowed herself," he said, "to indulge in comparisons in all three categories so grotesque that it confirms me in the belief that, for a party, litigation has greater refractive power than any other medium." Then, perhaps apprehensive that his metaphor might not convey the full burden of his meaning, he added bluntly: "Absurdity could not rise to greater heights." He exonerated O'Neill, and awarded him $17,500 as counsel fees.

Shortly afterward Judge Woolsey had another plagiarism case. The authors of the notable musical satire *Of Thee I Sing* were accused of having helped themselves to an obscure script entitled *U. S. A. with Music*. Again he was handed a massive analysis. "As is common in all cases of this kind," he said, with a touch of weariness, "I am faced with page after page of alleged parallelisms of phrase. Obviously, the plaintiff cannot claim a copyright on words in the dictionary, such as the names of the seasons in the principal lyrics, or on the usual English idioms, or on ideas." Once more he concluded there had been no infringement.

Here are some of the specifications which Myra Page Wiren relied on in the *Death Takes a Holiday* case to show that her play *Most* had been larcenously used:

| *Most* | *Death Takes a Holiday* |
|---|---|
| A brightness approaches. | I carry the lamp into your house. |
| He has such charm. | A divine smile. |
| You don't seem over twenty. | Youth. |
| How buoyantly she steps. | Athletic. |
| Where's Miss Hermoine [*sic*]? Is she up there alone? | Where is Grazia Maria? I shall go look for her. |
| I feel a strange presentiment. | This day it is better to be careful. |
| Shall you remain here long? | Will you stay on awhile? |
| I have lingered here. | It is my vacation. |
| One year later. | Three days have elapsed. |
| If you are tired . . . we'll find seats. | Poor girl! . . . Sit down. |
| Laughing ironically. | Ha, ha, ha. |
| 'Tis quite enough to make you mad. | Are you mad? |
| My love! | My love! |
| Now the wind is strong. | The wind howls. |
| Lightning. | Lightning. |
| I shall go with you. | Let us go. |

Mrs. Wiren found suspicious parallels in such age-old stage directions as "Enter X and Y," and in the fact that in her play a character "steps aside," while in the Italian play from which *Death Takes a Holiday* had been adapted a character "goes to the right, forward and stops." In each play, she said, a character fainted; in the one there was a minuet, and in the other a czardas; in the one there was a fair with gypsy fortunetellers, and in the other an autumn festival with singers and dancers.

Without reading one of these analyses in full, one cannot appreciate the immense amount of labor that goes into them, or the air of fantastic unreality that invests them.

Charging that *Gone with the Wind* plagiarized her *Authentic*

*History of the Ku Klux Klan*, Susan Lawrence Davis made much of the fact that both books were in "Confederate grey binding," and that both contained such words as scalawag, carpetbagger, States' rights, the fiery cross of the Klan, and such names as President Jefferson Davis, Fort Sumter (Fort Sumpter in the *Authentic History*!), Charleston and South Carolina. She spoke as though she had acquired exclusive rights to Southern names and history. Among the "similarities" she set forth were these:

| *Authentic History* | *Gone with the Wind* |
| --- | --- |
| [Dr. Richardson] was a very handsome man, immaculate in his attire at all times. | Dr. Meade . . . was tall and gaunt . . . and his clothes hung on his spare figure as though blown there by a hurricane. |
| Practically destitute. | Utterly impoverished. |
| Scotch-Irish. | Scotch Irish. |
| Stonewall Jackson was dead. | Stonewall Jackson was dead. |
| Mirrors above the mantel. | Gilt frame mirrors and long pier glasses. |
| Crimson plush sofas. | Red wallpaper and red velvet portières over the folding door. |

Mrs. Davis too met with defeat.

Then there was the case in which it was claimed that Edna Ferber and George Kaufman (who had collaborated on such hits as *The Royal Family* and *Dinner at Eight*) had lifted their successful play *Stage Door* from an unproduced, unpublished script called *Through the Looking Glass*. The plaintiff submitted several of the usual double-column analyses. I quote at random from the papers.

"In both plays," said the plaintiff, "the time element of the meeting of central character and male lead is substantially the same—during the action of the first act." The defense asked: "Isn't this also true of virtually every play that has ever been written?"

"In neither play," said the plaintiff, "is there a juvenile lead." The defense said: "It may also be noted that in neither play is there a grandmother or a midget or a whirling dervish. The type of approach which seeks to prove similarity by common omission would make every play a copy of every other play."

"In both plays," said the plaintiff, "there is, for low comedy, embarrassing reference to bathrooms." The defense said: "Does the plaintiff really believe that a chance reference to a girl staying in the bathroom overlong was purloined from her play? Has not the boardinghouse character who monopolizes the bathroom, while other boarders stamp and fume, been the stock subject of broad humor in books and plays for generations?"

"In neither play," said the plaintiff, "does the star appear in the early part of the performance. The words 'right away' are used in each play. In both plays there are characters that do not appear in the second act. In both plays the servants are colored. In both plays there is a 'stricken pause.' " The defense declined to dignify these items with an answer.

Judge Conger found no evidence of plagiarism. "The combined documents," he observed, referring to the plaintiff's analyses, "consist of 186 pages. In them plaintiff has digested and dissected to the minutest detail each of the plays. I confess that these documents have been of little help to me. I have labored through them with great care but have not been impressed. A great many of the alleged similarities are strained, forced and in many instances not correct. The only impression made upon me was that plaintiff was grasping at straws to prove her case."

## Pro and Con

Some people think parallel-hunting is a commendable enterprise, and view those engaged in it as public-spirited citizens resolved to put an end to the abduction of brain children. Others denounce the practice fiercely, claiming to detect in its operatives every frailty from fatuity to downright dishonesty.[4]

Intrinsically, the use of parallels is neither good nor bad. Their value—in the case of literary research, to the enhancement of knowledge, and in litigation, to the administration of the law—depends on the integrity with which they are prepared, the way they are presented, the uses to which they are put, and the conclusions that are drawn from them.

In research, parallels can render a service if the scholar is an open-minded inquirer, not a prosecuting attorney bent on conviction. They can shed a light on the germinative process. They can demonstrate, perhaps more vividly than anything else, the cumulativeness and interdependence of all creative effort. Many admirable accounts of this kind have been written. Professor Lowes' *The Road to Xanadu* (discussing Coleridge's gleanings) and Howard Vincent's *The Trying-Out of Moby Dick* (tracing Melville's sources) are good examples.

Employed with probity and intelligence, parallels can be of help—limited help—in plagiarism suits. By focusing the judge's attention on the culprit's fingerprints, they can clinch a genuine case of theft. But the narrow nature of their function must never be lost sight of. They must not be allowed to becloud or eclipse the paramount canon that the crucial test of plagiarism is and must be a reading of the rival works themselves in their entirety.

Whether the virtues of parallels outweigh the vices is open to debate. The fact remains that the vices are considerable.

1. Any method of comparison which lists and underscores similarities and suppresses or minimizes differences is necessarily misleading.

2. Parallels are too readily susceptible of manipulation. Superficial resemblances may be made to appear as of the essence.

3. Parallel-hunters do not, as a rule, set out to be truthful and impartial. They are hell-bent on proving a point.

4. Parallel-hunting is predicated on the use of lowest common denominators. Virtually all literature, even the most original, can be reduced to such terms, and thereby shown to be unoriginal. So viewed, Mark Twain's *The Prince and the Pauper* plagiarizes Dickens' *David Copperfield*. Both deal with England, both describe the slums of London, both see their hero exalted beyond his original station. To regard any two books in this light, however, is to ignore every factor that differentiates one man's thoughts, reactions and literary expression from another's.

5. Parallel columns operate piecemeal. They wrench phrases and passages out of context. A product of the imagination is indivisible. It depends on totality of effect. To remove details from their setting is to falsify them.

6. Parallels fail to indicate the proportion which the purportedly borrowed material bears to the sum total of the source, or to the

whole of the new work. Without such information a just appraisal
is impossible.

7. The practitioners of the technique resort too often to sleight
of hand. They employ language, not to record facts or to describe
things accurately, but as props in a rhetorical hocus-pocus which, by
describing different things in identical words, appears to make them
magically alike.

8. A double-column analysis is a dissection. An autopsy will reveal
a great deal about a cadaver, but very little about the spirit of the
man who once inhabited it.

9. Most parallels rest on the assumption that if two successive
things are similar, the second one was copied from the first. This
assumption disregards all the other possible causes of similarity.[5]

Whatever his vices or virtues, the parallel-hunter is a hardy
species. He is destined, as someone had said, to persist until Judgment Day, when he will doubtless find resemblances in the very
warrant that consigns him to the nether regions.

# 6

# A Glimpse into the Past:
# Homer to Milton

In literature as in life there is no spontaneous generation. There can be no flowering without a seed; and the seedlings of even the most individual genius must have been grown in the gardens of those who toiled before he began to till the soil.

—Brander Matthews: Molière

---

THE history of derivation in the creative arts is a threefold chronicle. It is a survey of influence in general, and borrowings in particular. It is an account of the awakening of literary conscience, and of the growth of criticism. And it is a register of the evolution and application of legal theories and techniques for the protection of property rights in books and plays, pictures and music.

It is a vast and variegated pageant, sharp with surprises.[1]

## The Uses of History

Without the perspective of time, terms like "tradition," "evolution" and "the ancestry of ideas" languish as abstractions. Given that perspective, they become concrete and graphic. But the past does more than give reality to these concepts. It demonstrates more vividly and persuasively than anything else the continuity and interdependence of all creative effort. For an artist is served no less by the recorded experiences of others than by his own contacts with life. If it were otherwise, society would be doomed to perpetual intellectual infancy.

History confirms the platitude that the greatest men have ever been the greatest borrowers. To reiterate this is to belabor the obvious. To pause and glance no further is to court error. Of course geniuses have persistently levied tribute. Borrowing is and always has been an integral part of the creative process.

"Commend me to a pilferer," says Byron; "you may laugh at it as a paradox, but I assure you the most original writers are the greatest thieves." This is an exaggeration, but like most exaggerations it has a germ of truth. To be sure, the elect have not always been content with borrowing. They have, on occasion, stolen. It was not wholly without reason that Molière was called *un grand et habile picoreur*. La Bruyère copied out whole pages of Publius Syrus. Seventeen of Beaumont and Fletcher's plays have been directly traced to Spanish originals. Sterne was a wizard with shears and paste-pot.

There is a pitfall here, and we must beware of it. It's much too easy to play up the debts and thefts of the great and the near great. It's considerably less easy to view those debts and thefts in the proper frame of reference, and to render an account which avoids overstatement and specious debunking. A catalogue of instances of appropriation is useful and valid only so long as we remember that the lesson to be learned from it is other than to tell us that there have always been pick-brains, and that men of stature have at times been of their number.

We must be careful, too, as we look back, not to confuse borrowing with theft. There is a world of difference between the winnowings of a Dante or a Chaucer and the outright looting of a Stendhal.

Genius borrows nobly. Impatient with attacks on Shakespeare, Walter Savage Landor says: "Yet he was more original than his originals. He breathed upon dead bodies and brought them to life." Voltaire exploited other writers, but with such superiority that Dubuc remarked: "He is like the false Amphitryon: although the stranger, it is always he who has the air of being master of the house."

A man's appropriations must be judged in the light of his total achievement. When everything has been said about the "depredations" of genius, when we have reckoned to the full Spenser's loot in *The Faerie Queene* and Ben Jonson's in *Timber* and Byron's in *Manfred*, the august ones still stand on their pedestals.[2]

Too, every instance of borrowing must be assessed in its time context. The laws of conscience derive from custom, and custom changes from age to age. What was accepted practice in Shakespeare's day is frowned upon today.

One of the deep-rooted myths in the lay mind is that artists are "inspired"—that they are activated by a mystic force of divine origin. The belief is an ancient one; the Greek philosopher Longinus first propounded it. It evokes a pictures of the artist receiving his celestial afflatus in a shaft of radiance from on high, something like Danaë receiving Zeus in a shower of gold. This notion has persisted throughout the ages; one of the uses of history is to explode it.

Finally, the past confirms the doctrine—that of good husbandry in the expenditure of creative energy—which virtually all the masters appear to have subscribed to. Much time and effort can be lost, the doctrine holds, in mere invention. Given a plot, characters and incidents, a writer can concentrate on the task of combining them and animating the result. He can avoid vain labor, sustain his vigor, enlarge his scope, and—in Goethe's words—"preserve his own fullness."

## Echoes in Hellas

Homer, whom Pope was later to hail as the most inventive writer the world had ever known, wrought the *Iliad* and the *Odyssey* out of the mass of myths and legends—chaotic, barbaric, extravagant—that flourished around the Aegean in his day. Whatever his sources, it was his imagination and organizing skill which imposed order on confusion, and fused disparate bits and pieces into sovereign entities. "For when primitive utterance is frozen into its ultimate and perfected artistic expression—as a folk air framed into the setting of a Tchaikovsky concerto or a Brahms dance—it is a single intelligence that directs the process."[3]

Whether Aesop ever actually existed is a matter of conjecture, but we do know that he did not invent the fables ascribed to him; he collected them and gave them currency. Some of them can be traced to the oldest literature of the Chinese; some to apologues incised on Babylonian tablets; some to the Jatakas of India; some to the great Sanskrit storybook, the *Panchatantra*. The fable of the lion and the mouse may be found intact in an Egyptian papyrus of about 1200 B.C.

Borrowing was a familiar practice in ancient Greece. Isocrates, Demosthenes, Aeschines, Menander and Plutarch indulged in it at times. Aristotle lifted whole pages from Democritus, the laughing philosopher of Abdera.

Aristophanes, himself a debtor to Cratinus and Eupolis, touched on the subject in his satire *The Frogs*. Wishing to deride his two famous contemporaries, Aeschylus and Euripides, he wrote them into a rowdy scene in which they pelted each other with insults. At one point Aeschylus, stung by a gibe, was made to retort to Euripides:

> You dare speak thus of me, you phrase-collector,
> Blind-beggar-bard and scum of rifled grab-bags!

Sophocles owed much to Aeschylus. And Plato, who scolded the author of the *Medea* and *Iphigenia at Aulis* for having lifted some of the ideas of his teacher Anaxagoras, himself annexed the earlier thought of Heraclitus, Empedocles and Pythagoras.

### The Hills of Rome

Just as ascendant Rome, its armies sweeping onward, conquered region after region on its way to imperial greatness, so it seized the wealth of Greece in philosophy, art and architecture. Roman literature developed slowly, and much of it was derivative. The comedies of Plautus and Terence were imitations of Hellenic models. In his *Prologues* Terence confessed that he had "translated" Menander. Lucretius' *De Rerum Natura* was based largely on Democritus and Epicurus. Indeed, Roman writers considered a Latin adaptation from the Greek a new work, and did not always trouble to acknowledge their sources.

Virgil patterned his *Eclogues* after the *idyls* of Theocritus. He laid under contribution Apollonius of Rhodes and Ennius, the father of Roman epic poetry. He copied the tale of Sinon and the taking of Troy almost word for word from Pisander, and the love story of Dido and Aeneas from that of Medea and Jason in Apollonius. So far-ranging were his forays that they provoked comment: Macrobius listed the master's borrowings in the sixth book of his *Saturnalia*, and Perillus Faustinus was supposed to have produced a whole treatise on them. Virgil was not insensitive to this implied criticism. Someone, finding him with a volume of Ennius in hand, asked pointedly what he was doing. He replied, with uncharacteristic acerbity, that he was plucking pearls from Ennius' dunghill.

Virgil's chief model was Homer. In *The Aeneid*, "the stateliest measure ever molded by the lips of man," he drew heavily on the *Iliad* and the *Odyssey*. If Homer gives a catalogue of an army, says Pope, Virgil draws up his forces in the same order. If he has funeral games for Patroclus, Virgil has the same for Anchises. If Ulysses visits the shades, Virgil sends Aeneas after him. If Ulysses is detained by the blandishments of Calypso, so is Aeneas by Dido. If Homer gives his hero a suit of celestial armor, Virgil makes the same present to his.

"Virgil's conscious imitation of Homer," says Auden, "is, of course, not due to a lack of invention; indeed, it is often precisely when he copies most closely that the novelty of his vision is clearest. . . . The *Iliad* is poetry of the highest order, but it is the poetry of barbarians, of a tribal culture; *The Aeneid* is the poetry of civilization, of world history. A child can enjoy Homer; anyone who has come to appreciate Virgil has already grown up."

Horace's position in the pantheon of letters is as secure as Virgil's, yet there are few precepts in his *Ars Poetica* which cannot be traced to Aristotle's *Poetics*. Longus' *Daphnis and Chloë* is full of Anacreon, Callimachus, Propertius and Menander; it has bred a long line of offspring, starting with Sannazaro's *Arcadia* and including Tasso's *Aminta*, Montemayor's *Diana*, and Saint-Pierre's *Paul et Virginie*.[4]

### The Attitude of the Ancients

Plato was praised for having "irrigated his style with ten thousand runnels from the great Homeric spring." Cicero believed that to imitate Demosthenes was to achieve an eloquence at once Attic and perfect. Quintilian saw in the desire to copy what we admire a universal rule of life.

The writers of antiquity deemed innovation hazardous, and imitation both necessary and laudable. They insisted, however, that the imitation be of superior models, and that the imitator make a contribution of his own.

While literary practitioners felt that copying was permissible so long as one disclosed the source, the proviso was often disregarded. "In comparing various works with one another," Pliny the Elder observed sternly in his *Historia Naturalis*, "I have discovered that some of the most eminent writers have transcribed, word for word, from other works, without acknowledgment."

Theft was not condoned, nor the wrong kind of imitation applauded. "He who studies to ape the poet Pindar," warned Horace, "relies on artificial wings fastened on with wax, and is sure to give his name to a glassy sea."

After the fall of the Roman Republic in 28 B.C., the Greek and Roman masters continued to reign in the schools of the Empire. But their works, instead of kindling a fire like their own, inspired only pale reflections. A cloud of jargoners and compilers darkened the face of learning.

### The Middle Ages

With the collapse of the Roman Empire, the line of classical tradition was broken. The ancient civilizations had run their course, and the achievements of their philosophers, writers and artists were not to be revived for a thousand years. And yet for all the visitations which shattered the grandeur of Rome, and struck afterward— corruption, conflagration, plague, barbarian incursions, pillage—it was not total darkness that ruled the Middle Ages.

Borrowing kept the low-flickering torch of learning from going out altogether. Although the Church Fathers rejected paganism and warred against it with unrelenting zeal, they could not strip themselves of its legacy. Christian doctrine was tinctured with old beliefs. Augustine took so much from the ancients, it is said, that Gregory VIII, to shield Augustine's name, burned all the works he had lifted from. Boethius' *De Consolatione Philosophiae*, which played such an important part in molding medieval thought, also had roots deep in the past.

Monks were the unsung heroes of the Middle Ages. Toiling in the scriptoria of monasteries, countless companies of them spent their lives engrossing old texts and early Christian devotional matter. As the demand for books grew, the art of illumination flowered, and the scope of subject matter expanded. The monkish artists produced a wealth of Books of Hours, bestiaries, herbals, psalters, missals, liturgies and copies of the Scriptures. Calligraphy and miniature painting were merged to yield a new art form of extraordinary beauty.

Conditions were favorable for plagiarism. Just as the cloistered scholar, embarked on a dissertation of his own, must have been tempted to seize upon every bit of antique lore and wisdom that fell his way, without bothering to credit his sources, so the lettered adventurer, happening on a rare and ancient manuscript and hoping it was the only copy extant, must have been tempted to transcribe it and launch the copy as his original. Certainly the early biographers of the saints suffered no literary scruples; their accounts of the supposed trials and tribulations of the martyrs were often nothing more than loose paraphrases of classical legends.

Like their counterparts of antiquity, medieval epics were suckled by the past and fed the future. The version of *Beowulf* we know goes back to the eighth century; there were doubtless earlier versions, each bard retelling and elaborating the old lays in his own way. The Caedmonian cycle was based on the Bible; Caedmon's metrical treatment of the Genesis may have been one of the sources of Milton's *Paradise Lost*. The Arthurian Romance sprang from Welsh or Celtic legends, took partial shape in the work of Nennius in the ninth century, emerged solidly in Geoffrey of Monmouth's twelfth-century *Historia Regum Britanniae*, was further elaborated by the Norman poet Wace, the Worcestershire priest Layamon, and the Provençal romancer Chrétien de Troyes, and culminated in Malory's *Morte d'Arthur* in the fifteenth century.

*Chansons de geste,* early French epic poems, grew by accretion too. *Chanson de Roland* dealt with Charlemagne and heroes of his time; it was sung, added to and carried far and wide by jongleurs. It was linked to the Arthurian tale in England, Ariosto's *Orlando* in Italy, and the *Poem of the Cid* in Spain. Corneille's *Le Cid* was its celebrated offspring. The *Nibelungenlied,* the high point of medieval German literature, probably originated in the old Scandinavian fables recounted in the *Edda* and the *Volsunga Saga*: it ultimately inspired Wagner's *Ring*.

With the *Gesta Romanorum* (strictly translated, the *Deeds of the Romans,* but better known as the *Tales of the Monks*) we come to less exalted material. The *Gesta* is a miscellany of brief and lively homiletic anecdotes drawn from Roman, Oriental and European folk sources. It has been a rich mine for writers. Among others, it gave

Chaucer "The Man of Law's Tale," and Shakespeare the plot of *Pericles* and the episode of the three caskets in *The Merchant of Venice*.

## Troubadours and Minstrels

Originating in Provençe in the eleventh century, chivalry attained full blossom at the court of Eleanor of Aquitaine. Platonic mysticism was one of its ingredients; Christian dogma—with its insistence on the denial of the flesh (the knight's pure lady was a secular version of the Virgin Mary)—was another. It was a cult of gallantry based on the idealization and veneration of women, and it had definite conventions. A knight had to worship his lady with unquenchable devotion. She had to be of stainless virtue. Since courtly love was deemed incompatible with marriage, the lady had to be unattainable, preferably because she was wedded to someone else. It was preferable, too, that her husband be the knight's liege lord, so that the lover would be doubly torn between the flesh and the spirit, between loyalty and passion. These rules naturally made for a measure of similarity among the romances typical of the period. The era made memorable such evocative names as Lyonesse and Carcassonne, and gave us the story of Tristan and Iseult, *Amadis of Gaul, Chanson de Roland,* Boiardo's *Orlando Innamorato,* and Ariosto's *Orlando Furioso.*

While the minnesingers and the meistersingers of twelfth- and thirteenth-century Germany also sang of love, they expanded their repertory to include nature, religion and patriotism. Wolfram, one of their number, wrote *Parzefal* (Parsifal) and a variant of the Tristan story.

It was not only at courtly games and baronial feasts, however, that minstrelsy flourished. Strolling entertainers went from inn to inn, town to town, fair to fair, singing lyrics and ballads to the accompaniment of their harps, recounting fables spiced with sexual infidelity, broad humor and ridicule of the clergy. Boccaccio later drew heavily on these fables, as did Chaucer and Balzac.

## Crusades and Cathedrals

The holy wars against the Turks and the Saracens for the recovery of the Holy Land forged a link between Europe and the Near East. The literature and learning which crusaders, pilgrims, merchants and adventurers brought back with them from the Mediterranean—like bees that pick up and carry generative pollen—took on a new vitality in the North.

The West felt the impact of the South also. Byzantine architecture gave way to the Romanesque, and the Romanesque laid the foundation for the Gothic. And though the builders of the Renaissance, proud of their rediscovery of the ideals of Greece and Rome, were later to scoff at medieval architecture, coining the word "Gothic" as the equivalent of "barbarian," we now regard the Gothic cathedral as the supreme expression of the Middle Ages, the life and aspirations of which it epitomized as nobly as had the Attic temples their own era. Chartres, Amiens, Notre Dame, Rheims, Salisbury, Gloucester and Winchester are magic images—images reflected in countless structures reared centuries after the first ogive window was set aflame with stained glass, after the first legend was writ in sculpture across a church façade.

## The Threshold of the Renaissance

It used to be said that the Renaissance marked man's discovery of himself and the world, and the liberation of the individual from the shackles of medieval uniformity and religious authority. Today it is regarded as a continuation of Christian humanism: a synthesis of classical reason and Christian faith. In any case, it was an age of glory, not only because of the upsurge of invention, exploration and commerce, but also because it flung all the wealth of ancient literature and art before the eyes of Europe. If poets and philosophers, painters and sculptors, composers and architects, dazzled as if they had burst into Ali Baba's cave, loaded themselves with precious things and carried them forth into the world, for all to behold and enjoy, society was the gainer; and if the disseminators forgot, as they often did, whence they had fetched their treasures, their neglect was understandable, and usually overlooked.

Historians differ as to the date on which the Middle Ages came to an end. Some say 1450, when printing was invented; some say 1453, when Constantinople fell; some say 1492, when Columbus planted the flag of Spain on the soil of America. Actually, the great revival which shook England in the early years of the sixteenth century had begun in Italy two hundred years before. Dante, Boccaccio and Petrarch furnished the initial impetus.

Dante, the man who "'gave voice to ten silent centuries," who single-handed molded the Tuscan dialect into the modern language of Italy, wove the strands of Greek and Roman mythology, of medieval erudition and fervor, into the prodigious tapestry of the *Divine Comedy*. More original, in a strict sense, than most other poets of the first magnitude—his masterpiece was unique in conception, range and form—yet did he, as he trod the corridors of Hell with his guide Virgil, pay homage to him as the master from whom he derived his style.

Throughout his life Petrarch strove to proclaim the greatness of the classics. He was an eloquent transition figure, composing epistles and treatises in Latin, and pouring out his heart to Laura in Italian.

Boccaccio is chiefly remembered for the *Decameron,* a collection of a hundred stories purportedly told by a group of people during the plague at Florence in 1348. The stories are variations on the themes of medieval fabliaux. Boccaccio derides virtue, gibes at cuckolds, applauds carnal passion, revels in ribaldry. True to the folk-fable convention, he misses no opportunity to belabor the clergy. Prelates are wont, he observes, to don the robes of sanctimony when, after a full measure of riotous years, they can no longer indulge their physical appetites. It is ironic that Boccaccio's own life mirrored the pattern he so merrily castigated in ecclesiastics. After many years of profligacy, with the end of his days drawing near, he repudiated his stories as licentious and blasphemous. His brain children fared none the worse for this unfatherly treatment. They found a thousand other authors to adopt and clothe them—and profit by their benefaction.

### "Le Grand Translateur"

Chaucer set forth his literary creed in *The Parliament of Fowls*:

> For out of olde feldes, as men seyth,
> Cometh al this newe corn from yere to yere,
> And out of olde bokes, in good feyth,
> Cometh al this new science that men lere.

Chaucer was a prodigious assimilator. He devoured Ovid, Statius, Boethius, Dante and Petrarch, the singers of Provençe, and a host

of others. He possessed himself of Latin legends and French fabliaux
with equal unconcern. In *The Book of the Duchess* he tapped
Froissart's *Le Paradys d'Amour*; in *Troilus and Criseyde*, Boccaccio's
*Il Filostrato*.

So thoroughly did Chaucer, in *The Canterbury Tales,* quarry Boccaccio that it has been said the book is *aut Decamerone, aut nullus.*
The statement is not true. Chaucer's raw materials were diverse; he
appropriated and refashioned *exempla* (anecdotal sermons), *mi-
racula* (accounts of miracles performed by saints), chivalric romances,
fables and legends. "And poor Gower he used as if he were only a
brick-kiln or a stone-quarry, out of which to build his house."[5] And
yet, no matter what he took, what he gave back was pure Chaucer.

### *The Elizabethans*

Borrowing flourished in sixteenth-century England. It was often
flagrant enough to constitute plagiarism. The Elizabethans did not
bother to devise plots, incidents and characters; they lifted them
from their predecessors and from each other.

The advent of the printing press had opened up a market of
shining promise for literary material. Writers saw, perhaps for the
first time in history, a possibility of earning a living at their craft,
other than through patronage; and they wanted to make the most of
it. They did not boggle at short cuts. What they needed they carried
off. The risk to reputation was slight, for the standards of ethics
were low; the legal hazard was nonexistent because there was no
copyright statute. The poet or playwright who found himself plundered had only to remember his own filchings to cool his indignation.
Besides, the intellectual excitement, the avid curiosity, the prodigal
outpouring of expression which marked the age, scorned quotation
marks and the niceties of acknowledgment. "Even the greatest of the
Elizabethan sonneteers did not disdain occasional transcription of
the language and sentiment of popular French or Italian poetry. . . .
The full story of the Elizabethan sonnet is, for the most part, a
suggestive chapter in the literary records of plagiarism."[6]

To be sure, here and there an author uttered a protest. Occasionally
a critic spoke up. In his *Arte of English Poesie,* Puttenham denounced Sothern for stealing Ronsard's verse, saying: "This man
deserves to be endited of petty larceny for pilfering other men's

devises from them and converting them to his own use, for in deede as I would wish their inventour, which is the very Poet, to receave the prayses of his invention, so would I not have the translatour to be ashamed to be acknowen of his translation."

## Spenser and Sidney

Edmund Spenser, whom Milton honored as "a better teacher than Aquinas," whom Charles Lamb called the poets' poet, whose imagery and rhythms stood Burns and Keats and Tennyson in good stead, found both the Pan-pipes of antiquity and the viols of the jongleurs to his liking. In *The Shepheardes Calender* he imitated Greek and Roman eclogues. And into the splendid mosaic of *The Faerie Queene* he set stones plucked from many sources: Virgil and Homer, Plato and Aristotle, the epics of chivalry such as Ariosto's *Orlando Furioso* and Malory's *Morte d'Arthur,* allegories like *Roman de la Rose* and *Piers the Plowman* and *The Parliament of Fowls.*

Professing a fine disdain for Italianate conceits and apostrophes, Spenser's friend Sir Philip Sidney chided his fellow-sonneteers for singing "poor Petrarch's long-deceased woes with new-born sighs and denizened wit." His own innocence he proclaimed in clarion tones:

> And this I sweare by blackest brooke of hell,
> I am no Pickepurse of an other's wit.

Yet there are unmistakable echoes of Petrarch in his own sonnets, and his *Arcadia* owes more than a little to Longus' *Daphnis and Chloë,* Tatius' *Clitophon and Leucippe,* Sannazaro's *Arcadia* and Montemayor's *Diana.*

## The Jackdaw's Feathers

Shakespeare is, of course, the prize exhibit of the source-hunters. He is also their nemesis, their bête noire. He bears out most of their charges of lifting. At the same time he demolishes the very foundations of their house of cavil.

That he evinced a marked propensity for avoiding unnecessary invention, need hardly be said. He was not a rebel. He was a man of the working theater, sensitive to public taste. Whenever people flocked to see a certain type of play, he was certain to try his hand at it, and do it better.

By the time he arrived in London, the English stage had acquired a tradition. Medieval miracle and morality plays, Tudor masques and pageants, and the output of the early dramatists constituted a prodigal accumulation. Shaped and reshaped by many hands, historical and legendary subjects had become the property of the theater. The classics had been translated and were gaining circulation.

The Elizabethan dramatist was the inheritor of this wealth. That Shakespeare should turn to it was natural; that he should exploit it without compunction was in keeping with the spirit of the times. He commandeered everything that suited his purpose—Greek biography, Roman history, the tales of the Middle Ages, long-familiar anecdotes, old farces, the plays of his predecessors—and cast them into forms popular in his day.[7]

He went to Holinshed for *Macbeth, Cymbeline,* and his English history plays; to Sir Thomas North for *Julius Caesar, Antony and Cleopatra, Timon of Athens,* and *Coriolanus*; to Arthur Brooke for *Romeo and Juliet*; to Lodge for *As You Like It*; to Cinthio for *Othello*; to Boccaccio for *All's Well That Ends Well*; to Chaucer for *Troilus and Cressida;* to Gower for *Pericles;* to Thomas Kyd for *Titus Andronicus* and *Hamlet.* He took the outlines of the chronicle play from Marlowe, of the tragedy-of-blood from Kyd, of romantic comedy from Greene, of dramatic romance from Beaumont and Fletcher. He wrote *King John* in imitation of Marlowe's *Tamburlaine* (some critics dispute this). The verbal tilts and contests of wit, the elaborate conceits, similes and metaphors in *Love's Labour's Lost*, owed their existence to John Lyly's *Euphues.*

But Shakespeare did more than adopt design, plot, character and episode. Sometimes he copied word for word. Sometimes he paraphrased so closely that we're forced to conclude he had the original at his elbow as he wrote. Gonzalo's description of the ideal state in *The Tempest*:

> I' the commonwealth, I would by contraries
> Execute all things; for no kind of traffic
> Would I admit; no name of magistrate;
> Letters should not be known; no use of service,

> Of riches or of poverty; no contracts,
> Succession; bound of land; tilth, vineyard, none;
> No use of metal, corn or wine or oil;
> No occupation; all idle men, all.

is straight out of Montaigne:

It is a nation (would I answer Plato) that hath no kind of traffic, no knowledge of letters, no intelligence of number, no name of magistrate, nor of politic superiority, no use of service, or riches, or of poverty; no contracts, no successions, no occupations, but idle . . . nor no use of wine, corn or metal.

Some of the most impressive passages in the Bard's Roman plays are Sir Thomas North's prose strung into blank verse. There are speeches in *Antony and Cleopatra* which are pure Plutarch. Malone painstakingly analyzed Parts I, II, and III of *Henry VI*, and came to the conclusion that out of the 6,033 lines, Shakespeare had copied 1,771 intact, and had paraphrased 2,373 others, so that only 1,889 were entirely his own.

Robert Greene, whose *Pandosto* Shakespeare had dipped into for *The Winter's Tale,* and from whom he had learned the craft of weaving rhymed couplets into blank verse, and of integrating the comic with the dramatic, violently resented Shakespeare's free-and-easy ways. He bade Marlowe and Lodge to abandon playwriting because "there is an upstart Crow, beautified with our feathers, that with his Tygers hart wrapt in a Players hyde, supposes he is an absolute Ioannes fac totum, is in his owne conceit the onely Shake-scene in the countrey."

Time has rendered its verdict. Lyly's extravagances have become a literary curiosity. Kyd's gory charades are as dead as the corpses with which he used to clutter up the stage at curtainfall. Despite his eloquence and dramatic power, Marlowe's bombast and bathos and lack of humor have exiled his plays from the theater. Holinshed and North languish in libraries. Greene himself is no more than a name in the annals of letters. Shakespeare lives.

### The Organ-toned Puritan

"That double-dyed thief of other men's brains," wrote Robert Stephen Hawker, the eccentric vicar of Morwenstow, "John Milton, the Puritan, one-half of whose lauded passages are, from my own knowledge, felonies committed in the course of his reading on the property of others; and who was never so rightly appreciated as by the publisher who gave him fifteen pounds for the copyright of his huge larcenies." Himself the perpetrator of a literary hoax that fooled Scott and Macaulay, Hawker shared with the Reverend William Lauder the doubtful distinction of being the most unsparing—and the most unjust—of Milton's critics.

Like Chaucer and Shakespeare, Milton was omnivorous. His universe was shaped and colored by the luxuriant resources of his reading. "The lilt of old songs was in his ears, the happy phrases of the old poets, the jewels five words long from old treasures. He had the opulent memory of the profound student, and these things crowded thickly into his thought with each new suggestion from without."[8] Indeed, so great was his indebtedness to the classics that it was said that if he soared, it was because he plucked feathers from the wings of Homer and Virgil.

In one instance, however, he was the victim of a deliberate plagiarism frame-up. In his *Eikonoklastes* he had excoriated Charles I and had paid tribute to his executioners. A hundred years later, Lauder, a Scot who for some obscure reason felt attached to the memory of the dead king, sought to avenge him. He undertook to demolish Milton by showing that considerable portions of *Paradise Lost* had been stolen from little-known foreign poets. His plan misfired. The Bishop of Salisbury proved that the passages in question had been taken not from "foreign poets" but from William Hog's Latin translation of *Paradise Lost*. The misguided Reverend was convicted of forgery.

Du Bartas' *La Première Sepmaine* and *La Seconde Sepmaine*, Caedmon's *Genesis*, Grotius' *Adamus Exul*, the *Adamo* of the Italian dramatist Giambattista Andreini, the Dutch poet Vondel's *Lucifer*, and particularly the *Sarcotis* of the Jesuit Masenius—one or another of these has been put forward from time to time by source-hunters as the original of *Paradise Lost*. Suppose Milton read all these books. *Paradise Lost* still remains his. "It is perfectly certain," says Saintsbury, "not merely that nobody else could have constructed it out of them, but that a syndicate composed of their authors, each in his happiest passion and working together as never collaborators worked, could not have come within measurable distance of it, or of him."[9]

Voltaire was a shade less generous to Milton. The *Sarcotis* bothered him. He noted that Masenius' poem was little known in Europe in Lauder's time; it could not be readily compared with Milton's. When a new edition of the *Sarcotis* came out in 1757, Voltaire had an opportunity to make such a comparison. He professed to discover striking parallels. "The exordium, the invocation, the description of the Garden of Eden, the portrait of Eve, that of the devil," he said, "are precisely the same as in Milton. Further, it is the same subject, the same plot, the same catastrophe. If the devil wishes, in Milton, to be revenged on man for the harm which God has done him, he has precisely the same plan in the work of the Jesuit Masenius. . . . One finds in both little episodes, trifling digressions, which are absolutely alike; both speak of Xerxes who covered the sea with his ships; both speak in the same tone of the tower of Babel; both give the same description of luxury, of pride, of avarice, of gluttony."

Although Voltaire found that Milton had reproduced more than two hundred verses from the *Sarcotis,* his admiration for the poet remained unshaken. "I daresay," he concluded, "that he imitated only what was worthy of being imitated. These two hundred verses are very beautiful; so are Milton's; and the total of Masenius' poem, despite these two hundred beautiful verses, is not worth anything at all."[10]

The subject of the paternity of *Paradise Lost* will not die. In 1845 Zicari, an Italian researcher, wrote an extensive monograph purporting to show that Milton's epic was sired by a sacred tragedy called *Adam Caduto,* written by Serafino della Salandra, a Calabrian monk. Norman Douglas translated the monograph in 1908, and thereafter repeatedly expressed irritated surprise at the fact that Milton scholars have taken no notice whatever of what he considered to be a discovery of prime importance in the history of English letters.

# 7

## A Glimpse into the Past:
## Ben Jonson to the Present

> A well-cultivated mind is, so to speak, made up of all the minds of
> proceeding ages; it is only one single mind which has been educated during
> all this time.
>
> —Bernard de Fontenelle: Dialogue des Morts

---

REALIST and self-made classical scholar, one-time King's Poet
and later arbiter of letters at the Mermaid Tavern, Ben Jonson
had a sharp ear for what went on around him, and an equally sharp
memory of what he read. His tragedy *Sejanus,* probably written because of the success of Shakespeare's *Julius Caesar*, has in it much of
Tacitus, with dashes of Juvenal, Suetonius and Seneca. His *Catiline*
is studded with paragraphs lifted from Cicero. Even the comedies—
*Volpone, Epicene* and *The Alchemist*—in which he satirized life and
people in the London of his day, and for which he is remembered,
bear the impress of Petronius, Lucian, Plautus, Ovid, Horace and
Erasmus.

His famous song "Drink to Me Only with Thine Eyes" is a paraphrase of Philostratus. And his *Timber*, which contains his memorable tribute to Shakespeare, esteemed by Swinburne to be worth all
his other work put together, comprises more plagiarized material
than any other book of its size by an author of rank, with the possible
exception of Sterne and Stendhal. It has twenty-five excerpts from
Quintilian, twenty-one from the younger Seneca, eleven from the
elder Seneca, four each from Horace, Plutarch, and the younger Pliny,
and a couple from Aristotle and Plato.

## The Angler and the Pilgrim

*The Compleat Angler,* too, is an omnibus; Izaak Walton poured into it precepts, anecdotes, characters, reflections and technical information he had culled from dozens of writers. "He might have said, if challenged, that he was paying them the compliment of treating them as the authors of standard textbooks on the subject. Perhaps he felt himself no more obliged to make full acknowledgment to them than a scientist writing today would feel it necessary to admit his indebtedness to Newton every time he mentioned the law of gravity."[1]

When John Bunyan's *The Pilgrim's Progress* appeared, there were those who viewed it as a patchwork of the Bible, De Guileville's *Pèlerinage de L'Homme,* Langland's *Piers the Plowman,* and Bernard's *Isle of Man.* This grieved Bunyan. "It came from my own heart, so to my head," he said of his allegory; "nor was it unto any mortal known till I had done it. The whole and every whit is mine."[2]

## Poet Laureate

"The genius of our countrymen," declared Dryden, "is rather to improve an invention than to invent themselves." This was more an *apologia pro se* than a general statement. So persistent and venomous were the aspersions on Dryden's originality that he felt impelled to clarify his position on the subject. "I am taxed with stealing all my plays," he wrote in his preface to *The Mock Astrologer,* "and that by some men, who should be the last men from whom I would steal any part of them. . . . It is true that wherever I have liked any story in a romance, novel, or foreign play, I have made no difficulty, nor ever shall, to take the foundation of it, to build it up, and to make it proper for the English stage. And I will be so vain to say, it has lost nothing in my hands."

He freely admitted that in writing *The Mock Astrologer* he had drawn on Calderón's *El Astrologo Fingido* and Corneille's *Le Feint Astrologue.* "What I have performed in this will best appear by comparing it with those: you will see that I have rejected some adventures which I judged were not diverting; that I have heightened those which I have chosen; and that I have added others which were neither in the French nor Spanish. . . . I have further to add, that I seldom use the wit and language of any romance or play which I undertake to alter: because my own invention (as bad as it is) can furnish me with nothing so dull as what is there."

In general, he said, a poet was like a gunsmith or watchmaker; the iron or silver was not his own; but they were the least part of that which created the value: the price lay wholly in the workmanship. "I shall but laugh at them hereafter, who accuse me with so little reason," he concluded, "and withal contemn their dulness, who, if they could ruin what little reputation I have got, and which I value not, yet would want both wit and learning to establish their own, or to be remembered in after ages for anything, but only that which makes them ridiculous in this."

### To His Coy Mistress

Andrew Marvell (1621-1678) is best remembered for his apostrophe to a playing-hard-to-get enchantress. Here are a few of his lines:

> Had we but world enough, and time,
> This coyness, Lady, were no crime.
> We would sit down and think which way
> To walk and pass our long love's day. . . .
>                       I would
> Love you ten years before the Flood,
> And you should, if you please, refuse
> Till the conversion of the Jews.

And here is what Joseph Addison wrote in *The Spectator* of June 12, 1711:

First of all I would have them seriously think on the Shortness of their Time. Life is not long enough for a Coquet to play all her Tricks in. . . . Were the Age of Man the same that it was before the Flood, a Lady might sacrifice half a Century to a Scruple, and be two or three Ages in demurring. Had she Nine Hundred Years good, she might hold out to the Conversion of the Jews before she thought fit to be prevailed upon.

### The Wicked Wasp of Twickenham

"I admired Mr. Pope's *Essay on Criticism* at first very much," wrote Lady Mary Wortley Montagu, "but I had not then read any of the ancient critics and did not know that it was all stolen." The stricture was not wholly unmerited. Though in the *Dunciad* Pope drew a derisive picture of a plagiarist:

> Next o'er his books his eyes begin to roll
> In pleased memory of all he stole;
> How here he sipped, how there he plundered snug
> And sucked all o'er like an industrious bug.
> Here lay poor Fletcher's half-eat scenes, and here
> The frippery of crucified Molière.

he was a pretty industrious bug himself. His *Pastorals* bear the stamp of Virgil's muse. His *Dunciad* harks back to Dryden's *Mac Flecknoe*. There is more than a little of Bolingbroke and Leibnitz in his *Essay on Man*. In *The Rape of the Lock*, the impact of Boileau's *Le Lutrin* and Tassoni's *Sacchia Rapita* is clear.

However, it is his epigrammatic utterances that reveal his obligations most strikingly. His famous aphorism—the proper study of mankind is man—was cribbed from the Frenchman Charron. Though the thought is different, the figure is identical in Dryden's

> Great wits are sure to madness near allied,
> And thin partitions do their bounds divide.

and in Pope's

> Remembrance and affection how allied!
> What thin partitions sense from thought divide.

On occasion he simply reverses the original; in his hands, Dryden's

> Truth has such an air, and such a mien
> As to be loved needs only to be seen.

becomes

> Vice is a monster of such hideous mien
> That to be hated needs but to be seen.

But as a rule Pope transfigures what he takes. Though he trespasses at will on Wycherly's preserve, the sum of the matter is that we still quote Pope but none of us reads the maunderings of Wycherly. Donne's "Who are a little wise the best fools be" is good; Pope's "A little learning is a dangerous thing" is better. Suckling says:

> But as when an authentic watch is shown,
> Each man winds up and rectifies his own,
> So in our very judgments.

Pope's version springs from shrewder observation:

> 'Tis with our judgments as our watches, none
> Go just alike, yet each believes his own.

Sometimes he does an inspired job of compression, as where he transmutes Phineas Fletcher's

> When needs he must, yet faintly when he praises;
> Somewhat the deed, much more the means he raises:
> So marreth what he makes, and praising most, dispraises.

into "Damn with faint praise, assent with civil leer."

### Ursa Major

A friend of Samuel Johnson, discussing the subject of criticism with him, remarked that critics of repute labored under a burden: they were expected to be saying witty and meaningful things all the time, and it was a heavy tax on them. "It is indeed a very heavy tax," said Dr. Johnson, "a tax which no man can pay who does not steal."

It was the task of writers, the learned Doctor held, to make familiar things new, and new things familiar. He warned against irresponsible imputations of piracy. The common field in which authors had to work, he observed, was comparatively small, and similarities unavoidable. "A man loves and hates, desires and avoids, exactly like his neighbor," he said. "Resentment and ambition, avarice and indolence, discover themselves by the same symptoms in minds distant a thousand years from one another. Nothing, therefore, can be more unjust than to charge an author with plagiarism, merely because he assigns to every cause its natural effect, and makes his personages act as others in like circumstances have always done."[3]

### Sterne and Goldsmith

For Sterne no explanation predicated on coincidence will suffice. The plain fact is that he stole, and stole extensively and without compunction. Burton, Swift and Bolingbroke were among those he cribbed from, as were Erasmus, Rabelais, Montaigne, Scarron and Cervantes. His celebrated line "God tempers the wind to the shorn lamb" he took from Henri Etienne's *"Dieu mesure le froid à la brebis tondue."* The irony was that he piously denounced the offense of plagiarism—using the words of Burton!

Yet in one respect posterity has done an injustice to Sterne. It has been said that there isn't a single paragraph in his *Koran* which may not be found, word for word, in the books of his contemporaries. The *Koran* was a hoax. It appeared in 1770, two years after Sterne's death. Its perpetrator was Richard Griffith the elder, who wagered with a friend that he could write a volume which would pass as Sterne's. Griffith won the bet; and ever since then commentator after commentator, unaware of the hoax, has cudgeled Sterne for his depredations in the *Koran.*

It is possible—though not likely—that Goldsmith, who gave us *The Vicar of Wakefield* and *She Stoops to Conquer,* and for whom Dr. Johnson coined the epitaph *Nullum quod tetigit non ornavit,* did not filch his

> Man wants but little here below
> Nor wants that little long.

from Young's "Man wants but little, nor that little long." But when it comes to his best-known stanzas

> When lovely woman stoops to folly,
>   And finds too late that men betray,
> What charm can soothe her melancholy?
>   What art can wash her guilt away?
>
> The only art her guilt to cover,
>   To hide her shame from every eye,
> To give repentance to her lover
>   And wring his bosom, is—to die.

the most fervent apologist for Goldsmith is hard put to it to find a noninvidious explanation when confronted with the following lines, penned by the French poet Ségur nine years before Goldsmith was born:

> Lorsqu'une femme, après trop de tendresse,
>   D'un homme sent la trahison,
> Comment pour cette si douce faiblesse,
>   Peut elle trouver une guérison?

Le seul remède qu'elle peut ressentir,
La seule revanche pour son tort,
Pour faire trop tard l'amant repentir,
Hélas! trop tard—est la mort.

## Suspension of Disbelief

Coleridge took whole pages of his *Biographia Literaria* practically intact from Schelling. As a critic and philosopher he levied on Kant and Schlegel. In his "Hymn" he simply appropriated a poem by Frederica Brunn.

His friend De Quincey wrote a long article chiding him for the cavalier way he helped himself to whatever he came across. For the light it sheds both on the author and his subject, the article merits the scrutiny of a psychiatrist. De Quincey starts out with expressions of admiration for Coleridge. When he gets down to business about plagiarism, he confesses his heart is wrung. Coleridge and he are Damon and Pythias; he hates to expose him. But if he doesn't do it, someone else less generous than he is will, and he may as well "forestall other discoverers who would make a more unfriendly use of the discovery."

Let it be said, though, to the Opium Eater's credit, that he concedes that in "Hymn" the dry bones of the German outline have been created by Coleridge into the fullness of life. He professes to be puzzled by the cribbing he exposes, implying that Coleridge was a kleptomaniac. "Had he any need," he asks, "to borrow from Schelling? Did he borrow *in forma pauperis*? Not at all: there lay the wonder. He spun daily and at all hours, for mere amusement of his own activities and from the loom of his own magical brain, theories more gorgeous by far than Schelling could have emulated in his dreams. With the riches of El Dorado lying about him, he would condescend to filch a handful of gold from any man whose purse he fancied . . ."[4]

There are, in the history of literature, few examples of alchemy as vivid and unassailable as "Kubla Khan" and *The Rime of the Ancient Mariner*. Coleridge poured the essence of dozens of strange and obscure travel books into his masterpieces. The more we scan his sources—Professor Lowes has made a remarkable study of them in *The Road to Xanadu*—the greater our wonder at the supreme skill with which he assimilated and metamorphosed what he took, and the keener our realization that the result was irrevocably his.[5]

## Byron and Keats

Charles Lamb suggested to Godwin, who was essaying a play, various dramatic works Godwin could profitably rifle, saying that from this method of "honest stealing much yet remains to be sucked."

Whether Godwin needed any such hint is not known. Byron certainly didn't. He transferred much of the action and some of the language of Goethe's *Faust* to his *Manfred*. He expressed his gratitude by roundly abusing the German master as a plagiarist. The latter's reaction was that of a tolerant adult to a fractious child. "The greater part of those fine things cited by Lord Byron," he said, "I have never even read, much less did I think of them when I was writing *Faust*. But Lord Byron is great only as a poet; as soon as he reflects he is a child. He knows not how to hold himself against the stupid attacks of the same kind made upon himself by his own countrymen. He ought to have expressed himself more strongly against them. 'What is there is mine,' he should have said, 'and whether I got it from a book or from life is of no consequence; the only point is whether I have made a right use of it.' Walter Scott used a scene from my *Egmont*, and he was entitled to do so; because he did it well he deserves praise. He has also copied the character of my Mignon in one of his romances; but whether with equal judgment is another question. . . . My Mephistopheles sings a song from Shakespeare, and why should he not? Why should I trouble to invent one of my own, when this said just what I wanted? If, too, the prologue of my *Faust* is something like the beginning of *Job*, that is again quite right, and I am rather to be praised than censured." Goethe might have been less royally indifferent if he had been more conversant with English and had known the full extent of Byron's levies on him.

Keats drew form, imagery and spirit from Spenser, phrases and passages from a multitude of others. You can almost trace his reading, says Gardiner, by the perfumed words he has ravished from other gardens, and to which he has given new and immortal setting. He "blended in the Indian maiden's song quite unsuspected scraps of Diodorus Siculus and Rabelais with the well-known fragments of

Sandys' *Ovid,* and reminiscences of a glowing masterpiece of Titian, and phrases touched with the magic of *The Ancient Mariner* itself. And into the four books of *Endymion,* after dipping out of every fountain-head to which he came, Keats emptied helter-skelter all his brim-filled bowls."[6]

## The Nineteenth Century

In *The Pickwick Papers* Dickens sifted Boswell's *Life of Johnson,* drew more heavily on Washington Irving (he copied some passages from Irving verbatim, lifted descriptions with slight alterations, and adapted some of Irving's tales), and plucked freely from contemporary papers and journals, song and travel books, comedies, fiction, poetry, essays, and biography. It has been said that *A Tale of Two Cities* owes its very existence to Carlyle's *French Revolution* (an ambiguous statement which does not necessarily betoken plagiarism), and that *A Child's History of England* is little more than a copy of Goldsmith's *History of England.*[7]

Owen Meredith, scion of the man who gave us *The Last Days of Pompeii,* was one of the most assiduous and audacious plagiarists that ever lived. Every memorable line, every striking incident in every one of his books has been traced to some other author. His *Gyges and Candaules* echoes Keats' *The Eve of St. Agnes;* his *Lucile,* George Sand's *Lavinia.* Dubbing him a seventh-rate poet, Swinburne parodied him mercilessly. Meredith's defense was epitomized in a single sentence: "Genius does what it must, and talent does what it can."

"Whistler," wrote Oscar Wilde in the *Pall Mall Gazette,* "is indeed one of the very greatest masters of painting in my opinion. And I may add that in this opinion Mr. Whistler himself entirely concurs." To which Whistler replied: "Oscar—the amiable, irresponsible, esurient Oscar—has the courage of the opinions . . . of others!"

Oscar Wilde's lecture on "The English Renaissance in Art," with which he diverted the curious who flocked to hear him on his American tour, was compounded largely of Whistler's views. The painter never forgave Wilde for "picking from our platters the plums for the puddings he peddles in the provinces," and he missed no opportunity to taunt the lily-bearing aesthete. Lord Alfred Douglas himself, whose association with Wilde resulted in the poet's downfall, and who rejected him utterly in his extremity, gave an extra twist to the screw by charging him with plagiarism from Milton, Keats, Hood, Tennyson, Elizabeth Barrett Browning and William Morris.

### The Voice of Victorian England

"I am sure," said Tennyson, "that I myself and many others find a peculiar charm in those passages of such great masters as Virgil or Milton, where they adopt the creation of a bygone poet, and re-clothe it, more or less, according to their fancy."

Like Dryden before him, he was indulging in a bit of self-exoneration. The practice which he ascribed to the masters was his own as well. He "re-clothed" goodly portions of Malory, Froude and Freeman. His "In Memoriam" reminds us of Petrarch, his "Dream of Fair Women" of Chaucer, his "Godiva" of Moultrie.

His foraging earned him much abuse during his lifetime. He faced up to his detractors, not with the truculence of a Byron or the scornful calm of a Dryden, but rather with the hurt bewilderment of a man who feels he's trod the path of righteousness all his days and yet finds himself set upon for wickedness. When he published *The Princess,* a critic charged that the lines

> A wind arose and rush'd upon the South,
> And shook the songs, the whispers and the shrieks
> Of the wild wood together; and a Voice
> Went with it, 'Follow, follow, thou shalt win.'

owed their existence to the quatrain in Shelley's *Prometheus:*

> A wind arose among the pines and shook
> The clinging music from their boughs, and then
> Low, sweet, faint sounds like the farewell of ghosts
> Were heard, 'O follow, follow, follow me.'

"I do not object," Tennyson wrote the critic, "to your finding parallelisms. They must always occur. A man (a Chinese scholar) some time ago wrote to me saying that in an unknown, untranslated Chinese poem there were two whole lines of mine almost word for word. Why not? . . . It is scarcely possible for anyone to say or write anything at this late time of the world to which, in the rest of the literature of the world, a parallel could not somewhere be found."

He admitted having read *Prometheus,* but denied copying Shelley or anyone else. He described how he came to compose the stanza in question. He made out a fairly persuasive, though perhaps labored, case of independent conception. He might have spared himself the effort. Actually, it mattered very little whether unconscious borrowing or pure accident lay at the root of the matter. For by no stretch of the imagination could *The Princess* be considered a duplication or approximation of *Prometheus.*

In his study of the sources of *In Memoriam,* A. C. Bradley notes that it contains a large number of phrases which recall those of other poets—a larger number than one would find in the same amount of verse by any other famous English author excepting Milton and Gray. He sees nothing wrong in this. "Sometimes," he observes, "a poet adopts the phrase of an earlier writer knowingly, and with the intention that the reader should recognize it; and if the reader fails to recognize it, he does not fully appreciate the passage. Milton and Gray often did this, and Tennyson does it to beautiful effect when he reproduces phrases of Virgil or Theocritus; and so in *In Memoriam,* when he writes 'change their sky' or 'brute earth' he means the Horatian phrases to be recognized. Sometimes, again, the similarity of phrase is due to mere coincidence; the second poet never read the words of the first, but he invents for himself what the first had invented for himself. A third cause is unconscious reproduction: a phrase is retained in memory perhaps for years, and is reproduced without any consciousness that it is not perfectly original. Lastly, a poet may use the words of a predecessor, knowing what he is doing but not intending the origin of the phrase to be observed. This is plagiarism, and it is the only one of the four cases in which any discredit attaches to the poet."[8]

### In France: Rabelais

When Gargantua was born, seventeen thousand nine hundred and thirteen cows were assigned to supply him with milk (which was no reflection on his mother, who could draw from her breasts two thousand one hundred and three hogsheads at a time); later, he inadvertently swallowed six pilgrims in a salad.

The mind of the man who conceived Gargantua displayed a voracity scarcely less astounding. Rabelais appropriated whatever he could get hold of: the classics, medieval legends, the romances of chivalry, religious and scientific treatises, folk tales. As Erich Auerbach has indicated in his *Mimesis,* almost all the elements of Rabelais' style—the earthy jokes, the animalistic concept of the human body, forthrightness in sexual matters, the mingling of realism with satire and didacticism, the prodigious store of learning—existed in the Middle Ages. Handling these elements with extraordinary ingenuity, skill and gusto, Rabelais synthesized them into a whole which, in spirit, was a rejection of medieval thinking. And so, with inherited materials, he produced one of the most original books of all time.

Speaking of Seneca and Plutarch, Montaigne said that his essays were "constructed wholly of their spoils." The very character of his discourses indicates that he was a note taker of unremitting industry. A vast library went into the making of his work. He was scrupulous about quotation marks, though he pretended not to be. "Amongst so many borrowed things," he wrote, "I am glad if I can steal one, disguising and altering it for some new service." Actually, he stole very little.

Like Shakespeare, Molière arrogated to himself all the drama known in his time, including French farces, Spanish plays and the repertory of the *commedia dell' arte. Les Précieuses Ridicules* was a refashioning of an Italian comedy which had been put on the boards two years before. He extracted the idea of *Tartuffe* from a novel called *The Punishment of Avarice.* His debt to Plautus and Terence was immense. There is an oft-repeated anecdote, one version of which unjustly depicts Molière as a callous and unregenerate plagiarist. He is supposed to have lifted two whole scenes from a play by Cyrano de Bergerac (the Cyrano who centuries later was to become the hero of Rostand's drama), and inserted them in his *Les Fourberies de Scapin*; and to have retorted, when confronted with the theft: *"Je prends mon bien où je le trouve.* I take my material where I find it." Marmontel offers a different version, with a different villain. The scenes in question, he says, were Molière's in the first place; Molière discussed them with his friend Cyrano, and Cyrano perfidiously slipped them into his *Pédant Joué.* When Molière discovered this, he angrily repossessed himself of his material, uttering the remark above attributed to him, with the exception that he said *reprends* instead of *prends*: "I recover what belongs to me wherever I find it."

On the subject of plagiarism the usually clear-eyed Voltaire betrays inconsistency of opinion. While he inveighs against it spiritedly in his *Dictionnaire Philosophique,* elsewhere he observes that of all forms of theft, plagiarism is the least dangerous and often proves beneficial. In any case his own *Temple du Goût* owes much to Pope's *Dunciad,* as does his *Micromegas* to *Gulliver's Travels.*

It remained for the literary notables of nineteenth-century France to demonstrate how far back the frontiers of borrowing could be pushed without impairing the reputation of the borrowers. [9]

Madame de Staël's *Corinne* owed its existence to Heinse's *Ardinghello.* Chateaubriand lifted whole sections from Marmontel's *Les Incas* and Aphra Behn's *Oroonoko*; the magnitude of his debt to others, including Gibbon, has been the subject of a doctoral dissertation which is in effect an indictment.[10]

Dumas the Elder—the man who, with his corps of ghosts, originated mass production in fiction—made substantial raids on Schiller, Scott, Chateaubriand, Hoffmann, and a host of early memoirists.

"Gautier," says Jacques Barzun, "makes no secret of his allusiveness and . . . boldly uses names and scenes from Balzac, phrases from George Sand, and finally, the plot of Shakespeare's *As You Like It* —itself a great example of art based on other art. Young men of genius are often tempted to set out in this way, and they are likely to succeed in eking out first-hand experience with second-hand because of the very strength of imagination which makes them young geniuses."

Victor Hugo dug deep into Chamberlayne's *L'Etat Present de L'Angleterre* for his *L'Homme Qui Rit,* cribbed from Mercier's *Paris Pendant La Revolution* and Count de Puisaye's *Mémoires* for his *Quatrevingt-Treize,* and poured a multitude of obscure Gothic chronicles into *The Hunchback of Notre Dame.*[11]

Throughout his career Zola was the butt of similarity-snufflers. "I have spent more than thirty years of my life creating," he cried, charged with plagiarism for the seventy-ninth time, "and there are offspring to the extent of some twelve hundred, all issued from me, a whole world of characters. Have I not proved my virility? . . . Run along, little man. You may assert that I appropriate everywhere. . . . You will never make anybody believe that my swarm of children does not belong to me!"[12]

A year after Anatole France died, Gabriel des Hons published a study in which he endeavored to prove that France took his cast of mind, his rhythm, and many of his phrases and images from Racine. Like many literary sleuths, des Hons professed an admiration for his subject. He was not concerned, he said, with plagiarism but with "parentage." Had France been alive, he would doubtless have regarded des Hons' performance with tranquil amusement. Concerning originality, as about most other things, he entertained no illusions. "When we see," he wrote, "that our ideas have been stolen, let us consider, before we cry out, whether they were really our own."

With Stendhal, however, we come to an apple off another tree. The man who said that whenever he wished to write a sentimental love story he first read a half-dozen pages from the Penal Code to set himself a tone, the man who proclaimed: "Whatever be the destiny that awaits me, I want to be able to say always with the great Corneille: 'To myself alone I owe my renown'; therefore I don't want to introduce into my works the least bit of imitation," was, on occasion, an out-and-out thief.

He stole the idea of his first novel *Lucien Leuwen* from a manuscript which one of his mistresses had given him for criticism. For his *L'Histoire de la Peinture en Italie,* he seized paragraphs, pages, almost entire chapters from Abbé Lanzi's *Histoire de la Peinture* and from Amoretti's *Mémoires Historiques.* He plundered Prosper Mérimée to enrich his *Mémoires d'un Touriste.* Having cribbed certain choice passages from *The Edinburgh Review* for an article of his, he chortled with sardonic glee when the *Review,* in appraising his volume, selected for special commendation the very sections which he had purloined from its columns.

His prize exploit, though, had to do with his *Vies de Haydn, de Mozart et de Métastase.* He took Carpani's life of Haydn, Schlichtegroll's life of Mozart, and Baretti's eulogy of Métastase and put them bodily into his biography. Fearing trouble, he presented the book under the pseudonym of Louis-César-Alexandre Bombet; and on the principle that an offensive is the best defense, he promptly and insolently accused Carpani of plagiarism. Choked with fury, Carpani struck back at "Bombet," giving facts which established conclusively the priority of his study. Stendhal had a flash of inspiration. He conjured up a Bombet, Jr., who belligerently took up the cudgels for his equally nonexistent sire, asserting that while the latter deemed it below his dignity to engage in a brawl with so vulgar a creature as Carpani, he, the son, could not suffer in silence the unjust and vicious blackening of his father's reputation![13]

Eventually Stendhal mended his ways. It is significant that the access of moral scruple that induced him to do so sprang largely, according to his frank admission, from the realization that stealing was more trouble than it was worth.

### In the New World

Poor Richard was anything but poor when it came to literary pickings. Dryden, Pope, Prior, Gay, Swift, Bacon, La Rochefoucauld, Rabelais—he combed them all. He claimed as his own a translation of *De Senectute* done by Logan. "The rustic philosopher," says Carl Van Doren, "drew also on the stream of popular adages, whether already gathered into printed collections or still only current in ordinary speech. In this profusion and uncertainty of sources Poor Richard never hesitated to rework his texts to suit his purpose and his audience." As an example of Franklin's method with his sources, Van Doren cites how the *Pantagruelian Prognostication* in the Urquhart-Motteux version of Rabelais became *True Prognostication* in the 1739 Almanac—a neat bit of adaptation which bears witness to the sharpness of Franklin's eye for usable material, no less than to his adroitness in reshaping it.[14] For nothing that passed through his mind came out quite the same.

"When I consider the true talent, the real force of Mr. Emerson," commented a harsh critic, "I am lost in amazement at finding him little more than a respectful imitation of Carlyle. Is it possible that Mr. Emerson has never seen a copy of Seneca? Scarcely—or he would long ago have abandoned his model in utter confusion at the parallel between his own worship of the author of *Sartor Resartus* and the aping of Sallust by Aruntius, as described in the 114th Epistle."

Bryant's "Thanatopsis," considered to be the first great poem written by an American, bears so close a relation, in mood and (occasionally) language, to Gray's "Elegy," Blair's "Grave," Porteus' "Death," Kirk White's "Time," and the other crepuscular pieces of the eighteenth-century melancholiacs that it has been called an echo of the graveyard poets.

It remained for the Little Longfellow War, however, to bring plagiarism really to the fore on the American scene.

No writer of consequence in this country was ever more savagely set upon or more persistently pounded for his borrowings than was Longfellow by Poe. The author of "The Raven"—Lowell called him three-fifths genius and two-fifths fudge—was a formidable adversary. His arsenal included a sharp—if not always sound—critical intelligence, a love of literature, a wide reading, a capacity for indignation, an unshakable belief in the correctness of his judgments, and a mastery of invective.

Himself a cribber of "learned" articles from encyclopedias, an expounder of aesthetic theories abstracted from Coleridge, a teller of tales steeped in the tradition of the Gothic novel, Poe deplored the predilection of American writers for aping European models. He singled out Longfellow as the prime exponent of this tendency.

When Longfellow's *Hyperion* appeared, Poe wrote: "Were it possible to throw into a bag the lofty thought and manner of the *Pilgrims of the Rhine*, together with the quirks and quibbles and the true humor of *Tristram Shandy*, not forgetting a few of the heartier drolleries of Rabelais, and one or two of the Phantasy Pieces of the Lorrainean Callôt, the whole, well shaken up, and thrown out, would be a very tolerable imitation of *Hyperion*."

Concerning Longfellow's *Midnight Mass for the Dying Year*, Poe said: "The general idea and matter are from Tennyson's *Death of the Old Year*, several of the most dramatic points are from the death scene of Cordelia in *Lear*, and the line about the 'hooded friars' is from the *Comus* of Milton." He deemed the poem a species of "plagiarism which is too palpable to be mistaken, and which belongs to the most barbarous class of literary robbery: that class in which, while the words of the wronged author are avoided, his most intangible and therefore his least defensible and least reclaimable property is purloined." Nor did he take a more charitable view of Longfellow's *The Spanish Student* and *The Beleaguered City*.

Everything that Poe lacked—financial security, recognition, social standing—Longfellow had in abundance. Each misfortune that befell Poe seemed to add vitriol to his pen. Yet it would be an oversimplification to suppose that his blasts proceeded from nothing more than frustration and envy. He was the first man of letters in America to give serious thought to the subject of originality and derivation, and there can be little doubt of the genuineness of his interest.[15]

It was a decidedly one-sided controversy. Longfellow refused to be drawn into it. He attributed Poe's outbursts to "the irritations of a sensitive nature, chafed by some indefinite sense of wrong." All that he would venture to say by way of defense was: "Of a truth, one cannot strike a spade into the soil of Parnassus without disturbing the bones of some dead poet."

It is idle to go on. The pattern is clear enough. Clear, too, are the admonitions implicit in the pattern.

First, there is a difference between research and plagiarism. Sometimes the two come dangerously close, but it is a mistake to confuse the one with the other. Gibbon was not a pirate because he availed himself of the resources of Montesquieu's *Considerations on the Grandeur and Decadence of Rome*; nor Flaubert because he took many of the incidents and characters in *Salammbô* from the Greek historian Polybius, and the background from Hotman; nor Melville because he poured into *Moby Dick* the altered essence of shelves of books on whaling.

Second, there is a difference between derivation and copying. La Fontaine constructed his *Fables* on the foundations laid by Aesop and the anonymous compilers of medieval bestiaries. La Bruyère modeled his chief work, *Les Caractères*, after Theophrastus. Yet both men are justly honored for their originality.

Third, just as one swallow doesn't make a summer, so a lapse or two doesn't make an author a rogue. Burns copied the third stanza of his "A Red, Red Rose" virtually word for word from "The Young Man's Farewell to His Love" in the Motherwell collection of chapbooks. Remembering his over-all contribution, posterity has gratefully forgiven him.

If we are to be instructed by history, we must not misread its precepts.

# 8

# Literary Property and Copyright

When 'Omer smote 'is bloomin' lyre,
    He'd 'eard men sing by land an' sea;
An' what he thought 'e might require,
    'E went an' took—the same as me!

—Kipling: Barrack Room Ballads

FORGETFUL of his own indebtedness, Virgil complains: "*Hos versiculos feci; tulit alter honores.* I penned these lines; another wears the bays." "Simpleton," cries Martial angrily in his *Epigrams*, "why do you mix your verses with mine? What have you to do, foolish man, with writings that convict you of larceny? Why do you seek to associate foxes with lions, and make owls pass for eagles?" Martial adds: "Report says that you, Fidentinus, recite my compositions in public as if they were your own. If you allow them to be called mine, I will send you my verses gratis; if you wish them to be called yours, pray buy them, that they may be mine no longer."

In Roman law, *plagium* was the stealing of a slave from his master, or the stealing of a freeman with intent to keep him or sell him as a slave. The act was a criminal offense—*crimen plagii*—and the wrongdoer was called *plagiarius*. In essence, plagium was kidnapping. It was Martial who first applied the term to literary theft (an indication that the ancients did give thought to property rights in writings), but it was not so used in England until the sixteenth century.

## The Economic Factor

Although Cicero is said to have made money from his literary endeavors, and although the sale of compositions for purposes of

95

recital and multiplication goes back to the days of Terence and Statius, the ancients were principally concerned, in cases of theft, with the deprivation of authorship credit.

The essence of copyright is precisely what the word indicates: the right to make copies. By necessary implication, this right carries with it the privilege of reaping profit from the sale of copies. While manuscripts were highly prized in antiquity and during the Middle Ages, the question as to whether any property rights existed in the making of copies, as distinguished from the manuscripts themselves, received very little attention. Duplication was a difficult and laborious process. Since most writers couldn't earn a living from their originals, they had scant hope of obtaining revenue from copies. And so they subsisted on the bounty of patrons, or, if they were less favored, took up other pursuits to keep body and soul together. It was Gutenberg who opened up a fabulous new vista, prompted men of letters and jurists to tackle the problem of literary property, and set in motion the train of events that culminated in statutory copyright.

### Literary Property

Literary property is the exclusive right which the creator of a work of the intellect—a story, a drama, a picture, a song—has to possess, use and dispose of what he has created. It is a comprehensive term. It includes common law copyright and statutory copyright.

Literary property is personal property. It is intangible. It is distinct from the physical form into which it is cast. The author of a completed novel owns the manuscript of it, just as he might own a suit of clothes or a piece of furniture. He also owns the right to produce copies of it for publication and sale. Though growing out of a single product of the mind, these two property rights are separate. The novelist may make a grant of publication rights and retain the ownership of the manuscript. Or he may sell the manuscript and reserve publication rights.

"Our first legislators," says Blackstone, "took great care to ascertain the rights and to direct the disposition of real property, but entertained a low opinion of all personal estate, which they regarded as a transient commodity. . . . Our ancient law books did not often condescend to notice personal property."

If the law in its early stages deemed tangible personal property of scant consequence, it was even more laggard in recognizing something as impalpable as literary property. Nor was progress quickened —once recognition came—by the fact that judges sought almost invariably to apply to works of the imagination rules which had been developed for the handling of a keg of nails, a coil of rope, livestock and produce.

Generally, property is something which is susceptible of ownership. It implies both a relationship between the owner and the object, and social and economic consequences. When you own an automobile, you have the right to possess it, use it, and dispose of it. Your right does not exist in a vacuum; it has certain concomitants which arise from the fact that you are a member of society. It enables you to prevent others from injuring or stealing your car, and to obtain redress if they do. It carries with it an obligation not to operate the car to the injury of others.

"Though the earth and all inferior creatures," says Locke, "be common to all men, yet every man has a property in his own person: this nobody has any right to but himself. The labor of his body, and the work of his hands, we may say, are properly his." This is true whether the labor is muscular or mental or both. "All arguments in support of the right of learned men in their works," said Lord Kenyon in an early English case, "must be heard with great favor by men of liberal minds." The Supreme Court of the United States has declared that the foundation of all rights of this kind is the natural dominion which everyone has over his ideas. Indeed, it may be said that there is no property more peculiarly a person's own than that wrought by his brains and his hands. It is a matter of simple justice, therefore, that the creative individual should derive two benefits from the thing he has created: money, so that he may exist, and authorship credit, so that he may build a reputation.

Books, manuscripts, plays, poems, letters, lectures, musical compositions, paintings, drawings, statuary, photographs, architectural plans—all these may constitute the subject matter of literary property.

### Common Law Copyright

When people speak of copyright, they usually mean statutory copyright. There is common law copyright as well.

Common law copyright exists independently of any statute. It is the exclusive, perpetual property right which an author has in his unpublished work. He may deal with that work as he wishes. He can destroy it; he can retain it; he can circulate it among his friends; he can withhold it from the public at large, and stop anyone who wrongfully gets hold of it from publishing it; he can transfer it; he can publish it and secure a statutory copyright.

Like many a genteel lady of her time, Queen Victoria dabbled in art. She and her consort Prince Albert made some etchings for their own amusement, and a few impressions were struck off for members of the royal family. Someone surreptitiously got hold of the prints and sold them to a publisher named Strange, who announced that he was going to place copies of them on the market. He reckoned without the interdict of the common law. Prince Albert went to court and obtained an injunction against him.

Back in 1876, Mark Twain hit on the idea of several authors' writing a story based upon a common plot. He prepared an outline in which he set forth a central theme he considered suitable for the purpose. The outline itself was not designed for publication. He submitted the idea to *The Atlantic Monthly,* which rejected it. The manuscript was missing from his papers when he died. In 1930 it turned up among the effects of a deceased collector. Someone purchased it from the collector's estate, and announced that he would publish it. The trustees under Mark Twain's will intervened, claiming that the common law rights in the composition belonged to them, notwithstanding the purchaser's ownership of the physical manuscript. Their position was upheld in court, and the purchaser was enjoined.

In a famous early English copyright case it was said that the ideas of an author are like "birds in a cage, which none but he can have a right to let fly, for till he thinks proper to emancipate them, they are under his dominion." However, the moment a creator publishes his work *generally*—I shall indicate in a moment what is meant by general publication—the common law right is extinguished. If the author wants protection after that, he must get a statutory copyright. Otherwise his work falls into the public domain.

Oliver Wendell Holmes, author of *The Autocrat of the Breakfast Table,* and father of the illustrious Justice, learned this to his sorrow.

*The Autocrat* appeared in twelve installments in *The Atlantic Monthly* back in 1857 and 1858. The various issues of the magazine were not copyrighted. The installments were then collected and published, with Holmes' permission, in a single volume on which statutory copyright was obtained. The book was pirated, and Holmes sued the unauthorized publisher for infringement. The Supreme Court of the United States told him, perhaps regretfully, that it could do nothing for him. Since the original installments of *The Autocrat* had not been copyrighted, the whole work had become part of the public domain. The later copyright could not rescue it.

Publication may be general or limited. General publication occurs where a work is offered for sale or distribution to the public at large with the author's consent and without any restrictions. For example, a book is generally published if it is printed and issued so that anyone may buy a copy. Limited publication occurs where a work is shown to or circulated among selected individuals or a small group on some particular occasion or for a particular purpose. The circulation, by a writer, of a number of copies of his manuscript among his friends or acquaintances for criticism and comment constitutes limited publication. Similarly, the presentation of a play on the stage—in the absence of its issuance in volume form—does not deprive the dramatist of his common law rights. The same is true of the performance of a musical composition, the delivery of a lecture to a class of students, and so on. It is important to distinguish clearly between general and limited publication, because the latter does not, even in the absence of statutory copyright, throw a work into the public domain, whereas the former does.

### Statutory Copyright

Statutory copyright is the exclusive property right granted by statute to authors for a limited time to make and sell copies of their works, and to perform and record them. In the United States the period is twenty-eight years, with a single renewal term of equal duration.

A statutory copyright is, in effect, a monopoly. Notwithstanding our avowed policy against monopolies, we sanction this one to stimulate intellectual productivity. However, the monopoly is limited in years, so that the eventual free use of all copyrighted material is assured. It is also restricted in scope. For example, the only rights which the law gives the author of a copyrighted novel are to print and sell copies of it, to translate it into other languages, and to dramatize it. And once the copyright expires, anyone else may publish the novel or turn it into a play or a movie or make any other use of it that he sees fit.

Not everything can be copyrighted. The law clearly specifies the classes of matter which are eligible. These include books, encyclopedic works, directories, and other compilations; periodicals and newspapers; lectures, sermons and addresses (prepared for oral delivery); dramatic and dramatico-musical compositions; musical compositions; maps; works of art, and models or designs for works of art; reproductions of works of art; drawings or plastic works of a scientific or technical character; photographs; prints, illustrations and labels used for articles of merchandise; and motion pictures.

The man who complains of infringement must have a copyright to begin with, and the copyright must be one that will stand up in court if challenged. This means that he must have complied with the legal requirements to secure a copyright; and his material must be of a character that qualifies it for copyright protection.

A copyright in, say, a book is ordinarily obtained by publishing it with the prescribed copyright notice, and by registering the claim of copyright in the Copyright Office. The registration is not essential to getting or preserving the copyright, but it must be completed before any infringement suit is started.

A copyright—to quote Sam B. Warner, formerly Register of Copyrights—"buys an author a ticket in the greatest sweepstake on earth— the attempt to catch the fancy of the American public. To the copyrighted winner, this means fame and fortune. To a writer who, like the Reverend Charles M. Sheldon, author of *In His Steps*, the all-time American best seller, neglects to secure copyright protection, victory means fame only. Though some twenty-five million copies of *In His Steps* were sold throughout the world, only one of its forty-odd publishers bothered to make a gift of any royalties to Dr. Sheldon." Beatrix Potter, author of *Peter Rabbit*, the most successful children's animal book ever issued, was similarly negligent; there have been at least a hundred different editions of it, with sales running into astronomical figures, but Miss Potter didn't benefit.

It is interesting to note that a large proportion of the literary and scientific works published each year in this country, as well as almost all newspapers, are not copyrighted. One simple (but not necessarily conclusive) way of finding out whether a publication is in copyright is to look for the copyright notice required by law. If it bears no such notice, it is in all probability in the public domain, unless it is a pirated edition from which the unauthorized publisher has willfully or negligently omitted the notice. If the book does bear a notice, then the *date* of the copyright becomes significant. Any date going back more than fifty-six years means the work is in the public domain.

The copyright law is a Federal statute. Infringement cases are heard in the Federal courts, which have exclusive jurisdiction. However, you can sue in the state courts for breach of common law copyright, since the latter exists independently of statute.

The Federal courts consist of the District Courts, the Circuit Courts of Appeals, and the United States Supreme Court. Infringement claims are heard in the first, and are appealable to the second. There is no direct right of appeal to the Supreme Court; it may hear a case if it wishes to.

## The Background of Copyright

It is almost *de rigueur* that every account of the historical origins of copyright start out with the case of *Finnian* v. *Columba*, which arose in A.D. 567. However, the economic implications of the case are sometimes overlooked.

It seems that there was a monastery in Ireland, of which one Finnian was abbot. The monastery owned an illuminated psalter of such exceptional beauty that people flocked from afar to see it. The monk Columba, who belonged to another abbey, secretly made a copy of it. When Finnian discovered this, he wrathfully demanded that the copy be surrendered to him. Columba refused, and the dispute was carried to King Dermott at Tara. The King decided in the abbot's favor. "To every cow her calf," he decreed; "and to every book its copy." Some time later the chronicler Andamnan set it all down, and *Finnian* v. *Columba* became the first reported copyright case.[1] Columba eventually rose to sainthood; whether he did so in spite of this incident or because of it, is not recorded.

It should be borne in mind that monasteries in those days throve on income derived from the offerings of pilgrims and travelers who paused within their gates. Having a holy relic or an extraordinary work of art assured a continuing flow of visitors. As a result, a brisk competition, based on the drawing power of their respective treasures, sprang up among monasteries. Columba's establishment had nothing to display to the faithful. So it is not unreasonable to suppose that the pious monk's exploit was inspired less by his love of jeweled calligraphy than by the hints of an alert and practical-minded superior.

Although the invention of printing vastly increased the potential audience of writers, it fell far short of solving their economic problems. Indeed, it created new hazards. In England the Crown quickly recognized that the press could be a powerful instrument of sedition, as well as a weapon against established religion. On the theory that since the King had imported the first printing press, the right to print belonged to him, unlimited royal authority was asserted over the press.

From 1556 to 1640 this authority was exercised through the Stationers' Company, and enforced by decrees of the Star Chamber. The decrees provided for the pre-licensing of books, and the regulation of printing presses throughout the land. The deposit of copies of licensed books was required, to guard against surreptitous changes in text after publication. The King and his favorites found a new source of revenue in the license fees.

The penalties for the issuance of unlicensed books were severe. "After his first publication," says Birrell, "the British author usually disappeared, and if he reappeared, it was in the pillory." It may well be, adds Rogers, that he was more interested in getting out of the pillory than in protecting the work that had got him there.

But the tide could not be stemmed. Printing presses appeared everywhere. Unlicensed books poured forth. Writers and printers risked mutilation and death. When the Star Chamber was abolished, the Long Parliament substantially re-enacted the Chamber's repressive measures on pre-licensing. This called forth Milton's *Areopagitica*, one of the most impassioned pleas for free expression in the history of letters. It was of little immediate avail. Pre-censorship continued for another fifty years until its abolition in 1695.

In 1709, more than two centuries after Caxton set up his press at Westminster, the first English copyright law was enacted. This was the famous Statute of Anne, the precursor of all English and American copyright legislation. The statute gave authors a monopoly in the publication of their works for a period from fourteen to twenty-eight years. Unauthorized reproduction became a legal offense.

It is a curious commentary on the evolution of copyright legislation that a measure designed for the protection of creative people had its historical roots in something utterly alien to such an objective: censorship.

While the new law was a tremendous forward step, it was no cure-all. It did not define infringement and provided no criteria for the detection of violation. And if it baffled authors because it failed to tell them where lawful borrowing ended and larceny began, it addled the courts no less on another score. Judges believed that under the common law there was a property right of *unlimited* duration in *printed* books, independently of legislation; the Statute of Anne had been passed, they said, to provide specific remedies in cases of infringement, not to destroy this perpetual right. On the other hand, they were faced with the plain mandate of the statute as to limited protection. In 1774 the judicial branch of the House of Lords finally settled the question. It ruled that an author had perpetual rights in his *unpublished* work, but that after publication his rights continued only for the period specified in the statute. In other words, general publication was held to extinguish common law rights forever. This remains the law of England to the present day, and is our law as well.

## Copyright in the United States

Colonial America was aware of the necessity for copyright protection. Before the Constitution was adopted, the several states had enacted copyright laws. However, there was a serious drawback. State laws could operate only within state borders; an author wishing to preserve his rights on a wider basis had to obtain multiple copyrights.

The Founding Fathers devised a simple solution. They took copyright out of the hands of the states and made it a Federal function. The Constitution gave Congress the power "to promote the progress of science and useful arts, by securing for limited times to authors and inventors the exclusive right to their respective writings and discoveries."

In 1790 the first Federal copyright statute came into being. It was badly needed. Literary piracy had become a grave abuse in the eighteenth century. Periodicals were egregious offenders. "When an editor hoisted the black flag of a magazine, he assumed the privilege of levying tribute upon all the other craft that sailed the literary seas. Nor was it any crime, or even misdemeanor: it was expected."[2]

The Act of 1790 was revised several times. It resulted in the Act of 1909, which, with amendments, is the law now in force.

The fundamental purpose of all copyright legislation was made clear in the Congressional report which accompanied the Act of 1909. The law was intended, said the report, primarily for the benefit of the public. It gave a bonus to authors and inventors, not to favor them, but to stimulate writing and invention for the good of "the great body of people."

With the past to give us perspective, we can now turn to consider plagiarism in current and near-current literature, drama, motion pictures, art, music, radio and television.

# 9

# Plagiarism in Books and Magazines

A good storyteller is a person who has a good memory and hopes other people haven't.

—Irvin S. Cobb: Exit Laughing

---

AN AUTHOR, unsung, impoverished and no longer young, encountered one of his ideas in a successful book. "There goes a child of mine," he said wryly, "who has prospered."

Whenever Brander Matthews discussed Kipling with his students, he adverted to the masters of narrative in whose footsteps the author of *The Light That Failed* trod. Meeting Kipling, he told him about this. The Englishman smiled. "Why give it away?" he asked. "Why not let them think it was just genius?"

"It seems to me," commented Zelda Fitzgerald on her husband's *The Beautiful and Damned*, "that on one page I recognize a portion of an old diary of mine which mysteriously disappeared shortly after my marriage, and also scraps of letters which, though considerably edited, sound to me vaguely familiar. In fact, Mr. Fitzgerald—I believe that is how he spells his name—seems to believe that plagiarism begins at home."

## Genesis, Copyrighted

Convinced that the contribution of women to the birth and growth of civilization had never been justly appraised, Florence Deeks undertook, thirty-odd years ago, to rectify this grievous male-inspired neglect. She penned a chronicle of her own, starting with the dawn of the world, and entitled it *The Web*. She submitted it to Macmillan's of Canada, a house affiliated with Macmillan's of London and Macmillan's of New York.

Miss Deeks' manuscript was examined and rejected. During the seven months that the publishers held it for consideration, H. G. Wells completed *The Outline of History*, which appeared in 1920.

Five years later Miss Deeks started suit against Macmillan's of Canada, H. G. Wells, and Macmillan's of New York, one of Wells' publishers, for copyright infringement. She asked for half a million dollars in damages.

Since the implication was that *The Web* had secretly found its way to Wells via the allied Macmillan firms, the editor in charge of the manuscript at Macmillan's of Canada testified at the trial that it had not left his possession at any time during the period in question. Wells too took the witness stand; he swore he had never seen nor heard of *The Web*.

As direct evidence of access was lacking, Miss Deeks based her attack on "similarities." She brought forward three literary experts who backed her up. Although on cross-examination the experts admitted that common sources existed which both writers could have independently utilized, they insisted that Miss Deeks had made some original additions and alterations, and that Wells had exploited these as well as the sources.

The Ontario Supreme Court—the case arose in Canada—ruled against Miss Deeks. She took an appeal. She lost again. Undaunted, she carried her claim to the tribunal of last resort: the Privy Council of the House of Lords. In 1932, seven years after the suit was brought, the tenacious lady went down to final defeat.

The Privy Council characterized some of her evidence as fantastic. It viewed with disfavor the fact that the testimony of the experts had not been kept within strict bounds. It felt that, given the undertaking, such resemblances as did exist between the two books were unavoidable. "After all," it said, "neither Miss Deeks nor Mr. Wells was present at the beginning of the world or until a very considerable time later, and they have had to rely upon the accumulation of information which has been made by many authors before them, and to which they have had to have recourse in writing such a book as this."

With a nice appreciation of the ways of plaintiffs, the Council added: "It is very doubtful whether anything any court says will be likely to alter Miss Deeks' opinion of the merits of her case, but at any rate she will have the satisfaction of knowing that it has now been very fully considered by three courts."

## Fair Game

A generation ago Zane Grey was accused of pirating, in his novel *The Thundering Herd*, a part of an autobiography entitled *The Border and the Buffalo*. Judge Cosgrave found no evidence of infringement and absolved Grey. "The entire plan, the foundation, the framework of the two books, and the treatment of the subject," he declared, "are entirely dissimilar. It can only be said that the stories are similar in the treatment of the Indians and description of buffalo herds and hunting. These, however, are historical facts. They are in the public domain. Situations quite similar to those described in *The Border and the Buffalo* are to be found in many stories of the West. Francis Parkman in *The Oregon Trail* describes them. Horace Greeley even in 1859, after apologizing, it may be noted, for discussing so trite a subject, believes that he saw ten thousand buffalo in one herd and one million in a single day. William Cullen Bryant speaks of the remote plains where 'roam the majestic brute in herds that shake the earth with thundering steps.' A large number of other writers of fact and fiction have found in this a fascinating subject. The history of the West is not complete without the story of the buffalo."

## Just for Practice

In a plagiarism case it's usually an unknown writer versus a celebrity. Rarely is it the other way around.

In the early 30's, a detective story called *Death in the Dark*, ostensibly the brain child of Cecil Henderson, an "amateur" English novelist, caused quite a stir in London. It became a success practically overnight, and it looked as though Henderson was a made man. Then *The Evening Standard* rudely pricked the bubble. It revealed that the book was virtually a replica of Dashiell Hammett's memorable *The Maltese Falcon*. In the plagiarism suit that followed, Henderson made no attempt to deny the charge. He had copied Hammett, he said, "for practice." He did not explain, however, why he had seen fit, after having had his practice, to submit his exercise under his own name to an innocent publisher. The court stopped the sale of *Death in the Dark*, and ordered Henderson and his publisher to surrender all unsold copies of it, account for the profits, and pay costs.

George Barr McCutcheon, of *Graustark* fame, was the victim of a similar theft. Somebody took his *The Sherrods*, altered the title, the dedication, the first four pages and a few names, and presented the result as a new invention. The thief had a neat wit. He added a touching inscription: "To my mother, the faith of this book being hers." Another plagiarist selected *Under False Colors* as the title for a volume he stole. And only recently a French writer was found guilty of lifting, word for word, two mystery stories, one of them by E. Phillips Oppenheim.

### Six and a Half Billion Dollars

The infringement action which was precipitated by Margaret Mitchell's phenomenally popular *Gone with the Wind* set an all-time high for damages demanded. Asserting that her *Authentic History of the Ku Klux Klan* had been pillaged, Susan Lawrence Davis sought to recover not less than five thousand dollars "for each act of infringement." Since over 1,300,000 copies of the Scarlett O'Hara epic had been snapped up by the public, and since every copy was technically an act of infringement, Miss Davis was shooting for six and a half billion dollars—a sum calculated to deplete the petty cash drawer of any publisher.

*Authentic History* purported to be a historical work confined to the actual doings of the Klan. In *Gone with the Wind* the Klan played a relatively small part; the Klan material that Miss Mitchell had used was routine historical stuff. Miss Davis' grievance seemed to be that certain incidents recorded in her book also appeared in Miss Mitchell's. That these incidents were part of history and were bound to be mentioned whenever the Civil War was dealt with apparently had not occurred to Miss Davis.

She presented a document consisting of 461 typewritten pages wherein she set forth the alleged similarities. I cited some of her specifications in Chapter 5. She found a culpable resemblance between "fired the shot that was heard around the world" (which she quoted, and which, of course, started the Revolution), and Miss Mitchell's "fired the shot that started the war" (i.e., the Civil War). She said that General Ben Butler of the Confederate Army, whom she referred to in her history, had been larcenously metamorphosed into Captain Rhett Butler in *Gone with the Wind*.

Judge Goddard threw the case out of court. He stated the law: no one could acquire a proprietary interest in historical facts. He found no evidence that Miss Mitchell had borrowed anything from Miss Davis. But even if she had, he said, there would have been no cause for complaint; the style and expression of the two works being essentially different, the taking would have been no more than fair use of a fact-source.

### Battle over Barton

The life that Clara Barton, founder of the American Red Cross, led from 1821 to 1912 was rich in usefulness and unselfish devotion to worthy causes, but—notwithstanding the vague hints of some of her biographers—regrettably lacking in love interest.

When Mercedes De Acosta undertook to fashion a screenplay based on Clara Barton's career, she was mindful that heart-throbs were a *sine qua non* in Hollywood. She proceeded to invent the romance that the facts declined to furnish. She gave her heroine a lover, calling him Tom Maxwell, after—as she later testified—the well-advertised coffee of the same name. She had Tom leave the East to go to California, where he died, bequeathing his beloved ten thousand dollars' worth of gold dust. Clara Barton was apprised of the death and the legacy by her brother, in a poignant letter of Miss De Acosta's coinage. Though drawing on historical material, Miss De Acosta accorded free rein to her fancy. She invented characters and gave a fictional twist to most of the factual episodes. When she completed her manuscript, she tried to sell it to the movies.

The idea of a film tribute to Clara Barton had also occurred to Beth Brown, a writer with a number of published stories to her credit. Before Miss De Acosta's treatment began to make the rounds, Miss Brown had produced an early draft; she completed her final version after the De Acosta screenplay had been put in circulation. Extracts from Miss Brown's final version, called *Dedicated to Life*, were published in *Cosmopolitan* magazine.

*Dedicated to Life* substantially duplicated the romance with Tom Maxwell. It reproduced the letter announcing Tom's demise. It mentioned a Patent Office clerk named Eyra Jenks—the same Eyra Jenks who strode across Miss De Acosta's pages. Miss De Acosta later told the court that she had called this fictitious figure Ezra, but her typist had misread her handwriting, and she had let the *y* stand in place of the *z* to save correction expense. In all, seven characters born of Miss De Acosta's imagination turned up in Miss Brown's work.

Miss De Acosta sued Miss Brown and *Cosmopolitan* for infringement. Miss Brown protested her innocence. Miss De Acosta won.

Judge Rifkind said that he was convinced that Miss Brown had had access to Miss De Acosta's screenplay, either directly or "indirectly through one or more of her numerous assistants, of varying degrees of literacy, whom she employed in what she euphemistically called 'research.'" He was equally certain that she had copied. He found the internal evidence "so overwhelming as to exclude coincidence almost to a mathematical certainty."

Although the plagiarized portion represented only a small part of Miss Brown's version, it was, the judge said, an essential part in the development of the story. True, no exclusive rights could be had in the facts of Clara Barton's life, or in the *idea* that she had had a lover. But Miss De Acosta had done more than repeat history. She had created a specific courtship, particular dramatis personae and distinct episodes. Of these she could not be deprived with impunity. Original treatment of material in the public domain was entitled to protection.

Judge Rifkind granted an injunction and ordered an accounting. There was an appeal. The higher court upheld Judge Rifkind.

### The Vicissitudes of Rebecca

When a book, as a result of soaring sales, earns the privilege of having its parentage impugned, the reprobation usually proceeds from a single quarter. In the case of Daphne du Maurier's *Rebecca*, it sprang from two unrelated ones.

The basis of the first attack was *A Sucesora*, a Portuguese-language novel from the pen of Carolina Nabuco, a Brazilian lady of wealth and social and literary standing. Set in South America, the story had to do with the tribulations of a second wife. It was published in Brazil in 1934, and was an instant hit.

Desiring a wider audience, Miss Nabuco translated her book into English and sent it to a literary agent in the United States. It went from publisher to publisher for several years and found no taker. The agent finally submitted it to an English house, which also turned it down.

*Rebecca* appeared in 1939. A friend wrote Miss Nabuco: "Have you read the English version of *A Sucesora*? I have just read *Rebecca* and thought I was reading *A Sucesora*."

When the Portuguese translation of *Rebecca* reached Brazil, the local critics almost without exception took Miss du Maurier severely to task, enumerating what they considered damning parallels between her book and Miss Nabuco's.

There were repercussions in this country too. One caustic commentator pointed out the following: Both novels had for their heroine a dead wife whose personality dominated the life of her timid, apprehensive successor. In both novels the second wife, before meeting her husband-to-be, heard tales of the loveliness and brilliance of the first wife, and of the husband's grief upon her death. In both novels the husband's ancestral home loomed large. In both, the second wife, on visiting the home for the first time, was struck by the menacing quality of the luxuriant vegetation around it. In both there was a hostile housekeeper who resented the new mistress and sought to torment her by harping on the beauty and accomplishments of her predecessor. In both, the husband had an only sister. When the second wife in *A Sucesora* entered a room, "it often seemed that Alice had just left it, that her departing steps might be heard, that her hands had touched the flowers in the vases, or her body had left its imprint on the sofa cushions." In *Rebecca* the second wife mused: "Someone had been before me, had surely left an imprint of her person on the cushions and on the arm where her hand had rested. . . . I thought Rebecca took the lilacs as I am doing and put the sprigs one by one in the white vase."

"Whether the explanation of this uncanny likeness," concluded the commentator, "lies in the plane of coincidence, clairvoyance or a more realistic explanation, as Brazilian critics insist, the fact remains that *A Sucesora* and *Rebecca* confront each other as literary doubles of an extraordinary order, even to a dispassionate eye."[1]

Miss du Maurier had her adherents. The basic plot of both narratives, they insisted, was more or less formula stuff; the motivation in *A Sucesora*, as distinguished from that in *Rebecca*, was alien to American and English social attitudes; and in any case the treatments were different.

The question which naturally suggested itself was where and how Miss du Maurier, four thousand miles removed from Miss Nabuco, could have had access to the Brazilian novel. Rumor supplied the answer. Miss du Maurier, it was said, had been a reader for the English publisher to whom *A Sucesora* had been sent, and she had studied it before producing *Rebecca*. Miss du Maurier's denial was succinct and sweeping. "I never heard of Carolina Nebuco or her novel," she said, "and have never been reader for any publishing house in Britain or the United States. *Rebecca* is entirely my own creation."

Although Spanish and Portuguese versions of *Rebecca* were circulated in Brazil and elsewhere in South America, Miss Nabuco took no legal steps. She would not stoop, it was reported, to engage in degrading traffic with the law.

Just about the time this controversy was at its height, Miss du Maurier was set upon from another quarter. The Nabuco partisans, it seemed, were all wrong; *Rebecca* had been drawn from another book.

### Blind Windows

The new complainant was Edwina MacDonald. In 1924 she had written a confession piece called *I Planned to Murder My Husband*. She had later expanded it into a novel, *Blind Windows*, published over a decade before the issuance of *Rebecca*. She was not too proud to sue.

Mrs. MacDonald's catalogue of "similarities" was, if anything, even more formidable than that which had been adduced for Miss Nabuco. Both stories, she charged, were told from the point of view of the second wife. In both, the second wife was young, poor and sensitive. In both, she married a rich and charming stranger twice her age whom she had known only for a short time. In both, the wedding had been hastily arranged, and the honeymoon lasted about six or seven weeks. In both, the husband took the second wife to his home, which figured prominently in the story. In both, they were greeted by servitors who had worked for the first wife and were so well-trained that the second one had very little to do. In both, the vivid personality of the first wife, evident everywhere in the house, haunted the second to the point of obsession. In both, the second wife, tortured by a sense of inferiority, convinced herself that her husband was still grieving for her predecessor. In both, she considered leaving her husband and was prevented from doing so by a fortuitous event and the discovery that her husband loved her.

After reading the two books, Judge Bondy found no merit in these claimed parallels. "The stories," he said, "are different." He indicated some of the differences. "Wilda [the second wife in *Blind Windows*] has self-assurance and is willful. Mrs. de Winter [the second wife in *Rebecca*] is exceedingly shy and submissive. Wilda eventually hates her husband and thinks of ridding herself of him by murdering him. Mrs. de Winter, actuated by love, thinks of ridding him of herself by killing herself. Dupré [the husband in *Blind Windows*] is vain, jealous, suspicious and temperamental; de Winter is not temperamental. He is not disclosed to be vain, jealous or suspicious. The first wife in *Blind Windows* is only flirtatious, her counterpart in *Rebecca* is immoral."

Judge Bondy felt that if there was any similarity of incident, it was due to the use of the basic plot, not to copying. He saw no reason for a trial. He dismissed the case on reading the two books.

Mrs. MacDonald appealed.

Two of the members of the Circuit Court—Judges Learned Hand and Swan—didn't like the idea of dispensing with a trial. To deprive Mrs. MacDonald of her day in court was, in their opinion, a "real vice." They reversed the dismissal and ordered a trial.

Judge Clark, the third member of the bench, dissented sharply. "For my part," he declared, "I must consider it as bordering rather on the fantastic, as implying callousness towards, if not derision of, real literary talent and skill, to suggest that such trifling and coincidental similarities as a microscopic examination of the two books is thought to bring out here be considered to weigh at all against the sharp differences between them in all matters which really should count—viz., in intended objective and type of reader appeal, in fashioning of the plot and in its progression, in the conception and delineation of characters, in the climax of the story and denouement of the plot, and in the effectiveness and, certainly in part at least, in the literary skill with which the chosen objective is reached."

The case was finally tried before Judge Bright in 1948, seven years after it was started. By that time a million and a half copies of *Rebecca* had been sold. The trial lasted seven days.

Harrison Smith, one of the editors of *The Saturday Review of Literature*, and a bookman of long experience, testified as an expert for the defense. He had read, he said, as many second-wife novels as he could find. It was astonishing to discover how alike they were, and in how many ways. For purposes of fiction, all second wives walked into luxurious ancestral seats; they were all shocked by the traces of occupancy their predecessor had left behind—the engraved silver, the embroidered linen, the portrait, the mirror in the bedroom wherein shimmered a wraith of the beautiful departed one. There was usually an aura of mystery about the first wife: in some she had been mad, in some she had been murdered, in others she had been unfaithful, in still others she had resembled her successor. Of them all, Smith held, *Rebecca* was the most original and the most vital.

Miss du Maurier took the witnesss stand. Certain occurrences in her own life, she said, had supplied part of the material for her book. Manderley, the de Winter mansion, was a composite of a half-dozen large houses she had known, including Menabilly, which had been her home since 1927. She had not read Mrs. MacDonald's work until the plagiarism suit was started.

On cross-examination, Mrs. MacDonald's attorney read to Miss du Maurier an excerpt from *The du Mauriers*, a family history which she had recorded.

"Did you write," he asked, " 'The du Mauriers have streaks in common, even distant branches down to the third and fourth generations who no longer bear the family name. They lie with grace and ease . . . and are forgiven just as easily'?"

"It is true," she said, "I wrote it."

"Are you an exception to the rule?"

Miss du Maurier thought that one over. The lawyer prodded: "It is true about you, isn't it?"

"No, it is not."

"Then you are an exception to the rule?"

"I don't know."

Judge Bright came to the same conclusion Judge Bondy had four years before. He found no proof of access or copying. "A large bulk of the parallelisms asserted," he declared, "would naturally be expected to be included in such a story, written, as both were, by ladies with their intuitive analysis of the emotions, thoughts and introspection of their own sex under like conditions."

### Versus Adverse

Where the purported source of a best seller is in the public domain, an infringement suit is, of course, out of the question. But that does not mean that parallel-hunters won't be heard from.

When Hervey Allen's *Anthony Adverse* burst upon the literary scene, letters and telephone calls streamed into the publisher's office, charging that parts of the book had been cribbed, and specifying the sources. Among the latter was Vincent Nolte's *Fifty Years in Both Hemispheres*.

Ordinarily, the best thing an author can do in a situation like this is to let the flurry pass unnoticed. Deeply troubled, Allen felt he had to explain. He admitted having consulted the works which the literary sleuths so triumphantly brought forward. He gave a full account of his sources: maps, newspapers, old prints and diaries, and shelves of volumes dealing with the places Adverse visited. "There is only one way to write a historical novel," he said, "and that is to use fully any material out of any books anywhere, always provided the material is reworked and reshaped into that new entity which is from the novelist's own mind." He added that if he had wished to conceal his indebtedness to Nolte, he certainly would not have made the man one of the characters in his tale. "To the thousands of the public who have enjoyed *Anthony Adverse* as a novel," he concluded, "I wish to extend my gratitude. To the comparatively few who have found their principal enjoyment in the book as something to be dissected for the purposes of historical research, I extend my sympathy, and regret that their pleasure in literature is confined to curiosity. To the insignificant number who regard the ordinary processes of the writing of historical fiction as merely so much 'second-story' work, I can only beg leave to part from them with the observation that they are confused in general and therefore wrong in particular."[2]

### Song Lyrics as Accessories

I indicated in Chapter 1 that there are two arrant misconceptions about fair use that appear to resist all efforts to explode them, and that one of them is the notion that none of the lyrics of a copyrighted song may be quoted without permission in fiction or non-fiction, even though the mention may be casual and for the purpose of establishing mood and background. I repeat: There is no legal warrant for this myth, even though music publishers have bedeviled people into believing that if they put so much as a line of a song into their stories, they must humbly ask the copyright owner for leave to do so, and must tack on the copyright notice.

*The Saturday Evening Post* published an article dealing with the formation and exploits of a professional football team called the Green Bay Packers. The article quoted, without dispensation from the copyright owner, eight lines from the chorus—words, not music —of a popular song, "Go! You Packers, Go!" which had been dedicated to the team. Judge Duffy ruled that the use was "incidental and illustrative," and hence fair.

When Pearl White died, *The New Yorker* magazine commented on her early triumphs as the star of the silent movie serial *Perils of Pauline*, and quoted without permission the words of the chorus of the copyrighted song "Poor Pauline." Again the use was held to be fair.

### Compilations

While the individual items contained in compilations—directories, lists and charts, tabulations, encyclopedias, almanacs, social registers, trade catalogues—may be in the public domain, the task of gathering the items together and arranging, classifying and editing them requires effort and skill. Hence a compilation is copyrightable. But the *field* covered by the work cannot be pre-empted. A subsequent investigator may seek out the same sources and assemble his own compendium. However, a compiler is protected against any borrower who, instead of starting from scratch and using his own judgment as to selection and arrangement, simply copies the pioneer.

"An author," said Mr. Justice Story in a century-old case that has been often cited and quoted, "has as much right in his plan and in his arrangements and in the combinations of his materials, as he has in his thoughts, sentiments, opinions, and in his modes of expressing them. The former as well as the latter may be more useful or less useful than those of another author; but that, although it may diminish or increase the relative values of their works in the market, is no ground to entitle either to appropriate to himself the labor or skill of the other, as embodied in his own work. It is a great mistake to suppose, because all the materials of a work or some parts of its plan and arrangements and modes of illustration may be found separately, or in a different form, or in a different arrangement, in other distinct works, that therefore, if the plan of arrangement or combination of these materials in another work is new, or for the first time made, the author, or compiler, or framer of it (call him what you please), is not entitled to a copyright. The reverse is the truth in law, and, as I think, in common sense also."

### Cribbage, Ivy-covered

That most school and college texts lack originality is obvious enough. The texts are not intended to blaze trails or to shine with novelty or to overflow with personality. They are designed, as Homer A. Watt has said, to serve as convenient vehicles for passing on the world's store of learning and lightening the burden of teaching; and if they present old facts in a fresh and attractive form or add a new device for making the student's recalcitrant brain more receptive, that's about all that can be expected of them.[3]

Text writers know that if they desire to quote from copyrighted material in excess of fair use, they can usually get permission without much trouble or expense, provided they credit the source. However, some authors are either so disdainful of the property rights of others, or so eager to invest their work with an aura of pristine revelation, that they overlook or begrudge acknowledgment. They're the ones that get publishers in trouble.

There is another kind of pilferage in the academic field which practically never finds its way to court, and which is all the more reprehensible because it is less open to detection and redress. "University professors of established reputation," says Watt, "are frequently unfair in the use they make of the work of graduate students and of underlings in their departments. I do not like to believe that many of them mean to be unfair; it is probable that in their eagerness for research, and sometimes for the added prestige which another successful investigation will bring them, they carelessly fail to give credit where credit is due." Watt mentions the case of a graduate student who attended a meeting of a literary club and was shocked to hear a professor put forth, with some elaboration but without any credit, a discovery which the student had made and imparted to the professor in a seminar paper. In another case a biology professor published as his own the results of an investigation which a student was about to incorporate in his doctoral dissertation. "A scoop of this sort," Watt observes, "is particularly despicable since it robs the younger scholar of the prestige to which he is justly entitled. Such injustices are so frequent that I heard a famous Harvard professor commended the other day because 'he always gives credit in his publications for contributions sent him,' as if this quality gave him distinction."

### Gunpowder in the Magazines

Some years ago a story called "At the Health Resort" arrived at the offices of a New York magazine. The editor liked it, and sent a check in payment. Deeming the title weak, he changed it to "Never Say No!"—a phrase which occurred several times in the dialogue. On publication it was discovered that the story had previously made its bow in an English journal under the very caption the editor had chosen. The thief had altered the title to cover up his tracks; by sheer coincidence the editor's act had nullified the switch and resulted in an immediate give-away.

When Charles Hanson Towne was at the helm of *The Delineator*, he received a poem accompanied by a note. The note dwelt on the time and effort that the sender had expended on the contribution, and expressed the hope that the remuneration would be commensurate. Towne instantly recognized the poem as one of his own. He wrote to the contributor:

> I beg to acknowledge receipt of your verses,
> and to inform you that I have found them ad-
> mirable. I cannot praise them highly enough.
> Indeed, I liked them so well that I wrote
> them myself two years ago.

A manuscript scribbled in pencil on dog-eared yellow paper found
its way to *Munsey's Magazine* back in the days when Robert H.
Davis was editor. It had journeyed all the way from Montana, and
bore the by-line of Joseph Smith, a miner. The name of it was "The
Luck of Roaring Camp," and it was an exact copy of Bret Harte's
famous tale. Davis penned what he later termed his best rejection
slip:

> As much as I admire the story you have sub-
> mitted, I am unable to publish it for a very
> peculiar reason. Many years ago I promised
> my old friend Bret Harte never to print "The
> Luck of Roaring Camp" by anyone else but
> himself.

"The Perlu," published in *Esquire* in 1935, paralleled and in
places duplicated Ambrose Bierce's "The Damned Thing." "The
Tale of Three Cities," printed in the same magazine a year later,
was an almost exact transcription of "The Eternal Triangle," published in *College Humor* in 1932. In the late 30's, a man in Indiana
went into the plagiarism business in a big way: he copied stories and
articles wholesale from religious and trade papers and pulp magazines and resold them under nine different aliases. He was trapped
when, through carelessness, he sent a piece to the very publication
from which he had stolen it.

It is difficult for magazines to guard against victimization of this
kind. There is no absolute defense against impostors. To be infallible
in spotting theft, an editor would have to be omniscient—he would
have to know everything that has ever been written, at any time and
in any language.

Yet many frauds are caught before publication. Periodicals are
constantly rejecting disguised copies of the works of master story-
tellers. And even if the stolen material gets by and is printed, exposure is inevitable. There is a super-police—the public—more

vigilant and industrious than the keenest private eye ever dreamed up by purveyors of detective fiction. No matter how old or well-hid the plundered original, some alert bloodhound of a reader will track it down and present it derisively to the editor, usually hinting that it must have been stupidity or rank carelessness not to have recognized it in the first place.

Whenever a hoax is brought to light, the red-faced editor turns on the contributor and demands an explanation. Sometimes he is met with silence, sometimes with abuse, sometimes with an abject and bewildered confession. On occasion—and here we glimpse one of the intriguing aspects of the subject—the response reveals a degree of ingenuity and a touch of the fanciful which, if placed at the service of unaided composition, might have obviated any need for copying.

### The Cribbers "Explain"

A good many years ago George Jean Nathan assembled a number of noteworthy examples of self-exculpation.[4] Among them was the case of the Seattle man who foisted an O. Henry story, with only the locale and the names of the characters changed, on an unsuspecting magazine. Taxed with his peculation, he wrote to the editor:

I am insulted at the insinuations you have made in your letter regarding my story. You say it is exactly like a story of O. Henry's, and I say in reply I have never heard of O. Henry or ever read any of his stuff. Similarity is often nothing more than coincidence. There is a man in Seattle who is a dead ringer for President Taft! Could you call him a plagiarist? And I am a dead ringer and often have been mistaken for Gypsy Mike, a notorious character hereabouts. Am I therefore a plagiarist? I do not think so. You will have to blame Nature!

Then there was the case of the man who sold a piece of fiction which, with the exception of a single detail, was a copy of one that had appeared in England years before. The detail had to do with the substitution, in the offender's version, of a candlestick for a small sculpture in the original. Caught, the plagiarist broke down. He was a somnambulist, he wailed; his affliction was incurable. He had done many strange things in his sleep. "Now comes this accusation," he said, "seemingly well-founded. Did I copy that story in my sleep, and did the candle I carry in my midnight wanderings insinuate itself through my subconscious mind into the copied story instead of the statuette? Who can tell? It would seem so. Do not censure me. Forgive and pity a man cursed with a habit like mine. Forgive and forget!"

And this is how the bard who purveyed stolen verses to a weekly paper accounted for it: He had composed hundreds of poems, which he kept in his desk at home. His young son was practicing penmanship, and was in the habit of copying things out of books. The verse in question must have been transcribed in this manner, and must have accidentally found its way to the literary drawer. "The rest you may appreciate," he told the editor of the weekly. "My wife took the poem out, believed it to be one of my own, typed it, and innocently sent it to you."

If the plagiarist is a thorn in the flesh of publishers, he is no less a nuisance to the authors he feeds on. Yet in one instance a larcenist actually benefited his victim. Charles E. Van Loan had been turning out baseball stories for years for the pulps, but he hadn't been able to get into the big time. Somebody cribbed one of his stories, and with a change or two got it printed in *The Saturday Evening Post*. A friend of Van Loan's, who happened to know George Horace Lorimer, then the overlord of the *Post*, wrote to Lorimer: "If you like Van Loan stories, why not buy them direct?" Lorimer did; and so began Van Loan's long and prosperous association with the *Post*.

# 10

# Plagiarism in Plays

There is probably not a play in the history of the world that has not something that is to be found in some previous publication, either in drama, or in fiction or poetry, or some form of literary endeavor; but infringement cases are never decided upon so narrow a basis.

—Judge Mayer: Underhill v. Belasco

---

J. M. BARRIE said he had never written a book but someone found out that he had taken all of it from somebody he had never heard of. "The case is still worse with my plays," he declared, "for a man proved first of all that I had taken them wholly from George Sand or someone else; and then, as an amiable secondly, that there was nothing in them to pay for the trouble and expense of the theft."

In the drama, as in other fields of creative expression, there is no private property in the soil. As William Archer put it, all a playwright can demand is security for the crop he raises; if it were otherwise, the whole cultivable area would long ago have been taken over by a syndicate of pestilent land-grabbers, named Menander, Calderon, Shakespeare & Co., and the dramatists of today would have no recourse but to emigrate to some other planet.

While each tiller of the soil sows and reaps in his own way, and while there may be differences in color and richness between one man's harvest and another's, there is little variation in the immemorial basic nature of the yield.

"The forms of both tragedy and comedy have changed a good deal in non-essentials [since the days of Greece], but in essentials they are in the main the same religious rites which grew up around the altars of Attica long ago. Old Greek comedy was dedicated to the spirits of lust and riot and earth, spirits which are certainly necessary to the health and continuance of the race. Greek tragedy was dedicated to man's aspiration, to his kinship with the gods, to his unending, blind attempt to lift himself above his lusts and his pure animalism into a world where there are other values than pleasure and survival. However unaware of it we may be, our theatre has followed the Greek patterns with no change in essence, from Aristophanes and Euripides to our own day. Our more ribald musical comedies are simply our approximation of the Bacchic rites of Old Comedy. In the rest of our theatre we sometimes follow Sophocles, whose tragedy is always an exaltation of the human spirit, sometimes Euripides, whose tragi-comedy follows the same pattern of an excellence achieved through suffering."[1]

### Some General Rules

A play ordinarily has a theme, characters, plot, setting, incidents, dialogue, and mood. It also has a title. Sometimes it conveys a moral or a message. To what extent can there be exclusive property rights in these components?

As I have already indicated, copyright does not protect themes or ideas as such, but only an author's individual presentation of them—the words in which he clothes them. "Upon any work," said Judge Learned Hand in the *Abie's Irish Rose* case, "and especially upon a play, a great number of patterns of increasing generality will fit equally well, as more and more of the incident is left out. The last may perhaps be no more than the most general statement of what the play is about, and at times might consist only of its title; but there is a point in this series of abstractions where they are no longer protected, since otherwise the playwright could prevent the use of his 'ideas,' to which, apart from their expression, his property is never extended."

Judge Hand went on to say that although this precise boundary could not be fixed, both plots and characters were susceptible of infringement. As to characters, he added: "If *Twelfth Night* were copyrighted, it is quite possible that a second comer might so closely imitate Sir Toby Belch or Malvolio as to infringe, but it would not be enough that for one of his characters he cast a riotous knight who kept wassail to the discomfort of the household, or a vain and foppish steward who became amorous of his mistress. These would be no more than Shakespeare's 'ideas' in the play, as little capable of monopoly as Einstein's Doctrine of Relativity, or Darwin's theory of the Origin of Species. It follows that the less developed the characters, the less they can be copyrighted; that is the penalty an author must bear for marking them too indistinctly."

It goes without saying that the word-for-word lifting of an entire play or of a vital scene or of an essential part of the dialogue makes out the clearest case of infringement. But there may be plagiarism *without* literal copying. The law will not permit a thief to do deviously—by resorting to paraphrasing—that which he may not do directly.

While a new plot is protectible, an old one is not. As to incidents, it is difficult to say where public domain ends and private property begins. For example, the court ruled in *The Spider* case that the interruption of a stage performance by the supposed murder of a member of the audience was not, in itself, a copyrightable dramatic incident. However, it does not take many incidents, nor much connection between them, to make what will, under proper circumstances, pass for a protectible plot.

Neither locale nor period, mood nor moral, is susceptible of exclusive appropriation. The dramatist who first conceives the notion of doing a play laid in Pago Pago or back in the days of Omar Khayyám can't complain if someone else follows suit, so long as the next man's interpretation is his own.

Copyright secures only the contents of a play, not its title. If the title acquires a secondary significance through its identification with the work, anyone wrongfully seeking to appropriate it can be enjoined under the doctrine of unfair competition.

Where a play is based on a novel in the public domain, and the play itself is copyrighted, the copyright protects the play, not the contents of the novel. A subsequent dramatist cannot be prevented from making a new stage version of the novel, but he must not avail himself of the earlier play in doing so.

## Measure and Mirage

It's one thing to define plagiarism; it's another to apply the definition to a specific case. The Copyright Act itself lays down no rules to guide us.

This lack has bothered judges and attorneys for a long time. It particularly bothered the late Moses L. Malevinsky, an able theatrical lawyer. Having pondered the problem, he came up with what he considered a sure-fire solution. It was his Algebraic Formula. He wrote a book about it.[2]

Let X, he said, equal a play—any play. X is the product of—I am quoting his own language—A, a basic emotion, or an element in or of a basic emotion; B, personified by character; C, motivated through (1) crucible, (2) conflict, (3) complications and/or intrigue to ultimate (4) crisis and climax; D, progressed by narrative, plot or story; E, compartmented by derivative situations; F, dressed up by incidental detailed construction; G, the underlying idea oriented through its constituent elements as dramatically expressed; H, articulated by words; and I, imagined with artistry.

"A plus B plus C of the Algebraic Formula," averred Malevinsky, "when paralleled in two plays, prove infringement, even though the other six elements of the plays may be more or less or altogether different." $C(2)$, $C(3)$, and $C(4)$, he added, did not have to coincide provided it was apparent that they had been deliberately altered to thwart detection. Nor did it matter if the infringer added or substracted characters or situations, so long as the "organic structure" of the play remained the same.

"Under the Algebraic Formula," asserted its inventor confidently, "two or more plays may be paralleled, squared and plumbed, with the certainty of an engineer's T, so that the understanding mind may be able to say with absolute assurance that they are or are not the same."

The formula was, of course, nonsense. It had a single virtue, a negative one: it demonstrated how futile it was to try to apply a mechanical gauge to imponderables.

If Malevinsky thought that judges would gratefully embrace his equation, he was mistaken. He urged it on behalf of the defendant in the *Polly Preferred* case and on behalf of the plaintiff in the

*Abie's Irish Rose* case. He won the first and lost the second; but in both instances the Circuit Court made it clear that it wanted no part of the Algebraic Formula. Dissection and analysis, the Court said, were not the proper way to diagnose plagiarism; the approach had to be more ingenuous, more like that of the average spectator. And in the *Strange Interlude* case Judge Woolsey hazarded the guess that the genesis of the suit, which he found without merit, was traceable to the effect on the plaintiff's mind of reading Malevinsky's book.

The court cases offer no easy test, no simple criterion, no automatic measuring rod for infringement. They do reveal the law of plagiarism in action; and we must look to them to bring the general principles into focus and to give those principles objective significance.

## Hardy Versus Pinero

Thomas Hardy, the noted Wessex novelist, composed *Far from the Madding Crowd* sometime before 1881. He dramatized it and sent the script to Comyns Carr, the art critic, for comment and correction. Carr revised it, adding a new character; and with Hardy's consent he submitted it to Hare, the manager of the St. James Theatre in London. Hare liked it; he encouraged Hardy and Carr to believe that he would shortly produce it. Then he abruptly rejected it.

In December 1881, Pinero's *The Squire* opened at the St. James. Many felt that it was an unacknowledged adaptation of Hardy's novel. Hardy was furious. "My drama," he cried in *The Times*, "is now rendered useless, for it is obviously not worth while for a manager to risk producing a play if the whole gist of it is already to be seen by the public at another theatre."

At first Pinero denied any knowledge of Hardy's work. "All I've done," he protested, "is put my horse's head to the open country and taken the same hedges and ditches." Later he modified his stand: he *had* read Hardy's novel, but only after he had fully formulated the outline of *The Squire* in his mind. "Nowadays," he declared with hurt dignity, "on the production of a successful play, the writer of any novel dealing with the same theme, however common the theme, and permeated with the same atmosphere, however common the atmosphere, may start up and claim the sole title to a common subject, and charge the playwright with theft."

To the very end Pinero maintained that he had never laid eyes on the Hardy-Carr script. There was one suspicious fact, however. A gypsy, who did not figure in the novel, had been added to this script by Carr for local color; the same gypsy had turned up in *The Squire*. And because Pinero was probably lying in one particular, a lot of people disbelieved his whole story.

Though feelings ran high, there was no litigation. Whether this was due to Hardy's awareness of his own vulnerability, is hard to say. But one mordant fact remains clear. Hardy, who objected to brain-picking so vehemently when he was the victim, not only felt otherwise when he was the aggressor—he did some drastic lifting in his *The Trumpet Major* and *A Laodicean*—but could calmly wait a dozen years after he was exposed to make amends.[3]

## *Tanks and Tracks*

Some of the early practitioners of the melodrama in this country were less reluctant than Hardy to invoke the law.

There was a play, back in the 1880's, in which the villain met his end by toppling off a bridge into a river. The river consisted of a concealed tank of water. The adoption of this inspired device in another drama precipitated an infringement suit. The sole basis of complaint was that in the second show, as in the first, the river was simulated with real water instead of the conventional painted canvas. The plaintiff argued that this was in itself a sufficiently novel dramatic invention to constitute intellectual property. The judge said no.

Twenty years before, Augustin Daly had had better luck with the famous "railroad scene" in his *Under the Gaslight*. In this scene, which was the high point of the drama, one of the characters was tied and laid helpless on the rails of a railroad track over which a train was momentarily expected to pass. Another character, struggling against odds, managed to reach the intended victim and drag him from the track a fraction of a second before the train thundered over the spot. There was much action and little dialogue in the scene. People were thrilled by it, and *Under the Gaslight* played to packed houses.

A manager named Palmer produced Dion Boucicault's *After Dark*, which contained an episode quite similar to Daly's. Daly sued. Palmer's defense was that there could be no literary property in a scene as such. Judge Blatchford ruled in Daly's favor. He was of the opinion that where a scene consisted of a series of incidents grouped in a certain sequence, it was entitled to protection against piracy. "The adaptation of such a series of events," he said, "to different characters who use different language is like the adaptation of a musical air to a different instrument, or the addition to it of variations or of an accompaniment. The original subject of invention, that which required genius to construct it and set in motion, remains the same in the adaptation. A mere mechanic in dramatic composition can make such adaptation, and it is piracy."

Having successfully launched his producing career with a purloined version of *Faust*, William Brady decided, a generation later, that he could prevail where Palmer had failed. He opened *After Dark* in New York. Daly was watchful; he sued again. Brady proved to be a tougher adversary than Palmer. He fought Daly tooth and nail for thirteen years, pouring fifty thousand dollars into the litigation. It was no use. Once more Daly came out on top.

Of course, said the Circuit Court in answer to Brady's contention that the railroad scene was old stuff and hence public property, there was nothing in mere peril and rescue which anyone could claim as his own. But the Court agreed with Judge Blatchford that the scene was a *new* combination of old elements, and hence deserving of the law's aid.

### Cyrano de Bergerac

Samuel Eberly Gross of Chicago wrote a play called *The Merchant Prince of Cornville,* and sent it to the Port St. Martin Theatre in Paris. The script was held there for six weeks, and then rejected. The famous actor Coquelin had been appearing at the Port St. Martin at the time, and his good friend Edmond Rostand, author of *L'Aiglon* and *Chantecler*, had frequently visited him in his dressing room. Not long thereafter Rostand's *Cyrano de Bergerac* had its première at the Port St. Martin, with Coquelin in the leading role. Gross proclaimed that he had been robbed.

An Illinois court adjudged Rostand a thief and stopped the

presentation of *Cyrano* there. A New York court came to the opposite conclusion. When the Illinois decision was cited in the course of another infringement trial elsewhere, Augustus Thomas, the playwright, decried it as "an attempt to influence this court by a decision that made another court ridiculous."

Many years later George Jean Nathan, who had known Gross, said: "Plagiarism? The hell with it! I thoroughly believe Rostand swiped my friend's play. But Rostand made it into a beautiful thing, didn't he, so what's the odds?"

### The Wizard of Oz

*The Wizard of Oz* was a hit musical half a century ago. Its special feature was a song called "Sammy," sung by Lotta Faust, one of the principals. The stage business Miss Faust used was new at the time. She would step forward to one of the proscenium boxes, single out a male seated there, and warble meaningfully to him alone. The number delighted the theatregoers, probably—as Judge McPherson later drily remarked—because of the impertinence of making a member of the audience acutely uncomfortable.

Fay Templeton was appearing at the time in a musical called *The Runaways*. She did parodies of five actresses, including Miss Faust delivering "Sammy." She used only the chorus of the tune; the take-off on Miss Faust was announced as such. Bloom, the producer of *The Wizard*, tried to get an injunction against her. Judge McPherson refused to grant one. "What is being represented [by Miss Templeton]," he said, "are the peculiar actions, gestures and tones of Miss Faust; and these were not copyrighted by the complainant Bloom, and could not be, since they were the subsequent device of other minds. It is the personality imitated that is the subject of Miss Templeton's act, modified, of course, by her own individuality, and it seems to me that the chorus of the song is a mere vehicle to carry the imitation along. Surely a parody would not infringe the copyright of the work parodied, merely because a few lines of the original might be textually reproduced."

The Judge added: "No doubt the good faith of such mimicry is an essential element; and if it appeared that the imitation was a mere attempt to evade the owner's copyright, the singer would be prohibited from doing in a roundabout way what could not be done directly."

The result was the same when, five years later, the producer of Franz Lehar's *The Merry Widow* tried to prevent a couple of vaudevillians from imitating and burlesquing Lina Barbanell and Donald Brian, who were starring in the Lehar show.

### Master of Stagecraft

David Belasco had one of the longest and most fruitful producing careers in the theater. Dramatist as well as director and manager, guiding spirit of the destinies of such stars as Mrs. Leslie Carter, Frances Starr and Lenore Ulric, he raised authenticity of stage detail to a fine art. He was the leading theatrical figure of his time. He was also the most-sued man in the history of plagiarism.

His first two encounters—those involving his productions *The Millionaire's Daughter* and *May Blossom*—didn't get beyond threats. He was a young man then, an impecunious novice, hardly an attractive target for plaintiffs. But as soon as he prospered, there began the series of suits that were to plague him for three decades and cost him a fortune to defend. There were seven suits. He won them all.

The first case arose in 1888. Fanny Ayman Matthews accused Belasco and Henry C. De Mille of stealing their drama *The Wife* from her script *Washington Life*. Judge Beach dismissed the complaint.

Belasco's production of *Du Barry* precipitated the next case. The French writer Jean Richepin considered *Du Barry* a piracy of one of his own plays, and he engaged the notorious law firm of Howe & Hummel to press his claim. Hummel plunged into action in his customary flamboyant fashion. "Instead of serving papers on Belasco himself or at the box office, he bought a first-row ticket for one of his servers and had him vault onto the stage a second after Mrs. Leslie Carter, the star, made her entrance. She met the applause of the audience and the outstretched hand of the process server at the same moment. The incident upset the temperamental Mrs. Carter so much that she had to retire for several minutes, summons in hand, and then begin all over again."[4] The type of tactics which had worked so well for Hummel in breach-of-promise affrays failed to intimidate

Belasco. The quick settlement the lawyer had hoped to extort did not materialize. The case never went to trial.

Two years later Belasco was sued again. The aggrieved individual this time was Grace B. Hughes, who asserted that Belasco's *Sweet Kitty Bellairs* plagiarized her *Sweet Jasmine*. Judge Lacombe didn't agree with her. "The climax of one act in each piece," he said, "was principally relied upon in argument, where the unexpected discovery of the title character in a place where she should not be makes a dramatic situation which is presumably helpful to the success of both plays. That is an old device. It was common property of all playwrights when Sheridan employed it in the *School for Scandal*. Analyzing the details of that situation as presented in these two plays, the points of essential difference so far outnumber the points of similarity that it is difficult to understand how any one could persuade himself that the one was borrowed from the other."

The fourth suit, brought in 1912, really got under Belasco's skin. It arose out of De Mille's *The Woman,* which Belasco had produced with great success. A Bath Beach barber charged that his own *Tainted Philanthropy* was the source of the play.

In court Belasco, ever the showman, made an unprecedented gesture. "I am heartily sick," he told Judge Holt, "of being sued by nursemaids, waiters and barbers every time I bring out a new piece. I should very much like to give a performance of both these plays before your Honor."

"Won't it be very expensive for you," asked the Judge, "to have the case decided this way?"

"Yes, sir; it will cost me a lot, but I want to show these unknown authors, once and for all, that they cannot come into the courts and attack every successful production I make without submitting their plays to a comparison that will dispose of their claims very quickly."

The two performances were given in the Belasco Theatre an hour apart. *Tainted Philanthropy* was enacted by capable actors exactly as written. It proved to be, to quote William Winter, "a veritable farrago of impalliable trash." After the final curtain the barber accosted De Mille and said: "Many people have told me that my play is better than yours." "My dear sir," replied De Mille, "I have denied the similarity, not the superiority, of your play."

Three days later Judge Holt dismissed the complaint. The plaintiff was chagrined but not wholly disconsolate. He went around boasting that he had had a play produced by the great Belasco.

If Belasco believed that he had now purchased peace, he was quickly disillusioned. The same year one Amelia Bachman came forward and challenged Edward Locke's *The Case of Becky,* which Belasco had put on, as a copy of her play *Etelle,* the script of which she had previously shown to the producer. The theme of *The Case of Becky* was dual personality; its heroine, a young lady alternately innocent and vicious. Public interest in the well-worn Jekyll-and-Hyde formula had been stimulated by the publication, shortly before, of Dr. Morton Prince's *The Dissociation of a Personality* (a case history) and of John Corbin's magazine story *How One Girl Lived Four Lives.*

The similarities stressed by Miss Bachman—among them the fact that a character in *Etelle* said "Oh, it's awful!" and another in *The Case of Becky* said "Ain't it awful, sir?"—failed to impress Judge Mayer. He decided against her.

On appeal she fared no better. "We have read," said the Circuit Court, "Corbin's story, have looked over Dr. Prince's book, and have read both plays, and have reached the conclusion that in the story and the book there is enough to suggest the plot, incidents, situations and dialogues of both plays, without any mutual assistance, the one from the other." A common source, the Court added, naturally suggested similar situations to anyone; the person who first built and copyrighted a play around those situations could not prevent another from doing the same, provided the later dramatist got his material from the common source, not from the copyrighted play.

Belasco's production of *The Boomerang* in 1916 provoked the sixth suit. The plaintiff was Lila Longson. Judge Sheppard held that her play *The Choice* had not been infringed. She tried to reopen the case ten years later, but without avail.

The final legal bout arose over Edward Knoblock's *Marie Odile,* one of Belasco's greatest successes. Gregorio Martinez-Sierra, a Spanish dramatist of note, had written a play called *The Cradle Song,* and had sent it to Belasco. The producer had liked it, and had been on the point of accepting it when—according to his story—he had got hold of Knoblock's script. He had considered this script superior, turned down Sierra's, and gone ahead with *Marie Odile.* Both plays dealt with life in a convent.

Judge Mayer found no evidence of plagiarism. "Most of the incidents that happen in the world," he said, "may be availed of in plays or books, and the question essentially is in what manner they are availed of. . . . There is rarely anything that is physically new. Convents are old. The theme of a foundling in some relation or another is old. The conduct of persons in any given walk or department of life—that is to say, the normal conduct—is ordinarily old and well known. . . . Except for the fact that the scene of both plays is in a convent and that of necessity there are some similarities of dialogue and language, the two plays are essentially and fundamentally different." He adverted to the fact that Belasco had held on to Sierra's script for nine months; he felt that if it hadn't been for this, there might have been no litigation at all.

The thirty-year siege was over. Belasco had withstood all assault. Yet there can be no doubt that he borrowed from produced plays; William Winter, his reverential biographer, admits this and cites proof.[5] Nor is it unlikely that he got hints from the hundreds of scripts that fledgling playwrights brought prayerfully to his door. What saved him was his instinctive ability to draw the line between permissible borrowing and illicit copying. And so his reputation remained intact. Only his exchequer suffered.

# 11

# Plagiarism in Plays (Continued)

We have often wondered why it was that the stupid ogres and other monsters of the fairy-tales, who wished to give an impossible task to the prince they had got into their clutches, never set him to tracing an idea to its source.
—William S. Walsh: Handy-Book of Literary Curiosities

THE cycle of legal proceedings against Belasco was a prelude. It ushered in the golden era of plagiarism litigation.

The era began around 1915, gained momentum in the roaring 20's, spurted through the troubled 30's, and bowled along merrily in the 40's. It was golden only in the sense that there were many cases. The plaintiffs rarely scored court victories. Some of them doubtless managed to wring settlements from their adversaries. In any event, the cases kept coming one after the other with unfailing regularity. And now in the 50's there is no indication of a let-up.

## The Array of the Aggrieved

Let's start with 1913. That was the year Max Marcin was sued on his *Cheating Cheaters*. He was supposed to have stolen it from an unproduced play called *Wedding Presents*. Judge Manton felt that the idea of a bunch of crooks insinuating themselves into a household as respectable servitors, as well as the device of a man's impersonating a girl to expose the skulduggery, was too old and commonplace to sustain a claim of exclusive ownership.

Two years later *At Bay* was similarly exonerated. The plaintiff said that a copy of his play *Threads of Destiny* had been previously sent to Augustus Thomas, co-author of *At Bay*. Thomas, who had half a hundred dramas to his credit, testified that he received many scripts from unknown writers for comment, and that for his own protection he made it a point never to so much as glance at unsolicited ones. The Court took his word for it.

The next stage hit to be attacked was *Arms and the Girl*, which was claimed to infringe a novel called *Little Comrade*. Both works dealt with World War I, espionage, a pretended or forced marriage, a forged or stolen passport. It would never do to hold, Judge Mayer felt, that just because an incident from a copyrighted book or play was later used here and there in another relation in another work, the latter necessarily infringed the former.

The controversy concerning Leroy Scott's *No. 13 Washington Square* and Joseph William Frankel's *Three Months Abroad* turned on the same point, and with the same result. In both plays persons announced they were going abroad, were prevented by money difficulties from doing so, and, embarrassed, decided to remain hidden in their nominally closed houses. "This incident or background," said Judge Hough, "is common property; no one can appropriate it, nowadays at all events. The happenings in a supposedly empty home have been too often exploited for literary purposes."

In 1925 the string of defendants' triumphs was broken. A plaintiff—Ida Vera Simonton—finally won. Her claim that Leon Gordon's drama *White Cargo* plagiarized her novel *Hell's Playground* was sustained. Both works were set in Africa, both explored the disintegrating effect of life in the tropics on white men; both contained an illicit mixed-blood love affair. There were, in addition, significant extrinsic facts. The novel had originally come to the attention of a playwright named Leroy Clemens. Clemens thought it had stage potentialities; he discussed it with Gordon, with whom he had collaborated before. Gordon was interested, and a contract was made with Miss Simonton. Clemens then broached the project to a theatrical producer, and got a discouraging response. The producer was certain the public wouldn't take kindly to a dramatization of sex relations between a white man and an African charmer. The contract with Miss Simonton was allowed to lapse.

Some time later Gordon's *White Cargo* was produced. It turned out to be a smash hit. The magnet that drew the crowds was the torrid and explicit love scenes between the hero and his dusky temptress, proving once more how wrong theatrical experts can be. Tondeleyo, the heroine, became overnight a symbol of sultry passion.

Faced on every side with parallels that could not be explained away, the defense adopted a last-ditch line. *Hell's Playground,* it argued, was a lewd and lascivious opus, and as such not entitled to the law's intervention. Judge Knox did not see it that way. While he found both works "coarse and sensual," he pointed out that they purported to depict actual conditions in the tropics; and he doubted whether, in the light of the frank contents of current magazines, novels and dramas, they could be considered immoral.

Shortly afterward Ossip Dymow sued Guy Bolton alleging that the latter's *Polly Preferred* had been appropriated from his *Personality.* Judge Hough agreed with Dymow, but the Circuit Court reversed him and dismissed the complaint.

What, then [said the Circuit Court] is the extent of similarity existing between these two plays? In each is presented an ambitious girl of at least potential charm, who is willing to have her ambition served by an ingenious young man in financial straits. In each the man, though by wholly different means, sails very close to the winds of finance and veracity in exploiting the girl as a mold of fashion (Dymow) or a "movie star" (Bolton). Result—gratification of ambition by girl, and requited affection on the man's part. This incomplete skeleton the two plays have in common, but it is with real difficulty that the flesh and blood, the incidental yet essential adornment and trimming, of the plays can be cut away to show similarity between a few bones. This difficulty is fatal to plaintiff's case; the copyright law, like all statutes, is made for plain people; and that copying which is infringement must be something "which ordinary observation would cause to be recognized as having been taken from" the work of another . . . It requires dissection rather than observation to discern any resemblance here. If there was copying (which we do not believe), it was permissible, because this mere subsection of a plot was not susceptible of copyright.

Like Belasco, Channing Pollock was attacked time and again for plagiarism. Like the maestro, he never lost a case. One of the court battles arose out of *The Fool,* which Abraham P. Waxman considered an ill-disguised version of his own *Soldiers of the Common Good.* Waxman made much of the fact that in his script a rejected suitor suggested to his lady, in case she changed her mind about him, that she raise the shade in her bedroom and pass a light across the window three times, whereas in *The Fool* a spurned adorer said to his loved one: "See how you feel in the morning. My telephone is Rhinelander 6942." Moreover, Waxman swore he had given his script to a third party who, in his presence, had handed it over to Pollock. Judge Thacher didn't believe him, and awarded Pollock five thousand dollars in counsel fees. Waxman promptly went into bankruptcy.

Sidney Howard too had to go to court to defend his integrity as author. The accusation was that he had lifted his play *They Knew What They Wanted* from a romantic tragedy called *The Full of the Moon*. On cross-examination he was shown a printed copy of his play.

"Do you recall," the plaintiff's attorney inquired, "writing a preface for this volume?"

"I do," said Howard.

"Are the views expressed in the preface the views you've always held and still hold with respect to authorship?"

"They are."

The attorney flung open the book with a triumphant flourish. "I ask you whether you recall saying in the preface that your play is, and I quote, shamelessly, consciously and even proudly derived from another source?"

"Yes."

"And do you also recall saying this: 'I advise all other young writers, who need plots and can't make up good ones of their own, to pick a good one out of the classics'?"

"I do."

Actually what Howard had written was: "The story of this play is shamelessly, consciously, and even proudly derived from the legend of Tristram and Yseult."[1]

Howard was absolved. "The only striking feature," said Judge Augustus N. Hand of the Circuit Court, "common to each [play] is the accident to the bridegroom on the day of the wedding. A physical injury to husband or wife has frequently been employed in literature to furnish a temptation to the remaining spouse to yield to the wooing of a lover. . . . The practical everyday philosophy of Howard's characters is as far removed as possible from that of the passion-driven figures that pass across complainant's stage."

Fulton Oursler and Lowell Brentano's thriller *The Spider* hung up a record of sorts in plagiarism litigation in 1930. Four separate offensives were mounted against it; four different works were put forward as its purported wellspring. Since all these compositions were claimed to resemble *The Spider*, they presumably also resembled each other; just how the several plaintiffs felt about the possibility of larcenous taking as among themselves, is shrouded in mystery. Two of the suits withered on the vine; the other two ripened into trial. Judge Thacher found no proof of piracy.

An ordinary observer of the three plays here involved [said the Judge] would undoubtedly form the impression that they were of the same type and had utilized the same material—that is, a shooting in a theater and the solution of the crime. But no impartial person would think that anything of importance in *The Spider* had been taken from either of the other two plays. . . . The authors having worked with the same material to construct the environment or setting in which the action is laid . . . similarities are inevitable, and the products of such labor are comparable to paintings of the same scene made by different artists. Similarities in the one case are of little more significance than in the other. When in such a case similarities are found not in the plot or in its dramatic development or in the lines or action of the principal characters, but only in incidental details necessary to the environment or setting, there is no basis upon which to found a charge of plagiarism, and it may usually be said that such material is so unimportant and so trvial that its appropriation by copying, even if shown, would not be a substantial taking of copyrighted material.

Frank Bacon's celebrated starring vehicle *Lightnin'* (one of the marathon champions of all time), R. C. Sheriff's notable *Journey's End*, the Kaufman-Ryskind-Gershwin Pulitzer Prize musical *Of Thee I Sing*, Walter Ferris' *Death Takes a Holiday*, Sidney Kingsley's *Dead End*, Kaufman and Hart's *You Can't Take It with You*, Kaufman and Ferber's *Stage Door*, Noel Coward's *Blithe Spirit*, Norman Krasna's *Dear Ruth*, Arnaud d'Usseau and James Gow's *Deep Are the Roots*, and Lindsay and Crouse's *State of the Union*— all these were set upon for plagiarism in their time, and all of them were cleared.

The comments of the Circuit Court in the *Stage Door* case merit quotation:

Such similarities as exist: i.e., the general theme, the *mise en scène*, the suicide and the rest, are easily accounted for upon the assumption of independent composition. Indeed the only thing which even faintly demands an explanation is that the lead in each play takes to the stage because of her mother's defeated histrionic ambitions. That might serve as corroboration, if there were really any tentative inference to corroborate; but there is none. In order to suppose that these two highly experienced and successful authors should have found in the plaintiff's play cues for the far-fetched similarities which she discovers, one must be obsessed, as apparently unsuccessful playwrights are commonly obsessed, with the unalterable conviction that no situation, no character, no detail of construction in their own plays can find even a remote analogue except as the result of piracy. "Trifles light as air are to the jealous confirmations strong as proof of holy writ."

In the *Blithe Spirit* case Judge Bernstein found that the only similarities between Coward's comedy and John O. Hewitt's *Spirits* were that they both had as characters the spirits of dead persons; that the name of one of the revenants in *Blithe Spirit* approximated phonetically the name of one of the living characters in Hewitt's play; and that a maid served as a comedy figure in both. All the other items of supposed similarity, the Judge indicated, were trifling; on the other hand, the differences were so marked and obvious that no ordinary observer could conceivably confuse one work with the other.

*Dear Ruth* and its supposed source both involved a meddlesome adolescent girl who dispatched ardent letters in her sister's name to a strange soldier, with the to-be-expected complications on the soldier's unannounced arrival at the girls' home. "Resemblance there may be," said Judge Null drily, "but only in the broad and general sense in which it may be said that one horse is like another."

These brief summaries cannot, of course, convey the full drama of litigation, nor the detailed rationale of the legal results. Let's take a closer look at a few of the outstanding cases.

## The Bird of Paradise

In the entire history of plagiarism court battles, no case was more stubbornly fought or left a deeper impress on the law than the one in which the competing works had as their background the land of the hula-hula, the grass skirt, and the ceremonial *lei*.

In 1910 Richard Walton Tully decided to do a play about Hawaii. He drew up a synopsis and sent it to Oliver Morosco, then a budding theatrical producer on the West Coast. By sheer coincidence, Grace A. Fendler gave her drama *In Hawaii* to Morosco at about the same time. There was no question that the scenario and the play had been independently conceived and written. Morosco liked Tully's synopsis. He rejected Mrs. Fendler's script. Tully went to the Coast, conferred with Morosco about the development of his outline, and then sailed for Hawaii to gather authentic data. He eventually completed his play, *The Bird of Paradise,* and Morosco presented it in New York, with Laurette Taylor as the star. It was a hit.

If Tully and Morosco were pleased, Mrs. Fendler wasn't. She felt sure the producer had shown her script to Tully, and Tully had made improper use of it. She had, on the surface, grounds for suspicion. Both plays dealt with a young American who went to the Islands to work and succumbed to the charms of a native girl; both plays stressed native rites and customs, music and folklore.

Mrs. Fendler started suit in New York for violation of her common law copyright. She asked for an injuction and an accounting of the profits of *The Bird of Paradise.* She lost the first skirmish: her application for a preliminary injunction was denied.

Although the case was started in 1912, it is a commentary on the law's delays that the trial was not held until a dozen years later.

At the trial Mrs. Fendler took the position that while Tully's scenario may have been an innocent conception, it differed in several material respects from the final version of *The Bird of Paradise,* and that Tully had made these changes as a result of having rifled *In Hawaii.* The heroine, in the scenario the daughter of a priest, had, in the final version, become a princess, the last of a royal line. A new character had been introduced in the play: an American trader who rose to a position of power in the local government. In Mrs. Fendler's script too, the heroine was the last of her royal line, and an American was prime minister of Hawaii.

Tully swore in court that he had never seen *In Hawaii.* He described at length how his own work had come into being. But there was one damaging fact he could not plausibly account for: the changes he had made in his synopsis. He failed to convince the

Court. Mrs. Fendler won a crushing victory. She was awarded more than $780,000.

Morosco and Tully lost their first appeal. However, in 1930, eighteen years after the litigation was started, the Court of Appeals—the tribunal of final resort—set aside the judgment and dismissed the complaint.

In its opinion, the Court conceded that there were many similarities. "Perhaps this is inevitable," it said, "in two plays about Hawaii. The very name Hawaii seems to suggest to Americans the hula dance and the sport of swimming, flowers and sunshine and music. It suggests too the dread disease of leprosy. All these things are introduced, though with varying emphasis, in both plays. Doubtless the value of the producing rights of the plaintiff's play must have suffered by the successful production of any play about Hawaii. Of that she cannot be heard to complain." The Court went on to say that although Mrs. Fendler had lived in Hawaii and had studied its traditions, she could not acquire a monopoly in those traditions by weaving them into a play. Others could use them at will in different forms and combinations.

Even assuming—the Court concluded—that a surreptitious reading of *In Hawaii* prompted Tully to insert some new material in *The Bird of Paradise*, there was still no ground for complaint. Where the similarity was close, the material was inconsequential; where the material was important, the treatment was different. "Details must be viewed in their setting; then resemblances vanish."

The man who had stood in the shadow of an accusation for twelve years, and who for another six had been pronounced a literary thief by the law, was finally acquitted. The long-delayed exoneration left him impoverished and exhausted, his creative faculty crippled. He never turned out anything of consequence thereafter. "I've lost the best years of my life," he said bitterly, "more completely than if I had been convicted and sent to prison, and the law gives me no redress."

### Strange Interlude

The play which won the encomiums of most critics—but which Alexander Woollcott ("rancor was his only form of exercise") disdained as the *Abie's Irish Rose* of the intelligentsia—also wound up in court on a question of parentage.

In 1924, Georges Lewys, a precocious young lady, completed an uncanonical opus entitled *The Temple of Pallas-Athenae* [*sic*]. A limited edition of a thousand copies was privately struck off for subscribers—"illuminati," the circular called them. The book was copyrighted. No copies were sent to reviewers or offered to the general public.

Not content with so limited an audience, Miss Lewys discussed with Boni & Liveright the possibility of general publication. Nothing came of it. She then sent a copy of her novel to the Theatre Guild, averring in her covering letter that in the opinion of one critic, the book "said the most terrible things in the divinest language," and that, in the opinion of another, it was a classic. She enclosed the outline of a proposed dramatic treatment, in which she described *The Temple* as a satire.

The story [she said] rests on a scientific foundation: the Greek custom of "specimen reproduction" or selective parenthood. Scientific reproduction of the human species was incorporated in a Greek ritual, practiced in the ancient Temple of Pallas-Athenae. . . . A house is built in Paris in the present day for the same purpose, six male specimens are incarcerated there, and the handsome American and European women who are married to senile, awkward, or debauched husbands visit this house without the knowledge of their husbands in order to obtain beautiful children and to improve the human race.

Unimpressed, the Theatre Guild declined the script. Some time later it staged Eugene O'Neill's *Strange Interlude*. Miss Lewys sued. The essence of her complaint was that the Theatre Guild had turned over her book and dramatic treatment to O'Neill, and that he had pirated both. She set her sights high. She asked for a million dollars.

When O'Neill was shown the 41-page list of supposed parallels that Miss Lewys had drawn up, his comments ranged from such mild remarks as "This is incomprehensible to me," "I see no possible connection," and "Nothing remotely reminiscent here" to such robust utterances as silly, ridiculous, absurd, far-fetched, laughable, idiotic and utter rot. He concluded by saying: "The subject of hereditary insanity has been often treated in literature before. And if it hadn't, there are many books on psychopathology open to any writer who wants data on such material. And the idea of a woman having a child by a man other than her husband, either because her husband cannot give her a child or because she doesn't want one by him but by her lover, is also nothing new. . . . The idea that I would wade through a gooey mess like this to pilfer ideas —I who have always, as can be proven, had enough plots for plays noted down to occupy me the rest of my life!—is about as plausible an assumption as that Rockefeller would steal pennies from a blind man's hat!"

The case was tried before Judge Woolsey in 1931. It was quite a show. The tone of it was set when the defense pointed out that the theme of selective paternity was paralleled in the Bible story of Elisha. "Yes," said the Judge with dead-pan solemnity, "I shall take judicial notice of the Bible."

Miss Lewys, tossing bright-red curls, made a lively witness. She testified that during her seven-year stay in New York she had been to the theater only three times. No, she had never seen an O'Neill play. She was a very serious person, she said; she did not like to be diverted from her work by "stupid comedies and the ordinary run of plays."

She was hard put to it to show access, but this did not daunt her. O'Neill, she argued, could have obtained from the charwomen at the Guild Theatre the key to the office of the Guild reader to whom *The Temple* had been entrusted. And she kept pounding away at the supposedly multitudinous similarities—she called them "finger-prints"—which, to her way of thinking, established O'Neill's guilt beyond a doubt.

Miss Lewys fought spiritedly and resourcefully. She made much of the fact that O'Neill's testimony was in the form of a deposition, and that he had not come to court in person to face cross-examination. However, she herself didn't do so well when the other side started firing questions at her. One bit of evidence counted heavily against her. She was forced to admit that the document which she presented in court as the outline she had originally forwarded to the Guild was *not* the one she had sent, but a later fabrication—prepared after she had read *Strange Interlude*—in which she had altered the story of *The Temple* to come closer to O'Neill's plot.

Characterizing Miss Lewys' assertions as preposterous, Judge Woolsey dismissed the complaint. The case, he said, was not without its usefulness. It illustrated how plagiarism claims arose and were fostered. Miss Lewys, like many plaintiffs before her, had become so obsessed with the idea of having been robbed that she had not flinched at any means, no matter how extreme or reckless, to abet her cause. As far as the "fingerprints" were concerned, "absurdity could not rise to greater heights." Since the lady had played for high stakes and lost, the Judge felt it fitting that she pay court costs and substantial counsel fees. He fixed the latter at $17,500.

The award was a victory for O'Neill in every sense but the financial. Miss Lewys, it turned out, had no means out of which the judgment against her could be satisfied.

### "Sketch of a Great Man"

George Bernard Shaw once called Frank Harris more pugnacious than six Queensberrys. He had good reason.

In the introduction to his play *Shakespeare and His Love*, published in 1910, Harris adverted to the fact that the National Shakespeare Memorial Committee was about to produce Shaw's *The Dark Lady of the Sonnets*. He indicated that fourteen years before, "provoked by the nonsense Mr. Shaw was then writing about Shakespeare," he had advanced an original theory about the Bard. "With admirable quickness," said Harris, "Mr. Bernard Shaw proceeded to annex as much of this theory of mine as he thought important; in preface after preface to his plays, notably in the preface to *Man and Superman*, he took my discovery and used it as if it were his."

This, fumed Harris, was not all. He had built a drama around Shakespeare; Shaw had seen it. "Now," he went on, "Mr. Shaw has written a play on the subject which I have been working on for these fifteen years, and from what he has said thereon in *The Observer* it looks as if he had annexed my theory bodily so far as he could understand it, and the characters to boot, using words of mine again and again as if they were his own. All this in the England of today is looked upon as honorable and customary. If Mr. Shaw can annex my work, it only shows that he is stronger than I or abler, and this fact in itself would be generally held to absolve or justify him: *vae victis* is the noble English motto in such cases. But if it turns out in the long struggle that Mr. Shaw is only more successful for the moment than I am, if my books and writings on

Shakespeare have come to stay, then I can safely leave the task of judging Mr. Shaw to the future. In any case I can console myself. It amused me years ago to see Mr. Shaw using scraps of my garments to cover his nakedness; he now struts about wearing my livery unashamed. I am delighted that so little of it makes him a complete suit. My wardrobe is still growing in spite of his predatory instincts, and he is welcome to as much of it as I have cast off and he can cut to fit."[2]

Shaw was unruffled. He was also admirably candid. "Harris," he said, "accuses me flatly of cribbing from him, which I do not deny, as I possess in a marked degree that characteristic of Shakespeare, Molière, and Handel, which is described as picking up a good thing where you find it. After all, what did Mr. Harris mean to do? He published certain views about Shakespeare, just as Darwin published certain views about the origin of species. But whereas Darwin did not expect biologists to continue writing as if Chambers' *Vestiges of Creation* were still the latest thing in their science, Mr. Harris seems seriously to believe that I ought to have treated the history of Shakespeare exactly as Cowden Clarkes left it, and to have regarded his observations as non-existent. The mischief of such literary ethics is shewn in Mr. Harris's own work. It is impoverished by his determination not to crib from me, just as my work is enriched by my determination to crib from him. Nothing that he ever said or wrote about Shakespeare was lost on me. Everything that I ever said or wrote about Shakespeare seems to have been lost on him. Consequently, my Shakespeare has everything that is good in Harris and Shaw. His Shakespeare has only what is good in Harris. I respectfully invite my friends and patrons to walk up to *my* booth, as offering, on his own shewing, a superior exhibition."[3]

Either Harris wasn't as angry as he pretended to be, or he tempered indignation with practicality. At any rate, he soon asked Shaw to add a note of personal reminiscence to his, Harris', *Oscar Wilde*. Shaw was glad to oblige.

## The Importance of Being Original

If Harris relished berating his more successful colleague for real or fancied borrowings, how much more would he have enjoyed, had he lived, the plagiarism imbroglio growing out of his biography of the lily-loving poet!

Harris' *Oscar Wilde* was copyrighted in this country in 1916. A generation later Leslie and Sewell Stokes fashioned a play called *Oscar Wilde,* depicting the rise and fall of Wilde. Proceeding on the theory that the facts as to Wilde were in the public domain, the Stokes brothers did not bother to get the permission of the Harris estate. Gilbert Miller produced the play with Robert Morley in the title role, and it ran for about eight months on Broadway.

Harris' widow charged that fifty-four items in the drama had been abstracted from her husband's biography. When she got to court, she abandoned seventeen of these. The other side conceded that five of the remainder had been taken bodily from Harris.

The defendants, as usual, had several strings to their bow.

They argued, first, that the borrowing was not substantial; second, that it was not of a kind protected by copyright, since Harris had merely recorded conversations he had had with Wilde, and these were "historical" in the sense that anyone could use them; and third, that Harris himself had been guilty of plagiarism in writing his book, as he had drawn too freely on two prior works, one of them André Gide's study of Oscar Wilde.

Judge Leibell rejected these arguments. As to the first, he said that it was not a question of quantity but of quality and value; although only a small part of the original had been lifted, it constituted a material part of the play, and most of it was verbatim. As to the second, he declared that the use of quotation marks by Harris had not put the quoted matter in the public domain; no stenographer had attended the talks; the report was Harris' personal version, involving the exercise of authorship quite apart from any bare recital of facts; and even if the dialogues in question were assumed to be literal transcriptions, Harris' part in them was original with him, and contributed to the creation of Wilde's part. As to the third, the Judge's answer was terse. "What the Stokes brothers took from the Harris biography," he said, "was not something Harris had taken from someone else."

Mrs. Harris carried the day. The profits of the infringing play were ultimately computed at eighty thousand dollars, and thirty thousand of this amount was awarded to her as the part attributable to the use of the appropriated material, as distinguished from what the Stokeses themselves had contributed to the show.

## The Man Who Came to Dinner

Unpredictable in mood and utterance, compact of incongruities, Alexander Woollcott must have struck more than a few writers as a character around whom an amusing stage piece could be built. He was a reviewer who combined a neat wit with a critical faculty capable of egregious howlers; an enthusiast who carried his projects to ridiculous lengths, and fell prey to hoaxes; a man of commodious frame who was given to baby talk; a writer whose style oscillated between mannered elegance and cuddlesome phrases; a sentimentalist who was unostentatiously kind and ostentatiously rude.

Vincent McConnor was one of those who saw dramatic possibilities in Woollcott. In 1936 he prepared a script called *Sticks and Stones*, and through Arthur Levy, a press agent, sent it to George S. Kaufman. A few days later Kaufman wrote to Levy:

I think this is pretty good, but there's just nothing I can do about it. I *have* to work on my own things if I am ever going to get anything done; twice this season I dabbled in outside shows and each time they ran a week. So I'm cured, for the present at least. Specifically, I think the Woollcott character is fine, but Ross is rather dull—too much whining and prodding. The scenes in which he is involved seemed repetitious. Also, the general swinging of the finger of suspicion, in Act Two, is somewhat conventional and not always sufficiently motivated. But it's pretty good and I don't know why someone shouldn't put it on with you. It just can't be me, and I regret it.

For the next two years McConnor tried hard to market his play. He couldn't find a producer.

Toward the end of 1937, Woollcott paid a visit to Moss Hart's country home in Pennsylvania. He proved himself a presumptuous and disagreeable guest. On his departure he inscribed the following token of thanks in Hart's guest book:

This is to certify that on my first visit to Moss Hart's manor house I had one of the most unpleasant evenings I can recall ever having spent.

Hart, who knew Kaufman, told him about this, and they fell to discussing their mutual friend's eccentricities. They had been thinking on and off for years about doing a comedy about him, but somehow their ideas hadn't clicked. They thought some more, and *The Man Who Came to Dinner* was the result. The play prospered on the stage, on the screen, and in book form.

In the plagiarism proceedings that followed, McConnor hammered away at access and similarity. The note to Levy, he said, proved conclusively that Kaufman had not only had an opportunity to study *Sticks and Stones*, but had actually done so. A Woollcott-like character dominated both plays; Tiny Tim, Florence Nightingale and Little Lord Fauntleroy were mentioned in both; a love triangle and a radio broadcast embellished both; in one there was a reference to Max Steuer and in the other to Samuel J. Leibowitz; calf's-foot jelly and a hatchet-murder were spoken of in both; in one a character said: "I have seen you some place before . . . been trying to place your face for a week," and in the other: "You know, I've seen that face before somewhere." How could these duplications occur, asked McConnor, except through copying?

Kaufman swore he hadn't read *Sticks and Stones*. He said that when he got it, he turned it over to his secretary to glance over. She had given him a verbal report, and it was on the basis of that report, not personal perusal, that he had penned his note to Levy.

On cross-examination McConnor's attorney undertook to show that Kaufman was possessed of such insatiable curiosity that, having in his hands a script dealing with a crony of his, he could not have resisted the temptation to examine it. The attorney read the following passage about Kaufman from *A Peculiar Treasure* by Edna Ferber, who had collaborated with Kaufman on several plays:

No written word is safe from his gaze. A letter, telegram or note left lying about will sooner or later be read by the Paul Pry of playwrights. He can't help it. His curiosity is seemingly overpowering. I thought of a plan to punish him for this habit. Before he was due to arrive at 11, I typed a telegram on a Western Union blank and placed it face up on my desk, almost completely covered by another sheet of paper. Only one corner of the telegram peeped out, folded and creased, as though it had been read and reread. There wasn't enough of it exposed to make its reading possible, but one could see it was a telegram left open. Immediately his gaze lighted on this. As we talked he stalked his prey. He would walk over to it and eye it hungrily. He would walk away from it, cast a longing glance over his shoulder. He bent his head and screwed it around to see if he couldn't thus make out a word or two. Finally, "Damn it, what's in this telegram," he said, and picked it up. I have heard that people's jaws drop with surprise. I never had hoped actually to see this. I saw it now. This was the telegram I had typed, "Georgie Kaufman is an old snooper."

"Did this incident," McConnor's lawyer demanded, "ever actually happen?"

The question did not catch Kaufman unawares. In the *Stage Door* case he had been confronted with the same passage. He did not have to answer; the question was objected to, and the objection sustained.

"Mr. Kaufman," persisted the attorney, "were you ever at Miss Ferber's house, and did you ever pick up a telegram that was covered and find on it that phrase 'Georgie Kaufman is an old snooper'?"

"The telegram was not covered. Miss Ferber is a fiction writer, and has made a good story out of it."

McConnor lost the case. Judge Galston was not persuaded that there had been any theft. Kaufman and Hart, he felt, had been far more abundantly served by material in the public domain than by access to McConnor's work. He pointed out that Tiny Tim, Florence Nightingale and Little Lord Fauntleroy, when used as conversational props, were not copyrightable.

"Even on the assumption," the Judge continued, "that all the suggested similarities stemmed from the plaintiff's play, there remains such gross dissimilarity in all the other aspects of the two plays, particularly in the important subjects of theme, dialogue, setting and sequence, as to defeat the charge of substantial copying. . . . Neither the ordinary observer nor the keenest critic could recognize *The Man Who Came to Dinner* as a reproduction or copy of *Sticks and Stones*. It would take more than a play doctor to transmute one into the other."

The Circuit Court of Appeals, to which McConnor carried his case, agreed with Judge Galston.

## The Non-Legal Arena

Many a plagiarism charge never reaches the bar of justice, but is aired in the press, with highly vocal disputants on both sides.

The reaction of the critical fraternity to the production of *The*

*Skin of Our Teeth* in 1942 was sharply divided. Some thought it superb; indeed, one connoisseur addicted to breathless and extravagant eulogies exclaimed: "Thornton Wilder's dauntless and heartening comedy stands head and shoulders above anything ever written for our stage." Others were less ecstatic, though they too applauded Wilder for breaking fresh ground in the drama. It remained for Joseph Campbell and Henry Morton Robinson to register harsh dissent.

"While thousands cheer," they wrote in *The Saturday Review of Literature*, "no one has yet pointed out that Mr. Thornton Wilder's exciting play is not an entirely original creation, but an Americanized re-creation, thinly disguised, of James Joyce's *Finnegan's Wake*. Mr. Wilder goes out of his way to wink at the knowing one or two in the audience, by quoting from and actually naming some of his characters after the main figures of Joyce's masterpiece. Important plot elements, characters, devices of presentation, as well as major themes and many of the speeches, are directly and frankly imitated, with but the flimsiest veneer to lend an American touch to the original features. . . . It is a strange performance that Mr. Wilder has turned in. Is he hoaxing us? On the one hand, he gives no credit to his source, masking it with an Olsen and Johnson technique. On the other hand, he makes no attempt to conceal his borrowings, emphasizing them rather, sometimes even stressing details which with a minimum of ingenuity he could have suppressed or altered. But if puzzlement strikes us here, it grows when we consider the critics—those literary advisors who four years ago dismissed *Finnegan's Wake* as a literary abortion not worth the modern reader's time, yet today hail with rave notices its Broadway reaction. The banquet was rejected but the Hellzapoppin' scrap that fell from the table they clutch to their bosom."[4]

This touched off a literary controversy of considerable liveliness. Edmund Wilson, while agreeing that the Wilder work had been written in a "state of saturation with Joyce," observed that "Joyce is a great quarry, like Flaubert, out of which a variety of writers have been getting and will continue to get a variety of different things." Others seized the occasion to refer to Wilder's debts elsewhere; his *The Woman of Andros*, they insisted, was based on Terence's *Andria*, and the most striking personalities in *The Bridge of San Luis Rey* had been lifted from Prosper Mérimée's *Le Carosse du Saint Sacrement*. Amid the cheerless gravity of the parallel-pundits, Wolcott Gibbs supplied welcome comic relief; the experts were mistaken, he declared. *The Skin of Our Teeth* had been taken almost in toto from an early novel of his called *Nabisco*, proclaimed by Alexander Woollcott to be "head and shoulders above Shakespeare."[5]

Wilder, then in the Air Force, stood aloof. His sole comment was: "When I get to it, I'll write an article myself and poke fun too." He didn't have to. The critical flurry died down quickly, and Wilder's reputation was none the worse for it. All that had been proved was the old truism: all creative people borrow.

# 12

# Plagiarism in Motion Pictures

In copyright we have been accustomed to actions without shadow of merit. Apparently the conviction of which authors and composers cannot be disabused [is] that the finest gossamer of similarity can be made to serve. The prizes are large; the security of the foundation often seems to be in inverse proportion.

—Judge Learned Hand: Rosen v. Loew's

COMPARED with fiction, the drama, art and music, the screen has had a very brief career. It's hard to believe that it was only fifty years ago that commercial movies were first flashed on the screen in Koster and Bial's Music Hall on Herald Square in New York City. Yet the medium has generated more infringement litigation than any other.

Actually, Hollywood, conscious of the risks, rarely steals. It imitates. And it exploits trends and vogues with an assiduity that bespeaks idolatrous worship of the success formula.

## The Endemic Fallacy

Ruling that the movie *Roman Scandals* did not plagiarize the play *Oh, Shah!*, Judge Woolsey said: "It seems to me that—putting the case more favorably for the plaintiffs than a comparison of the works here involved justifies—the most that can be said for them is that they brought this suit for literary larceny because they were infected with the fallacy, which seems to be endemic among writers, that copyright may be claimed on a theme or an idea, which, of course, is not and never has been the law."

The fanatic tenacity with which plaintiffs cling to this fallacy has brought grief to many of them. A long line of cases—among them those growing out of *A Circus Romance* (life under the big tent); RKO's screen operetta *I Dream Too Much* (a wife sacrifices her career to save her marriage); *I Married an Angel* (love between a celestial visitor and an earth dweller); *My Man Godfrey* (during the depression of the 1930's a once-affluent young man takes a butler's job); *Show Business* (a salute to vaudeville in its heyday); the Borden case (rules for successful selling); *Test Pilot* (exploits in the wild blue yonder)—bears witness to this.

As we've seen, old plots are no more protectible than themes. Although Warner's *Alcatraz Prison* bore more than a casual resemblance to the play *Ex-Racketeer*—in both a person is engaged in a shady business; he has a child (or relative) to whom he is devoted and whom he keeps in ignorance of his illicit affairs; having made his fortune, he suffers the usual pangs of conscience, and decides to reform and devote himself to his cherished one—Judge Symes felt that the story line was too hackneyed to permit of infringement. Moreover, he noted that in 1934, when the picture was produced, Alcatraz Prison had figured prominently in the public prints as "the abode of desperate criminals"; he felt that Warner's could have gotten the idea of doing a film on it just as easily from the newspapers as from the play.

A religious miracle constituted the climax of a play called *The Christ of the Alley*. A pair of lovers plighted their troth before an image of Christ; later, when the girl was in mortal peril, the image came to life and testified for her. A similar episode embellished Goldwyn's *Night of Love*, except that in the picture it was no miracle that caused the sacred statue to stir and speak: a live mortal had surreptitiously taken the place of the image, and had spoken up when the needful moment arrived. The basic incident, Goldwyn contended, was in the public domain; it stemmed from medieval legends, and had been retold many times; one version of it could be found in a poem by Don José Zorilla, from which the plaintiff had apparently taken it. The plaintiff lost.

So did Allen Caruthers, who claimed that RKO's *Cimarron*, based on Edna Ferber's novel, infringed his unpublished work *The Sooners*. The picture and the book both described the early days of the settling of Oklahoma. "The incidents mentioned in *The Sooners* and shown in *Cimarron*," said Judge Woolsey, "are certainly, with one exception, familiar to all readers of stories of the Western frontier and the rough life led by the early settlers." The exception had to do with a little Negro boy charged with the task of fanning a dinner table to shoo away the flies. He became so absorbed in what was going on that, in *The Sooners*, he inadvertently struck one of the diners with his whisk, and in *Cimarron*, lost his balance (he was perched above the table) and fell into a frosted cake. The Judge thought that this episode was of such slight consequence that Caruthers had no cause for complaint even if it had originated with him.

James Oliver Curwood's novel *The River's End* was laid in the Canadian Northwest and featured a Chinese den equipped with the usual props: inscrutable Orientals, tinkling music, incense and opium. The appearance of the movie *I Am the Law*, with the same locale and trappings, convinced Curwood that he had a good plagiarism case. Judge Knox felt otherwise. "One must remember," said the Judge, "that Chinese dens are more or less indigenous to stories of the Western and Northern frontiers, and that between most of them there must necessarily be points of similarity."

Marie Cooper Dieckhaus had better luck—or so it seemed at the outset. The Trial Judge held that Twentieth Century-Fox's *Alexander's Ragtime Band* infringed her *Love Girl*. Said the Judge:

The book and the picture have a gag about a bootlegger concealing bottles of liquor in a baby carriage; a gag about a soldier in camp putting on a sweater too small for him; a gag about a soldier in the first war (shown sleeping in long underwear) hating to get up in the morning; in both a girl in a Pullman listens to a phonograph played by sentimental young folks "necking" there (the plaintiff called the song being played "Remember" but in the picture the words and music are of one of Berlin's most famous songs which was old at that time); an old music professor protests against his pupil playing jazz; musicians have trouble starting to play a new song; young women flutter around a handsome young musician at a musical affair; a lover composes a song to his beloved (in the picture it is one of Berlin's); a young man objects to a girl's costume; parted lovers meet each other in a theater; a returned soldier finds his sweetheart married to another man and she tells him of it; a love scene on a moonlit balcony between a leader of musicians who has turned the lead over to the pianist and joined his lady; lovers parted as soldiers leave for camp or war; an approach is made to the interest of a prospective employer through a good meal provided him; a music professor uses the word *pizzicato* in speaking to his pupil, though in a different sense in the book and the picture; the heroine rides in a taxi, overhears music and converses with the driver who makes a small charge.

The Circuit Court of Appeals was of different mind. It found nothing significant of theft in the similarities, and reversed the Trial Judge.

The plagiarism attacks on Warner's *Across the Pacific*, Howard Hughes' *Hell's Angels*, Charlie Chaplin's *Modern Times*, RKO's *Condemned Women*, Warner's *Meet John Doe*, Loew's *The Mortal Storm*, and Twentieth Century-Fox's *Miracle on Thirty-fourth Street* and *Wilson* were equally unsuccessful.

When James M. Cain, who won acclaim with his *The Postman Always Rings Twice*, sued Universal, charging that the movie *When Tomorrow Comes* infringed his novel *Serenade*, the picture company pleaded the usual defense of non-access, and, for good measure, threw in that of immorality. The church scene in *Serenade*, Universal argued, was so lewd and lascivious as to vitiate Cain's copyright and deprive him of any standing in court.

Judge Yankwich decided in Universal's favor. He deplored the prestidigitation of literary experts who, by reducing incidents to abstractions, conjured up similarity where none existed. He reminded Cain that auxiliary details which sprang naturally from setting or environment were not copyrightable. Since the Judge found no evidence of copying, he didn't have to weigh the defense of immorality. He felt impelled to do so in justice to Cain.

"The church scene, if it stood alone," he said, "could be considered not only indecent and vulgar, but immoral and sacrilegious. To use a church, especially one of a denomination which teaches the living presence of God on the altar, for the purpose for which *Serenade* uses the little church at Acapulco, Mexico, is an act of impious desecration. However, I think that whatever immorality or sacrilege there be in this scene is cured by the last scene in the book." Here a hint of the Hollywood decalogue crept into the Judge's opinion. Noting that the two transgressors expiated their act, the one by death and the other by suffering and contrition, the Judge added: "A narrative can have no immoral tendency where derelictions end in punishment or suffering and contrition, followed by merciful forgiveness. . . ."

It was arrant imposture, not misguided belief, that gave rise to *The Road to Glory* case. The complaint of Robert H. Sheets, a Tennessee store clerk, was, up to a point, familiar enough: he had prepared a scenario entitled *The Road to Glory*; he had sent it to the studio; it had been turned down; the studio had thereafter made a picture using his scenario. In one respect, however, the situation was out of the ordinary. Sheets seemed to have an absolutely airtight case. The parallels were villainously close and damningly many.

Sheets' claim was eventually blown sky-high, but it took an eight-week trial, seven thousand pages of testimony, and an appalling amount of money to do it. At the trial Sheets swore that he had typed his script on a certain typewriter. Twentieth Century-Fox proved that the machine had not come into his possession until almost a year *after* the picture had been released. Sheets had simply copied his scenario from a synopsis of the film which had appeared in a trade magazine. No wonder his story had looked so irrefutable!

## The Silver Lining

It is not to be supposed that defeat has been the invariable lot of movie plagiarism plaintiffs.

Harper & Brothers, owners of the copyright in Lew Wallace's novel *Ben Hur*, got an injunction against the Kalem Company restraining it from marketing its unauthorized film version. Kalem protested that it had utilized only a small portion of the book. Harper's showed that virtually all the important scenes—such as the attack on the Roman procurator, Ben Hur in the galleys, and the chariot race—had been lifted.

The picture *The Strength of Donald MacKenzie* was held to infringe the play *The Woodsman*. In the play a young hunting guide of primitive ways falls in love with a rich and sophisticated city girl. She is engaged to marry a man of her social class. This man, who serves as the villain, suspects that his fiancée's heart is more than a little inclined to her child-of-nature admirer, and he realizes that drastic measures are called for. He bribes a half-breed to change the markers on the trail that the guide and the girl are to follow

into the forest. The couple lose their way. The girl suspects the guide
of treachery hatched in aid of seduction, and she hovers on the verge
of disillusion. In the nick of time, however, the half-breed confesses,
the villain is exposed, and the guide and the girl wind up—with
benefit of clergy—in each other's arms.

The same characters and the same narrative figured in the picture. Though the general idea was hoary with age, Judge Learned
Hand found piracy. "A man may take an old story and work it over,"
he said, "and if another copies, not only what is old, but what the
author has added to it when he worked it up, the copyright is infringed. It cannot be a good copyright, in the broader sense that all
features of the plot or the bare outlines of the plot can be protected;
but it is a good copyright insofar as the embellishments and additions
to the plot are new and have been contributed by the author."

The movie *Hotel for Women* was found to plagiarize Myrtle
Louise Stonesifer's play *Women's Hotel*; Twentieth Century-Fox had
to pay damages and counsel fees. When Harold Lloyd showed that
fifty-seven consecutive scenes from his *Movie Crazy* had been copied
in Universal's *So's Your Uncle*, he won an award also. And a jury
found that RKO had built its *Ghost Ship* on a drama called *The
Man and His Shadow*, and gave the playwrights twenty-five thousand
dollars in damages.

### Amor Omnia Vincit

Among the many movie plagiarism cases, those involving Universal's *The Cohens and the Kellys*, Harold Lloyd's *The Freshman*,
and Metro-Goldwyn's *Letty Lynton*, stand out as milestones in the
law.

Anne Nichols' comedy of interracial love and conflict, *Abie's
Irish Rose*, made its bow on the New York stage in 1922. It chron-
icled, with scant subtlety and an abundance of old vaudeville gags
and situations, the romance between a Jewish boy and a Catholic
girl. A smash hit, it ran for years.

In 1925, Universal tried to buy the screen rights. The deal fell
through. Universal then produced *The Cohens and the Kellys*, which
was allegedly based on Aaron Hoffman's play *Two Blocks Away*.
It later developed, however, that while the script of the film had
been in the process of preparation, the scenarists had "studied" the

synopsis of *Abie's Irish Rose*. Moreover, Universal had boasted in the press that the picture would be to the screen what *Abie's Irish Rose* was to the stage.

Miss Nichols sued. She was represented by Moses L. Malevinsky, inventor of the "Algebraic Formula" for plagiarism-detection discussed in Chapter 10.

At the trial Malevinsky took the witness stand as an expert. He testified at great length about his supposedly infallible yardstick. Applied to the movie and the play before the Court, he said, it established theft beyond the shadow of a doubt.

The gist of Universal's defense was that the substance of *Abie's Irish Rose* was nothing but vintage stage hokum, and common property. In support of this, the company produced Billy Watson, of renown in burlesque, who testified that all the situations of consequence in the play had been anticipated in *Krausmeyer's Alley*, a farce in which he had acted years before.

Judge Goddard found Malevinsky's formula less than a touchstone for instant solution.

Mr. Malevinsky's theoretical test [he said] does not meet the full requirements of a correct test. . . . That two productions display the same trend of emotions is not enough to show plagiarism. Emotions, like mere ideas, are not subject to preemption; they are common property. It is the incidents or elements, or grouping of them, which produce the emotion that are to be compared. Similar emotions may be caused by very different ideas. It is obvious that the underlying emotions reflected by the principal characters in a play or book may be similar, and yet the characters and expression of the same emotions may be different. While it is true that a sequence of like events will awaken in the average person like emotions, it does not follow that . . . like emotions were produced by the same events. . . .

Although Judge Goddard felt that a "fairly strong inference" could be drawn that the creators of the picture had made use of the play, he concluded that whatever they had abstracted was not sufficient to constitute infringement. Miss Nichols appealed.

The Circuit Court upheld Judge Goddard. "We think," said Judge Learned Hand, speaking for the Court, "the defendant took no more —assuming that it took anything at all—than the law allowed. . . . The only matter common to the two [works] is a quarrel between a

Jewish and an Irish father, the marriage of their children, and a reconciliation."

Miss Nichols, he declared, could assert no monopoly in her theme or background. Nor could she arrogate exclusive title in her characters. "It is indeed scarcely credible," the Judge said, "that she should not have been aware of those stock figures, the low-comedy Jew and Irishman. The defendant has not taken from her more than their prototypes have contained for many decades. If so, obviously so to generalize her copyright would allow her to cover what was not original with her. But we need not hold this as matter of fact, much as we might be justified. Even though we take it that she devised her figures out of her brain *de novo*, still the defendant was within its rights."

There are [he went on to say] but four characters common to both plays, the lovers and the fathers. The lovers are so faintly indicated as to be no more than stage properties. They are loving and fertile; that is really all that can be said of them, and anyone else is quite within his rights if he puts loving and fertile lovers in a play of his own, wherever he gets the cue. The plaintiff's Jew is quite unlike the defendant's. His obsession is his religion, on which depends such racial animosity as he has. He is affectionate, warm and patriarchal. None of these fit the defendant's Jew, who shows affection for his daughter only once, and who has none but the most superficial interest in his grandchild. He is tricky, ostentatious and vulgar, only by misfortune redeemed into honesty. Both are grotesque, extravagant and quarrelsome; both are fond of display; but these common qualities make up only a small part of their simple pictures, no more than any one might lift if he chose. The Irish fathers are even more unlike; the plaintiff's a mere symbol for religious fanaticism and patriarchal pride, scarcely a character at all. Neither quality appears in the defendant's, for while he goes to get his grandchild, it is rather out of a truculent determination not to be forbidden, than from pride in his progeny. For the rest he is only a grotesque hobbledehoy, used for low comedy of the most conventional sort, which any one might borrow, if he chanced not to know the exemplar.

## Ten Seconds to Play

The picture which was chiefly responsible for establishing agile and bespectacled Harold Lloyd as a topflight screen comedian also got him into serious legal difficulties.

In 1915, H. C. Witwer, who had been contributing to periodicals for some years, wrote a story called "The Emancipation of Rodney." It had to do with a shy and lonely boy who went to college, aspired to be popular, fell in love, went out for football to impress his girl, proved a dub, but through a fluke won the crucial game of the season. *Popular Magazine* paid seventy-five dollars for the story, published it, and assigned the copyright on it to Witwer.

In 1924, Lloyd's business manager brought Witwer around to see the comedian. They explored the possibility of Witwer's doing a picture for Lloyd. Asked whether he had any ideas, Witwer outlined the plot of "Rodney." Lloyd was interested. For years he had been planning to do a college football comedy—his staff had filmed many sequences at major football games—but somehow he'd been unable to hit on the right formula. He told Witwer he wanted to read the story, and Witwer gave him a copy of the magazine.

Lloyd then discussed the project with Sam Taylor, one of the men who later worked with him on *The Freshman*. Taylor took a dim view of the potentialities of "Rodney," and the thought of screening it was abandoned.

Lloyd was disappointed. He had played around with the football theme so long that he couldn't bring himself to drop it. He and his associates kept plugging at it, and finally found an approach that satisfied them. They roughed out the general features of *The Freshman*. Lloyd was gratified, but one thing worried him. What if he produced the film and Witwer came along with a plagiarism suit? He decided to play it safe. He invited Witwer to the studio and told him what he proposed to do. Witwer, Lloyd's staff subsequently swore, raised no objections.

When *The Freshman* was released, to the delight of millions of movie-goers, the blow Lloyd had feared and had sought to avoid fell. Witwer sent word that he felt "Rodney" had been wrongfully utilized. Then he sat by for more than three years, presumably waiting for the film to roll up profits. Finally he started suit. He died before the trial, and his widow carried on in his place.

Lloyd told the Court that if Witwer had demurred upon hearing the synopsis of *The Freshman*, he would not have gone on with it. He admitted having heard Witwer relate the substance of "Rodney," but insisted he had never read the story itself, and didn't know what had become of the copy of the magazine Witwer had given him.

In view of the final result, it is particularly illuminating to peruse the opinion of Judge Cosgrave, who tried the case.

From a comparison of the two works [he wrote] I am convinced that plaintiff's charge of plagiarism is well founded. The features common to both are a country boy ambitious to be a popular athletic college hero. He is of non-athletic type. He practices college yells before a mirror in the privacy of his room. He has the college letter inscribed upon his sweater, and admires it in secrecy. He meets a girl to whom he tells exaggerated stories of his athletic prowess and who is sympathetic. He longs to be called by a familiar name. He studies the literature of athletics. In his actual athletic work he is pitifully weak. . . . He inspires in the students feelings ranging from contempt to grudging toleration. He is generously allowed to think himself a member of the college athletic team when in reality he is not. He enjoys the bliss of this deception for a brief period. Finally realizing that he is an object of ridicule and contempt, he resolves to throw away pretense and be his real self . . . He decides that his only hope for athletic eminence and consequent popularity is to take part in the football game with his college's traditional rival. The game is going badly against the home team. The team is reduced to the last available man. He grasps the coach in appeal and argument to be allowed to enter the play. He forces his way into the game. By an extremely unusual play he wins for the home team. The girl justifies her faith in him, in the one case telling his rival, "Didn't I tell you Rod would do it?" and in the other to him, "I knew you could do it." He is the hero of the hour, attains the coveted nickname, and is naturally successful in his suit. The foregoing is the substance or plot of the infringed and of the infringing production. One is the counterpart of the other. A comparison produces the conviction that . . . the work of Witwer was appropriated by the defendants.

By a vote of two to one, the Circuit Court reversed Judge Cosgrave. The two pronouncements of the appellate bench—that of the majority and that of the dissenter—came to about forty-five thousand words; and coupled with Judge Cosgrave's views, they constituted a vivid illustration of the kind of difference of opinion that not only makes horse races but fills plagiarism litigation with exhilarating—and exasperating—uncertainty.

After having read [said the majority opinion of the Circuit Court] the critical analysis of the story and the play contained in the briefs and argument, it is not easy to place oneself in the attitude of a fairly indifferent and disinterested spectator of the moving picture play, *The Freshman*, but we think it is fairly clear that, given an interval of two or three weeks between a casual reading of the story and a similar uncritical view of *The Freshman*, it would not occur to such a spectator, in the absence of suggestion to that effect, that he was seeing in moving picture form the story or any part of the story of *The Emancipation of Rodney*, this because of the differences in the appearance, name, and character of Rodney and Harold, and in the football scene. If this is true, there is no copying and no infringement. If we can see at first blush that there is no such similarity as would impress the ordinary observer, it is unnecessary to consider the question of novelty or copyrightability of such similarities as exist. We are of opinion that such similarities as exist between the play and the story, and there are many, are such as require analysis and critical comparison in order to manifest themselves. The outstanding feature, the climax of both story and play, is the football game, with necessarily some similarity, but there is nothing new and novel in that other than the unusual participation of the heroes in their respective games, and on analysis these are neither identical nor similar in scene nor in conception of the two productions, but, if this be doubted, as was done by the trial court, then it is clear that there is no such similarity as overcomes the positive testimony that there was in fact no copying.

Four Judges had weighed the case. On the same facts, on the same exhibits, on the same law, two had ruled for one side and two for the other. Mrs. Witwer wanted the Supreme Court of the United States to act as final arbiter, but it declined to do so.

### The Trail of the Serpent

A sensational criminal case burst like a thunderclap on customarily staid Glasgow in 1857. Madeleine Smith, the daughter of a well-to-do architect, was accused of poisoning her lover, Emile L'Angelier. Since Madeleine was young, beautiful and spirited, and her lover a dashing Frenchman, and since all the titillating elements of a *crime passionel*—infatuation, illicit intercourse, quarreling, sudden and violent death—were present, the prosecution became a *cause célèbre* overnight. In England as well as in Scotland the newspapers were full of it. What added particular zest to the occasion was that almost everybody was convinced of Madeleine's guilt, and excitedly debated her chances of getting away with it.

She did get away with it. The jury returned a verdict of "not proven"—which was tantamount to saying: "We think you did it, all right; it's your luck the evidence wasn't quite as overwhelming as it should have been."

A description of the trial was published in 1905 in a series of books dealing with notable Scottish trials. It was reprinted several times. In 1928, Edward Sheldon and Margaret Bayer Barnes collaborated on *Dishonored Lady*. Copyrighted in 1930, the script bore this legend: "The authors salute with gratitude Miss Madeleine Smith of Glasgow whose conduct in 1857 suggested to them this play. Accordingly they make a friendly and admiring bow to her across the years."

Shortly afterward Mrs. Belloc Lowndes wrote a novel called *Letty Lynton*. She indicated in the foreword that although the two chief characters had been suggested by "a famous Scottish murder trial," she had not consulted any of the numerous accounts of the case. Her story, she said, was fiction.

*Dishonored Lady* opened in New York in 1930, with Katherine Cornell in the title role. It had a four-month run. The screen rights were then offered to Metro-Goldwyn Pictures. Metro returned the script, saying that Will Hays (then film censor) had raised objections to it. Too much sex.

Anxious for a movie deal, the playwrights got busy and hammered out a new version in which they sought to meet Hays' exceptions. They dispatched it to Metro. Apparently the company was as eager to buy as the dramatists were to sell; a contract was drawn up and the purchase price fixed at thirty thousand dollars. Getting Hays' approval was made a condition of the deal. That sturdy guardian of morals stood firm. The negotiations came to nothing.

Shortly afterward Metro bought the movie rights to Mrs. Lowndes' novel for thirty-five hundred dollars. The facts blur at this point; just why Hays gave the nod to *Letty Lynton* after repeatedly condemning *Dishonored Lady*, though both were fictional treatments of the same occurrence, is not clear. At any rate, the release of the picture in 1932 was, for Sheldon and Mrs. Barnes, a clarion call to battle.

In the movie as in the play, a girl of good family plunges impetuously into an affair with an adventurer to whom she is sexually drawn but for whom she has no real affection. Eventually she falls in love with someone else. She desires to sever the unholy bonds. Her unchivalrous lover refuses to oblige. Worse than that, he threatens, if his mistress persists in discarding him, to expose her. He has compromising letters of hers in his possession. The girl is desperate. She arranges to meet the blackguard, and they have a stormy session. In the course of it the man takes a drink and dies of poison. There is an investigation. The girl is suspected of having administered the fatal potion. She is rigorously questioned, and hovers on the brink of confession. At the last moment she is saved by a false alibi: a man comes forward and swears that she spent the crucial night with him in his rooms.

In the play, the denouement is tragic; the girl loses her true love and marries the stranger who saved her, for whom she doesn't care. In the movie, true to cinema tradition, there's a happy ending.

Metro's contention was, of course, that the film was a picturization of Mrs. Lowndes' novel, and that it had taken nothing from the play. Then how did it come about, asked Sheldon and Mrs. Barnes, that there were ingredients common to the picture and the play which were *not* to be found either in the novel or in the facts of the original case?

The details of the murder case, Judge Woolsey noted, had been in the public domain for many years; Mrs. Lowndes and Metro were no less entitled to exploit these details than the two dramatists. While he felt that Metro's scenarists had doubtless had access to the play and had borne it in mind, he didn't think they had copied anything that was protectible by copyright. He dismissed the complaint.

The Circuit Court of Appeals took the contrary view. Said Judge Learned Hand:

It makes no difference how far the play was anticipated by works in the public demesne which the plaintiffs did not use. The defendants appear not to recognize this, for they have filled the record with earlier instances of the same dramatic incidents and devices, as though, like a patent, a copyrighted work must be not only original, but new. That is not, however, the law as is obvious in the case of maps or compendia, where later works will necessarily be anticipated. At times, in discussing how much of the substance of a play the copyright protects, courts have indeed used language which seems to give countenance to the notion that if a plot were old, it could not be copyrighted. . . . But we understand by this no more than that in its broader outline a plot is never copyrightable, for it is plain beyond peradventure that anticipation as such cannot invalidate a copyright. Borrowed the work must indeed not be, for a plagiarist is not himself pro tanto an "author"; but if by some magic a man who had never known it were to compose a new "Ode on a Grecian Urn," he would be an "author," and, if he copyrighted it, others might not copy that poem, though they might of course copy Keats'.

To Metro's argument that not a jot or iota of the dialogue of *Dishonored Lady* had been lifted, Judge Hand's reply was the blunt reminder that a play was susceptible of piracy *without* using the dialogue. Indeed, he said, theft could often be most effectively achieved by leaving out the speech, for which a substitute could be found, and by keeping the whole dramatic meaning.

That [he added] is exactly what the defendants have done here; the dramatic significance of the scenes we have recited is the same, almost to the letter. True, much of the picture owes nothing to the play; some of it is plainly drawn from the novel; but that is entirely immaterial; it is enough that substantial parts were lifted; no plagiarist can excuse the wrong by showing how much of his work he did not pirate. We cannot avoid the conviction that, if the picture was not an infringement of the play, there can be none short of taking the dialogue.

Metro had to pay Sheldon and Mrs. Barnes quite a tidy sum. And if it hadn't been for another important court decision, which we shall come to in a moment, the figure would have been five times as much.

### Paying the Piper

What is the measure, in dollars, of the penalty that an infringer must pay?

The Copyright Act says that he must make good the damages that the copyright owner has suffered, and must in addition turn over all the profits he has made as a result of his wrongdoing.

It should be noted at this point that there is a difference between plagiarism via a book and plagiarism via a play or a movie. The sole creative agency in a book is the author. In a play or a movie, the story is but one element, however important; the finished product is the result of the combined efforts of a number of individuals:

director, actors, scenic artist, costume designer, lighting expert, composer of incidental music, and, in the case of a film, scenarist and photographer.

To be sure, even where the infringing medium is a novel, the culprit may say: "All right, you've caught me. I'll pay for what I stole. But look: I didn't take all of the original, and I added a lot of stuff of my own. It isn't fair to make me give up *all* the money I made on the book. There should be some kind of apportioning."

This was precisely the argument advanced in the defendant's behalf in an infringement case back in 1888. It didn't work. Casting a respectful glance at an earlier English decision by the distinguished Lord Eldon, the Supreme Court of the United States said:

The only proper rule to be adopted is to deduct from the selling price [of the book] the actual and legitimate manufacturing cost. If the volume contains matter to which a copyright could not properly extend, incorporated with matter proper to be covered by a copyright, the two necessarily going together when the volume is sold, as a unit, and it being impossible to separate the profits on the one from the profits on the other, and the lawful matter being useless without the unlawful, it is the defendants who are responsible for having blended the lawful with the unlawful, and they must abide the consequences, on the same principle that he who has wrongfully produced a confusion of goods must alone suffer. . . . The present is one of those cases in which the value of the book depends on its completeness and integrity. It is sold as a book, and not as the fragments of a book. In such a case, as the profits result from the sale of the book as a whole, the owner of the copyright will be entitled to recover the entire profits on the sale of the book.

For many years afterward it was taken for granted, on the basis of the Supreme Court's pronouncement, that there could *never* be apportionment in any medium. The fact that the allocation of profits had been denied in this particular instance only because it wasn't feasible, was overlooked.

Then came the *Letty Lynton* case. Metro's profits were computed at $587,604.37. Confident of recovering the entire amount, the victors were jubilant. The people at Metro were perceptibly less so. So staggering an award, they protested, would be unconscionable. They fetched into court an array of experts who testified that the success of the picture had been due largely to the box-office appeal of the stars, Joan Crawford and Robert Montgomery, and that the maximum value of *Dishonored Lady* to the movie couldn't have exceeded 10 per cent of the profits. And so the Circuit Court was squarely faced with the issue of apportionment.

We are resolved [said Judge Learned Hand] to avoid the one certainly unjust course of giving the plaintiffs everything, because the defendants cannot with certainty compute their share . . . the only question is what evidence of separation courts will accept. Strictly and literally, it is true that the problem is insoluble. The profits from a picture consist of admission fees, which the playgoers pay because the picture attracts them with the hope of enjoyment. That enjoyment, which is one source of its further popularity, is made up of many factors: the actors, the work of the producer and director, the story, the scenery and costumes. The attraction and the hope which first draw them are principally aroused by advertisements, and the reputation of the stars and the producing company. These factors have no unit common to all, and are therefore incommensurable; in that, the situation is not different from the usual case of copyright infringement where the pirated material has been mixed with matter in the public demesne. The difficulties of separation have generally prevented infringers from attempting any apportionment; they have contented themselves with getting down the net profits as low as possible.

Judge Hand recognized that out of all this, no real standard emerged. "It is not our best guess that must prevail," he said, "but a figure which will favor the plaintiffs in every reasonable chance of error. With this in mind we fix their share of the profits at one fifth."

And so Sheldon and Mrs. Barnes got an award of about $117,500, plus $33,000 in counsel fees, and costs. They went to the Supreme Court, insisting that on the basis of the 1888 decision they were entitled to all, not a part, of Metro's profits. The Circuit Court was sustained; and a question that had long vexed plagiarism attorneys and litigants was clarified.

In the *Hotel for Women* case, the same formula of division was followed. The net profits of the movie were $19,800; of this sum, Miss Stonesifer got one fifth, plus $1,000 counsel fees. In the *So's Your Uncle* case, the fraction was reduced. The profits were $400,000; all that Harold Lloyd got was $40,000, and $10,000 counsel fees.

# 13

## Plagiarism in Art

Through all art there is a filiation. If you see a great master, you will always find that he has used what was good in his predecessors, and that it was this which made him great. Men like Raphael do not spring out of the ground. They took their root in the antique and in the best that has been done before them. Had they not used the advantages of their time there would be little to say about them.

—Goethe: Conversations with Ackermann

---

IN A sense every artist of the representational school "copies." He tries to set down what he sees.

The Copyright Act is concerned with a different kind of copying —the duplication of material in copyright. Only the copyright owner (or his assignee) has the right to make and sell copies of a copyrighted work. Unauthorized multiplication is forbidden, and the prohibition applies no less to a single copy than to a number. It is infringement to make and sell facsimiles of a protected painting without permission. It is also infringement—and plagiarism if the offender poses as author—to produce a single copy, whether in the same medium as the original or any other. Works in the public domain may, of course, be freely reproduced.

Plagiarism in art usually, though not necessarily, involves the making of single copies. Infringement arises as a rule from wholesale duplication.

### Copying

Curiously enough, there are many laymen who admire literal rendering from nature, and who at the same time regard copying from art as ignoble. The word "copying" evokes, for them, the image of a hack toiling dully in a museum, or of an untalented amateur bent on fabricating a replica of a chromo. Yet to condemn copying unqualifiedly is to ignore the vital rôle it has played in the development of painting and sculpture, and to disregard the fact that copies may be works of art in their own right.

A copy of a picture by a primitive—a primitive is an unschooled artist with a direct emotional approach—is often just as fresh and individual as anything the artist depicts on the basis of direct observation. Astonishingly enough, a primitive's copy may well excel the original in aesthetic merit. Susan Whitcomb's primitive version of Alexander Robertson's "Mount Vernon" has infinitely more richness and charm than the source. Darley's "Hunting Buffaloe" is a competent but unimpressive illustration; the copy of it by an unknown primitive displays a bold simplicity, a rhythm of line, a vitality which make for a compelling painting.[1]

For artists great and small, copying serves as a form of exercise, as a steppingstone to self-realization, and as a means of tribute to the Olympians they esteem.

Back in the days of the old masters, gifted youngsters joined the ateliers of the illustrious ones and worked as apprentices until they gained painter-status and could join the guilds. In those days, copying was an accepted custom and an integral part of art training. When the novice was not grinding pigment or cleaning brushes, he copied his teacher's pictures. This familiarized him with the master's style; when he became adept enough, he assisted in the production of actual paintings. At this stage of his education, too much individuality was a handicap.

Leonardo da Vinci did not hesitate, while in Verrocchio's workshop, to use the latter's drawings in his compositions. His fellow apprentices Lorenzo di Credi and Pietro Perugino copied from him in turn, as did his pupils when he himself became master.[2]

Nor was copying limited to the ateliers. Throughout the Renaissance a spirit of healthy give-and-take prevailed in the arts. Michelangelo, Vasari tells us, was an inveterate copyist of old drawings; his skill was so great that his copies (which he took the trouble to smoke and tint) could not be distinguished from the originals. His first attempt in marble, when he was fifteen, was a copy of an antique mask. Dürer copied the horse in his famous "Knight, Death and the

Devil" from a pen drawing by Leonardo. In turn, Andrea del Sarto copied many of Dürer's engravings.

Although the nineteenth century witnessed the emergence of the aesthetic philosophy that made a fetish of originality, copying persisted in its threefold function. Géricault duplicated dozens of canvases by the men he honored. "Only on one's knees should one pronounce the name of Delacroix!" cried Cézanne, and he proceeded to copy—as Manet had done before him—the great man's "Barque of Dante."

"We painters," wrote Van Gogh, "are always asked to *compose* of ourselves. . . . But in music it is not like that—if some person or other plays Beethoven he adds his personal interpretation. . . . I pose the black and white of Delacroix and Millet or something taken from them before me as a subject. And then I improvise color on it, not, you understand, altogether as myself, but searching for memories of *their* pictures—but the memory, 'the vague consonance of colors,' which are right in feeling at least—that is my own interpretation. Heaps of people do not copy; heaps of others do—I started it by chance, and I find it teaches me things, and above all it sometimes gives me consolation. And then my brush goes between my fingers just as a bow would on the violin."

Barye's "Nude," in oils, is an exact transcription (plus an arm) of an ancient bronze. Derain copied Ghirlandaio's "Christ on the Way to Calvary." Ensor copied Callot's "Le Pisseur." Some of Utrillo's Paris street scenes were done from commercial postcards; Toulouse-Lautrec's "At La Mie" and Rousseau's "Artillerymen," from photographs.

The copies made by these men are regarded as authentic works of art. We don't think any less of Van Gogh because he chose to pay homage to Millet by copying him. The point to remember, though, is that if someone were to do the same thing today, and the original happened to be in copyright, he'd run the risk of legal trouble.

### Borrowing—with Honor

Copying and borrowing are not synonymous. The one is adoption; the other is adaptation. The copyist hews close to the model; the borrower absorbs, transmutes, reinterprets.

Like copying, borrowing is a stout staff for the neophyte to lean on. But whereas the time comes, in the course of every artist's growth, when copying has fulfilled its purpose and should be relinquished, borrowing survives the stage of maturation and persists as part of the artist's creative activity for the rest of his life. It is the vehicle by which influence is transmitted. It is, in its cumulative form, the foundation of tradition.

"The choice of becoming a painter," says Jean Cassau, the French critic, "implies the acceptance of sharing in the domain of painting. There you find predecessors; you have to use their language; and anything you do will be related to something that has been done before."

Phidias evolved his renowned statue, the ivory-and-gold "Athena" of the Parthenon (now unhappily lost), from previous archaic images of the goddess. Praxiteles got the idea for his "Hermes" from Kephisodotos.

Original as he was, Mantegna owed a debt to Donatello and the carvers of antiquity. Pollaiuolo paved the way for Michelangelo in painting, as Jacopo della Quercia did in sculpture. Raphael persuaded Bramante, who had a key, to let him in to see the unfinished Sistine Chapel while Michelangelo was away; he carried off conceptions which he promptly incorporated in his work in the church of San Agostino.

Tintoretto's motto was: "Michelangelo's design and Titian's color." Bosch and Brueghel drew their surrealist monsters from the bestiaries so popular in the late Middle Ages.

Manet's debt to Velasquez and Goya was so enormous that he was openly accused of plagiarism. His "Dead Torero" is a vivid reminder of Velasquez' "Dead Warrior." The link between his "Olympia" and Goya's "Maja Desnuda" is equally clear. All that Baudelaire, who defended him vociferously against the jibes of the critics, could say for him on this score was: "In him Spanish genius is reborn in France!"

And so it goes. Caravaggio takes Correggio's chiaroscuro, bends it to his own uses, founds the school of "new realism," and leaves a profound impress on generations of painters. Jan Van Eyck's "Arnolfini and His Wife" may well have been the source of such divergent progeny as Cézanne's multiple perspective, and Tenniel's Mad Hatter. Blake looks at old tarot cards, and they haunt his illustrations for the Book of Job. Chirico's canvases seem, to the uninitiated, to open up vistas never before explored; a glance at Piero di Cosimo proves otherwise. Japanese prints reveal a new world to Degas and Cassatt, Toulouse-Lautrec and Whistler, as do Persian miniatures to Matisse. What Han sculpture has done for Marini, calligraphy does for Tobey. To enumerate all the springs of Picasso's many-faceted art, and all the men who trespass on him, is to write a history of painting.

### Sticks and Stones

In the hands of the Greeks, the post-and-lintel construction of the Egyptians shed its ponderosity and became a thing of beauty. Vitality was added to strength; form and function met in perfect fusion. The result was a style of architecture as felicitously expressive of the logic, poise and serenity of the Greek mind as it was responsive to need.

What the Romans lacked in creative imagination they made up for in boldness and engineering skill. To their wholesale borrowings from the Greeks, they added the arch, and proceeded to alter the face of the empire with imposing piles. Basilicas and amphitheaters, baths and aqueducts and bridges sprang up. Yet the arch—the one thing commonly pointed to as the Romans' unique contribution to architecture—they did not invent. They got it from the Etruscans, and the Estruscans took it from an earlier civilization.

If the scale and massiveness of Roman structures compel admiration their integument does not. The Romans seized Greek ornament and applied it lavishly and without meaning. They took the noble Attic column, split it or flattened it into a pilaster, and affixed it to walls. Stripped of its function as a means of support, the column became parasitic ornament, hiding whatever naked dignity the edifices had.

With the Gothic architects it was a different story. Inventing the flying buttress, they did away with the cumbrous walls the Romans had devised to parry the side thrust of the arches. They narrowed the arch so that it rose to a point; they made the pillars high and slender, set them in clusters, and crowned them with ribbed vaults; they filled their windows with the jeweled radiance of stained glass; they raised spires and pinnacles to the sky. The cathedral came into being: the consummate glory of the perpendicular.

The Renaissance, "that first transcendent springtime of the modern world," worked miracles for literature; it did less well for architecture. For while the heady draughts of the classics spurred the writers of the period to creative efforts of their own, the architects were overwhelmed by their models. The Roman arch, with Romanized Greek columns, became the basis of construction. Although occasionally the dignity and fine proportions of an edifice broke through the welter of meaningless cornices, pediments and entablatures, the fundamental style was derivative. Decoration had become a covering unrelated to function or the times.

"When the early Renaissance designers," says Sheldon Cheney, "dug up the elements of Roman construction and Roman-adapted Greek ornament, instead of creating a new art for a new forward push of the human spirit, they initiated a sort of architectural slavery that persisted five hundred years."

The chronic and illogical cultivation of traditional styles, despite radical changes in human need and even more radical advances in technology, reached its apogee in the Victorian era. Gothic became *de rigueur* for our schools and churches, Renaissance for our banks and public buildings, and eighteenth-century Georgian for our homes and state houses.

Where, in the other arts, copying has been a means to an end, in architecture it has been the end. Where, in the other arts, borrowing has been a fecundating factor, in architecture it has been mortmain.

"There is one profession, and only one, architecture," wrote Le Corbusier in 1927, "in which progress is not considered necessary, where laziness is enthroned, and in which the reference is always to yesterday. Everywhere else, taking thought for tomorrow is almost a fever and brings its inevitable solution: if a man does not move forward, he becomes bankrupt."

"How the beauty-sophisticated Greek," says Frank Lloyd Wright, "would shudder with impotent disgust if he could see the chaste proportions of his work mummified in your whitewashed imitations of his legitimately beautiful creations! . . . All architecture worthy of the name is a growth in accord with natural feeling and industrial means to serve actual needs. It cannot be put on from without." He adds: "I have been accused of having contempt for my fellow architects. I have no contempt for them, only for their work."[3]

We no longer wear togas or ply the seas in triremes or treat disease with bloodletting and quacksalves. But as far as the façades of most of our buildings are concerned, we're still living in the past. Look at the Washington Monument, and you see an Egyptian obelisk. Look at our triumphal arches, and you see the Arch of Titus. Look at our armories, and you see feudal castles, complete with turrets, slit windows and crenellations. Look at our schools and universities, and you see Salisbury and Gloucester, Winchester and Westminster. Look at the cinema palaces of the Golden Twenties, and you see Byzantine bombast.

The shackles of the past have fortunately begun to loosen. The modern movement, sparked by men like Sullivan and Wright, is making headway. The spirit of Beaux Arts and Prix de Rome is on the wane, though it dies hard. The new philosophy views a structure as a living organism. It tries to synthesize form and function, individual need and social utility, new materials and new methods. The aping of the monuments of dead ages may eventually be recognized for what it is—plagiarism.

## Art before the Bar

So far as litigation is involved, plagiarism in art differs sharply from plagiarism in the other media.

For every couple of dozen court cases involving books or plays, movies or songs, there's only one dealing with pictures or sculpture. It's hard to say whether this is because there's less pilfering in art or because artists have a keener awareness of the interdependence of all creative expression or because they prefer to shy clear of the machinery of the law. The reason may be wholly a matter of money. The huge profits of a *Gone with the Wind* or a "Bei Mir Bist Du Schön" or a *Night of Love* are tempting bait. But unless the artist is the creator of comic strips or animated cartoons or pin-ups, the sale of reproductions of a "successful" work of his will not make him the income-tax collector's pet. This is true even where his canvas wins first prize at the Carnegie International. There are no private swimming pools in Bohemia.

The obsessive misconception which leads so many plagiarism claimants astray—that exclusive property rights can be had in ideas or subjects as such—is much less prevalent in art than elsewhere. The man who writes a play about a historic personage will burn with indignation if someone else chooses to dramatize the same figure, and the absence of access will not avail to cool his ire. Yet no limner of a bowl of chrysanthemums or a spied-upon Susanna or La Rue St. Rustique would dream of scurrying to the law under comparable circumstances. The art student who met the eminent landscapist Harpignies in one of the villages of the Sologne, and cried beseechingly: "You know, sir, I have reserved this countryside for myself," was hardly typical of his calling.

## Drawing the Line

The few art-plagiarism cases that have reached the courts make up a curious—even ludicrous—assortment. Properly speaking, they don't touch art at all. They have to do with such things as strip cartoons, commercial lithographs and the like. Leonardo would, I'm sure, shake his head in tranquil amusement if he could contemplate the strange company the titans are made to keep in this chapter; Caravaggio would let loose one of the purple oaths he was noted for.

We start with Superman, the atomic-age combination of Hercules, St. George and Robin Hood. Although the valor and epic achievements of this mighty figure in fields other than the law have become matters of common knowledge, his prowess in the halls of justice has been less widely noted.

A decade or so ago, while Superman was doing his stuff in a magazine called *Action Comics*, a rival—Wonderman—materialized in another periodical to challenge him. The appearance, attributes and exploits of the two colossi were quite similar. Each wore a cloak which, when flung aside, revealed a skintight acrobatic costume. At times each donned ordinary raiment. Each espoused the cause of the oppressed. Each was shown, on one occasion, racing toward a full moon "off into the night," and on another, crushing a gun in his Brobdingnagian grip. Superman stopped bullets with his person, and leaped over a twenty-story building. Wonderman caught shells with his bare hands and flung them back, and soared from rooftop to rooftop.

Judge Woolsey found that short of making "Chinese copies," the publisher of Wonderman could hardly have gone further in invading the rights of *Action Comics*. "In dealing with a comic cartoon," he said, "it has to be remembered that such a cartoon embodies a conception of humor or surprise or incredibility . . . and what the owner of the copyright is entitled to is the protection of that embodiment of his concept." And so Superman won the first round.

On appeal Wonderman's sponsors argued that Superman was not protectible by copyright because his exploits and characteristics were old stuff, and he himself was nothing more than the modern prototype of the heroes of mythology. The Circuit Court was not receptive to this view. "Irrespective of the sources from which the author of a work may derive the material he uses," wrote Judge Augustus N. Hand, "a picture or a writing which is his own production cannot be copied. The prior art is only relevant as bearing on the question whether the alleged infringer has copied the author or has taken his material direct from the prior art. So far as the pictorial representations and verbal descriptions of Superman are not a mere delineation of a benevolent Hercules, but embody an arrangement of incidents and literary expressions original with the author, they are proper subjects of copyright and susceptible of infringement." Superman carried the day once more.

In another case, the infringer's defense was that the circus posters which he had copied were wholly devoid of artistic merit, and hence not entitled to copyright protection. The Supreme Court of the United States rejected the contention.

It would be a dangerous undertaking [said Mr. Justice Holmes] for persons trained only in the law to constitute themselves final judges of the worth of pictorial illustrations, outside of the narrowest and most obvious limits. At the one extreme, some works of genius would be sure to miss appreciation. Their very novelty would make them repulsive until the public had learned the new language in which their author spoke. It may be more than doubted, for instance, whether the etchings of Goya or the paintings of Manet would have been sure of protection when seen for the first time. At the other end, copyright would be denied to pictures which appealed to a public less educated than the judge.

An advertising chromo of carrots and beets, cabbages and radishes, was similarly adjudged worthy of the benefits of copyright. So long as the conception was the plaintiff's own, said the Court, neither the humble character of the objects depicted nor the mediocrity of execution made any difference.

## Switching Media

I discussed in Chapter 1 the legal effect of transplanting a copyrighted work, without license, from one medium into another. Instances of this kind of lifting occur now and then in connection with comic strips and screen cartoons.

The strip cartoon "Alphonse and Gaston" endeared itself to a vast public in the early 1900's. It was a daily feature of *The New York Journal*. With the permission of the copyright owner, a farce celebrating the antics of the two paragons of politeness was put on the boards. The show, too, was a success. Then a rival comedy exploiting the same characters was staged without authorization. In the ensuing court battle the piratical producer defended on the ground that there were no dramatic rights in a cartoon which were protectible by copyright. Judge Lowell disabused him of this notion.

The same question came up in the "Mutt and Jeff" case ten years later, with the same result. There, however, the defense was different. The culprits, keeping straight faces, protested that their *Cartoonland* was legitimate parody. Judge Rose told them that while a copyrighted work was open to criticism via lampooning, appropriation in the guise of parody would not be tolerated.

A toy company made and sold a stuffed horse in imitation of Barney Google's Spark Plug, familiar to millions of newspaper readers. The company was promptly enjoined. The law intervened with equal firmness on behalf of Popeye the Sailor when certain toys and jewelry in his image were sought to be marketed.

Born in the never-never land of the animated cartoon, Betty Boop achieved great vogue. When an unauthorized attempt was made to invest her round baby face, coquettish eyes, pouting mouth and incongruous grown-up bosom with a third dimension via a doll, the bench rallied gallantly to her side. Finding her "a unique combination of infancy and maturity, innocence and sophistication," Judge Coleman gave her a preliminary injunction, and Judge Woolsey made it permanent.

But where a concern, having made a plaster miniature of a religious shrine and sold copies of it as souvenirs, found that a competitor had put a similar replica on the market, and applied for an injunction, the application was denied. Judge Welch felt that the competitor could just as readily have based his product on the shrine itself; and since the pioneer firm couldn't prove that the competitor had copied *its* replica, it had no tenable cause for complaint.

### The Lens and the Lady

A camera artist photographed a girl in the nude, called the picture "Grace of Youth," copyrighted it, and sold the copyright for a small sum. Something in the girl's eyes must have enchanted connoisseurs of bright innocence; reproductions sold by the thousands. Regretting the lack of business foresight which had led him to part with his rights so cheaply, the photographer got hold of the original model, placed her in the same pose, except that now he bade her to smile and to hold a cherry stem between her lips. He called the new print "Cherry Ripe" and began to distribute it. The copyright owner of "Grace of Youth" stepped in and got an injunction against him.

The Court made it clear that if two artists successively used the same model to express the same idea, even to the point of resorting to the same pose, background and lighting, the earlier artist would have no cause for complaint so long as the later one worked independently. In this case, however, the Court felt that there had been a deliberate attempt to simulate a copyrighted product and cash in on its success.

The eye of an artist [said the Court] will no doubt, find differences between these two photographs. The backgrounds are not identical, the model in one case is sedate, in the other smiling; moreover the young woman was two years older when the later photograph was taken, and some slight changes in the contours of her figure are discoverable. But the identities are much greater than the differences, and it seems to us that the artist was careful to introduce only enough differences to argue about, while undertaking to make what would seem to be a copy to the ordinary purchaser who did not have both photographs before him at the same time. In this undertaking we think he succeeded.

Accordingly the Court restrained further sales of "Cherry Ripe."

## Reproductions

Under the Copyright Law it is possible to protect the *reproduction* of a work of art, even though the work itself is in the public domain. Anyone else may seek out the original and make his own copy of it, for it remains in the pool of general availability. But no one may copy the copyrighted reproduction.

Accordingly it has been held to be an infringement to transfer a copyrighted facsimile of an old master without permission onto silk scarves. The making of unlicensed color lithographs from copyrighted mezzotints of paintings in the public domain has likewise been frowned on. In the latter case Judge Smith emphasized the fact that the creation of a mezzotint engraving required individual skill and judgment. "No two engravers," he said, "can produce identical interpretations of the same oil painting. This would appear to be sufficient to meet the requirement of some originality to entitle a work to the protection of the copyright law."

# Plagiarism in Music

The ordinary words of the English language, used by the average person, amount to ordinary speech. The same words, woven into poetic speech by Keats or Shelley, or any other great poet, sound like the most poetic words in the English language. Certainly, before we find plagiarism in a song, we should be able to find some substantial part of it which can be traced to and discerned by the ordinary listener in the composition which it is claimed to infringe.

—Judge Yankwich: Carew v. RKO Radio Pictures

MUSIC is full of echoes.
There are single echoes, as where a later song repeats all or part of an earlier one. There are multiple ones, as in the case of "wandering airs." A melody in a Gregorian chant, born around A.D. 600, wandered about for more than a millennium before it turned up in the infernal regions in Gluck's *Orpheus and Eurydice*. Thereafter it found haven successively in a piano-violin sonata by Beethoven and in Schumann's "Soldier's March." Another air, an old Spanish folk tune, runs like a vagabond stream through the varied landscape of Yradier's *Chanson Havanaise,* Bizet's *Carmen,* one of MacDowell's *Sea Pieces,* and a scene in Victor Herbert's *It Happened in Nordland.* An even older strain, a Russian hymn, lends its cadence to Beethoven's Rasoumovsky string quartets, and to the Coronation Scene in Moussorgsky's *Boris Godunov.*

## The Resources of Music

Much has been said of the smallness of the musical alphabet as a powerful factor in inducing similarity in music.

It is true that the alphabet is limited. Musical notes available for combinations are twelve in number. They represent the tones produced by striking the white and black keys of a single octave on the piano. These tones constitute the chromatic scale, and all music is essentially a combination of them. They are the raw materials every composer starts out with. As a result, a certain amount of similarity of tone succession is inevitable in music.

The chromatic scale, however, does not define the range of creativity in the medium. The basic stuff of composition is more than twelve notes; it is as many multiples of twelve as there are octaves in our instruments. The mathematical possibilities of the scale are thus vastly extended. Harmony, rhythm, accent and tempo, the timbres of our instruments, are further sources of variety.[1]

Actually such factors as borrowing, the use of folk tunes, the practice of variations, and conscious and unconscious quotation are much more influential in causing similarity in music than the meagerness of the scale.

## The Old Refrain

Few masters of music have escaped the charge of borrowing or plagiarism.

Bach's inability to invent melodies has become a staple of musical commentary. Given a theme which he could develop, he was supreme. But he needed sparks from the outside to kindle his genius. He got them from traditional airs, and from the compositions of his predecessors and contemporaries. He wrote sixteen Concerti "after" Vivaldi; six of these were actually no more than arrangements. He took the beginning and the thematic development of the first movement of his *Italienisches Concerto* from a symphony by Georg Muffat, and the slow movement from an opera by Francesco Provenzale. The C Major Prelude in the first part of his *Well-Tempered Clavichord* had its inception in a prelude by Johann Kuhnau. "But what wondrous tones," says Dr. Paul Nettl, the critic, "have developed from the dry chirpings of Kuhnau!"[2]

Handel has been called the most unblushing and persistent musical plagiarist that ever lived. His admirers as well as his detractors have dwelt on the range of his peculations. He was extraordinarily sensitive to influence. In his youth he was swayed by Mattheson and Keiser in Hamburg; in Italy he leaned on Scarlatti, and in England on Purcell. However, it wasn't only a matter of influence. In 1831 Crotch listed twenty-nine composers from whom Handel had appropriated pieces. Recent studies have disclosed more. Stradella, Clari, Muffat, Kerll, Buxtehude, Carissimi, Lotti and Erba were all his substantial creditors. Dr. Chryander, the authority on Handel, thought it a disservice to the master to deny his obligations; they were, he felt, of no consequence; what counted was that Handel had glorified every composer he had drawn on.[3]

During a rehearsal of *Die Walküre* in 1876, Richard Wagner suddenly turned to Liszt and said: "Here comes a theme I got from you." "Never mind," replied Liszt, "that will at least give it a chance to be heard." When Wagner's *Parsifal* was first performed in New York, a critic wrote: "There is more honesty in a single measure of one of Liszt's oratorios than there is in the whole *Parsifal* score. Wagner stole one of his principal motifs from a Belgian bell-chimes suite. The lamenting of Amfortas is primarily an echo from the Italian operas. On every page of Wagner's work one finds signs of musical poverty."

More recently it has been suggested that Wagner got the opening motif of his *Tristan and Isolde* from the Romeo-seul theme of Berlioz's *Romeo and Juliet* symphony, and the Eucharist theme of *Parsifal* from the opening of Berlioz's *Requiem*.[4] Whether—as some insist—Wagner derived the whole idea of sustained narrative music from the *Symphonie Fantastique* of Berlioz, is open to debate; but there is little doubt that the German master took substantial hints from Weber and Marschner, Schubert and Mendelssohn.

Nor did Brahms hesitate to help himself when the need arose. Delving into sixteenth-century music, he resurrected melodies and formulas long forgotten, without bothering to specify his sources. So profound was the debt he owed to his idol Beethoven that unfriendly commentators dubbed his First Symphony Beethoven's Tenth. Most of the time he withstood the dispraise calmly enough. But when his "Sonata in A Major" was derisively labeled the "Meistersinger Sonata" because the first few notes of the opening movement resembled the first notes of Wagner's "Prize Song," he lost his temper. "Any donkey," he exclaimed, "can see that!" He himself was plundered often enough. A composer who had trespassed heavily on him had the misfortune of being present one day while a work of his (the composer's) was being played to the Master. Feigning innocent puzzlement, Brahms asked him: "But what piece of mine is that?"

Stung by the charge that he aped the hierarch of the *Gesammtkunstwerke*, Bizet wrote in righteous indignation: "If I thought I imitated Wagner, I should not write another note in my life, in spite of my admiration for him. It is better to work badly in one's own style than in that of others. And besides, the more beautiful the model, the more ridiculous the imitation!" Yet his scruples did not deter him from lifting his famous "Habanera" from Yradier.

Not so long ago two women came forward to claim authorship of the opera *Turandot*. "The thousands of Puccini admirers," said *The New York Times*, "who love to sing or whistle any of his charming melodies, without the faintest notion whether it is from *La Bohème* or *Tosca*, *Madame Butterfly* or *Manon*, would cite their ignorance as proof that nobody but Puccini could have written *Turandot*. The tune they hum all day slides from one opera to the next so smoothly that the singers cannot place the aria; they know only that it is Puccini."

## Beyond Censure

While stealing from a known composer is frowned on, tapping unknown ones is, under certain circumstances, not only condoned but commended.

"We talk of Brahms' *Hungarian Dances* and Liszt's *Hungarian Rhapsodies*," says Deems Taylor. "The 'rhapsody' part is all right, but neither Brahms nor Liszt made up the tunes on which the dances and rhapsodies are based. They are Hungarian gypsy tunes that existed long before Brahms or Liszt was born."[5]

Taylor points out that the Holy Grail theme in *Parsifal* is an old German amen, known as the "Dresden Amen"; that a French folk song called "The March of the Kings" adorns a movement of Bizet's *L'Arlesienne*; and that half the score of *Boris Godunov*, as well as of Stravinsky's *Petrushka*, is Russian folk tunes. He might have added that Haydn drew on Croatian melodies, and that Grieg built his *Peer Gynt Suite* on Norwegian ones.

## Adaptation and Quotation

The term "borrowing" usually implies concealment of source. There are, however, two forms of musical borrowing which are innocent of intent to deceive.

One of these has to do with the practice of writing variations—taking a theme or a melody from another composer, paraphrasing it, adapting it, ringing changes on it, arranging it for other instruments. The reshaping of musical thought can be an authentic creative activity. Liszt was a wizard at it; most of the august ones—Handel, Haydn, Schubert, Schumann, Chopin, Brahms, Tchaikovsky—turned to it from time to time. Mozart left an unfinished piano suite "in the style of Handel." Beethoven wrote variations on Mozart. Schönberg has done "Three Choruses on Sixteenth-Century Folk Songs."[6]

In the case of a variation, the source is expressly indicated in the title of the piece. In the case of quotation, the source is implied, and is intended to be recognized. The difference between ordinary borrowing and quotation is the appositeness and explicitness of the latter. When Mozart quoted from Martins and Sarti in *Don Giovanni*, the public was delighted. The pieces were old favorites of theirs, and were sung and played everywhere.

In his opera *Ariadne and Blaubart*, Paul Dukas quotes the heroine-motif from Debussy's *Pelléas et Mélisande*. Berlioz quotes *Dies Irae* in his *Symphonie Fantastique*; Tchaikovsky, the "Marseillaise" in his *1812 Overture*; Puccini, "The Star-Spangled Banner" in *Madame Butterfly*.[7]

Of these two modes of expression, as of some others, law and art take divergent views. While anyone is free to do variations on a theme in the public domain, the same treatment of a copyrighted composition—assuming that the basic melody remains recognizable—may well be an infringement. Nor will it do the arranger any good to argue, when haled into court, that he has bettered the original.

By the same token, quotation from a copyrighted song is taboo if it goes beyond fair use.

## With Malice—

Here and there we encounter instances of appropriation that cannot be dismissed as the legitimate result of influence, variation or quotation. They are, simply, thefts.

Robert Führer, an organist, brazenly published Mozart's *Mass in G* as his own. The harpsichordist Giuseppi Jozzi stole eight sonatas from his teacher Domenico Alberti. The English composer Henry Eccles took credit for pieces he had filched from Arcangelo Corelli and Giuseppi Valentini. Bononcini cribbed a madrigal from Lotti and with a lofty gesture dedicated it to the Academy of Ancient Music; he persisted in claiming paternity even when Lotti presented incontrovertible proof that the madrigal was his. Musicologists are still battling over the question as to whether the ceaseless and intensive foraging of Handel was a justifiable pursuit, or—to the extent of his exploitation of works like Urio's *Te Deum* and Stradella's serenata— larceny.

### —and Without

Theft may, of course, be unintentional. A composer lives in a world of music. His ears are filled with melodies. When a theme comes to him, he can't always tell whether it's his own or someone else's. Indeed, he can be tricked into disowning his own brain child.

Ferenc Molnár, the Hungarian playwright, likes to play practical jokes. Walking past the house of Viktor Jacobi, the composer, in Budapest one day, he overheard Jacobi playing a song he had just written. Molnár, who has a good ear, eavesdropped long enough to memorize the piece. Meeting Jacobi a few days later, he began to hum the tune. Jacobi was flabbergasted. "Where did you hear that?" he asked anxiously. "In Paris," fibbed Molnár; "it's quite a hit there." "Impossible," cried Jacobi, "it's a new piece I've just finished!" "You plagiarized it," said Molnár, "and I can prove it." He hummed the song to the end. Convinced, Jacobi shook his head sadly. "And I thought it was original," he said. "I should have known better. It did sound a bit familiar!"

### Tin-Pan Alley

If echoes abound in serious music, they fairly make the welkin ring in popular songs. There are cynics who profess to find in the output of Tin-Pan Alley nothing but faint and debased reverberations from the classics, from folk tunes, and from primitive rhythms.

To be sure, "Marcheta" is reminiscent of the Overture to *The Merry Wives of Windsor*; "Ti-Pi-Tin," of the Waldteufel Waltzes; "Let's Fall in Love," of the Garden Scene in *Faust*; "Love in Bloom," of a passage in Johann Strauss' *Voices of Spring*; Jerome Kern's "Till the Clouds Roll By," of an old German folk song.[8]

The catalogue is endless. "Chickory Chick" is Beethoven's Fifth Symphony at faster tempo. "Yes, We Have No Bananas" harks back to Handel's *Messiah*. "I'm Always Chasing Rainbows" repeats the melodic theme of Chopin's *Fantaisie Impromptu* in C-Sharp Minor. "Moonlight and Roses" and "Castles in the Air" owe their inspiration to Chopin too. "Full Moon and Empty Arms" can be traced to Rachmaninoff's Second Piano Concerto.

To say that this convicts tunesmiths of poverty of invention is to render judgment on insufficient evidence. There are plenty of popular songs—good ones too—that can't be traced back to antecedent sources. It may well be that some of the obvious analogies have arisen from coincidence, not copying. The fact that derivative composers far outnumber the original ones should not blind us to the existence of the latter.

The derivative fellow can cite several factors in extenuation of his acts. One is the voracity of the market. The life span of the average popular song is brief; the journeyman composer must keep on grinding out stuff without waiting for the prod of fresh ideas. Another is the elastic ethics of certain segments of the profession—ethics expressed in the motto: "Why shouldn't I grab what I can? Everybody else does."

Still another factor is the structure of the popular song. The form is more or less arbitrarily set; only the audacious and inventive depart from it. The chorus has three parts: the opening strain, which runs for eight bars and is repeated for another eight, a middle tune of eight bars which is in the nature of a variation, and a concluding group of eight bars which repeat the first strain. The notes must be within the range of the ordinary voice and the skill of the average player. And as if these limitations were not enough, the melody must be catchy and the lyrics of general appeal. No wonder a genuinely new song is a rarity.

Then, too, the popular composer is acutely sensitive to the influence of his contemporaries, particularly if he is of scant talent and they exceptionally gifted. "Waves of plagiarism accompany prosperous musical times, when two or three brilliant writers soar far above mediocrity, acting powerfully on the current of ideas. Into their mood are swept not only many willing proselytes but composers of sturdier stuff whose bells must be made to ring in key with the popular ensemble."[9]

It is a sardonic fact that the man in the street who shies away from serious music will embrace it with joyful enthusiasm if clad in simple melodic guise. "Till the End of Time," based on a Chopin theme, has sold well over two million copies of sheet music and five million records; twenty thousand dollars was paid for its use in a single movie. Songs based on Tchaikovsky's compositions—"Moon Love" on his Fifth Symphony, "Tonight We Love" on his Piano Concerto, and "Our Love" on *Romeo and Juliet*—have done as well. In most cases the revenue from commercial adaptations flows into the pockets of strangers, since the creator has died and his work has fallen into the public domain. One of the few exceptions is Debussy, whose estate got more money from "My Reverie," the popular version of a Debussy theme, than the composer earned from all his efforts during his lifetime. The publisher who went to Igor Stravinsky to persuade him to convert a melody from his celebrated *Firebird Suite* into a popular song was armed with a persuasive argument. "Do you want to be like Tchaikovsky and Chopin," asked the publisher, "and wait for everyone to pick your bones after you're dead? Do it yourself while you're still able to enjoy the money." And so Stravinsky rewrote the melody into a slow dreamy number called "Summer Moon."[10]

Some people look upon this kind of adaptation as a means of bringing at least a modicum of good music to a vast audience. Others condemn it as vulgarization, if not downright profanation. There is one point, though, on which both sides are apt to agree. It is that there should be no deception. An adapted number should be presented as such. It is one thing for Sigmund Romberg to resurrect Schubert's music in *Blossom Time*, since the show deals with Schubert's life and there's no pretense that Schubert's work is Romberg's. It is quite another for composers to usurp authorship, as some have done, of folk tunes which they've merely arranged.

There was a time when "Tin-Pan Alley" was a term of disparagement and derision. The epithet has lost a good deal of its sting. The profession, like any other, has its hacks, its scroungers, its leeches. Many "new" songs sound like a thousand others that have gone before them. But surely there is nothing inherently tin-pan about a medium of expression that has known such men as Victor Herbert and Irving Berlin, Vincent Youmans and Jerome Kern, George Gershwin and Cole Porter, Richard Rodgers and Frank Loesser.

### Music and the Law

The law gives the copyright owner of a musical composition the exclusive right:

(a)  To print, publish and sell copies of it;
(b)  To give public performances of it; and
(c)  To arrange and adapt it.

The basic principles summarized in Chapter 1 govern the protection of this right.

### Similarity

There can be no plagiarism without copying, and no copying without similarity. A slight resemblance in the progression of a few bars of music is something that occurs frequently. A case of piracy cannot be built on this alone.

Similarity is a question of fact to be determined by comparison. Comparison is usually made by having the rival works sung or played in court. The test is whether the similarity is noticeable to the average listener.

In the "Chatterbox" case the plaintiff's experts strove to establish resemblance by detailed technical analysis, but admitted that the two melodies involved, if sung or played in the ordinary course, did not sound alike. Judge Yankwich held for the defendant. What counted, he said, was the impression conveyed to the untrained ear, not the findings of musicians predicated on dissection.

The same point came up in the case involving one of the hit songs in Walt Disney's *Snow White*. There the claim was that Frank Churchill's "Some Day My Prince Will Come" had been lifted from "Old Eli." "Some Day" was a waltz, "Old Eli" a marching song; the latter had been written in 1909, the former in 1934. The plaintiff contended that both were in the same key and tempo, had the same rhythm and harmonic structure, had the theme repeated in the same place the same way, had a unique interval of a sixth instead of the customary fourth twice in the same place and between the same notes, had the same note progression at the same place, and had the same notes in the theme as repeated, with two minor changes. Both sides produced experts. "The opinions of these men of music," said Judge Conger in dismissing the complaint, "are so wide apart that it is impossible to reconcile them. I have heard the compositions played, and to my ear there is a similarity, but not such as would impress one. . . . I would not take one for the other."

## Copying

In the legal battle between Jack Darrell's "Does Anybody Want a Little Kewpie" (1928) and Sherman, Meskill and Silver's "On the Beach at Bali-Bali" (1936), the Circuit Court of Appeals observed: "The strength of the plaintiff's case lies in the substantial identity of a sequence of eight notes in his song and theirs; and indeed that hardly does justice to the similarity between the two, because the sequence reappears in each song so frequently as to constitute the greater part of each. This makes the two, when rendered, so much alike to the ear that the supposed piracy appears almost inevitable." From this you would have thought that the Court was about to award victory to Darrell. Not so. The court went on: "Nevertheless we are not convinced that that conclusion is inescapable. . . . Such simple, trite themes as these are likely to recur spontaneously; indeed, the defendants have been able to discover substantial equivalents of that at bar in a number of pieces which appeared earlier than plaintiff's. . . . Recurrence is not therefore an inevitable badge of plagiarism." The Court declined to overrule Judge Mandelbaum, who had found no infringement.

Nor could Judge Rifkind see any occasion for the law to intervene on behalf of "Hubba Hubba" as against "Dig You Later: A Hubba Hubba Hubba." Here the plaintiff's grievance was predicated on the alleged lifting, not of any music, but of the words "Hubba Hubba." Taking judicial notice that these words connoted "that which in the Gay Nineties was expressed by a male's whistle, evoked whenever a wind-rustled skirt revealed a well-turned feminine ankle," the Judge went on to say:

Should the suspicion arise that the defendants' use of these strange words is the product of copying, it is immediately dissipated by the fact that between April 18, 1944, and June 20, 1945, five distinct hubba hubba songs, so entitled, were copyrighted in the Copyright Office, before either of the songs in issue. The words had become common. They frequently appeared in cartoons and in comic strips in the newspapers. By April 19, 1946, the number of copyrighted hubba hubba songs had grown to fifteen. Apparently there was great fecundity in these words. For some reason, hidden from judges, these words released the poetic muse and conveyed myriad thoughts which conventional English was quite incapable of expressing. In any event such common usage dissipates the suspicion that might otherwise arise.

But Judge Learned Hand felt that the similarity between "I Didn't Raise My Boy to Be a Soldier" and "You Will Never Know How Much I Really Cared" exceeded "the bounds of mere accident," and he ruled that the former infringed the latter.

Access is essential to copying. Direct access is hard to establish. It may be inferred from parallels. To warrant a judgment in the plaintiff's favor, however, the parallels must do more than engender a suspicion; they must demonstrate piracy with reasonable certainty.

If the defendant has had access to material which could have served him as well as the plaintiff's, his denial of copying becomes the more credible, and a heavier burden of proof is cast on the plaintiff.

Copying must be substantial or material. Either a considerable part of the original must be appropriated, or its essential ingredient abstracted. In the case of a popular song, the essential ingredient may be the entire chorus or the theme (usually eight bars) or the accompaniment or a significant sequence of notes.

In holding that "Confessing" plagiarized "Starlight," Judge Cox said: "Unquestionably the melodies are strikingly alike in sound, and a comparison of the note structures shows almost complete identity in the first eight bars of the introduction, and in the first fifteen and the last ten bars of the chorus, or over three-quarters of the most significant parts of the two songs." In this case the use of only the music of "Starlight" was litigated. Some years later another fight arose—against a different song—over the title and the lyrics. This time the plaintiff did not fare so well. Noting that the lyrics were but a slight variant of the old rhyme "Starlight, starbright," and that thirteen previous songs had borne the title "Starlight" or "Starlight, Starbright," Judge Conger found no reason for complaint.

## Dardanella

Most court decisions on plagiarism in music make sense. The "Dardanella" case is a puzzler.

As the suit arose more than a quarter of a century ago, and a lot of other music-infringement disputes have gone through the judicial mill since then, the case would not merit extended discussion if it weren't for two facts. First, the case was decided by Judge Learned Hand, the foremost expounder of the law of plagiarism. Second, it has been often cited as authoritative precedent, and is still being cited.

Judge Hand ruled that Jerome Kern's "Kalua" infringed "Dardanella." The ruling was predicated on the duplication of eight notes. The notes were used the same way in both pieces: as an *ostinato* accompaniment.

Now the only kind of similarity noticeable to the average listener—whose ear, the cases say again and again, is the only proper testing device—is that of melody. There was no such similarity between "Dardanella" and "Kalua." The link between the two was the *ostinato*, repeated over and over again as a continuous rhythmic bass. It appeared in the chorus of "Kalua," and in the verse (not the chorus) of "Dardanella." The ordinary layman pays no attention to the accompaniment of a song.

What was it, then, that tipped the scales against Kern, a man of integrity and proven skill? He took the stand and swore he hadn't copied. Judge Hand said he believed him, yet from the mere fact that "Dardanella" had had a great vogue and that Kern must have heard it, the Judge assumed that Kern had lifted it unconsciously. He found infringement notwithstanding evidence that the musical figure in issue had been used long before by Wagner, Schumann and Kummer (thought not as an *ostinato*), and by Landon as an *ostinato*.

Judge Hand did not believe that the accompaniment was at all as important to the success of "Dardanella" as the plaintiff urged. "I admit," he said, "that it was a good bass and helped, but I think the piece won its success substantially on the melody." Moreover, "Dardanella" had apparently run its course when "Kalua" arrived; the likelihood of competition and injury was so remote that Judge Hand, calling the whole business a trivial pother, refused to give the plaintiff more than $250 minimum damages. "Such victories," he said, "I may properly enough make a luxury to the winner." Why, then, was the winner the winner?

And if the success of the plaintiff's song was in itself sufficient to overcome Kern's categoric disclaimer of copying and to raise a conclusive presumption of unconscious plagiarism, what was the purpose of allowing Kern to go into the witness box to say he hadn't copied?

## Originality

Once the requisite amount of copying is established, the existence of slight differences between the original and the copy will not defeat a recovery.

To support an infringement suit, a musical composition must be in copyright. It must also be copyrightable. To be copyrightable, it must be "original." This doesn't mean that it has to be fresh or striking or excellent, but only the spontaneous product of its creator's imagination.

The composer of "Lady of Love" lost her plagiarism suit against "Without a Word of Warning" when it was shown that the material which she claimed Paramount Pictures had stolen from her, she had taken from Johann Strauss' *Die Fledermaus*. The Strauss source was in the public domain; and the plaintiff had not, the Court felt, added to it enough of her own devising to entitle her to a claim of originality. Infringement could result, the Court made clear, from copying a work based on material in the public domain, but only where the creator of the work transformed the material to such an extent as to make it his own.

Faced with Emery Heim's charge that his Hungarian song had been plagiarized by Aldo Franchetti and used under the title of "Perhaps" in the movie *Nice Girl*, Universal Pictures admitted that there was substantial identity between the two pieces. It insisted, however, that this was due to both composers having borrowed the same phrase from Dvorak's *Humoreske*. Universal won.

## Song Titles

There is no copyright in the title of a song as distinguished from the song itself. If the title has, by sufficient usage, acquired a secondary significance, the courts will protect it under the theory of unfair competition. To sustain this theory, the plaintiff must show that the public has been, or is likely to be, deceived. When the owner of a song called "The Man Who Broke the Bank at Monte Carlo" sued Twentieth Century-Fox for issuing a film by the same name (the song itself was not used in the picture), the Court said:

The member of the public who is supposed to be deceived must, to start with, be assumed to know what he is wanting to see or hear. Thus in the present case he must be presumed to know that what he wanted was to hear the song "The Man Who Broke the Bank at Monte Carlo." It seems inconceivable that when or if he bought a ticket for the motion picture, he imagined he was going to hear a performance of the familiar song. The two things are completely different, and incapable of comparison in any reasonable sense. The thing said to be passed off must resemble the thing for which it is passed off. A frying pan cannot be passed off as a kettle.

This case arose in 1939. Since then we have had a run of nostalgic screen musicals built around—and in several instances bearing the name—of a popular song. The legal result of borrowing the title of a hit tune would doubtless be different today.

### A Risqué Business

An obscene song is at the mercy of any infringer. This is so even if the composition wears the badge of copyright. In any plagiarism tilt between the originator of an immoral work and its purloiner, the latter has all the advantage—not because the law favors him, but because it won't help the originator.

However, a song must be more than merely tawdry or tasteless or ribald to forfeit the law's benefits. In the "Rum and Coca-Cola" case, the defense was that the Calypso song, which "Rum and Coca-Cola" was claimed to plagiarize, was obscene, since it commemorated carnal traffic between American soldiers and Trinidad women. Judge Byers felt that it would be absurd to suppose "that the rather cheap and vulgar verses would tend to promote lust." He gave the plaintiff an injunction and ordered an accounting.

### The Stone of Sisyphus

If Belasco shone peerless among plagiarism defendants, Ira B. Arnstein stands sovereign among plaintiffs. Belasco never lost a case. Arnstein has lost six.

By his own declaration Arnstein is a classicist who pauses now and then in the midst of his serious endeavors to turn out light pieces. His career in the courts goes back a generation. It began when he sued Nathaniel Shilkret, orchestra conductor and composer, over the latter's "Lady Divine." He said that he had shown his "Light My Life with Love" to Shilkret, that Shilkret had liked the middle theme and had offered to buy it, that the deal had fallen through, and that Shilkret had later cribbed the theme. Judge Coleman dismissed the complaint.

Arnstein's next offensive was against "Play, Fiddle, Play," which he said plagiarized his "I Love You Madly." Judge Symes conceded that there was some resemblance between the two, but not enough to establish infringement.

Four years later Arnstein was in court again—this time against ASCAP, the American Society of Composers, Authors and Publishers. ASCAP is a nonprofit organization engaged in protecting the copyrighted works of its members from being publicly performed for profit without permission. ASCAP as a powerful entity; no one can accuse Arnstein of courting feeble opposition. His story was that five hit numbers handled by ASCAP—"The World Is Mine Tonight," "My Wishing Song," "Be Still My Heart," "Take Me in Your Arms," and "Bei Mir Bist Du Schön"—had been pirated from him. Judge Conger didn't see it that way.

Arnstein then sued Broadcast Music, ASCAP's rival. Again his grievance concerned five successful songs. Again he met defeat.

Having been repeatedly wrecked on the reefs of similarity, Arnstein plotted his course in his fifth action with an extra measure of artful seamanship. The defendant this time was Twentieth Century-Fox, and the song in question was "Kalamazoo" (used in one of the company's pictures), which Arnstein said had been stolen from his "I've got a Girl in Kalamazoo." "By ingenious manipulation of his composition," said Judge Bondy, "the plaintiff attempts to establish similarity. For instance, to do so, he transfers notes from accompaniment in the bass to melody in the treble, he omits and changes notes and the rhythm of some of his phrases, and separates parts of some of his phrases and places them in different parts of his composition. It has frequently been held that similarity cannot be established in this manner."

## L'Affaire Cole Porter

A less hardy soul than Arnstein would have been disheartened long before this. Not he. He plunged into his sixth campaign with hope undimmed and ardor unabated. It turned out to be an exciting venture, giving him a taste of victory and a brief burst of glory.

Charging that six of Cole Porter's brilliant hits—"Begin the Beguine," "My Heart Belongs to Daddy," "I Love You," "Night and Day," "You'd Be So Nice to Come Home To," and "Don't Fence Me In"—were larcenous replicas of his own compositions, Arnstein sued for a million dollars. He demanded a jury trial.

In the course of his examination before trial, he unfolded a tale reminiscent of a Hitchcock thriller. He said that Porter had "had stooges right along to follow me, watch me, and live in the same apartment with me," and that his room had been ransacked several times. Asked what basis he had for saying that Porter had had anything to do with all this, Arnstein replied: "I don't know that he had anything to do with it; I only know that he could have." It must have occurred to him that this was a tenuous basis indeed for so grave a charge, for he did a face-about. "Many of my compositions have been published," he said. "No one had to break in to steal them. They were sung publicly."

Porter submitted to the Court phonograph records of piano renditions of his songs and Arnstein's. He pointed to Arnstein's background: five suits, five defeats. The claim, he pleaded, was transparently preposterous and vexatious; a trial would be an unnecessary hardship for him. He asked that the case be thrown out. Judge Caffey granted the request.

Arnstein appealed.

He had taken appeals before. He had never won a reversal. This time Lady Luck smiled on him. By a vote of two to one, the Circuit Court of Appeals upset the dismissal and sent the case back for trial.

Judge Frank wrote the majority opinion of the Court. He noted that there were similarities between Arnstein's songs and Porter's. While these similarities did not, he said, compel the conclusion that there had been copying, they were sufficient—assuming there was evidence of access—to let the case go to the jury. The fact that Arnstein's claim had taxed Judge Caffey's credulity did not justify dismissal. "If evidence is always to be disbelieved because the story told seems remarkable or impossible," he said, "then a party whose rights depend on the proof of some facts out of the usual course of events will always be denied justice simply because his story is improbable. We shouldn't overlook the shrewd proverbial admonition that sometimes truth is stranger than fiction."

Nor did the Circuit Court deem it proper to attach any weight to Arnstein's previous failures. Each case, said Judge Frank, had to stand or fall on its own facts.

He then proceeded to restate some of the principles of plagiarism applicable to music, and to specify the circumstances under which expert testimony could be received.

1. If there are no similarities, no amount of evidence of access will suffice to prove copying.
2. If there is evidence of access and similarities do exist, then the question is whether the similarities are sufficient to prove copying. On this issue, analysis ("dissection") is relevant, and the testimony of experts may be received.
3. If evidence of access is lacking, similarities must be so striking as to preclude the possibility that both parties arrived independently at the same result.
4. If copying is established, then only does there arise the second issue, that of *illicit* copying, i.e., unlawful appropriation.
5. Each of these elements—copying and improper appropriation—is an issue of fact.
6. Where access is denied, the credibility of the denial also raises an issue of fact.

Generally speaking, concluded Judge Frank, there should be trials in plagiarism suits. For one thing, the plaintiff must not be deprived of the invaluable privilege of cross-examining the defendant. For another, the plaintiff is entitled to have the jury observe the witnesses while testifying. The appearance and behavior of a witness are often a complete antidote to what he testifies; he may convince all who hear and see him that he is disingenuous and untruthful, and yet his testimony when read may convey a most favorable impression. Mere words on paper "cannot give the look or manner of the witness: his hesitation, his doubts, his variations of language, his confidence or precipitancy, his calmness or consideration; they are the dead body of the evidence, without its spirit."

It is of importance to note that while Judge Frank referred to the long-accepted lay-listener test in his opinion, he indicated that expert testimony *could* properly be received on the question as to whether the similarities betokened copying.

Judge Clark of the Circuit Court disagreed emphatically with his colleagues. He considered Judge Caffey's disposition of the case simple and appropriate. However, he suggested that Porter had perhaps made a tactical error on the motion for dismissal.

In an endeavor to assist us [he said], he caused to be prepared records of all the musical pieces here involved, and presented these transcriptions through the medium of the affidavit of his pianist. Though he himself did not stress these records and properly met plaintiff's claims as to the written music with his own analysis, yet the tinny tintinnabulations of the music thus canned resounded through the United States Courthouse to the exclusion of all else, including the real issues in the case. Of course, sound is important in a case of this kind, but it is not so important as to falsify what the eye reports and the mind teaches. Otherwise plagiarism would be suggested by the mere drumming of repetitious sound from our usual popular music, as it issues from a piano, orchestra, or hurdy-gurdy—particularly when ears may be dulled by long usage, possibly artistic repugnance or boredom, or mere distance which causes all sounds to merge.

Judge Clark had something to say, too, about the technique of analysis so dear to plagiarism claimants. He restated the established rule: even where dissection and "theoretical disquisition" dredge up some points of similarity, it's still the total impression that counts. Arnstein, the Judge observed, did not and could not claim extensive copying, measure for measure. That was why he resorted to a comparative analysis of small detached portions which were really fillers between the better known parts of the melodies.

Plaintiff's compositions [Judge Clark went on] are of the simple and trite character where small repetitive sequences are not hard to discover. It is as though we found Shakespeare a plagiarist on the basis of his use of articles, pronouns, prepositions and adjectives also used by others. The surprising thing, however, is to note the small amount of even this type of reproduction which plaintiff by dint of extreme dissection has been able to find.

Judge Clark felt it would be idle to cite Arnstein's showing of "plagiarism" as to each song in issue. He took one example: Porter's "Don't Fence Me In," which Arnstein insisted had been taken from his "A Modern Messiah." The first was written in common or 4/4 time, the second in 6/8 time; there was only one place where there was a duplicate group of as many as five consecutive notes, and these without the same values. As to the other songs, Arnstein's claim rested on a sequence of three, four or five—never more than five—identical notes, usually of different rhythmical values.

Since Judge Clark was unwilling to believe that his colleagues would, on such flimsy evidence, uphold a judgment in Arnstein's favor even if he recovered one, he saw no sense in sending the case back for trial. "The present holding," he said, "is therefore one of those procedural mountains which develop when it is thought that justice must be temporarily sacrificed lest a mistaken precedent be set at large." His colleagues, he was convinced, were in effect issuing a clear invitation to the exploitation of slight musical analogies by clever musical tricks in the hope of getting juries to divide the wealth of Tin-Pan Alley.

Judge Clark's prophecy proved correct. Arnstein's victory was short-lived. The case went to trial before a jury, and the jury returned a verdict for Porter. But Arnstein wasn't through yet. Once more he appealed to the Circuit Court. This time the judgment was upheld. The Supreme Court of the United States refused to review the case.

## Sleuths of Song

The tune detective is a by-product of infringement litigation. He is the defendants' tower of strength, and the plaintiffs' nemesis. A genealogist, he delves into the ancestry of latter-day compositions and traces them back to classical material, drinking songs, folk airs, hymns. When he testifies as an expert for the defendant, he undertakes to show that the plaintiff's melody is not original—and hence not entitled to copyright protection—by exposing its source. Dr. Sigmund Spaeth is probably the most accomplished performer in the field. He has displayed his erudition in books and magazine articles, on the witness stand and over the radio.[11] It is said that he made more money explaining how "Yes, We Have No Bananas" was inspired by

Handel's *Messiah* than Handel earned in royalties on a half-dozen of his major works.

Legally or otherwise, the tune detective's word is never conclusive. When, in a controversy in which X accuses Y, the sleuth has demonstrated that X went to the public domain for his song, three questions still remain. Where did Y get *his* tune? Did he too go to the public domain, working independently, or did he take a short cut via X? And what did each composer do with and to what he took?

Among music critics, reminiscence-seeking is not as prevalent as it once was. It still persists, though, and occasionally the parallel-hunter is hoist on his own petard. When the Metropolitan Opera put on Deems Taylor's *Peter Ibbetson*, one reviewer professed to discern in it gleanings from Puccini, Massenet, Wagner, Debussy and Strauss. The only thing he could bring himself to praise was Taylor's treatment of old French folk songs, "particularly the lovely old *Dors, Mignonne*." Actually, Taylor *had* woven several French folk songs into the score for atmosphere, but as it happened the very number which the reviewer had singled out—and which, since he liked it, he had found impossible to credit to Taylor—*was* the latter's original.[12]

# Plagiarism in Miscellaneous Fields

> What goes on around him, of course, and what he remembers from the
> past, the writer appropriates for his own use . . . He must essentially draw
> from life as he sees it, lives it, overhears it, or steals it, and the truer
> the writer, perhaps, the bigger the blackguard.
>
> —Charles Jackson: The Sunnier Side

A MAN went into an inn and asked for a drink. The innkeeper gave it to him in a glass about half the usual size, saying: "That glass you're drinking out of is fifty years old." "Well," remarked the thirsty guest, "it's certainly the smallest thing of its age I've ever seen."

George Washington, it is said, used to tell this story with an air of here's-what-happened-the-other-day. The anecdote was current in Athens four hundred years before the birth of Christ.

A farmer told Lincoln a thumping fib about the size of his hay crop. Lincoln drawled: "I've been cutting hay, too." "Good crop?" the farmer asked. "Fair," said Lincoln. "How many tons?" "Well, I don't exactly know how many tons," said Lincoln, "but my men stacked all they could outdoors and stored the rest in the barn." Lincoln was probably unaware that he owed this one to Quintilian.

### The Longevity of Jests

Few facets of the study of plagiarism are as absorbing as the ancestry of anecdotes, jokes and aphorisms.

Take the story of the man who met a friend who said to him:

"Why, I heard you were dead!" "Well," said the man, "you can see that I'm not." "Oh, no," replied the friend, "I'd sooner believe the man who told me than you." This one too first saw light in Hellas. Groucho Marx has used variants of it.

Horace Walpole's favorite Irish gag—of the man who said: "I would have been a handsome man but they changed me in the cradle"—came from Don Quixote. Cervantes got it from the Greeks, and the Greeks got it from the Egyptians.

Hierocles, who has been called the Greek Joe Miller, tells two stories that bring to mind our modern nonsense fables.

An avaricious carter, wishing to teach his horse not to eat much, cut down his ration of hay each day until he finally fed him nothing. The horse died of starvation. "I have suffered a great loss," the carter lamented to his friends. "Just when I had taught my horse to live on nothing, he died."

A merchant bought some wine and stored it in a large glass jar. Distrustful of his household, he sealed the jar. His slave bored a hole and drew off some of the wine. The merchant was amazed to find that, though the seal was unbroken, the wine gradually diminished. His neighbor suggested that he examine the bottom. "Fool," he replied, "it isn't the lower part that's gone, it's the upper!"[1]

When De Bussy, Comte de Rabutin, sang in the seventeenth century:

> Je ne vous aime pas, Hylas;
> Je n'en saurais dire la cause,
> Je sais seulement une chose;
> C'est que je ne vous aime pas.

he was merely repeating Martial's thirty-third epigram, then sixteen hundred years old:

> Non amo te Sabidi, nec
>     possum dicere quare;
> Hoc tantum possum dicere
>     non amo te.

Dr. Fell, Dean of Christchurch in De Bussy's days, told an expelled pupil—Tom Brown—that he would reinstate him if he translated Martial's epigram. Brown submitted the following:

I do not like thee, Doctor Fell,
The reason why I cannot tell;
But this alone I know full well,
I do not like thee, Doctor Fell.

There is a strong resemblance between Roman humor and our own. When Horace tells of the bore you can't get rid of, or of the habit musicians have of refusing to play when asked but never stopping once they get started, we get more than a glimmer of recognition. Nor are we strangers to the sport Martial and Juvenal make of mothers-in-law, prodigal sons and irate fathers, bald-headed men, fat women, wearers of false teeth or hair, guests who tarry too long, shoppers who never buy, debtors who never pay.[2]

An attorney, endeavoring to break down a doctor who was a hostile expert witness, said to him: "You'll admit, won't you, that doctors make mistakes?" "Yes, the same as lawyers." "But doctors' mistakes are buried underground," said the lawyer triumphantly. "True," countered the doctor, "but lawyers' mistakes are left swinging in the air." This item, frequently recounted as a contemporary occurrence, was circulated, in one form or another, in the days when Cicero raked Catiline over the coals. It had become a staple by the seventeenth century, when Francis Quarles observed: "Physicians of all men are most happy. Whatever success they have the world proclaimeth, and what faults they commit the earth covereth."

## Of Adages and Kings

Cowper says: "God made the country and man made the town." The Latin poet Varro said the same thing long before.

The French proverb *"Le mariage est comme une forteresse assiégée: ceux qui sont dehors veulent y entrer, et ceux qui sont dedans en sortir,"* originated in the Middle Ages. It emerges as a fresh pearl of wisdom in three Renaissance works: Sir John Davies' *The Married State*, John Webster's *The White Devil*, and Montaigne's essay on Virgil, with inconsequential switches in metaphor.

The estimable lawyer of our own day, who, rebuked by the court for submitting a voluminous brief, said with a seeming burst of inspiration: "If I had had more time, Your Honor, I'd have written a shorter one," was taking a leaf out of Dr. Johnson. The learned Doctor himself had taken a leaf out of Pliny the Elder.

Voltaire says: *"L'histoire n'est que le tableau des crimes et des malheurs."* Gibbon says: "History is little more than the register of the crimes, follies, and misfortunes of mankind," and gives Voltaire no credit. Washington Irving says: "History is but a kind of Newgate Calendar, a register of the crimes and miseries that man has inflicted on his fellow-man," and *he* bows neither to Gibbon nor Voltaire.

Daniel Webster was held something of a wit for the three rules he professed to have evolved for the guidance of his actions: first, never to do today what he could defer till tomorow; second, never to do himself what he could get another to do for him; and third, never to pay his debts today. He omitted to mention that he was merely quoting Sheridan, who echoed the witty D'Argenson, who in turn probably tapped an obscure source.

When Baron Alderson said of Brougham, one of the worthies of British jurisprudence: "What a wonderful, versatile mind is Brougham! He knows politics, Greek, history, science; if he only knew a little of law, he would know a little of everything!"—the target was new but the gibe was not. Louis XVI had made the same observation about Abbé Maury's knowledge of religion.

Napoleon had a rich collection of snuffboxes which he amassed by the simple expedient of asking for snuff whenever he saw a box that struck his fancy, and omitting to return the box. He was as cavalier about the annexation of aphorisms. His famous one about there being but one step from the sublime to the ridiculous appears first in Marmontel, then in Blair, and then in Tom Paine, from whom Napoleon probably got it.

A lady told the Duke of Wellington that she passionately desired to witness a great victory. "Madam," said the Duke, "there is nothing as dreadful as a great victory—excepting a great defeat." This dictum too echoed D'Argenson.

A single glance at Burton Stevenson's *Book of Quotations* will reveal that most maxims, epigrams and aphorisms have been uttered again and again throughout the ages, with but slight variations, and almost always as original. Disraeli's "You know who the critics are: men who have failed in literature and art," appears almost word for word in Pope, Dryden, Landor, Balzac and Dumas. "Might makes right," says Thucydides, and Plautus, Lucan, Seneca and Schiller say the same thing. Adages like Samuel Butler's "'Tis better to have loved and lost than never to have loved at all," and Smedley's "All's fair in love and war," and Goldsmith's "I love everything that's old: old friends, old times, old manners, old books, old wine," spring from a long line of forebears, and have sired an equally long line of descendants.

Wilson Mizner, gold prospector, brawler, fight manager, coiner of mordant bon mots, probably threw more quips into the public domain than any other individual of his time. His appraisal of Hollywood—"a trip through a sewer in a glass-bottomed boat"—became Mayor Jimmy Walker's "A reformer is a guy who rides through a sewer in a glass-bottomed boat." His "If you steal from one author, it's plagiarism; if you steal from many, it's research," has been repeated—without quotation marks—by many others.

The taking of a single copyrighted anecdote or a single copyrighted joke does not constitute infringement. *De minimis non curat lex.* The law doesn't bother with trifles.[3]

### Hardy Perennials

If humor is immemorial, it is also ubiquitous and multiform. The same jest, the same gag, the same gibe is apt to crop up again and again about different people, in different situations, at different times, in different localities. In his *Folk Laughter on the American Frontier*, Mody C. Boatright tells a lot of stories as Western; B. A. Botkin tells the same ones as Southern in his *Treasury of Southern Folklore*.

During World War II, a G.I. was reported to have wisecracked, when served a steak that was too rare: "Take this back and cook it some more. I've seen cows hurt worse than this get well." This utterance has been traced to Oklahoma, Texas, Wyoming and elsewhere, and goes back three generations or more.

Thinking to confound the great man, some students of the naturalist Agassiz constructed an insect of parts taken from various bugs. "What kind of bug is this?" they asked him. "A humbug," he replied. The identical anecdote has been told of George Washington Carver, and a dozen other eminent scientists.

Ed Wynn's 1912 gag—"Woodrow Wilson's got his eye on the Presidential chair, but look what Taft's got on it"—came to life in 1944 about Dewey and F.D.R., and in 1948 about Eisenhower and Truman.

When, according to Damon Runyon, Sailor Tom Sharkey, the old heavyweight, was served a lobster with a claw missing, he demanded to know why. "Oh, he had a fight with another lobster," said the waiter. "Well, then," roared Sharkey, "bring me the winner." The way Gene Fowler tells it, the obstreperous diner was John Barrymore.

A man visited the office of the late Bob (Believe It or Not) Ripley. Out of his head sprouted three petunias and a geranium. Ripley's secretary looked him over coolly. "And what," she asked, "do you wish to see Mr. Ripley about?" This is a particularly durable exhibit; it has been told of practically every well-known hard-boiled theatrical agent in New York.

Euripides noted, twenty-five hundreds years ago, that a remark which would pass unnoticed if made by a nonentity was apt to be hailed as a scintillant gem when emitted by a celebrity. Ennius echoed this sentiment in *Hecuba*, and so did Plautus in one of his comedies. Molière lifted it from Plautus:

> Tous les discours sont des sottises
> Partant d'un homme sans éclat;
> Ce seroient paroles exquises,
> Si c'étoit un grand qui parlât.

And Pope from Molière:

> What woful [*sic*] stuff this madrigal would be,
> In some starved hackney sonneteer—or me!
> But let a lord once own the happy lines
> How the wit brightens, how the style refines!

By the same token, anecdotes gain added fillip if linked with people of fame or notoriety. Stories cluster around big names. The more vivid the personality, the stronger its attraction for the stuff of legend. The fact that a reported episode is apocryphal makes no difference.

Nor does it appear to matter that the same anecdote has done service—long and arduous service—in other contexts. The story of how Lincoln, as a rising young lawyer, confounded a witness who swore he saw murder done by moonlight, by showing that there was no moon that night, may be found in Plutarch's account of Alcibiades in connection with the desecration of the statue of Hermes, and also in Chambers' *Book of Days* in another court scene.

Some of the duplications cited above may have been due to coincidence. But most of them were obviously the products of borrowing.

## Joe Miller

There is truth as well as paradox in Harry Hershfield's comment that Joe Miller's jokes have lived on and on, but not as long as comedians have lived on them.

Joe Miller has, of course, become a symbol. He stands for old wheezes. He belongs—nominally, not literally—in that omnivorous company of joke-gatherers who run all the way from the Attic Hierocles to the Bennett Cerf of today.

A man who could neither read nor write, Joe Miller was one of the decidedly lesser lights of the English stage two hundred years ago. He was taciturn to the point of surliness. At the Black Jack, the pub he frequented, his morose disposition and humorless rejoinders became an occasion for raillery. The patrons fell in the habit of derisively hailing as "Joe Miller's jest" any joke that fell flat. When Miller died, leaving his family penniless, the dramatist John Mottley collected all the stray jokes current in London and published them under Miller's name to raise some money for the actor's kin. The book was a huge success, and the grumpy old performer undeservedly won a place in history.

The compilation was by no means a trail blazer. *Hundred Merry Tales* appeared as far back as 1526; its vast popularity was due less to its mirth-provoking qualities than to its preoccupation with sex. Shakespeare knew about it; Beatrice says in *Much Ado about Nothing*: "I had my good wit out of the Hundred Merry Tales." *Tarlton's Jests* followed soon after. Richard Tarlton was a comic whose admirers are said to have included Queen Elizabeth. John Taylor, better known as the Water Poet (he earned his living as a collector of revenue on ship-borne wines), put forth his compendium in 1633. Then Archie Armstrong, court jester to James VI and Charles I, joined the procession with his *Banquet of Jests*.[4]

Read today, none of these volumes is likely to provoke gales of laughter. Their significance lies in the evolutionary relationship between them and modern humor. Here are a few examples.

Taylor's *Wit and Mirth:* A man unused to the sport was taken on a hunt. Someone asked him how he liked the cry. "A pox on the dogs," said he, "they make such a bawling I cannot hear the cry." A latter-day version: Two sightseers passed a church famous for its carillon. The bells began to peal full-throated. One of the sightseers said to the other: "Aren't those bells wonderful?" Unable to hear, his companion cupped a hand at his ear. "What did you say?" "I said, aren't those bells wonderful?" The second fellow shook his head in exasperation. "Can't hear a thing," he shouted, "for those damn bells!"

Armstrong's *Banquet of Jests:* Conversing with two gentlemen at dinner, a Court Lady assured them that she was but forty years old. When the Lady's back was turned, one of the gallants said: "It would require a stronger faith than I have in me to believe this." To which the other replied: "I must believe her, for I have heard her say so time and again during the last ten years." Ancient version: As Cicero advanced in years, it irritated him that his friend and onetime school-mate Vibius Curius persisted in lying about his age. "Then I take it," he told Vibius, "that when we used to practice declamation together, you had not yet been born." Modern version: Jack Benny and his perennial thirty-nine.

*Joe Miller's Jests:* At a public levee at the Court of St. James's, a gentleman said to Lord Chesterfield: "Pray, my Lord, who is that tall awkward woman yonder?" "That lady, sir," replied his Lordship, "is my sister." The gentleman reddened with confusion, and stammered: "No, no, my Lord, I crave your pardon: I meant that ugly woman who stands next to the Queen." "That lady, sir," answered Lord Chesterfield, "is my wife." Modern version: ditto, with switches in time and cast of characters.

## Gag-Stealing

"To accuse a comedian," says John Crosby, the New York *Herald Tribune's* radio and television critic, "of buying material that he can just as easily steal is an affront to the comedian's intelligence. It's a well-recognized fact that money, that filthy stuff, takes some of the bloom off a joke."

In the old days a good comic routine lasted for years. There were vaudeville acts that ran unchanged for decades. Audiences were small. No matter how often a joke was repeated, there were always some people who hadn't heard it before.

The advent of radio changed all that. Practically overnight the humor-supply business was revolutionized as violently as the silent screen had been by the arrival of sound. A monster of devastating voracity had been spawned. If a comedian hoped to stay on the air, he couldn't keep on using his old stuff. He had to assemble a sanhedrin of writers to supply fresh fodder for the insatiable maw. Gag-stealing went big time.

Radio did not initiate larceny; it intensified it. The vaudevillians of yesterday were no innocents. George Burns, Gracie Allen's co-worker, tells of a well-known comedian who made it a practice to drop in at variety and burlesque shows in small towns outside New York. Whenever he heard a joke that struck his fancy, he'd send a wire to the performer, saying: "That's my gag. You've no right to use it. I'll sue you." Since the comic had in all probability stolen it and had a guilty conscience, he'd capitulate without protest.

Burns himself was once the target of attempted hijacking of this kind. While he and Gracie were playing in Buffalo, he ran across a news item which he thought amusing enough to include in their act. A few days later a rival comic met him. "I caught your act the other night," said the comic. "It was good, but that joke happens to be mine." George got angry. "Like hell it is," he said, "I read it in *The Buffalo Courier.*" "Maybe you did," said the comic, "but not in the first edition."[5]

A comedian copied a whole routine from Fred Allen, and used it on the stage. Allen didn't mind; but when the fellow got bold and carried the material to the screen, Allen became angry. He threatened to take legal steps. He knew he couldn't win, but the culprit didn't know it, and made a cash settlement. "The fact is," Allen later confessed to Henry Morgan, "I had taken it all from an Englishman named Hill. He's dead now, or I'd ask him where *he* got it."

All comics borrow; but the champion borrower is probably Milton Berle. Bert Lahr watched Berle on television one evening and was displeased to find that Berle had lifted some of his best stuff. He wired him: DEAR MILTON: SAW YOUR SHOW. I WAS NEVER BETTER. Unable to attend a testimonial dinner to Berle, Morey Amsterdam— who is not a fellow to be casting stones—sent a message that he'd be there in material if not in spirit. "When you see Milton," says Bob Hope, "you're seeing the best things of everybody who has ever been on Broadway." Hope adds: "I enjoy Berle on television. I like to see my jokes as well as hear them." "There was a time," says a critic, "when Berle stole indiscriminately. Now he steals only from the best shows." Berle himself is disarmingly candid about all this. "I listened to Jack Benny the other night," he said on one occasion. "I laughed so hard I almost dropped my pencil and paper."

Gag-stealing has given rise to a special category of gags. Jokesmith Coleman Jacoby, who is improvident enough to squander some of his stock in trade in conversation, met a man who made a habit of eavesdropping on him and selling the gleanings. "I want to congratulate you," Jacoby told him, "on your witty ears."

There is a sharp division of opinion about the ethics of joke-stealing. Some people profess to see no distinction between gag-lifting and the theft of money or physical wares. Others are frankly cynical. The average comic who cries he's been robbed, say the latter, deserves little sympathy because he's probably guilty too; everybody preys on everybody else; all jokes are public property anyhow.

In any case nothing can be done about it. The registration of gags with some agency has been suggested from time to time. The unworkability of any such scheme is only too apparent.

## Pots of Gold

Nowhere is the operation of the success-formula more sharply illustrated than in radio. Let a show prosper, and a flock of imitators will instantly spring into being. There must have been a time, now lost in the mists of the past, when housewives had only *one* soap opera to wring their hearts as they went about their daily chores. There must have been a time when there was only one quiz program to shower dollars on contestants bright enough to know who is buried in Grant's Tomb. There must have been a time when there was only one give-away program, only one amateur show. Look at us now.

Aside from gag-stealing, plagiarism on the radio usually involves the appropriation of a program-idea or a specific program-format or a character or a plot.

As I have already indicated, the law recognizes property rights only in the arrangement, combination and expression of ideas, not in the ideas themselves. Disc-jockey shows, round-tables, old-record programs keep multiplying; so long as the later ones borrow no more than the central concept, there's nothing that the originator can do to stop them. However, if a person copies the originator's individual elaboration of an idea, he becomes liable for infringement, and it makes no difference whether the idea is old or new.

A jury recently returned a staggering verdict—$800,000—in favor of the owners of the *Bride and Groom* show in their million-dollar suit against Station KLAC-TV. The owners had charged that the television program *Wedding Bells* was a piracy of the format of *Bride and Groom*. The case was reported settled for $50,000.

A radio entrepreneur named Jack Stanley devised a program-idea which he called *Hollywood Preview*. It had to do with broadcasting a play over the air and seeking audience participation—with prizes, of course—in the selection of stories and stars for movie production. He had a recording made of a sample program, and tried without success to sell the idea to Columbia Broadcasting. C.B.S. then put on a program of its own called *Hollywood Preview* embodying the same features. While there was nothing new, the Court said, in broadcasting a play, or in the use of the words "Hollywood Preview" in connection with the first public showing of a movie, or in audience participation, the combination of all these elements was novel enough to be entitled to protection. Stanley was awarded $35,000.

Don Ettlinger asked for a quarter of a million dollars, charging that the *Our Miss Brooks* show had been taken from a script he wrote before the series went on the air. He won a judgment for $6,250.

Arthur Kurlan started suit against C.B.S. and others a few years ago over *My Friend Irma*. His story was that he had spent $10,000 in developing a radio program built around *My Sister Eileen;* that he had given the defendants an audition transcription of it; and that they had appropriated it for *My Friend Irma*. He demanded $150,000 in damages. Judge Ashburn summarily dismissed the complaint. The appellate court reversed, and ordered a trial. Since *My Friend Irma* had been on a sustaining basis when the action was started and had afterward gained considerably in popularity and value, Kurlan announced that he would raise his request for damages to $1,500,000. The case is pending.

Neither Gracie Allen nor Jane Ace can afford to point a finger at each other. There was a Dulcy once, and before her, Mrs. Mala-prop.

There are many parallels in radio plots. "The least plausible explanation," says John Crosby, "is that there aren't enough plots to keep the radio fires burning year in and year out, and sooner or later the same device is bound to occur to different writers. Another—and to my skeptical mind more logical—explanation is that the writers are stealing from the same sources and not infrequently from each other."[6]

Where a radio program has been on the air for some time, and has been advertised and generally promoted, the title of it—like the name of a book or a play or a movie—cannot be annexed with impunity.

But there is nothing to prevent the appropriation of a vocal trick. Comedian Mel Blanc lost his half-million dollar suit when he tried to stop the use of his Woody Woodpecker laugh in an unauthorized song.

## Political Thunder

The epitaph that Jefferson penned for his tomb proclaimed him the author of the Declaration of Independence. Accused of having quarried Locke's *Essay on Government,* a tract by James Otis, Richard Henry Lee's resolution on independence, George Mason's draft of the Virginia Bill of Rights, and other sources, Jefferson calmly replied: "I did not consider it as any particular of my charge to invent new ideas altogether and to offer no sentiment which had never been exposed before."

To point out that the phrase "life, liberty and the pursuit of happi-ness" is Locke's and the dictum "all men are born free and equal," Ulpian's, is to miss the essence of the Declaration. It was both the strength and the virtue of Jefferson's conception that he saw the Republic as the logical outgrowth of the roots of liberal tradition that reached back to England and other European countries, and beyond them to the ancient world. He was no solitary oracle, but the eloquent mouthpiece of the people, bent on drawing up a document that would be an expression of the American mind.[7]

On the subject of the borrowing of political ideas generally, I can do no better than to quote Alvin Johnson, President Emeritus of the New School for Social Research:

The theft of thunder is a well-established principle of Democratic polity. Grover Cleveland stole the thunder of Karl Schurz and the Liberal Republicans when he went in for civil service reform. The Populists stole the thunder of the Farmers' Alliance when they adopted the then radical program of regulation of railway rates and the progressive income tax. . . . Bryan, whose silver tongue had sounded ineffectively from the depths of traditional Democratic free trade, stole all the usable thunder of the Populists: free silver, railway regulation, the progressive income tax. . . . Roosevelt the First saw the thunderbolts lying around in Bryan's yard, and stole them. Honest Taft stole nothing and was nothing, but Wilson grabbed thunderbolts where he could find them. Follow the lamentable crew of non-stealers—Harding, Coolidge and Hoover, who came near reducing the U.S.A. to a desolation and a waste. . . . Roosevelt the Second was elected, and what a market for rusty thunderbolts! When the people are a reality, no party can survive on a static program. If either party has something the people want, the other party must steal it, if it can. . . . There is no private property in thunder. It goes to the stronger.[8]

In 1949, Franklin Hugh Ellison, a Brooklyn slot-machine manufacturer, told the newspapers he was entitled to remuneration from the United States to the tune of a billion dollars for the ten-point plan he had devised and tendered to the government in the early 1930's to combat the depression. His ideas had included, he said, the World Bank, the Voice of America, and the devaluation of gold; and F.D.R. had plagiarized them all. He declared that the government had made at least twenty billion dollars from his measures, and he felt that 5 per cent of this was no more than fair compensation. The nation has not thus far evinced any disposition to express its gratitude to Ellison in monetary terms.

Toward the end of World War II, James A. Sullivan, then vice mayor of Yonkers, sent out scores of condolence letters to the families of Yonkers service men whose names appeared on the casualty lists. The letters were remarkable for their depth of feeling and classic simplicity. No wonder. They had been copied practically word for word from Lincoln's poignant note to Mrs. Bixby on the death of her five sons in the Union Army.

## *Without Protection—*

When you devise a new method of bookkeeping or a new way of freezing foods or a new machine for curling hair, you acquire no monopoly in your discovery by writing a book about it and getting a copyright. The Supreme Court of the United States made this clear over seventy years ago:

A treatise on the composition and use of medicines, be they old or new; on the construction and use of ploughs or watches or churns; or on the mixture and application of colors for painting or dyeing; or on the mode of drawing lines to produce the effect of perspective, would be the subject of copyright; but no one would contend that the copyright of the treatise would give the exclusive right to the art or manufacture described therein. To give to the author of the book an exclusive property in the art described therein, when no examination of its novelty has ever been officially made, would be a surprise and a fraud upon the public. That is the province of letters-patent, not of copyright. The claim to an invention or discovery of an art or manufacture must be subjected to the examination of the Patent Office before an exclusive right therein can be obtained; and it can only be secured by a patent from the government. The copyright of a work on mathematical science cannot give to the author an exclusive right to the methods of operation which he propounds, or to the diagrams which he employs to explain them, so as to prevent an engineer from using them whenever occasion requires. The very object of publishing a book on science or the useful arts is to communicate to the world the useful knowledge which it contains. But this object would be frustrated if the knowledge could not be used without incurring the guilt of piracy of the book. And where the art it teaches cannot be used without employing the methods and diagrams used to illustrate the book, or such as are similar to them, such methods and diagrams are to be considered as necessary incidents to the art, and given therewith to the public; not given for the purpose of publication in other works explanatory of the art, but for the purpose of practical application.

Nor can you copyright business ideas like movie theater Bank Nights, curb-service drive-ins, dance marathons, premium schemes, pitch-and-putt golf courses, midget car races, whippet races, beauty contests or roller derbies.

What I've said above applies to cases where the originator puts his idea in operation, and someone else comes along and sets up a similar business. In cases of this kind there's no question of a contractual relationship between the parties involved.

## —and With

The legal picture changes where a man conceives a commercial scheme and communicates it to a specific person. Generally speaking, the originator of an idea can get a court award for its use where there has been an express contract—written or verbal—embodying the understanding of the parties; and if such a contract can be proved, it doesn't matter whether the idea is old or abstract. In the absence of an express contract, however, the originator can recover only if he can show that the idea is novel; that it was reduced to concrete form before disclosure; and that it was revealed under circumstances indicating expectation of pay if it was adopted.

Where a concern affixes a distinctive name or trademark to its goods or services, and builds up a market and a substantial good will, the law will not allow another concern to usurp the same name or mark, or a colorable simulation. Nor will the courts suffer any other business dodge whereby an imitator may pass off his wares for another's. Relief will be given to the injured party under the doctrine of unfair competition.

The Oneida Community Plate people had for years marketed a certain pattern of table silver under the name "Coronation." A competitor sought to market a similar design under a related name. There was evidence that retail dealers were induced to pass off the imitation for the original, and that buyers often confused the two. Judge Davis granted an injunction.

## The Glass of Fashion

"Hundreds of keen-eyed, quick-witted young women earn their living in the garment industry by helping to pirate dress designs. Some scout their employer's rivals. Others concentrate on the high-fashion designers who originate the styles. These are high-class operators. There are perhaps two dozen in New York—young women whose blue-blooded family backgrounds give them unquestioned *entrée* to the salons of the *haute couture* but whose anemic bank accounts do not permit them to buy there. They attend exclusive fashion showings, purchase what seem to be the most likely or striking models and turn them over to the mass manufacturers who copy them. The spy's reward is usually keeping the expensive original."[9]

The law on the subject of design-pilfering is complex and technical. We cannot explore its intricacies within the compass of this book. It will be sufficient, I think, to note that as things now stand, there's no effective way to stop depredations of this kind.

"The piracy of styles or designs," said Judge Shientag in a case, "is a problem of much concern in many important industries, particularly the ladies' garment industry. The formulation of a comprehensive policy is for the legislature rather than the courts. Many elements enter into it. . . . The whole situation is in a state of transition. The problem is how to retain for a man the benefits of his creative genius without at the same time unduly restricting manufacture and trade."

About a decade ago the apparel industry made a determined bid to stamp out the abuse. It organized the Fashion Originators' Guild, the members of which were pledged not to deal with style thieves. The attempt was futile. The Supreme Court deemed the scheme a violation of the antitrust laws, and struck it down.

### Reflections in Stained Glass

Plagiarism has left its impress on pulpit oratory no less than on the physiognomy of houses of worship. So rife was sermon-snatching in nineteenth-century England that it ushered in a whole school of anecdotes.[10] Here are a few:

Dr. South, a distinguished divine widely known for his homiletic talents, was visiting in Sussex and dropped in at a small country church one Sunday morning. The local rector did not know him, but greeted him as a brother of the cloth when the service was over. Dr. South thanked the rector for the edifying sermon he had preached, and suggested that it must have taken a lot of time to prepare. "Oh, no," said the rector with a wave of the hand, "I work rather quickly. It took me just one afternoon to prepare it." "Is that possible?" observed Dr. South. "It took me three weeks to write that very sermon." "Your name is not Dr. South?" said the rector. "It is, sir," said the visitor. "Then," beamed the rector, making a rapid recovery, "I can only say that I am proud to have preached a sermon by the great Dr. South."

Bishop Burnet received a number of complaints about an old cleric on the score of his sermons. He sent for the man and told him: "I am informed that your parish is well satisfied with you in every respect but one. They don't like your preaching. There is no excuse for this. Instead of discoursing at random as I am advised you sometimes do, or giving your own compositions, you have only to preach good printed sermons, and they will have no cause to complain." "May it please your Lordship," replied the parson, "you have been wholly misinformed. I have long been in the habit of preaching printed sermons, and the ones I have preferred have been your Lordship's."

A clergyman who made it a practice to bolster his limited talents with rhetoric borrowed from great divines, put on his customary performance one day. As he thundered forth one grandiloquent passage after another, an erudite and pitiless back-pew critic began to tick off his sources in a penetrating whisper audible to the victim. "That's Hooker," muttered the critic, "that's Barrow, that's South," and so on. Unnerved, the preacher suffered a lapse of memory, and blurted out something witless and ill-phrased. *"That,"* said the critic maliciously, "is your own."

# 16

## The Byways of Plagiarism

What is a great man, but one of great affinities, who takes up into himself all arts, sciences, all knowables, as his food? He can spare nothing; he can dispose of everything. What is not good for virtue, is good for knowledge. Hence his contemporaries tax him with plagiarism.

—Ralph Waldo Emerson: Representative Men

---

OLIVER WENDELL HOLMES—the Autocrat of the Breakfast Table—tells how, having once made a bright impromptu remark to a lady whose guest he was while on a lecture tour, he caught himself repeating the same witticism to the same person at the same place on a later visit. He had given no thought to the remark after he had first uttered it; it had leaped to his lips spontaneously the second time. It did not please him to reflect that his hostess probably believed he made a point of tossing off the identical bon mot wherever he went.

The episode must have bothered him, for he later wrote, with a touch of asperity: "You don't suppose that my remarks are like so many postage stamps, do you—each to be only once uttered? If you do, you are mistaken. He must be a poor creature that does not often repeat himself. Imagine the author of the excellent piece of advice, 'Know thyself,' never alluding to that sentiment again during the course of a protracted existence! Why, the truths a man carries about with him are his tools; and do you think a carpenter is bound to use the same plane but once to smooth a knotty board with, or to hang up his hammer after it has driven its first nail? I shall never repeat a conversation, but an idea often. I shall use the same types when I like, but not commonly the same stereotypes. A thought is often original, though you have uttered it a hundred times. It has come to you over a new route, by a new and express train of associations."

## Self-Plagiarism

The term self-plagiarism is actually a misnomer. When you repeat yourself, there's no false assumption of authorship.[1]

A man can't steal his own umbrella or his own automobile. He *can* (though he may not) steal his own brain child. If he takes a published work of his, alters it here and there, and puts it forward under a new title, he wrongs his first publisher, cheats the second, and swindles his readers. And if the original copyright is held by someone else, both he and his second publisher become liable for infringement.

There are several varieties of self-plagiarism—actual and total duplication; development and elaboration without literal copying; derivation and adaptation; the lifting of passages; recourse to the same themes, views, characters, plots and situations. Some of these uses are unlawful; some are innocent. The legal rules that govern them are the same as those applicable to plagiarism generally.

While Oscar Wilde was a student at Oxford, he won the Newdigate Prize with his poem "Ravenna." To enrich this composition he had plucked generous portions from his earlier "Magdalen Walks" and from his sonnet on Keats' grave. Later he inscribed a sonnet to Lily Langtry which began: "A lily-girl, not made for this world's pain," heedless of the fact that he had previously eulogized a boy in practically the same strain in "Wasted Days," the opening line of which was: "A fair, slim boy, not made for this world's pain."[2]

W. S. Gilbert, of the celebrated team of Gilbert and Sullivan, first made his mark with *The Bab Ballads*. Afterwards he freely confessed that whenever he needed material for the light operas, he simply went to the *Ballads* for it.

In *The Bridge of San Luis Rey* (1927), Thornton Wilder describes Captain Alvarado this way:

He was blackened and cured by all weathers. He stood in the Square with feet apart as though they were planted on a shifting deck. His eyes were strange, unaccustomed to the short range, too used to seizing the appearances of a constellation between a cloud and a cloud, and the outline of a cape in rain. His reticence was sufficiently explained for most of us by his voyages, but the Marquesa de Montemayor had other light on the matter.

The Marquesa explains that Alvarado's daughter had died, and adds: "I think he goes about the hemispheres to pass the time between now and his old age."

Here is the portrait of Captain Philocles from Wilder's *The Woman of Andros* (1930):

He was blackened and cured by all weathers. He stood in the squares of his various ports of call, his feet apart as though they were forever planted on a shifting deck. He seemed to be too large for daily life; his very eyes were strange—unaccustomed to the shorter range, too used to seizing the appearances of a constellation between a cloud and a cloud, and the outlines of a headland in rain. . . . He had been one of the persons whom Chrysis had most loved in her life, and it was she who had discovered his secret. . . . He was passing the time and filling the hours in anticipation of release from a life that had lost its savor with the death of his daughter.

## Motives and Reasons

An author may deliberately repeat something he has already published. He may do so because he feels it's been neglected and deserves reviving, or because he finds it particularly apposite to his new work or because he is badly in need of money, or because his creative energy is unequal to the demands of the public.

Commissions piled up so fast on Perugino, Vasari tells us, that he began to incorporate the same figures and objects in several paintings. His output became mannered and monotonous. When his fellow artists denounced a certain picture of his on this score, Perugino exclaimed: "I have painted in this work the figures you formerly admired. What more can I do?"

Self-plagiarism may be unconscious. Thornton Wilder is a gifted and resourceful writer; he didn't have to duplicate the description of Captain Alvarado. A fair guess is that he first set down the passage in his notebook, took it from there for *The Bridge*, made no entry to that effect, forgot about it, and picked it up again for *The Woman*.

In a broad sense every example of an artist's work bears a resemblance to every other. This resemblance is individuality made manifest.

For whenever a creative person is faced with a certain problem of expression, he will solve it in a way *characteristic* of him—that is to say, in a way consistent with his gifts, his experience, his temperament. Let him encounter the same problem a dozen times in his life, and all the solutions will be similar.[3]

Self-plagiarism must not be confused with the making of replicas for the same patron. The British National Gallery version (*c.* 1506) of Leonardo's "The Virgin of the Rocks" is a virtual transcription of the Louvre version (*c.* 1483) of the same subject by the same master; both were commissioned by the Confraternity of the Immaculate Conception at Milan. Reynolds' portrait of Lavinia, wife of the second Earl Spencer, pleased the Earl so much that he ordered another to give to a member of his family. The copy was faithful enough to cause a lawsuit afterward on a question of authentication.

### Development; Elaboration; Variation

There is a fundamental difference between repetition and reworking. A writer may be so obsessed by an idea, so passionately bent on giving it ultimate perfection of embodiment, that he may return to it again and again, probing deeper, experimenting, rejecting, adding, distilling. A vignette may evolve into a short story, a short story into a novel or a play, a simple refrain into a concerto, a lone figure into a complex pictorial arrangement.

Tennyson's *Lady of Shalott* became the lily maid of Astolat in his *Idylls of the King*. Bulwer-Lytton elaborated an early sketch of his into the Gothic thriller *Zanoni*. Thackeray turned out several treatments of his burlesque story of Richard Coeur de Lion before he hit it off triumphantly in *Rebecca and Rowena*. Joyce's *Stephen Hero* is a sort of first draft of *A Portrait of the Artist as a Young Man*.

There are three variants of Goya's "Majas on a Balcony"; two of Poussin's "The Rape of the Sabine Women"; six of Edvard Munch's "Sick Child."

### Themes; Characters; Devices

"People say these days that I'm stealing from myself," remarks Irving Berlin. "Sure I am. What's wrong with that? Everybody does it. The only difference is that I admit it. I've written fifteen or twenty songs in my life that were *firsts*—new ideas. That's a lot. You write one of those only every five years or so. The rest of the time you have to use the old ideas and try to give them a new twist."

Berlin goes on to say that while he was working on *This Is the Army,* he needed a rhythm number and couldn't get an idea. He went back to "Puttin' on the Ritz," played it and thought about it until he hit on a variation—"What the Well Dressed Man in Harlem Will Wear." "That's all that song is—a remake," says Berlin. "But why should I be ashamed of it? It's a good, workmanlike number. And that's how I keep going. I keep turning out sound, competent songs like that, and people like them. Then, bang, I get a new idea, and there's a great song."

When his *Sixteen Self Sketches* (1949) appeared, George Bernard Shaw warned: "You mustn't expect anything new in it. It is all a repeat of all the things I have said in my other books the last fifty years."

While other creative people aren't as clear-eyed and candid as Berlin and Shaw, their practices bear the same testimony. At any rate, the artist who is distressed to find that he's repeating himself can draw a measure of consolation from the past. He can reflect that about a thousand lines in the *Iliad* are repeated in the *Odyssey*; that Edmund in *King Lear* is no more than Iago's anemic counterpart; that half a dozen of Molière's comedies have identical plots; and that the protagonists in all the Stendhal novels are brothers under the skin.

The younger Dumas' play *Denise* is a rewrite of his earlier *Les Idées de Mme. Aubray.* Many of the characters and episodes that went into de Maupassant's *Bel-Ami, Une Vie, Fort Comme la Morte* and *Notre Cœur* came from his *Le Père Milon,* an obscure volume of fragmentary sketches.[4]

Pirandello was haunted by the theme of the multiple-faceted nature of truth—that the essence of reality is elusive, that each person involved in a situation sees it his own way and rejects everyone else's view. He returned to this idea again and again; it became the central thesis of four of his plays, including *Six Characters in Search of an Author.*

## Ghost Writing

Many publishers appear to be committed to the proposition that readers are consumed by an insatiable curiosity about the affairs and opinions of individuals in the limelight. The proposition may be sound. With the printed page's promise of brief immortality, the publishers do not find it difficult to persuade the luminaries to erect prose memorials for themselves. There is, as a rule, only one hitch. Most of the conquering heroes, sports demigods, ex-monarchs, wonder-medicos, big-game hunters, prima donnas, explorers, ex-office-holders and murderers Who Tell All can't write a line fit to read.

That's where the ghost writer comes in. He gets things down on paper. Sometimes he sticks to what he's told; sometimes he embroiders and exaggerates; sometimes he lets his imagination run wild. But always he remains faceless. The by-line goes to the hero or the heroine.

The coverage of the World Series by noted ballplayers is almost exclusively ghosted by experienced sports writers. Without batting an eyelash, the latter have been known to differ, in their own columns, with the opinions expressed by themselves in ghosted pieces.

Only recently the American University in Washington announced a new course in ghost writing, and the Washington *Post* published an advertisement reading: "The Ghost Artists—We Paint It—You Sign It—Why Not Give an Exhibition?"

The purchasers of a ghosted work don't get what they bargained for: the *ipse dixit* of the man whose signature the work bears. Mr. Justice Frankfurter of the Supreme Court doubtless had this in mind when he said in a recent case: "Ghost-writing has debased the intellectual currency in circulation here, and is a type of counterfeiting which invites no defense. Perhaps this Court renders a public service in treating phantom authors and ghost-writers as legal frauds, and disguised authorship as a deception."

Anita Roddy-Eden sued Milton Berle a short while ago for $250,-000 for breach of a ghost-writing contract. According to her story, the comedian had asked her to write a novel to be published under his name "in order to gain recognition in the literary field"; Berle and she were to share equally in the proceeds; she had done the job and delivered the manuscript; and Berle had refused to let it be published under his name. Berle's defense was that the contract was contrary to public policy and therefore unenforceable. Judge Eder of the New York State Supreme Court agreed with him. He found that the whole plan was "a scheme concocted and devised by the parties to deliberately foist a fraud on the public."

Harsh words, these. But those who discern no mortal sin in literary spooking will argue that the learned judges are taking the matter too seriously; that what's involved mostly is inconsequential and ephemeral screed, not literature; that without ghost writing some valuable facts would either be never revealed or wretchedly presented; and that the public isn't really fooled at all because it is disingenuous enough to know that the majority of the intimate accounts are ghosted.

In any case ghost writing is firmly imbedded in our mores. It is a large-scale, pervasive practice. It reaches way beyond the book, magazine and newspaper business.

The "personal opinions" on national and international affairs that a certain cosmic thinker commits to the air each week with apostolic authority are largely the lucubrations of assistants. Many of the ringing speeches delivered at banquets by captains of finance and industry are skillfully prefabricated by high-priced public relations men.

When screen siren Shelley Winters brightly remarks: "I got one perfect rose for my birthday; I wonder why someone doesn't give me one perfect Cadillac," she's talking pure Dorothy Parker. But it's not Shelley that's speaking. It's the studio publicity man.

Recently a Hollywood director discussed with the studio head a scenario that the company was having a lot of trouble with. "Give me two new writers," said the director, "and I'll do it myself."

Since men of state are generally subjected to every kind of calumny, it is only natural that the employment of literary spooks should be imputed to them. George Washington was accused of having his addresses ghostwritten by Madison. One of the lesser iniquities ascribed to Franklin Delano Roosevelt by his enemies was that all his speeches were a patchwork of the efforts of other men. To be sure, F.D.R. got aid from a battery of adjutants; but even Raymond Moley, who had no love for F.D.R. and broke with him long before he died, has acknowledged the basic inaccuracy of the charge. And Judge Rosenman says: "Nobody ever wrote a speech for the President. We helped him with the speeches. But by the time he got through tearing them to pieces and putting them back together again, they were all his."

There have been some flagrant instances of quasi-ghosting in which the ghost, unaware that he was intended to serve as such, was misled no less than the public. When Mozart agreed to accept a hundred ducats from an emissary of Count Walsegg to compose a requiem, he was not told that it was the Count's intention (which he later carried out) to have the work performed as his own.[5]

## Ghosts: Wholesale

Marcus Licinius Crassus, the Roman politico who served as triumvir with Pompey and Caesar two thousand years ago, may have been the first man to assemble and maintain a staff of ghost writers. He followed all the slave auctions zealously, and bid high whenever a serviceable poet was put on the block.

Van Dyck's apprentices painted large portions of his portraits. Since the Flemish master had a regular scale of prices depending on the amount of his personal contribution to each commission—the charge was less if he did only the face and hands, more if he added the clothing, and still more if he completed the background—there was no question of imposture. With Rossetti and Corot it was a different story. At the height of his vogue Rossetti took delight in foisting on gullible millionaires his pupils' work as his own. To assist his less fortunate colleagues, Corot would add a few of his characteristic touches to their pictures, and affix his name.

But it was the elder Dumas who pushed production-by-ghosts to the limit. To judge by the Calmann-Lévy edition of his works, his output totaled three hundred solid volumes, which included ninety-two novels and sixty-seven plays. He was a man of prodigious industry and phenomenal fertility of invention: he once made a bet of a hundred louis that he could complete the first volume of his projected *Chevalier de Maison Rouge* in seventy-two hours, including time out for sleep and meals, and he did it in sixty-six hours. Even so no single individual could have produced so mountainous a quantity of material unaided. He ran a literary factory.

He was bitterly criticized. An envious contemporary of his, Eugene de Mirecourt, haled him before the Société des Gens de Lettres, and denounced his activities as a fraud on the public, an injury to his assistants, and a blot on literature. The Société listened politely and did nothing.

Dumas took a good-natured view of the shafts leveled against him. One day an admirer, having praised his books, told him that he had found a geographical error in one of them. "Which one?" asked Dumas. "*Le Chevalier d' Harmontal.*" "The devil!" said Dumas. "I haven't read it. Let me see, who was it that wrote that one for me? Why, that rascal Auguste! I'll take care of *him*!"

On another occasion Dumas visited a village to get some historical data for a novel. "And so, Monsieur Dumas," the local antiquarian taunted him, "you're going to write a novel yourself this time?" "Oh, yes," replied Dumas. "I got my valet to do the last one, but as it was very successful the scoundrel demanded such an exorbitant raise that to my great regret I've had to let him go."

In his *Souvenirs Dramatiques*, Dumas wrote: "Of two collaborators one is generally the dupe, and that one is the man of talent. For your collaborator is like a passenger who has embarked on the same ship with you and who gradually reveals to you that he cannot swim. When shipwreck comes you have to keep him afloat at the risk of drowning yourself; and when you reach land, he goes around telling everybody that without him you would have perished."

The truth is that Dumas was anything but a false-front. His "collaborators" weren't collaborators at all; they merely supplied him the clay into which he infused miraculous life. Auguste Maquet, said to have been the ablest of Dumas' helpers, wrote on his own too. Without the master, Maquet was nothing. Without Maquet, Dumas was still Dumas.

Colette, hailed by Glenway Wescott as the greatest living French fiction-writer, got her start in a literary factory. She ran away from home when she was under twenty, and married Henri Gauthier-Villars. Henri was a small-time entrepreneur with a string of starveling novelists on his payroll; he purveyed their output as his own, under the pen-name Willy. Colette became one of the factory hands. Her first six books appeared under Henri's pseudonym, and captured the public.

### Plagiarism in Reverse

To gain a wider and more heedful audience, the early Christian preceptors often ascribed the authorship of their commentaries to one or another of the apostles.

Olivier Basselin was a fifteenth-century scapegrace notorious in his time for his unquenchable thirst, and remembered in ours for the rollicking drinking songs attributed to him. Actually the songs were composed by Jean le Houx, a Catholic lawyer of Vire, who followed Basselin by some two hundred years. Le Houx was a pillar of respectability in his community. While it gave him pleasure, in the privacy of his study, to celebrate the delights of the cup in many a lusty stanza, he was not disposed to associate himself with his dithyrambs. So he credited them to Basselin. He achieved three things by this simple expedient: he gave currency to his poems, he remained anonymous, and he had his secret joke.

Rudolf Erich Raspe, court professor and privy councilor to Frederik II, Landgrave of Hess, and later a fugitive in England—he had thoughtlessly pawned some of the Landgrave's medallions to pay his creditors—denied to the end of his days that he was the author of *Baron Munchausen.*

Early in his career Fritz Kreisler began playing violin pieces which he listed on the programs as arrangements of compositions by such long-dead men as Vivaldi, Couperin, Pugnani and Padre Martini. He kept this up for thirty years. In 1935, Olin Downes, music critic of *The New York Times,* thought he'd like to take a look at the originals. He couldn't find them. They didn't exist. Irked by the limitations of his repertoire, and fearful of censure if he openly played too many of his own pieces, Kreisler had simply made them up and ascribed them to the masters.

Several of the compositions of Dr. Hans Kindler, founder and conductor of the National Symphony Orchestra, got rough handling from the critics. In 1946 he conducted *Pacific Nocturne* which, according to the program note, had been written by "Phillip Henry, a young naval lieutenant, while on duty in the Pacific." The reviewers extolled it. A year and a half later Dr. Kindler made a confession. Phillip Henry was a figment of his fancy; he had invented him to have some fun at the critics' expense.

Many an embittered literary novice, faced with a mounting pile of rejection slips, has made the complaint that publishers and producers buy names, not works. There's a story about a little-known playwright who went to Hollywood and, his wares under arm, knocked on the doors of all the studios. He was met with stony disinterest. He then removed the title page of each play, and substituted another specifying Ferenc Molnár as the dramatist. Posing as

Molnár's agent, he resubmitted the plays. One of the major companies rose to the bait. The purported agent was sent for; he stood by while the story editor praised the script and began to discuss terms. The playwright's big moment was at hand. "Mr. Molnár has authorized me to say," he told the man, "that if the play wasn't good enough for you when I wrote it, it can't be any better even if he's supposed to have written it."

## Pseudonyms

While Max Marcin's play *The House of Glass* was in rehearsal, Sam Harris, who was producing the show with George M. Cohan, summoned Marcin and pounced on him with vials of wrath overflowing. "I've just seen a short story called 'The Probationer,' " he stormed. "It's by Hilary Blake, and you've stolen your play from it!" "I am Hilary Blake," Marcin told him. "I am also Christopher Wright, Creighton Tolerance and Donald Dawson. In fact, Mr. Harris, I'm even Lillian Larkin."[6]

Fear of hurt to reputation, predilection for privacy, excessive modesty, desire to avoid reprisal, sheer prankishness, recognition of the unwisdom of glutting the market—any one of these things may impel an author to dissociate himself from his brain child.

Defoe, Swift, Pope, Dr. Johnson, Gibbon, Walpole and Goldsmith all used pseudonyms on occasion. Dodgson the mathematician steadfastly refused to recognize his alter ego, the Lewis Carroll of *Alice in Wonderland* and *Through the Looking-Glass*. When Queen Victoria, charmed by Alice, sent word that she would be glad to sponsor Dodgson's next work, he responded by gravely tendering to her the manuscript of his new book. It was *An Elementary Treatise on Determinants*.

Eminent as an art scholar and critic, Willard Huntington Wright thought it might be fun to try his hand at whodunits. He was apprehensive about jeopardizing his name. He became famous as S. S. Van Dine, the creator of Philo Vance.

Boswell availed himself of about fifty different pseudonyms during his career. He may well be the all-time champion. However, there are plenty of others who run close. The indefatigable Frederick Faust, better known as Max Brand, used dozens of aliases in connection with his hundred and thirty published novels. Georges Simenon, memorialist of the adventures of Inspector Maigret, has a string of seventeen of them.[7]

It need hardly be said that a writer can sue for infringement if the copyrighted work to which his pen name is affixed is plagiarized.

### Hoaxes and Forgeries

During the Renaissance many an ancient text was presented as a new work, and many a new work bore a name ancient and celebrated. Indeed, Jean Hardouin, the skeptical Jesuit, asserted that practically all classical literature—including *The Aeneid* and the *Odes* of Horace —had been fabricated in the thirteenth century by a society of monastic scholars.[8]

Sigonius was a sixteenth-century master of the style of Cicero. Emboldened by his imitative skill, he published a dissertation entitled *De Consolatione* as a recently discovered composition by the Roman orator. The counterfeit deceived many until it was exposed by Lipsius three hundred years later.

Edmund Burke made a wager that he could ape Lord Bolingbroke to the point of confounding the experts. So faithfully did he, in his "Vindication of Natural Society," reproduce the manner and the spirit of his model that the essay passed for a long time as Bolingbroke's.

Thomas Chatterton, the youthful prodigy who came to a tragic end at the age of eighteen, ascribed the authorship of his *Rowley Poems* to an imaginary fifteenth-century monk, and deceived many antiquarians. In the latter part of the eighteenth century James Macpherson published a collection of poems of his own composition, claiming to have translated them from an ancient manuscript by the legendary Gaelic bard Ossian.

Two elaborate hoaxes marked the launching of Prosper Mérimée's literary career. He published *Théâtre de Clara Gazul,* a set of plays purportedly written by a beautiful Spanish actress, whose fictitious picture and biography were given; and *La Guzla,* a book of ballads said to have been translated from the Illyrian.[9]

Michelangelo carved a sleeping Cupid, broke off an arm, and buried the statue in a place where he knew it would soon be found. Unearthed, it was acclaimed as a precious relic of antiquity. It was sold to the Cardinal of St. George, to whom Michelangelo ultimately exposed the hoax by joining to the Cupid the arm he had kept.

Embittered by the recognition given to the works of Dürer, Lucas of Leyden and others of that school, while he himself languished in obscurity, the Renaissance painter Hendrik Goltzius engraved six plates in the manner of these masters to demonstrate he was as good as they were. His "Dürer" was hailed immediately as one of the finest things the famous German had ever turned out.

The trouble with a hoax is that, however innocuous its inception, it may get out of hand and do damage. Michelangelo doubtless got a lot of sardonic amusement out of the Cupid affair. It is conceivable that the Cardinal of St. George, who had parted with a thousand crowns for the disinterred "antiquity," considered the episode less hilarious.

The dividing line between a hoax and forgery is narrow but clear. It is intent and result that count. A hoax that keeps within the bounds of a practical joke won't land its perpetrator in court. A fake sold as an original probably will.

"There was some years since," observed the London *Weekly Oracle* in 1737, "a Painter (now dead) who had a dexterous Hand at making a Titian, a Guido, or an Angelo, by roasting them in a Chimney over a proper fire. This Painter, for want of a Name, could scarce get three guineas for an original of his own, but has had as many hundred for a copy from a Man of Quality, who imagined himself one of the greater Connoisseurs of the Age."

In our own time, the Dutch painter Han Van Meegeren made nearly three million dollars by faking seventeenth-century masterpieces, one of which he managed to sell to that noble-spirited art lover Hermann Göring. Discredited, Van Meegeren died in prison in 1947.[10]

### Piracy Primers

Of all the oddities in plagiarism, perhaps the oddest is that which has to do with instruction in thievery.

In 1677 Sieur de Richesource gave the world a manual of literary larceny, *Le Masque des Orateurs*, in which he described at length methods for altering filched material in such a way as to escape detection.

Then there was that engaging compatriot of Richesource, Count de Maubec de la Dentdulynx. A picturesque rakehell who enlivened the social scene in eighteenth-century Provençe, the Count penned a treatise, *A la Louange des Plagiats*, in which he ridiculed contemporaries of his who dabbled in verse and whose borrowings were only too apparent. He gave them these rules for covering up their tracks:

1. Shun the literal language of the poetaster (*rimailleur*) you propose to pluck. Where he is verbose, be concise. Where he is laconic, have a glib tongue (*la langue bien pendue*).
2. Disguise the characters. Shift the places. Advance or reverse the time.
3. Gather your booty from sources not readily accessible.
4. Steal from a number of authors, and so commingle your spoils that no single person may denounce you with certainty of success.
5. Be discreet. Guard against suspicion. Confide in no one.
6. If you are accused, make a flat denial. Present a countenance of hurt dignity.
7. When all else fails, smile amiably, spread your hands and confess. Remind those who denounce you that in the field of letters, as in many others, everything is at the mercy of anyone (*tout y est au pillage*).

Unhappily the Count was cut down in his prime. Finding, in an anonymous volume, some amatory poems that struck his fancy, he copied them and—in disregard of his own precepts—made no changes. He presented them as his own to Mademoiselle de La Troumelle, whose favor he was ardently seeking at the time. The Mademoiselle was the mistress of Prince des Boscénos. She showed the tender apostrophes to the Prince. He, as it turned out, was the anonymous poet. He killed the Count in a duel, proving that plagiarism can on occasion be fatal.[11]

# 17

# The Ethics of Plagiarism

*The anatomy of mind, as that of the body, must perpetually exhibit the same appearances.*
—Samuel Johnson: The Adventurer, No. 95

ONCE a piece of literary property is put in circulation, it becomes highly pilferable. You can't fence in a story or chain it down or lock it in a safe deposit box. You can copyright it, of course, and erect a NO TRESPASSING sign in the form of a copyright notice, but all that does is give you remedies against a larcenist *after* he's done his deed.

The theft of a product of the mind is more than a legal wrong. It is a moral wrong as well.

Voltaire assayed the moral issue with characteristic tolerance. "Of all the forms of theft," he averred, "plagiarism is the least dangerous to society." Erasmus was cynical, or pretended to be. "Those are wise," he said, "who publish under their names the works of another, thinking that if accused of plagiarism they will in the meantime have profited by it."

There are others who see in piracy the quintessence of meanness, with the meanness in direct ratio to the amount of honor attained by the misdeed. Edgar Allan Poe was a vigorous exponent of this school. "The ordinary pickpocket," he wrote, "filches a purse, and the matter is at an end. He neither takes honor to himself, openly, on the score of the purloined purse, nor does he subject the individual robbed to the charge of pickpocketism in his own person. By so much the less odious is he, then, than the filcher of literary property. It is impossible to imagine a more sickening spectacle than that of the plagiarist, who walks among mankind with an erecter step, and who feels his heart beat with a prouder impulse on account of plaudits which he is conscious are the due of another. It is the purity, the nobility, the ethereality of just fame, it is the contrast between this ethereality and the grossness of the crime, which places the sin of plagiarism in so detestable a light. We are horror-stricken to find existing in the same bosom the soul-uplifting thirst for fame and the debasing propensity to pilfer. It is the anomaly, the discord, which so gravely offends."[1]

## The Clashing Triad

The fact that ethics, art and the law take divergent views of borrowing has done much to confuse appraisals of plagiarism.

Ethics asks: Has the borrower acted fairly and honorably in taking and using the material involved?

Art asks: What has he done with it? Has he debased it? Or has he refashioned and improved it?

The law asks: Has he copied an essential or substantial portion of copyrighted and copyrightable matter?

Ethics is primarily concerned with intent. It takes for granted that the artist, like his fellows, can tell right from wrong. It condemns him only if he steals knowingly and willfully. It condones unconscious plagiarism, but it forbids the conscious variety even where the taker has bettered the original.

Art disregards ethics. It deems intent irrelevant. It addresses itself solely to the quality of the result. It deprecates copying that disfigures. It justifies any taking that yields a superior work. Hume said of the Puritans: "Bear-baiting was esteemed heathenish and un-Christian: the sport, not the inhumanity, gave offense." Art forgives Macaulay for cribbing the thought, for he has expressed it with greater incisiveness and felicity: "The Puritans hated bear-baiting, not because it gave pain to the bear but because it gave pleasure to the spectators."

The law heeds neither good faith nor excellence of result. It holds the unconscious plagiarist liable. It recognizes that qualitative appraisals are at the mercy of shifting values and warring critical standards. It knows that the super-sage does not exist who can say with unerring certainty that one story or picture or song is better than another. For over two hundred years Vermeer languished in obscurity; today he is enthroned among the immortals. The nineteenth century paid homage to Bouguereau and neglected Rousseau; Bouguereau's stock has gone way down and Rousseau's way up. No wonder judges fear to rush in where critics boldly tread.

In historical studies, manifestoes, debates and critical evaluations, ethics and aesthetics hold sway. In the courts, the law is sovereign. To reconcile the warring criteria of the three seems impossible.

## Ethics and the Artist

Morality is a perplexing subject. It is particularly knotty and contradictory in art.

It's easy enough to reel off the vintage platitudes: that art spurns conventions; that it has a higher morality of its own; that it's a law unto itself; that an artist who is striving with all his might to give shape to his conception can't be expected to pause and ponder the niceties of property rights; and that it's forgivable for a man to put himself in another's debt as long as he puts the world in *his* debt.

These generalizations are true enough. But they don't go to the heart of the matter.

First of all, they imply that the artist, in placing himself above the law, symbolizes a kind of moral anarchy peculiar to his breed, while his uncreative fellows adhere to the standards of honor that he scorns. To be sure, there have been artists who beat their wives, starved their children, cheated their creditors, indulged in profligacy. Yet there is no evidence that, on the whole, the man of talent is any more prone to rascality than his ungifted fellows. It's just that his delinquencies, having the glamour of Bohemia, have been more widely publicized.

Second, a distinction must be made between ethics in art and ethics in personal conduct. The artist who lies, steals, betrays and seduces without a qualm may be the soul of honor in his work. Marlowe was killed by a man he sought to knife. Villon was a marauding rogue. Coleridge took drugs. Suckling was a cardsharp. Toulouse-Lautrec preferred brothels to salons. No one has impugned the artistic integrity of any of these men.

Third, the artist is a member of society. Try as he may, he can't put himself beyond the law. It's all very well to speak of the split between art as expression and art as communication, and to argue that the creative process ceases the moment the last word of a sonnet is recorded, the last brush-stroke applied to a canvas, the last musical note set down on ruled paper. The process may cease, but the career of the product has just begun. The artist must have an audience. He certainly must have one if he's to earn a living or build a reputation. The moment he publishes his work he must reckon with the law— the libel law, the obscenity law, the copyright law.

Finally, the copyright law is a shield as well as a sword. Sooner or later every artist with a modicum of sense comes to realize that if the law deters him from robbing his neighbor's orchard, it also deters his neighbor from robbing his. It is usually the pretender-to-talent, not the genuine creator, who, caught in the act of cribbing, bombilates fiercely in favor of unfettered borrowing, but roars with even greater ferocity when someone lifts a paragraph from him.

### Thrust and Parry

The reactions, responses and attitudes of artists charged with theft afford an illuminating and diverting insight into ethics-in-action.

Some men confess their guilt with disarming readiness. Some avow their innocence. Some content themselves with a shrug. Some are coldly contemptuous. Some blaze up with indignation. A few offer ingenious explanations. Many submit pleas in extenuation.

"If that severe doom of Synesius be true," says Burton in *The Anatomy of Melancholy,* "that it is a greater offense to steal dead men's labours than their clothes, what shall become of most writers? I hold up my head at the bar among others, and am guilty of felony of this kind. . . . I am content to be pressed with the rest." "We do not disdain," says Fielding, "to borrow wit or wisdom from any man who is capable of lending us either."

The French poet Desportes stole wholesale from the Italians. Exposed, he calmly informed the critic who had denounced him that if he had known the critic's design, he could have furnished him with many more damning instances than the critic had marshalled. André Chénier echoed this centuries later:

Un juge sourcilleux, épiant mes ouvrages,
Tout à coup, à grands cris, dénonce vingt passages,
Traduits de tel auteur qu'il nomme; et, les trouvant,
Il s'admire et se plaît a se croire si savant.
Que ne vient-il vers moi? Je lui ferai connaître
Mille de mes larcins qu'il ignore peut-être. . . .

"I am not so often witty as I should like to be," writes C. E. M. Joad, "and I have been accustomed to make good the deficiency by remembering the wit of others. I defend myself by pointing out that appropriate remarks are meant to be appropriated." Gouverneur Morris says: "I wish people wouldn't write and tell me that my story "The Malaga Grapes" is stolen out of *The Arabian Nights*. I know it!"

## *The Bold Front*

A rival of Byron's came upon him in the act of marking up a volume he was reading. "What are you doing?" asked the man pointedly. Byron replied: "I am trying to crib, as I do whenever I can, and that's the way I get the character of an original poet."

When an acquaintance chaffed the elder Dumas about material he had lifted from Chateaubriand, the master retorted: "*Mon ami*, that passage is a daughter I've saved from bad company."

Charles Reade, who gave us *The Cloister and the Hearth*, put considerable chunks of Swift's *Polite Conversation* into his *The Wandering Air*; his *Knightsbridge Mystery* was an almost literal reproduction of *The Murder at the Swan Inn*. Excoriated by anonymous critics, he dodged the issue and instead blasted his accusers as "anonymuncula, pseudonymuncula and skunkula, ambushed behind masked batteries." But when his play *White Lies* turned out to be a direct translation of a drama by Auguste Maquet—the Maquet of Dumas' fiction-factory—Reade found it impossible to deflect the mounting censure with abuse. He changed his tack. He took the position that he had bought the original from Maquet; having paid for it, he saw no reason why he shouldn't use it any way he wished, even to the point of affixing his name to it.

"My plots and characters," Israel Zangwill told a heckler, "I get from manuscripts submitted to me by young authors whose clever but crude ideas I hate to see wasted."

When Pierre Jean Jouve's

> Voir un univers dans un grain de sable
> Et dans une fleur sauvage le Ciel
> Et dans la paume de votre main la Sacrée Infinité
> Et dans une heure l'éternité.

was exposed as a word-for-word translation—without so stating— of Blake's

> To see the World in a grain of sand,
> And a Heaven in a wild flower,
> Hold Infinity in the palm of your hand,
> And Eternity in a hour.

the French poet asserted, with icy snobbishness, that he had acted with malice aforethought; his contemporaries were stupid clods unaware of Blake, and it gave him pleasure to pull the wool over their eyes.

### Pleas in Mitigation

"Though there were many giants of old in Physics and Philosophy," says Donne, "yet I say with Didacus Stella: a dwarf standing on the shoulder of a giant may see farther than the giant himself."

"Nothing is sillier," says Heine, "than this talk of plagiarism. There is no sixth commandment in art. The poet dare help himself wherever he wishes—wherever he finds material suited to his work. He may even appropriate entire columns with their carved capitals, if the temple he thus supports is a beautiful one." Dr. Johnson's dictum, that authors are like privateers, always fair game for one another, is echoed in Bernard De Voto's "All writers are cannibals; they've got to live on each other."

Since the days of Aristophanes, men of letters have tried to justify borrowing on a variety of grounds. Here are some of their excuses:

1. *Everything has been said. We can do no more than repeat what others have uttered before us.* Terence made this observation two thousand years ago. It was not new then, it has since been reiterated times without number. The French playwright Alexandre Piron gave it a twist: the writings of the ancients, he said, were thoughts stolen from us in anticipation.

2. *He who rescues material from oblivion and gives it fresh currency deserves praise, not reproof.* "If I take an old plot from a play that has been a dead failure and redress it, put living words into the mouths of its characters, give it the proper technique and action that it lacks, make it an actable play and so a successful one," says Dion Boucicault, "I claim that the play is mine, for I have made from a dead a living thing."

3. *Our cultural heritage is a storehouse anyone may freely draw from.* If, while exploring this treasure-chamber, a writer finds a perfect vestment for his thought, there's no reason why he shouldn't carry it off. The wealth is there to be taken, circulated and enjoyed, not to be hoarded. "The ancients," says Fielding, "may be considered as a rich common, where every person who hath the smallest tenement in Parnassus hath a free right to fatten his muse. Or, to place it in a clearer light, we moderns are to the ancients what the poor are to the rich."

4. *A man can't be blamed for the wiles and deceits of his unconscious.* "It is almost impossible," says Sterne, "for anyone who reads much and reflects a good deal, to be able on every occasion to determine whether a thought is another's or his own. I have several times quoted sentences out of my own writings, in aid of my own arguments, thinking that I was supporting them by better authority."[2]

5. *Everybody steals, and it all evens up at the end.* Said Charles Nodier: "I have plagiarized the plagiarists of Sterne, who plagiarized Swift, who plagiarized Reboul, who plagiarized Guillaume des Autels, who plagiarized Rabelais, who plagiarized Morus, who plagiarized Erasmus, who plagiarized Lucian—or Lucius of Patras or Apuleius—for you can't tell which one of these three stole from the other two." Since Arthur Brooke's metrical romance about the Montagus and the Capulets was founded on a French translation of Bandello's story, which in turn was based on an old Italian tale, there was little reason for Shakespeare to have qualms about quarrying the Brooke version for *Romeo and Juliet.* That the Bard was not unaware of the endless chain of borrowing—that, indeed, he saw it as a rule of life—we find evidence of in *Timon of Athens*:

> The sun's a thief, and with his great attraction
> Robs the vast sea; the moon's an arrant thief,
> And her pale fire she snatches from the sun:

> The sea's a thief, whose liquid surge resolves
> The moon into salt tears: the earth's a thief,
> That feeds and breeds by a composture stolen
> From general excrement: each thing's a thief;
> The laws, your curb and whip, in their rough power
> Have uncheck'd theft.

6. *It's all right to lift material so long as you improve it.* "The bees pillage the flowers here and there," says Montaigne, "but they make honey of them which is all their own; it is no longer thyme or marjolaine. So the pieces borrowed from others [the artist] will transform and mix up into a work all his own." "Let no one argue," warns Pascal, "that I have said nothing new. The arrangement of the matter is new. In a game of tennis, both players use the same ball; but one of the players is better than the other." And Lowell: "Though old the thought and oft expressed, 'Tis his at last who says it best."

7. *There's nothing wrong in exploiting the classics.* "If I have taken anything from the Greeks and Romans," says Scudéry, postulating a criterion based on time, "I've taken nothing from the Italians, the Spaniards or the French, for it seems to me that what constitutes study among the ancients is theft among the moderns." The Chevalier Marin offers a geographical yardstick: "To take from one's compatriots is theft; to take from foreigners, conquest."

8. *Great men are a class apart, with special privileges and immunities.* "He invades authors like a monarch," says Dryden, speaking of Jonson, "and what would be theft in other poets is only victory in him." "As crowned heads have the right," says the creator of *Tristram Shandy*, "to call in the specie of a state and raise its value by their own impression, so there are certain prerogative geniuses who are above plagiaries, who cannot be said to steal, but, from their improvement of a thought, rather to borrow it, and repay the commonwealth of letters with interest; and may more properly be said to adopt than to kidnap a sentiment, by leaving it heir to their own fame." "The man of genius," insists the elder Dumas, "does not steal. He conquers, and what he conquers he annexes to his empire. He makes laws for it, peoples it with his subjects and extends his golden sceptre over it. And where is the man who, on surveying this beautiful kingdom, shall dare to assert that this or that piece of land is not part of the conqueror's property?"

9. *Plagiarism is a form of tribute.* A man takes only what he admires. "Milton's borrowings from Dante," says Alfred George Gardiner, "are abundant, but they are done in the grand manner, as of a prince taking a loan from an equal, not because he needs it, but because of their high companionship and their starry discourse. To be plagiarized by Milton would be no grievance, but a crowning distinction. It would be a title deed to immortality."[3]

## Credit Bestowed

A borrower may acknowledge his source. Or he may decide to make no reference to it. The ethical nature of his act or omission will depend on (a) the amount of his appropriation, (b) whether the source is so familiar as to need no specification, and (c) the form of the acknowledgment, if there is one.

Layamon, the thirteenth-century English priest, freely admits that in composing *Brut* (*c.* 1200) "he took the English book that Saint Bede made; another he took, in Latin, that Saint Albin made, and the fair Austin who brought baptism in hither; the third book he took that a French clerk made, who was named Wace and who well could write."

*"Omne meum, nihil meum,"* writes Burton. "I have wronged no authors, but given every man his own. . . . I cite and quote mine originals."

In the prologue to his version of *Titus Andronicus*, Edward Ravenscroft tells the reader that

> Like other poets, he'll not proudly scorn
> To own that he but winnowed Shakespeare's corn.

"Because I have had many of these jests by relation and hearsay," says John Taylor, the Water Poet, in the foreword to his compilation of jokes, "some of them may be in print in some other authors, which I do assure you is more than I do know. If it be so, I pray you but to condone and tolerate, and let the authors make twice as bold with me at any time."

"I claim as a notable merit in the authorship of this play," says George Bernard Shaw of *Captain Brassbound's Conversion*, which is laid in Mogador, a seaport on the west coast of Morocco, "that I have been intelligent enough to steal its scenery, its surroundings, its atmosphere, its geography, its knowledge of the east, its fascinating Cadis and Krooboys and Sheikhs and mud castles from an excellent book of philosophic travel and vivid adventure entitled *Mogreb-el-Acksa* (Morocco the Most Holy) by Cunninghame Graham. My own first hand knowledge of Morocco is based on a morning's walk through Tangier, and a cursory observation of the coast through a binocular from the deck of an Orient steamer, both later in date than the writing of the play."

Some authors are neurotically over-scrupulous in avowing their obligations. They're not content to doff their hats and bow: they must render an itemization.

Thomas Watson, the sixteenth-century poet, appended to each poem in *Hecatompathia, or Passionate Century of Love* a glossary of the French, Italian and classical compositions from which he drew his inspiration. Thomas Gray did the same thing in the 1768 edition of his poems. "The parallel passages," he remarked, "I insert out of justice to those writers from whom I happened to take the hint of any line, as far as I can recollect." T. S. Eliot affixed to *The Waste Land* seven pages of notes indicating his Elizabethan and Italian sources.

Acknowledgment may be specific, as where quotation marks or footnotes are used to identify the source. It may be general, as where an author states in his foreword that in assembling his book he has drawn on such-and-such works. Ordinarily the giving of credit is a badge of good faith. But excessive quotation marks and footnotes may also be evidence of timidity or ostentatious erudition, just as a blanket acknowledgment, while conveying an air of generosity, may be a cover-up for unconscionable borrowing.

About thirty years ago Dr. Eaglefield-Hull said in the preface to his *Music: Classical, Romantic and Modern*:

This book I have made for my own pleasure; I have taken stones for my walls, and tiles for my floors wherever good material came to hand, without always troubling to acknowledge it when the lifting is as apparent as the use of the stones and columns from Hadrian's Wall by the church-builders of Northumberland. Such an adaptation of warlike material to peaceful ends I hold entirely justifiable.

With ostensible magnanimity Dr. Hull then named a few writers whose works he had profited by. It was soon discovered that his conception of stones and tiles was a weird one: he had taken whole walls and chambers from the literary structures of two men whom he did not even mention. He was exposed by the musicologist Percy A. Scholes, who pointed out that a blanket acknowledgment was no moral justification for extensive lifting without quotation or ascription, and that a borrower compounded his wrong where, though he gave general credit to specific persons, he levied substantially on someone unnamed.

### Credit Withheld

Gustavus Myers, master researcher, spent long and weary years digging out the data that went into his weighty *History of the Great American Fortunes*. It darkened his life that the glib writers who followed him dipped so cavalierly into the wealth of facts he had assembled, and never troubled to admit it.

Writers who omit credit do so for a variety of reasons: because they desire to convey the impression that all the nuggets imbedded in their handiwork are their own; because they're negligent; because they realize that in a plagiarism suit non-access is a strong defense, and that acknowledgment destroys this plea.

Too, a man may quote something in the honest belief that his source is so well known as to call for no identification. When you say: "He jests at scars who never felt a wound" or "For men may come and men may go but I go on forever" or "Hope is a good breakfast but it is a bad supper" without citing Shakespeare, Tennyson and Bacon, respectively, you've not trying to impose on the public or to deprive the great of their due. You simply assume your audience will know that you're quoting, and whom.

"My borrowings," said Montaigne in his essay "On Books," "are all or very nearly all from names so famous and ancient that they seem to me to declare themselves without me." He gave an added reason for not specifying his sources:

As for opinions, comparisons, arguments, if I transplant some of those into my fields and mingle them with my own, I have purposely concealed the author, thereby to hold in check the temerity of those hasty judgments which fall upon every sort of writing, especially the recent writings of men still living and in the vulgar tongue, which permits all the world to talk of them and seems to prove the conception and the design to be vulgar, also. I would have them give Plutarch a fillip on my nose, and excite themselves to insult Seneca in me.

When George Bernard Shaw dramatized his novel *Cashel Byron's Profession*, he sounded a similar warning. He had purposely inserted in the script, he said, choice bits from Shakespeare and Marlowe. If anyone was minded to deride this passage or that, he'd run the risk of disparaging *Hamlet* or *Doctor Faustus*.

Goldsmith—whose own escutcheon was not wholly without stain—once reproached a borrower for his ungenerosity, saying that "a trifling acknowledgment would have made that a lawful prize which may now be considered as plunder." Goldsmith was expressing an ethical judgment, not a legal one. Credit is primarily a matter of conscience. The giving of it doesn't make an unlawful use lawful. The withholding of it doesn't make a lawful use unlawful.

## Lyons Versus Cerf

Granted the most generous salute, a moral question still remains. *How much* may a man lift? At what point does reference to one's creditor cease to be a gracious gesture and become an excuse for picking his pockets? Does it make any difference, for ethical purposes, whether the victim is dead or alive, whether the material is in or out of copyright?

More specifically, can anyone acquire exclusive rights in a gag or sally of general currency? In the utterance, public or private, of a celebrity? In an actual incident? If so, under what circumstances? And if these items are not ordinarily susceptible of ownership, does it alter the situation if the original chronicler obtained them by direct contact and not by hearsay? What, if any, is the relevance and impact of such factors as the first gatherer's calling, the borrower's purpose, the ratio between the quantity taken and the total source, and the ratio between the quantity taken and the borrower's whole work?

All these questions came to the fore in the controversy which flared up a few years ago between newspaper columnist Leonard Lyons and publisher Bennett Cerf. The bone of contention was Cerf's *Try and Stop Me*, a collection of anecdotes. In the preface Cerf indicated the method he had used in compiling it. To supplement his memory, he said, he had pored through countless issues of magazines. He had devoured reams of columns by Winchell, Lyons, Sobol, Wilson,

Skolsky, Hoffman, and others. He had listened to radio programs, combed books old and new.

"I have tried to give credit wherever possible," said Cerf, "but anecdotes are bandied about so generally and new stories sweep the country so quickly that it is often impossible even to discover who put a story into the public prints first, let alone find out who actually originated it." He went on to say that column conductors and radio comics were engaged in a highly competitive business, and that their anxiety to establish the originality of their material was understandable. "It has always struck me as faintly ridiculous, however, for them to cry Thief! Thief! at rivals who very possibly overheard the gem in dispute at the same night-club table or in the same gentlemen's room. They seem to forget that they actually create very few of the bright quips and amusing anecdotes they chronicle, and that the people who tell *them* their stories probably repeat them to a dozen others that very evening."

Implicit in this *apologia pro se* was the anticipation of criticism, and criticism came. Lyons denounced Cerf as a pirate, and cited Cerf's foreword as a confession of piracy. "To argue," wrote Lyons, "that it's all right to steal our stories because we didn't make them up— Cerf, incidentally, brazenly put a copyright mark on his collection of stories taken from others—is as ridiculous as it would be to argue that it's all right to lift stories from Gunther's *Inside Europe*. We spent years interviewing thousands of people in thousands of places to get this material. It is elementary that no one has the right to the fruit of our labor; no man, using only scissors and paste-pot, should benefit from another's leg-ear-and-eyework, and devour, without permission, reams of our columns."

To Cerf's observation that a luminary might utter the same scintillating *jeu d'esprit* several times of an evening, Lyons retorted that his wife Sylvia had thought up a number of quips which Lyons had, as a lark, ascribed to celebrities, and Cerf had recorded them as actually uttered. How was Cerf going to explain *that*?

The antagonists never carried their quarrel to court. There's no way of knowing for certain what the outcome would have been if they had.

It's hardly necessary to point out that fair use can be made of columnists' efforts, as well as of any other protected matter. A biographer of, say, Winston Churchill would doubtless be justified in borrowing a few copyrighted anecdotes to enliven his pages. But were someone to do an article on Churchill composed entirely or almost entirely of stories culled from a single source, he'd be acting counter to the law as well as the dictates of conscience. Nor would it do him any good to argue that since there can be no exclusive appropriation of news as such, he shouldn't be blamed because he cribbed only reports of what actually happened. There *can* be exclusive property in the treatment of news.

The next question is whether the legal and ethical considerations are any different where numerous sources, not just one, are exploited. Analogies are tricky, to be sure, and they're particularly so when things of the mind are sought to be equated with ordinary tangible objects. But would a man who built a house out of stolen materials be heard to plead innocence, when challenged by someone he plundered, on the ground that he raided a dozen brickyards instead of one?

Compilations vary in kind; the rules applicable to them vary too. The maker of an almanac is free to pick up scattered facts and figures from a multiplicity of copyrighted sources. The editor of a poetry anthology is not free to include a copyrighted poem, even though the poem constitutes a small part of the original copyrighted book, and a small part of the anthology. In discussing the work of a poet, a critic is permitted to quote a number of copyrighted poems. The biographer of a poet has the same privilege. So has the literary historian. The distinction rests on reason. In an anthology, the collected pieces are paramount; the selection and arrangement are subordinate; the public buys the collection for the poems, not for the compiler's comments. In a critical or historical study, the contribution of the critic or historian is primary; the quoted examples serve merely as illustrative incidents.

What can be said to the man of good will who wants to obey the dictates of the law and fair dealing, and would like to have a few simple and categoric rules for his guidance? This: Stand on your own legs. Assimilate and remold your raw materials, whether in or out of copyright, so that the result is authentically yours. Express yourself your own way. Don't hesitate to draw on our cultural heritage, but don't presume on it. Declare your obligations. Respect the property rights of others. Where your borrowing of copyrighted material is fair use, don't be intimidated into buying something that's legally yours. If you exceed fair use, get permission; if a reasonable fee is asked, pay it. When you're the one whose permission is sought, don't be arbitrary in refusing it; don't exact harsh terms. And if you're ever in doubt as to what you ought to do, just put yourself in the other fellow's shoes.

# The Psychology of Plagiarism

Memory is a friend of wit, but a treacherous ally of invention; and there are many books that owe their success to two things: the good memory of those who write them, and the bad memory of those who read them.

—Caleb Charles Colton: Lacon

IN EXPLORING the psychology of plagiarism, we're principally concerned with three things: the dynamics of the creative process, with particular reference to the vagaries of memory and unconscious plagiarism; the reasons why people commit literary theft; and the motivation of plagiarism-criers.

## The Creative Process

We can duplicate in a test tube all the chemical ingredients that are found in living organisms, and yet fail to bring the combination to life. So, too, we can isolate and analyze the elements that enter into the making of a work of art, and still not discover the precise nature of the process by which those elements are synthesized into an animate whole.

Psychology gives us a clue or two.

Art is the end product of a series of intricate inner operations, of which stimulation, reaction, and articulation are progressive stages. We are connected with the outside world by means of our sense organs: eyes, ears, nose, tongue, skin. The sensations that reach our consciousness via the nervous system are impersonal messages. The instant they arrive, they lose their abstract quality; they are modified and interpreted by our minds. They become perceptions. On seeing blue, for instance, we cannot retain it as an absolute color. We associate it with whatever blueness we've experienced in the past: the color of the sky, perhaps, or of the sea, or of someone's eyes. It may revive a memory, stir a dormant desire, quicken an old fear.

In the ordinary course we ignore sensations or respond to them casually: with an exclamation, a sigh, a smile or a hummed tune. The function of the response is to give release from the pressure set up by the stimulus; when the function has been performed, the response ceases to exist. The "Ouch!" that a man utters when he stubs his toe, the wolf-whistle elicited by the sight of a well-constructed female, the "Ah!" that is wrung from a circus crowd when an aerialist misses the trapeze and plummets into the net—these are simple, instantaneous and ephemeral reactions to stimuli.

The artist's response is complex, delayed, and non-transitory. It assumes concrete form. Poetry is often defined as emotion recollected in tranquillity. Thousands saw the bullfight that Claude Debussy attended at San Sebastian around 1905. The crowd's answer to the drama of blood and sand was roaring and applause; Debussy's was the tone poem *Iberia*.

### Flashes and Flights

The writers of antiquity invoked the Muses, believing that the nine daughters of Zeus and Mnemosyne were dispensers of divine afflatus. Many of the early Church Fathers ascribed their pronouncements to the promptings of the Holy Spirit. Raphael spoke of a mystic force guiding his brush. "One does not work," declared de Musset, "one listens." Lehmbruck told a friend: "When my work goes well, a daemon stands at my elbow." And nowadays we hear of short stories flowing flawless and complete from the pen (or the typewriter) of an "inspired" person in a single sitting, or a three-act play getting written in white heat in a week, with the implication that there was a sudden seizure and a miraculous outpouring, without prelude or gestation.

While a few expressionist art chroniclers like Elie Faure still cling to the notion that artists see, feel and explode into paint the way a bird bursts into song, today the artist is not regarded as a creature abruptly swept into the creative act, or as the passive instrument of a power outside himself—except in the myths that flourish in the slick magazines, radio serials, and the movies.

In the view of modern psychology, when an artist is "waiting for the spirit to move him," when he is biding his time for "the right mood," he is really waiting for his unconscious to complete its work; and inspiration is nothing more occult than the critical moment when the inchoate mass of ideas, impressions, intuitions, memories, fancies and emotions that have been streaming in and out of the artist's consciousness suddenly fuse into a coherent and meaningful whole, ready to be expressed.

Shakespeare knew this. In *Love's Labour's Lost*, he wrote: "This is a gift that I have, simple, simple; a foolish extravagant spirit, full of forms, figures, shapes, objects, ideas, apprehensions, motions, revolutions; these are begot in the ventricle of memory, nourished in the womb of *pia mater*, and delivered upon the mellowing of occasion."

"The point should be stressed," says Professor Downey, "that all so-called inspirations occur strictly within the limits of the individual's capacity, training and previous cogitations. . . . Inspiration may be a flash-up from the unconscious, but it is no chance inspiration occurring indifferently in feeble-minded or genius. Moreover, no intuitions, as such, are guaranteed; their value is in direct ratio to the mind that has them."[1]

Imagination is the faculty of the mind which conceives mental pictures. It is activated by sensations, perceptions and emotions. It varies in intensity, function and result with individuals. In the artist, imagination takes over the materials stored in memory, breaks them up, selects and arranges the fragments, and integrates them into a new entity. The transition from chaos to clarity and order is, except in the case of so-called automatic art, directed by some dominating concept. Because, given a large number of elements, the possible permutations and combinations are infinite, fancy has no limits except this: the mind cannot feed upon itself, it can conjure its marvels only out of the stuff that has been supplied to it from the outside.

The common daydream, born of evasion and nourished by inaction, is an offspring of the imagination. So are Cretan vases, Persian manuscripts, Gothic images, Renaissance textiles, and modern skyscrapers.

## No Star Is Lost

Man is a remembering animal.

Memory has been apostrophized as the cabinet of the imagination, the treasury of reason, the registry of conscience, and the council chamber of thought. And it is particularly significant that the Muses identified with the various arts and sciences were originally goddesses of memory.

Memory is the act of reviving the past and recognizing it as such. It is also the sum total of a person's experiences as actually or possibly recalled. It involves four steps: the original impression, its retention, its recall, and the recognition of it as being of the past.

There is probably no such thing as complete forgetting. "A thousand accidents may and will interpose a veil between our present consciousness and the secret inscriptions of the mind; accidents of the same sort will also rend away this veil; but whether veiled or unveiled, the inscription remains forever; just as the stars seem to withdraw before the common light of day; whereas in fact we all know that it is the light which is drawn over them as a veil, and that they are waiting to be revealed when the obscuring daylight shall have withdrawn." It was the Opium Eater who said this a hundred and thirty years ago; it's considered scientifically true today.

A momentary glimpse of a stranger's face, a scent, a chance melody, may cause the withdrawal of "the obscuring daylight," and there will emerge from our unconscious, with the utmost clarity of detail and in full poignancy, some long-forgotten episode in our lives.

We can recall not only things that have actually happened to us but also what we have gleaned from art, literature and music. The countrysides we see are enhanced by—and enhance—the painted landscapes we gaze upon. We listen to majestic strains with Bach, plunge into Gehenna with Bosch, savor serenity with Bonnard, know terror and anguish with Kafka. Our experiences are more than any lifetime could offer, for they are the sum of a thousand lifetimes.

When we realize that our five senses are accumulating sensations every moment of our lives, and that these are translated into impressions which are imperishable, we get some idea of the incredible variety and opulence of the contents of the human brain.

## The Unconscious in Creation

There are psychologists who hold that the creative process is largely a function of the unconscious. They speak of incubation, of the threshold of the conscious, of flashes from hidden depths, of up-rushes from the subliminal.[2]

Writers have long been aware of the help they get from the unconscious. Dryden tells of his play *The Rival Ladies* "when it was only a confus'd Mass of Thoughts, tumbling over one another in the Dark; when the Fancy was yet in its first Work, moving the Sleeping Images of things toward the Light, there to be distinguish'd, and then either chosen or rejected by the Judgment." *"Le poète,"* says Voltaire, *"fait des vers en dormant."* For two years Goethe struggled with the stuff of Werther without finding the key to the form he wanted. Then one day the plan suddenly emerged—"the whole shot together from all directions and became a solid mass, as the water in a vase, which is just at the freezing point, is changed by the slightest concussion into ice."

When Henry James conceived the idea of *The American,* he says he "dropped it for the time being into the deep well of unconscious cerebration: not without the hope, doubtless, that it might eventually emerge from that reservoir, as one had already known the buried treasure to come to light, with a firm iridescent surface and a notable increase in weight."[3]

Robert Louis Stevenson flashed through the first half of *Treasure Island* like a blue streak. Then the rocket of narrative invention abruptly fizzled out. It did him no good to cudgel his brain. He decided to drop the story and to give it no more thought. He idled about for a few weeks. Then, for no reason he could name, he just as abruptly got started again. He completed the book swiftly and effortlessly.

"Much of a novelist's writing," says Graham Greene, "takes place in the unconscious. . . . One may be preoccupied with shopping and income-tax returns and chance conversation, but the stream of the unconscious continues to flow undisturbed, solving problems, planning ahead; one sits down sterile and dispirited at the desk, and suddenly the words come, the situations that seemed blocked in a hopeless impasse move forward; the work has been done while one slept or shopped or talked with friends."

The theme of the beautiful quintet in *The Magic Flute* came to Mozart in the midst of a game of billiards. Hamilton conceived his theory of quaternions while walking with his wife in Dublin. Poincaré the mathematician claimed that he was able to solve difficult problems unconsciously that baffled him completely while conscious. Professor Kekulé was riding on top of a London bus when he saw atoms dancing in the air in a pattern expressive of his hypothesis of atomic grouping.[4]

## Unconscious Memory

Omit the fourth element of memory—recognition that the thing remembered relates to past experience—and you have a case of unconscious memory.

George would like to pass for an entertaining fellow; he seizes and saves up every funny story he hears; his unconscious may trick him into telling Harry the very joke Harry told him.

Just as an obliging unconscious may beguile us into adopting as our personal experience an agreeable occurrence which has been related to us, so we may be trapped into presenting as our own creation something we've read or seen or heard.

"Faded ideas," says Sheridan in his preface to *The Rivals*, "float in memory like half-forgotten dreams; and the imagination in its fullest enjoyment becomes suspicious of its offspring and doubts whether it has created or adopted." "I have often felt," declares Oliver Wendell Holmes, "after writing a line that pleased me more than common, that it was not new and was perhaps not my own."

Doubt vanishes, however, when the unconscious has done a thorough job of suppressing recognition. A moral obstacle is then removed; and the artist feels free to exploit the avails of his recollection. For the artist's mind is an old curiosity shop, crammed to bursting with trophies, relics, odds and ends. Some of these were rightfully come by, some stolen. When imagination pays a visit to make a purchase, memory—the keeper of the shop—scurries about and fetches forth what the customer wants. But the wily merchant knows that if the object happens to be loot and he so declares it, he'll probably lose the sale. And so he assumes a pious air, obliterates all traces of origin, fools the customer, and clinches the bargain.

## Unconscious Plagiarism

Poe, who was so fiercely intolerant of deliberate theft, understood unconscious plagiarism. "What the poet intensely admires," he wrote, "becomes in very fact, although only partially, a portion of his own intellect. It has a secondary origination within his own soul—an origination altogether apart, although springing from, its primary origination from without. The poet is thus possessed by another's thought, and cannot be said to take possession of it. But, in either view, he thoroughly feels it *his own*—and this feeling is counteracted only by the sensible presence of its true, palpable origin in the volume from which he has derived it—an origin, in the long lapse of years it is almost impossible *not* to forget—for in the meantime the thought itself is forgotten. But the frailest association will regenerate it—it springs up with all the vigor of a new birth—its absolute originality is not even a matter of suspicion—and when the poet has written it and printed it, and on its account is charged with plagiarism, there will be no one in the world more astounded than himself."[5]

When William Dean Howells pointed out to James Russell Lowell that a poem Lowell had penned was virtually identical with one that had adorned the pages of *The Atlantic Monthly* two years before, the poet laureate of Cambridge wrote to him: "Last night I found The Atlantic for May, '66, and was astonished at your mildness. You should have cried 'Stop, thief!' at the top of your lungs . . . Why, Mrs. A [the original author] could have brought suit before any court in Christendom. I was taken red-handed and with the goods under my arm. I had utterly forgotten the confounded woman's verses—not that I should have hesitated to bag her idea, *more majorum,* if I had been starving. But I wasn't. There is no defense whatever . . . Anyhow, I am much obliged for your friendliness, which would not let me walk straight into the hands of the police with the evidence on my person."

Disraeli delivered a stirring panegyric on the death of the Duke of Wellington. The speech turned out to be a literal translation of Louis Adolphe Thiers' funeral oration for General Saint-Cyr. Dis-

raeli's explanation was that he had copied the address into his commonplace book and had mistaken it for his own. (The alibi doesn't
ring true. Jottings are jottings, and may get mixed up; a long piece
is something else. When Disraeli copied Thiers' composition, why
did he omit Thiers' name? And Saint-Cyr's?)

The quantity and nature of the borrowed material are often telling—but not necessarily conclusive—indications of the presence or
absence of intent. It's easy enough to set down a phrase, a line, a
paragraph, a simple image, a few musical notes, without knowing
that they're borrowed. As the quantity of the taking increases, the
likelihood that the taking is involuntary decreases.

### In the Courts

As I've repeatedly indicated, the copying of a substantial or material portion of copyrighted and copyrightable material constitutes
infringement. It makes no difference whether the copying is from
memory or direct from the original, whether the borrower acts with
premeditation or without.

In the "Dardanella" case Jerome Kern took the witness stand and
swore he had not consciously plagiarized the plaintiff's song for his
"Kalua." Judge Learned Hand believed him, but decided against
him. "Whether he unconsciously copied," said the Judge, "he cannot
say and does not try to. Everything registers somewhere in our
memories, and no one can tell what may evoke it."

In the *Letty Lynton* case, which Metro lost, Metro's witnesses had
sworn that they had not rifled the play *Dishonored Lady* in preparing
the movie. "In concluding that the defendants used the play," said the
Circuit Court of Appeals, "we need not charge their witnesses with
perjury. With so many sources before them, they might quite honestly
forget what they took; nobody knows the origin of his inventions;
memory and fancy merge even in adults."

### Why Do People Plagiarize?

Individuals steal, of course, for reasons other than the shifts and
stratagems of the unconscious.

They steal for money. The petty swindler who copies a tale by
Ambrose Bierce, changes the title and the names of the characters,

and sends it off to a magazine hopes to deceive the editor and collect some cash.

They steal because they admire. Admiration induces imitation; the closer the imitation, the narrower the dividing line between it and outright copying.

They steal for glory. The boy who cribs a passage from Hawthorne or Melville for his school paper may be doing so because of his desire for praise and prestige. Half a millennium has passed since the invention of printing, and innumerable books of utter worthlessness have seen the light of day in the interval; yet there still persists in the laity—perhaps as a vestigial remnant of the awe in which the unlettered masses of the Middle Ages held the scholars and clerics who could read and write—a respect for the man who can string words together and get them published.

They steal because they're ignorant of the law. Paul Armstrong was a successful Broadway dramatist, with *Alias Jimmy Valentine* to his credit; he did a stage version of one of Bret Harte's stories without bothering to get the consent of the Harte estate; he said he assumed that Harte had become a sort of classic and was therefore public property; he was shocked to find that his assumption was wrong, and that he had to make good to the estate.

They steal because they're sick. The psychopathic plagiarist is a kleptomaniac; he is just as much a medical case as the pathological liar or compulsive arsonist.

### Why Do People Charge Plagiarism?

Here too we encounter a variety of reasons. People complain:

Because they honestly feel that something they've created has been stolen.

Because, though they know their claim is spurious, they hope to extort a settlement.

Because they suffer from a sense of guilt. Castil Blaze inserted in his *Dictionary of Modern Music* three hundred and forty passages from Rousseau's treatise on the same subject, and roundly abused the latter for his ignorance and derivativeness. Sterne lifted some of the most incisive parts of *Tristram Shandy* from his predecessors, and denounced piracy in ringing phrases—filched from Burton.

Because they are obsessed and irrational. "The court," cried a de-

ranged plaintiff some years ago when his claim was thrown out by
the judge, "was plainly in this conspiracy. A man who made all the
money that crook made out of my story could afford to buy up all
the courts he needed, and this explains why there are so few decisions
in favor of the real but poor authors."

Because, tormented by a sense of inadequacy and frustration, they
envy those who have talent and can fulfill themselves. To achieve
fame is to incur hostility. Ill will is quick to seize every opportunity
to cry down achievement, and there's no swifter, crueler way of
piercing the artist's Achilles heel than to brand him plagiarist. "It is
an old trick of detraction," says Moore in his *Life of Sheridan*, "and
one of which it never tires, to father the works of eminent writers
upon others; or, at least, while it kindly leaves an author the credit
for his worst performances, to find someone in the background to
ease him of the fame of his best. Indeed, if mankind were to be influenced by those *Qui tam* critics, Aristotle must refund to one Ocellus
Lucanus, Virgil must make a *cessio bonorum* in favor of Pisander,
the *Metamorphoses* of Ovid must be credited to the account of Par-
thenius of Nicaea."

Doctor Johnson remarks in *The Rambler*: "When the excellence
of a new composition can no longer be contested, and malice is compelled to give way to the unanimity of applause, there is yet this
one expedient [i.e., the charge of plagiarism] to be tried, by which
the author may be degraded, though his work be reverenced; and the
excellence which we cannot obscure, may be set at such a distance as
not to overpower our fainter lustre."

It is in the fabrication of myths that plagiarism-crying reaches the
highest peaks of absurdity.

Defoe, we're told, didn't write *Robinson Crusoe*. He stole it from
Alexander Selkirk, the seaman who was cast away on a desert island,
and who set down an account of his adventures and gave the manuscript to Defoe to polish up.

The crown of laurel for *The School For Scandal* does not belong to
Sheridan. It belongs to a brilliant young girl with whom Sheridan
had a brief affair. He robbed her of her script, and then brutally
deserted her. She died of consumption, unsung and nameless.

Irving Berlin has a little colored boy tucked away somewhere who
writes all his songs.

The last item illustrates the imperviousness of myth to logic. Berlin has been around for a long time, and little colored boys, however well hid, grow up. Berlin recently attempted to shed some light on the subject. "Once when I had just returned from Palm Beach with a very deep tan, I ran into Harry Ruby, and he cried: 'At last I've actually *seen* the little colored boy who writes for Irving Berlin!' "

Legends die hard, and those born of disappointment and rancor and envy die the hardest.

# 19

## Commentary

It was the original owner of King Solomon's mines who asserted that there was nothing new under the sun; and after a lapse of hundreds of years one may suggest that a ready acceptance of the charge of plagiarism is a sign of low culture, and that a frequent bringing of the accusation is a sign of defective education and defective intelligence.

—Brander Matthews: Pen and Ink

THE value of even the most cursory glance at the psychology of plagiarism is that it reminds us that we're dealing with something more concrete than legal abstractions, something more flesh-and-blood than printed words or pigments on canvas. Plagiarism is a drama of human beings—adversaries, witnesses, lawyers, judges.

### The Pros and Cons of Suit

A new movie comes out. You're convinced it plagiarizes a published story of yours. You write a letter to the movie company demanding reimbursement. The company rejects your claim. What's your next move? Should you sue? Or should you swallow your sense of injury and drop the matter?

Here are the considerations that urge you to go ahead: (1) You may have a strong case. (2) You may be able to persuade your lawyer to handle it on a contingency basis, which means that you won't have to lay out any money. (3) If the company sees you mean business, it may settle before trial. That's what happened in *The Great Dictator* case, in which Konrad Bercovici got $95,000 from Charlie Chaplin. Ferdinand Lundberg settled his $250,000 suit against RKO and others over *Citizen Kane* for $15,000. (4) Litigation lets you blow off steam. Also, it brings you into the limelight and feeds your ego. (5) If you win, you may make a killing. The award in the *Letty Lynton* case was $117,500.

Here are the factors that tell you to beware: (1) You may have a weak case. Don't rely on your own judgment on this; you're prejudiced. Ask your lawyer. (2) You may have to pay a retainer. (3) In any event you'll have to defray expenses. If depositions have to be taken out of town, the disbursements may run high. (4) You will have to submit to an examination before trial. (5) The odds will be against you on the final result. Most plagiarism suits are won by the defendants. (6) If you lose, you may be ordered to pay the movie company's counsel fees. The fees may be substantial. (7) Even if you win in the trial court, you won't be sure of ultimate victory. The company may appeal, and the higher court may reverse the award. (8) Whatever the outcome, you may get to be known as a troublemaker, and hurt your career. Purchasers of literary material don't like to deal with plagiarism-criers.

### Settle or Fight?

If a suit is started, the movie company too faces a choice. It has to compromise or fight.

The arguments in favor of settlement, from the company's standpoint, are: (1) The claim may be well-founded. (2) Litigation means adverse publicity. (3) Infringement suits are expensive to defend. Belasco spent a fortune fighting off plagiarism plaintiffs. It cost Twentieth Century-Fox over fifty-thousand dollars to explode the false claim in *The Road to Glory* case. As a rule it's cheaper to settle. (4) Pre-trial legal moves entail inconvenience, irritation, and —if the plaintiff's lawyer insists on interrogating the company's executives, writers and story editors—possible disruption of studio schedules. (5) If the plaintiff wins, he may recover a thumping amount. (6) If he loses, the company may be unable to collect any counsel fees from him. Confronted with an order to pay counsel fees of five thousand dollars, the plaintiff in *The Fool* case promptly went into bankruptcy. (7) If the company prevails in the trial court, the plaintiff may carry the case higher and get a reversal.

The counter-arguments are: (1) The claim may be utterly worthless. (2) It's impossible to keep a settlement a secret. The public usually interprets it as an admission of guilt. (3) While it may be cheaper to buy off one plaintiff than to fight him, in the long run a give-in policy is bound to prove more costly. Once a company gets to be known as an easy mark, it becomes a prey for sharpers. (4) It's morally wrong to capitulate to a baseless demand. It fosters extortion. (5) If the company tells the plaintiff bluntly that it won't settle, he may get discouraged and drop the suit. (6) The plaintiff may be solvent. If he loses, he may be good for counsel fees.

## Advocatus Diavoli

Speaking of the nuisance of plagiarism suits at a Book and Author Luncheon some years ago, George S. Kaufman, the playwright, who had good reason to be bitter, said: "I'm telling you all this in the hope that if any of you have lawyers in the family, you will kill them."

Criticism of men of the law began in ancient times, and has been going on briskly since. By now the refrain is thoroughly familiar. We know all its variations, from the Biblical "Woe unto you lawyers, for ye took away the key of knowledge, yet entered not in yourselves, and them that would ye hindered" to Coleridge's designation of the devil as arch lawyer, and Southey's characterization of every lawyer as *advocatus diavoli*. We have perused Gargantua's inscription on the gate of the Abbey of Thélème, bidding all contemptible folk—cheats, cowards, thieves, drunkards, gluttons, usurers, misers, bigots, hypocrites, fools, *and lawyers*—to stay away. We have heard Jeremy Bentham indict lawyers as "a passive and enervate race, ready to swallow anything, and to acquiesce in anything; with intellects incapable of distinguishing right from wrong, and with affections alike indifferent to either; insensible, short-sighted, obstinate, lethargic, yet liable to be driven into convulsions by false terrors; deaf to the voice of reason and public utility; obsequious only to the whisper of interest and the beck of power."

These generalizations have begun to pall. They have been uttered too often, always with the same ill-humored querulousness, and with the same debatable justification. I doubt that the men of the bar are an ethically inferior breed. I suspect that many of their alleged sins would, on closer examination, turn out to be no more than failings common to the human species.[1]

I don't propose to take up the cudgels here for the profession. I do think that two points should be made. One is that the pious lay-man who rails against pettifoggery doesn't, deep down in his heart, disapprove of it; he condemns it only when it's used against him; he stands by without a murmur—and very likely with secret satisfaction —when it's employed to advance *his* cause. The other is that the man who thinks that lawyers are to blame for all infringement suits has obviously never met up with plagiarism claimants. A good pro-portion of these claimants are fanatics. I've known of many cases where the implacable plagiarism client all but fought with his lawyer to take his case. I've never known of a case where a guileful attorney inveigled his reluctant client into suing, though I suppose that does happen now and then.

A cynic has remarked somewhere that few clients tell their attorneys the truth, the whole truth, and nothing but the truth. People sup-press, invent, color, distort. When a plagiarism client descends on his counsel, as he often does, with a parallel-analysis which is an adroit hodgepodge of exaggeration and fabrication, the attorney may be gulled into accepting a case he would otherwise decline (he may not be an infringement expert)—a situation hardly consistent with the Johnsonian picture of "the fell attorney prowling for his prey."

## In the Courts

In traditional murals, justice is usually depicted as a majestic lady with a blindfold and a flowing robe, holding a sword in one hand and a pair of scales in the other. So attired and equipped, even Diana would have found it hard to be fleet.

One of the numerous lay grievances against the law is its delays. Justice does grind slowly. There is no need to cite the classic English cases that went on with a fate-like inexorableness decade after decade, until the subject matter had long vanished and all the participants had gone bankrupt. We can find plenty of examples in the plagiarism arena in this country.

The *Bird of Paradise* case was in the courts eighteen years; *The Heir to the Hoorah* case, sixteen years; the *Letty Lynton* case, seven years. To be sure, many proceedings have been disposed of in less time. Yet for the man who feels that his work has been stolen, as for the man accused of the stealing, it's scant comfort to be told that in a year or two the law will tell him where he stands. He wants a quick decision, and you can scarcely blame him.

It has been often said that justice delayed is justice denied. It has not been said often enough that the maneuverings of lawyers are only partly responsible for the lag. Procedural requirements, the congestion of court calendars, the tardiness of judges in handing down decisions —all these contribute to it. And litigants too. There are plaintiffs who sedulously shun a showdown, relying on the continuing irritant of suit to force a settlement. There are defendants who demand that every expedient be resorted to in order to postpone the day of reckoning, hoping to tire out their adversaries.

## The Expert Witness

"We cannot approve," said the Circuit Court of Appeals in the *Abie's Irish Rose* case, "the length of the record, which was due chiefly to the use of expert witnesses. Argument is argument whether in the box or at the bar, and its proper place is the last. The testimony of an expert upon such issues, especially his cross-examination, greatly extends the trial and contributes nothing which cannot be better heard after the evidence is all submitted. It ought not to be allowed at all; and while its admission is not a ground for reversal, it cumbers the case and tends to confusion, for the more the court is led into the intricacies of dramatic craftsmanship, the less likely it is to stand upon the firmer, if more naive, ground of its considered impressions upon its own perusal. We hope that in this class of cases such evidence may in the future be entirely excluded, and the case confined to the actual issues; that is, whether the copyrighted work was original, and whether the defendant copied it, so far as the supposed infringement is identical."

As I stated in Chapter 12, it was Metro's contention in the *Letty Lynton* case—in which the movie was adjudged to infringe the play *Dishonored Lady*—that the value of the picture depended only slightly on the parts found to have been lifted from the play, and that Metro should therefore be accountable for a correspondingly small part of the profits of the picture. Metro produced expert witnesses—movie producers and exhibitors—who were asked to appraise, in percentages of revenue, the extent of the play's contribution to the picture. The estimates ran between 5 per cent and 12 per cent.

The plaintiffs called no expert witnesses on this issue. They insisted right along that a willful infringer like Metro had to give up *all* its profits, and that any apportionment was out of the question.

While the Circuit Court of Appeals disagreed with the plaintiffs, it was by no means eager to embrace as gospel the views of the producers and exhibitors. "Except in the most general way," said the Court, "the percentages of experts cannot be used to solve a problem in which there is no common measure; yet it would be a mistake to deny all weight to them. Men often make quantitative judgments and act upon them in matters which logically admit of them as little as this. If one says that he likes one kind of music twice as much as another, we do not charge him with talking nonsense."

The Court deemed the estimates of the experts as nothing more than expressions of very decided opinions that the play should count for little. The Court fixed the plaintiffs' share of the net profits of *Letty Lynton* at 20 per cent.

One wonders how the Court arrived at this magic figure. One wonders too what part the experts' computations played in the Court's deliberations. Would the result have been any different if the Court hadn't plowed through reams and reams of opinion testimony?

While expert witnesses are no favorites of the courts—the appellate judges had particularly harsh words for them in the *Outline of History* case—their testimony appears to be admissible for the purpose of showing (a) the lack of originality of the plaintiff's work, (b) whether similarities exist sufficient to prove copying, and (c) where an apportionment of the defendant's net profits is feasible, how much the plaintiff's work contributed to the defendant's.

## The Law in Action

Laymen have weird notions about how cases are decided. Cynics mutter about political influence and corruption. (Wilson Mizner said he could bribe a judge with a peanut, and his only fear was that the man would hold out for a walnut.) Self-styled realists aver that it's all a matter of which side has the more crooked counsel. The mechanical-minded think that the law is a sort of slot machine—you insert the facts, pull the lever, listen to the whir while the legal rules packed in the contraption act upon the facts, and presto! out pops the result.

Though justice is subverted now and then through the improbity of the bench or the bar, and though precedents are sometimes applied automatically and without regard to the realities, fundamentally the judicial process is neither a game of knavery nor an exercise in syllogistic logic. It isn't revelation either. It is a human activity, attended by human fallibilities.[2]

Judges are the key figures in the process. More than three hundred years ago Sir Francis Bacon adjured them "to be more learned than witty, more reverend than plausible, and more advised than confident," and pressed them to remember, above all things, that integrity is their portion and proper virtue.

Judges err, of course, but their errors flow less from venality or sloth or ignorance than from the fact that it's impossible for any mortal to attain the state of serene detachment necessary for ideal judicature.

When a judge in a plagiarism case compares two products of the imagination and weighs the testimony of witnesses, he interprets data. Interpretation permits of wide variation of deduction and inference. It is affected by elements in the judge's make-up—permanent factors such as his upbringing, education, habits, tastes, predilections and prejudices, and transitory ones like his mood or state of health. If a judge doesn't read books or look at pictures or listen to music, he can know very little about the continuity and cumulative nature of art. He may easily mistake legitimate borrowing for theft.

Judges, the legal empiricists insist, decide most cases by feeling and hunches, not by ratiocination, and reasoning appears on the scene only when the judges sit down to write opinions to support their decisions.[3] This is a half-truth. Judges aren't wholly swayed by emotion. They aren't governed solely by reason. Emotion and reason interact; they both have an impact. And it isn't fair to imply, as the empiricists sometimes do, that intuition is necessarily a mischievous guide. An intuitive disposition, though unattended by cerebration, may still be just and reasonable.[4]

The law is not something dispensed from on high and imposed on society. It springs from the beliefs, habits and practices of men. It grows and changes because men grow and change. It is a means to an end. The end is an orderly community in which individuals are afforded an opportunity to realize themselves. As Justice Holmes put it a long time ago, "the true grounds of decision are considerations of policy and social advantage, and it is vain to suppose that solutions can be attained merely by logic and the general propositions of law which nobody disputes."

## Expounding the Conclusion

When a judge has made up his mind about a case, he hands down a decision. A decision is a terse statement: it tells who wins. That's as far as the judge has to go. He may go further, and explain why he decided the case in the way he did. The explanation is called an opinion.

The average trial-court plagiarism opinion contains an indication of the nature of the case, a recital of the facts, outlines of the two works in question, an exposition of the legal rules purportedly pertinent, an application of the rules to the facts, a refutation of the defendant's contentions where the plaintiff prevails (or vice versa), and the final disposition. The pattern of appellate opinions is pretty much the same, except that where there is a reversal, the higher tribunal indicates where the lower one went off base.

Opinions are of prime importance in plagiarism matters. The Copyright Act does not define unfair use. The rules of infringement—unlike, say, the criteria of burglary or forgery or arson—are wholly *case* law. They are encompassed in the ever-growing body of judges' opinions on the subject.

One striking feature of many of these opinions is extended analyses of the rival works before the court. It's true enough that if a judge's pronouncement is to serve as a guide for the future, it must describe the works sufficiently to highlight the points of resemblance and the points of difference. But see what actually happens. A judge reaches a decision. He proceeds to verbalize his reasons. Rationalization takes over. If the judge holds for the plaintiff, he advisedly or unwittingly plays up the similarities and soft-pedals the dissimilarities. If he rules for the defendant, he does the reverse. While the result may be just, the performance yields dim illumination to those who study it afterward as precedent.

Take *The Freshman* case. Judge Cosgrave, who presided at the trial, felt that plagiarism had been proved. The appellate bench didn't think so. Place the two opinions side by side. Both contain lengthy synopses of Witwer's story "Rodney" and Harold Lloyd's movie. You'll say that the two courts couldn't possibly have been talking about the same things.

But even where plagiarism opinions seem to be models of dispassion, lucidity and wisdom, we must not embrace them as the Last Word. Each case turns on its own facts, and no new case is quite like any other that went before it.

## Thrust and Riposte

When the Académie Francaise gave the Grand Prix du Roman to Pierre Benoît for his *L'Atlantide* in 1919, the French *Quarterly Review* unfeelingly marred Benoît's triumph by accusing him of looting Rider Haggard's *She* for his tale. Benoît retaliated with a libel suit.

The heroine of both novels is a mysterious white queen, immune to time and death, reigning over a savage tribe in an inaccessible corner of Africa. In Haggard's *King Solomon's Mines* (not, it should be noted, in *She*) the departed members of the royal line are turned into stalagmites by the action of calciferous water which gradually deposits a transparent stony film over the bodies. In *L'Atlantide*, the hapless lovers of the enchantress queen, who are successively driven to suicide when she tires of them, are similarly preserved.

The Paris court that heard the case paid little heed to the fact that the magazine had charged undue borrowing from *She*, not from *King Solomon's Mines*. It dismissed Benoît's suit with costs.

Charged with stealing her drama *A Dark Crown*, based on the life of Edgar Allan Poe, Michael Strange retaliated with a $300,000 defamation suit. The case never went to trial.

While Maxell Anderson's *Anne of the Thousand Days* was playing to packed houses on Broadway, Francis Hackett called in newspaper reporters and told them that he felt Anderson had made unfair use of three volumes of his dealing with Henry VIII and Anne Boleyn. He asserted that he had "invented a number of episodes for which there were historical suggestions, some, in fact, that looked like episodes in the public domain of history but were not." He said that his characterizations of the personages involved were original with him, and that Anderson had appropriated them. "Many phrases personal to me," he added, "turned up in *Anne of the Thousand Days*."

He added that he had asked his attorney to look into the matter with a view to starting a suit for infringement. Anderson's reply, delivered virtually overnight, was a hundred thousand dollar libel action. The outcome was amicable. Hackett apologized and withdrew his accusation, and Anderson dropped his suit.

The relationship between plagiarism and libel has some intriguing aspects.

If Sharp tells the press that Straight has pirated a book of his, and a newspaper prints it, Straight can sue both for defamation. Sharp and the newspaper can plead that the imputation is true, but if they can't prove it, Straight can recover damages from both of them.

Let's change the facts. Suppose Sharp makes no statement; he goes direct to court with an infringement complaint. The newspapers report the case. A trial is had, and Sharp loses. Can Straight sue Sharp and the papers for libel? No, he cannot. Why not? Is not a plagiarism suit, for the person attacked, a much more serious matter than a mere published blast? Doesn't it generate more notoriety, cost more money to defend, consume more time?

The legal rule which bars a libel action by Straight rests on public policy. If every allegation of, say, fraud exposed a litigant to reprisal via a defamation suit, people would hesitate to go to law, and many a just grievance would remain unredressed. If a paper ran a libel risk every time it reported anything connected with a court proceeding, the free flow of information essential to a democratic society would be impeded. And so any averment, no matter how hurtful, contained in pleadings or uttered in open court cannot be made the basis of a libel action so long as it is relevant and material to the subject matter in controversy. Too, a fair report of a judicial proceeding is privileged.

There's an additional reason for the legal rule. When Sharp assails Straight in the columns of a paper, shunning the courts, Straight can't conclusively clear his name; no matter how categoric his denial, how full and open the journalistic debate, it's still his word against Sharp's. The only way he can legally vindicate himself is to sue for libel. On the other hand, when Sharp brings an action for plagiarism against him, Straight is assured of his day in court: he *can* be judicially absolved.

## The Plagiarism Racket

The fact that anyone can charge plagiarism with virtual impunity so long as he puts it in legal papers, has had its consequences.

Of the authors whose plays had two hundred performances or more on Broadway between 1910 and 1930, well over a third were confronted with plagiarism suits. Two Pulitzer Prize winners were among the supposed culprits. Every one of the defendants was held blameless. It probably cost each of them at least five thousand dollars in fees and expenses to repel litigation that should never have been started.

By 1930 plagiarism attacks had assumed the proportions of a racket —not a big-time operation, to be sure, but a brisk, lucrative hold-up game just the same. The racket rested on the proposition that if people were sued for a staggering amount, they'd be so appalled by the trouble and expense of defense—and the possibility of a huge judgment—that they'd be glad to settle for a lesser sum even if the claim was phony.

A crew of hirelings were said to be busily engaged in the Library of Congress making synopses of all the unproduced plays copyrighted by obscure authors. The synopses were forwarded to the New York office of the ring, where monitors scanned Broadway openings for similarities. When they hit on a likely quarry, they'd communicate with the copyright owner of the prior script, buy his rights for a pittance, and launch their suit against the show.

Another syndicate, it was reported, made a practice of procuring worthless unpublished songs. The syndicate would submit a song to a music publisher, taking care to establish direct access. The composition would be rejected. The blackmail boys would then lie in wait until the publisher had a hit. They'd fabricate a new number closely resembling the hit, declare that it was the song they had originally sent to the publisher, and pounce on the victim with an infringement action.

Many a defendant paid blood money to be let off. The few doughty ones who put up a fight and won had good reason to be rueful about their victory. Contemplating their depleted purses, they could understand why it's so often said that in a plagiarism set-to, the defendant never wins.

The situation got so bad that the Dramatists' Guild, whose roster of members includes virtually every playwright of consequence in the country, was stung into action. It called for the amendment of the Copyright Act to provide for the following procedure:

1. A plagiarism claimant would be required to present to the Federal Court, together with his complaint, a copy of his work and a copy of the allegedly infringing work.
2. The court would designate a referee or master to read the two exhibits and decide whether there was any merit in the claim.
3. If the referee or master ruled that there was a genuine issue of plagiarism, the case would be sent to trial in the usual course.
4. If the ruling was to the contrary, the plaintiff would be obliged to furnish a bond in a sum sufficient to assure to the defendant his reasonable expenses if the plaintiff lost.

The essence of the plan was, of course, the bond requirement. The Guild believed that cranks and crooks would think twice before reaching into their pocketbooks and backing their ventures with hard cash. The Guild felt confident that the proposed procedure would put no financial obstacle in the way of bona fide claims.

The plan was vulnerable on several grounds. For one thing, if the referee erred and the plaintiff had no means, a man with a just cause would be deprived of his day in court. For another, the scheme was discriminatory: it gave a moneyed party an advantage which it denied a moneyless one. For still another, the probable effect of raising a financial hurdle was to place writers and composers at the mercy of predatory interests, particularly those in Hollywood.[5]

Failing to win support, the proposal—like so many others designed to reform the copyright statute—subsided and died. There can be little doubt that it had a fatal flaw. Instead of providing for the swift suppression of false demands, it prolonged their life at a price. No one could have contended with certainty that the bond provision would not have frustrated more impoverished individuals with genuine grievances than it would have sharks or monomaniacs. Also, a defendant whose peace of mind was destroyed for four or five years by continuing litigation would have found less than complete solace in the fact that he was not out of pocket on expenses.

## Forcing the Issue

As a matter of fact, a method exists today—it existed in the days of the Guild's plan—whereby a plagiarism defendant can force a quick showdown. The moment he is served with suit papers he can march into court, present copies of the rival works, argue that the dissimilarity is such as to obviate the need of trial, and ask the judge to throw the case out.

This is known as "making a motion for summary judgment." If the motion is granted, the litigation is over, unless the plaintiff appeals. If the motion is denied, the case goes to trial.

This approach resembles the Guild's proposal, except that on a motion (1) it is the judge, not a referee or a master, who makes the preliminary appraisal; (2) the judge can dismiss the complaint without offering the plaintiff the alternative of giving security; and (3) the judge cannot require a bond.

"The procedure," said Judge Woolsey in the *Of Thee I Sing* case, "is bold and intelligent and, it seems to me, constitutes an appropriate method of dealing with a copyright suit of this kind, for it enables me, on the record before me, to decide this case by following the pragmatic method of comparing the two books."

The motion technique put an end to the *Of Thee I Sing* case in 1932, the *Death Takes a Holiday* case in 1933, the *Blonde Venus* case in 1935, the *Cimarron* case in 1937, and the *I Dream Too Much* case in 1938.

A year later, however, the Circuit Court of Appeals for the Second Circuit—there are ten circuits in the United States—sounded a note of warning. The Court below had, on a motion, thrown out a claim against Samuel Goldwyn's movie *Roman Scandals*. The Circuit Court reversed the dismissal and ordered a trial, saying:

To do justice to the plaintiff, the judge [i.e., the judge who decides the motion] must assume, not only that the defendant has had "access" to the book or play (which alone means nothing), but that he has actually copied those parts common to it and the film. That is not always easy to remember; and when it is remembered, the decision does not dispose of the case unless it goes against the plaintiff; if he wins, the issue of copying remains to be tried. We doubt the convenience of dividing the trial in this way; the issue of fair use, which alone is decided, is the most troublesome in the whole law of copyright, and ought not to be resolved in cases where it may turn out to be moot, unless the advantage is very plain. At least we should regret seeing the procedure become the custom. . . .

A trial was had, and the defendant won. Hence all that the Circuit Court's decision accomplished—aside from expressing a general admonition—was to give the plaintiff a taste of blood. He fought all the way up to the Supreme Court of the United States, without avail.

In 1946, in the Cole Porter case, the Circuit Court reiterated its caveat. Generally speaking, the Court declared, plagiarism suits should be tried; the plaintiff should have an opportunity to cross-examine the defendant, and to have the jury observe the witnesses while testifying. And so the rigmarole of the *Roman Scandals* case was repeated. The plaintiff had his day in court, lost, appealed, and was twice rebuffed by the Supreme Court.

Whatever impact the views of the Circuit Court may have had on the Federal District Courts within the circuit, New York State judges did not heed them. In 1946 Judge Null disposed of the *Dear Ruth* case on motion; and in 1948 Judge Eder did the same in the *Deep Are the Roots* case.

And in 1950, an undaunted Federal judge—Judge Rifkind—saw no reason to deny a motion to throw the claim against the *State of the Union* out of court. The alleged source of Howard Lindsay and Russel Crouse's stage hit was a meager script called *A Lady Goes to Congress*. "Neither in plot, theme, characterization or language," said the Judge incisively, "does the one bear resemblance to the other. Under the circumstances I see no issue of fact to be tried either to the court or to a jury. I have not the slightest doubt that the plaintiff's claim is the product of nothing but hope that, to avoid the expense and irritation of litigation, the owner of a successful play would buy his peace."

Motion procedure has manifest advantages. It is expeditious and simple; where meritorious claims are sustained, it encourages settlement; it extinguishes worthless claims before they become a galling nuisance; it saves time and money for the courts and the parties; it militates against extortion. It can't hurt the plaintiff because if the motion is erroneously granted, he can appeal. It can't hurt the defendant because if the motion is denied—access being assumed—he can still prove absence of access at the trial.

Since the doctrine of summary relief is deeply rooted in our law, the Second Circuit's aversion to it in plagiarism cases is puzzling. When a palpably fraudulent contract claim is asserted, no one will argue that the interests of justice will be jeopardized if, without further ado, the plaintiff is sent packing. Why should a man with a palpably fraudulent plagiarism claim be treated otherwise?

It may well be that the Circuit Court feels the way it does because it knows that plagiarism plaintiffs are monstrously persistent. The Court may reason that a defeat on motion does not stop these people, and that needless appeals are therefore generated. But is there any justification for the assumption that the plaintiffs would be less likely to appeal from an adverse decision after trial than from a dismissal on motion?

# 20

# Summing Up

Most of us would think it unlikely that men and women of admitted probity, who have spent years learning their trade and achieving distinction in it, should suddenly be tempted beyond their strength by the literary treasures created by barbers and stage-hands. Why should an expert in values rob a junk-shop while priceless jewels are to be had free—that is, while the masterpieces of three thousand years are in the public domain?

—Channing Pollock: The Plagiarism Racket

---

NEXT to the question of what constitutes fair use, the problem that bothers people most in connection with infringement is where to draw the line between what is protectible and what is not. Granted that copyright does not protect subject matter as such but does protect an original plot or treatment, granted too that copyright does not secure a stereotype but does secure a character, at what precise point does a theme or a character cease to be public property and become something that permits of exclusive private ownership?

A sort of working rule is the only guide we have. To the extent that a writer inclines toward simple abstraction in the handling of an idea or a theme, his work moves *away* from the realm of property rights; to the extent that he achieves particularity his work moves *toward* that realm. The vanity of human desire is an abstract theme; no matter how often it has been dealt with, no matter how many interpretations of it have been copyrighted, it may be treated afresh by any newcomer. However, if a novelist takes hold of the theme, colors it with his imagination, and develops it by means of dramatis personae, a story line, incidents, observations and language of his own, he attains individuality, and acquires exclusive rights in his version. A stage-struck novice actress is an abstraction; she cannot be pre-empted. Nor does she cease to be an abstraction if an author invests her with the long-familiar trappings: idealism, hope and devotion in the face of tribulations and disappointments. Nevertheless, if she is so delineated that she sheds generality and assumes the traits and dimensions of a human being distinguishable from type, she becomes her creator's girl, and anyone who abducts her acts at his peril.

### Review and Reflection

It may be helpful at this point to record a few observations on the various facets of plagiarism which we've been discussing now for nineteen chapters. These observations are offered not as axioms or as pontifical pronouncements, but rather as generalizations attended by exceptions.

1. Historically viewed, all artistic creativity is related and interdependent, continuous and cumulative. Every work, past and present, is but a link in the chain.

2. All artists borrow, the great nobly, the small without distinction. It's not what a man borrows that counts, or when or where or why, but what he does with it.

3. The plagiarism which, in the case of a genius (especially a dead genius) is hailed as an exercise of royal prerogative, may, in the case of a humble practitioner, be condemned as larceny.

4. No one damns a scientist for making a discovery, the groundwork for which was laid by a hundred predecessors. But if a writer levies on our cultural heritage, he may be assailed even though he so transforms what he takes as to create a new work.

5. The word-eating dragons—radio and television—have generated conditions highly conducive to borrowing and theft.

6. A certain amount of stealing is doubtless going on all the time. The preponderance of borrowing, however, is legitimate. There is too much unwarranted plagiarism-crying.

7. Neither exemplary conduct nor high position is a guaranty of exemption from attack. No less a personage than Lord Campbell, one of the immortals of the English bench, was accused (with little justification) of cribbing his study of legal references in Shakespeare.

8. Plagiarism claimants are, as a class, woefully ignorant of the elementary canons of infringement.

9. Nobody ever gets sued on a novel that winds up on the remainder counters or on a play that folds in three days or on a movie that doesn't click. Indeed, there are some hard-bitten practitioners who refuse to believe they have a hit on their hands until they've been served with infringement papers.

10. The dexterity which plaintiffs display in conjuring up parallels where none exist is matched by the ingenuity of defendants in fabricating defenses. The technique of the latter is reminiscent of the plea of the man who was sued because he borrowed a pitcher and returned it broken—he never borrowed the pitcher; it was broken when he got it; it was whole when he returned it. There's no similarity, says plagiarism defendant Black, between his opus and plaintiff White's; if there is, it's inconsequential; if it is substantial or material, then it's because both of them went to the same sources; anyway he had no access to White's work; even if he did have access he didn't take advantage of it; if he did take advantage of it, he didn't overstep the bounds of fair use.

11. It's depressing to contemplate the abysmal quality of the average plaintiff's work which was supposedly rifled to yield a successful product.

12. Most of the infringement cases appear to have been justly decided.

13. The extent of the plagiarism nuisance is not to be measured by the number of cases that run their course in the courts. The claims that are settled or dropped before or after proceedings are started outnumber by far those memorialized in the law books.

14. Precedents can be found to support either side of almost every legal question. No court decision is conclusively determinative of a later case, no definition is immutable, no judge-uttered rule sacrosanct.[1]

## The Copyright Act

The Copyright Act was passed in 1909. It's an outmoded edifice, cumbersome and cluttered. It's badly in need of renovation.[2]

As things now stand, the copyright owner of literary (as distinguished from dramatic) material is a sort of stepchild. The law

accords to the authors of stories, poems and books the exclusive rights
of publication, translation and dramatization, but arbitrarily with-
holds from them the exclusive rights of public performance and
recording which are granted to playwrights. As a result, anyone may,
without the copyright owner's permission, read a copyrighted story
in public for profit, and may make a recording of it, likewise for
profit. The unfairness of this is obvious. The law should be amended
to extend to literary works the exclusive rights now withheld.

In order to qualify for copyright protection at the present time,
books and magazines in the English language must comply with the
manufacturing provisions of the Copyright Act. The type from which
the publications are printed must be set in the United States, the
plates must be made here, the printing and the binding must be done
here. These requirements have made it virtually impossible for us to
reach any kind of agreement with other countries on international
copyright, and have severely handicapped American authors who for
various reasons find it necessary to have their books published abroad
and cannot arrange for subsequent publication here. The law should
be amended so as to eliminate the manufacturing provisions altogether.

The entire statute is poorly worded and clumsily arranged. The
infringement section, for example, is a veritable verbal jungle.
A thorough job of simplification is called for.

One of the most important provisions of the law—that dealing
with the duration of copyright—is arbitrary, and should be reap-
praised. A copyright, as we have seen, is good for twenty-eight years,
and may be renewed for twenty-eight years more. It has never been
established that these periods bear any realistic or justifiable relation
to individual need or social expediency.

Theoretically, a copyright should last as long as the author derives
benefit from it, subject to an outside limit dictated by the public
interest. But how can we translate this vague goal into a concrete
formula? If the continuance of demand is to be the yardstick, how
are we to determine when the demand has ceased? Wouldn't such a
criterion be unfair to the man who turned out an early nonselling
novel, say, and whose later success created a fresh market for his
previous book? And what kind of demand would we require to keep

the monopoly alive? Would the sale of a dozen copies a year be enough? Fifty? A hundred?

Or should we permit copyright to continue as long as the author is alive? What if he writes something at the age of twenty and lives to be ninety—should his monopoly persist for seventy years? What if he dies a year after he produces his work—should his family be deprived of its benefits? Or should the protection be for the author's lifetime, plus a fixed period? Material might then be tied up much longer than under the existing law. Should we retain the present term of twenty-eight years but abolish the renewal? Should there be different periods of protection for the various media? Should a copyright in the hands of a non-creator—a publisher or a movie company or a radio broadcaster—be endowed with lesser life than one in the hands of a writer, an artist, or a composer? And since it is of the utmost importance to society that the expiration date of a copyright should be readily discoverable, how would we deal with such unascertained and prospectively unascertainable dates as that of an author's death, or that of the cessation of demand?[3]

The entire problem ought to be thoroughly surveyed and a constructive policy formulated on the basis of the facts found.

## The Artist and Society

Certain basic propositions are sometimes lost sight of in copyright debates. One is that monopoly and liberty are essentially incompatible. Another is that copyright is a legalized monopoly. Still another is that the constitutional purpose of copyright is primarily to benefit the public, and only secondarily to promote the artist's welfare.[4]

Up to a point the interests of the artist and those of society coincide. The artist wants to create, and society wants him to create. But once the work is done, a clash arises. Just as the possessive parent seeks to dominate the destiny of his offspring, so the artist desires control over his brain child. But the unimpeded flow of ideas is indispensable to the welfare of society; and exclusive ownership of a product of the mind hampers the flow. Then, too, the artist's own wishes are ambivalent: he'd like his own property to be inviolate and at the same time he'd like to be free to utilize the property of others.

The artist must be made to understand that fair use is a two-way street. And where his interests and those of society come into conflict, a balance must be struck. The principle of the equilibration of interests is not new. It is an indispensable feature of our way of life. It is a process that is going on all the time in every field. We endeavor to offset the restriction inherent in copyright (1) by limiting the duration of the monopoly; (2) by applying the doctrine of fair use (the statute makes no mention of the doctrine; it is a creature of case law); (3) by emphasizing again and again that ideas as such cannot be removed from the stockpile available to all; and (4) by making copyright protection an instrument of salutary flexibility through judicial interpretations in specific cases.

If there were no copyright, we could say what we wished, and profit by it, even though we took the words out of someone else's mouth, and robbed him of his property and means of livelihood. To the extent that the law forbids us to do this, it inhibits our speech. But it's imperative to remember that there is a further factor which has a vital bearing on the conflict between originator and borrower. When anyone's utterance is inhibited, society's right to hear is impaired. And so, whatever the equities between the parties themselves, we must be doubly vigilant to resist any application of the law which extends the monopoly beyond the confines of strict necessity.

## In Search of a Remedy

Can anything be done to curb the activities of the litigious crank or the settlement-seeking schemer?

If an extortioner sues you, you must join battle with him as though he were the soul of honor. You can't go into court and say: "Judge, this is blackmail pure and simple." Nor will it do you any good, if your adversary is a crackpot, to proclaim that fact in the halls of justice. You must treat him as though he were sane.

At the present time the sole deterrent to bringing suit is the provision in the Copyright Act under which the loser may be required to pay the winner's counsel fees. The provision has proved ineffectual. Time and again victorious defendants have received awards of fees, in some cases in high amounts; time and again they've found it impossible to recover a penny, either because the plaintiff had nothing to begin with, or because he was crafty enough to transfer whatever he had to a friend or a relative before bringing suit.

Arbitration has been suggested as a solution. It has many virtues. It is private; its machinery is informal and unhampered by strict rules of evidence; it is inexpensive; it offers experts as arbitrators; it affords conclusive results, with scant opportunity for prolonged appeals; and above all, it is quick. There's only one catch: arbitration is voluntary. You can't compel a man to arbitrate if he doesn't want to. The very merits of the process repel the sharper, who sees in the sluggard pace of litigation his strongest weapon, and the fanatic, to whom the excitement of a court battle is the wine of life.[5]

Since the effect of plagiarism disputes is to cast a cloud on First Amendment material, a persuasive argument can be made that such disputes should have a priority on our court calendars. For hold-up men the interval between the start of the suit and the final showdown is a welcome period of attrition, during which hapless defendants may be badgered into settling. A priority would do away with this. To be sure, the expedient would be a palliative, not a cure, since the defendant would still be faced with the vexation and expense of a trial.

Unless a defendant can persuade his adversary to arbitrate, the only swift course open to him is the motion procedure described in the previous chapter.

### How to Avoid Trouble

People who are likely targets for plagiarism attacks often say: What can I do to protect myself? Is there any precaution I can take? Is there any armor I can don?

Absolute immunity from idiotic or dishonest claims is reserved for the mute and the inglorious: the people who never write, paint, carve or compose. For the creative individual there can be no complete safety; if he insists on the nearest approach to it, the advice is simple. Let him make sure he never has a success.

Beyond that, the most that anyone can hope to do is to reduce the risk. Here are a few suggestions:

If you're an author, respect the rules of fair use. If your borrowing is substantial or material, get permission. Date your notes and keep them. They'll help you prove priority of conception, absence of copying, and the diverse sources of your research. Don't use the "personal experiences" your friends pour into your ears unless you're reasonably sure they're genuine, and not reckless or unwitting repetitions of copyrighted works.

If you're a publisher or a theatrical manager, treat writers like human beings. Above all, don't hang onto their scripts. Nothing feeds their suspicion and rancor more than long retention capped with rejection. Many a plagiarism suit which cost the defendant months of worry and thousands of dollars could have been avoided by considerate handling of the potential plaintiff at the outset.

If you're a movie producer, adopt a clear-cut policy as to unsolicited submissions. If you decide not to look at them, ship them back immediately, unopened if possible. If you do examine them, act promptly. Learn to recognize as danger signals extravagant communications received in advance of scripts. Caution your staff. You may be scrupulous; they, conceivably less so. Many a bright idea ostensibly originating in the scenario department of a studio has been found to have its roots in refused works that the top executives never saw. Keep a fully documented record of the time and circumstances of the genesis and development of staff-created stories. Be particularly careful when you produce a film along the lines of a book or a play that you negotiated for and failed to acquire. Remember the *Marie Odile* case, the *White Cargo* case, the *Letty Lynton* case, and—a recent example—the *Ghost Ship* case. Don't settle any claim unless you're satisfied it's well-grounded. Build a reputation for being a tough opponent.

### L'Envoi

There is a truism which lies at the heart of practically everything we've been talking about throughout this book. I've stressed it again and again. It cannot be said too often. I'd like to repeat it once more.

Our cultural wealth is made up of the legacy of the past and the yield of the present. The growth of literature, art and music depends on contributions to this wealth, and withdrawals from it. Every poet owes a debt to Homer; every painter treads in the footsteps of the prehistoric hunter who traced bison on the cave walls of Altamira; every composer is moved by immemorial rhythms. By the same token, every creative person is influenced by, and influences, his contemporaries. What he takes and what he gives determines whether he is pirate or paragon.

As the elder Dumas put it, one cannot build from nothing. Not even God could avoid a prototype. When He created man, He could not or dared not invent him. He made him after His own image.

# Notes and Legal Material

## CHAPTER 1

## NOTES

1. For a detailed discussion of the various causes of similarity which are unrelated to copying, see Chapters 3 and 4.
2. For unconscious plagiarism, see Chapter 18.
3. For further discussion of this subject, see Chapter 20.

## LEGAL MATERIAL

### Plagiarism and Infringement

Plagiarism defined: Tamas v. Twentieth Century-Fox Film Corporation, 25 N. Y. S. 2d 899 (1941).

Infringement defined: Perris v. Hexamer, 99 U. S. 674, 25 L. Ed. 308 (1879). See *infra* under Copyright Infringement.

### What Copyright Does and Does Not Protect

"The right thus secured by the copyright act is not a right to the use of certain words, because they are the common property of the human race, and are as little susceptible of private appropriation as air or sunlight; nor is it the right to ideas alone, since in the absence of means of communicating them they are of value to no one but the author. But the right is to that arrangement of words which the author has selected to express his ideas. Or, as Lord Mansfield describes it, 'an incorporeal right to print a set of intellectual ideas, or modes of thinking, communicated in a set of words and sentences, and modes of expression. It is equally detached from the manuscript, or any other physical existence whatsoever.' 4 Burr. 2396. The nature of this property is perhaps best defined by Mr. Justice Erle in *Jefferys v. Boosey,* 4 H. L. Cas. 815, 867: 'The subject of property is the order of words in the author's composition; not the words themselves, they being analogous to the elements of matter, which are not appropriated unless combined; nor the ideas expressed by those words, they existing in the mind alone, which is not capable of appropriation.' " Holmes v. Hurst, 174 U. S. 82, 19 S. Ct. 606, 43 L. Ed. 904 (1898).

Ideas, as such, are not protected by copyright: Becker v. Loew's, Inc., 133 F. 2d 889 (C. C. A. 7th 1943); cert. den. 319 U. S. 772, 63 S. Ct. 1438, 87 L. Ed. 1720; reh. den. 320 U. S. 811, 64 S. Ct. 30, 88 L. Ed. 490; Nichols v. Universal Pictures Corp., 34 F. 2d 145 (D. C. N. Y. 1929), aff'd 45 F. 2d 119 (C. C. A. 2d 1930), cert. den. 282 U. S. 902, 51 S. Ct. 216, 75 L. Ed. 795; Kalem Co. v. Harper & Brothers, 169 Fed. 61 (C. C. A. 2d 1909), aff'd 222 U. S. 55, 32 S. Ct. 20, 56 L. Ed. 92 (1911), Ann. Cas. 1913 A, 1285; Ansehl v. Puritan Pharmaceutical, 61 F. 2d 131 (C. C. A. 8th 1932); Solomon v. RKO Radio Pictures, 44 F. Supp. 780 (D. C. N. Y. 1942); Borden v. General Motors Corporation, 28 F. Supp. 330 (D. C. N. Y. 1939); Long v. Jordan, 29 F. Supp. 287 (D. C. Cal. 1939); Eichel v. Marcin, 241 Fed. 404 (D. C. N. Y. 1913).

In International News Service v. Associated Press, 248 U. S. 215, 254, 39 S. Ct. 68, 78, 63 L. Ed. 211, 2 A. L. R. 293, affirming 245 Fed. 244 (C. C. A. 2d 1917), Mr. Justice Brandeis said: "At common law, as under the copyright acts, the element in intellectual productions, which secures such protection, is not the knowledge, truths, ideas, or emotions which the composition expresses, but the form or sequence in which they are expressed; that is, 'some new collocation of visible or audible points—of lines, colors, sounds, or words.' "

The purpose of copyright is to promote science and the useful arts. If it were possible by means of copyright to withdraw ideas from the stock of materials to be used by other authors, the field of thought open for development would be dangerously narrowed. Becker v. Loew's, Inc., 133 F. 2d 889 (C. C. A. 7th 1943); cert. den. 319 U. S. 772, 63 S. Ct. 1438, 87 L. Ed. 1720; reh. den. 320 U. S. 811, 64 S. Ct. 30, 88 L. Ed. 490.

But the means of expressing an idea is subject to copyright protection. Where one uses his own way of expressing an idea, such expression constitutes a protectible work. Universal Pictures Co. v. Harold Lloyd Corp., 162 F. 2d 354 (C. C. A. 9th 1947).

Copyrights and patents distinguished: Wheaton v. Peters, 33 U. S. 591, 8 Pet. 591, 8 L. Ed. 1055 (1834); Seip v. Commonwealth Plastics, 85 F. Supp. 741 (D. C. Mass. 1943); Aldrich v. Remington Rand, 52. F. Supp. 732 (D. C. Tex. 1942).

The "metaphysics of the law": Folsom v. Marsh, 2 Story 100, Fed. Cas. No. 4901 (C. C. Mass. 1841).

Classes of matter eligible for statutory copyright specified: 17 U. S. Code, Section 5. See Herbert A. Howell, "The Scope of the Law of Copyright," 4 Virginia L. Rev. 385 (1917).

There is no copyright in general subject matter: A Jewish boy falling in love with a Catholic girl, and the two meeting with parental objections: Nichols v. Universal Pictures Corporation, 34 F. 2d 145 (D. C. N. Y. 1929), aff'd 45 F. 2d 119 (C. C. A. 2d 1930), cert. den. 282 U. S. 902, 51 S. Ct. 216, 75 L. Ed. 795. The deterioration of a white man in the tropics: Simonton v. Gordon, 297 Fed. 625 (D. C. N. Y. 1924) ; but see same case, 12 F. 2d 116 (D. C. N. Y. 1925). Wild horses: Roe-Lawton v. Hal E. Roach Studios, 18 F. 2d 126 (D. C. Cal. 1927). Vendetta: Stephens v. Howells Sales Co., 16 F. 2d 805 (D. C. N. Y. 1926). Life in a convent: Underhill v. Belasco, 254 Fed. 838 (D. C. N. Y. 1918). War espionage: Stevenson v. Harris, 238 Fed. 432 (D. C. N. Y. 1917). Crooks masquerading as respectable people: Eichel v. Marcin, 241 Fed. 404 (D. C. N. Y. 1913). Congressional life in Washington: Maxwell v. Goodwin, 93 Fed. 665 (C. C. Ill. 1899).

News, as such, is not the subject of copyright; but insofar as an article involves literary quality and style, apart from the bare recital of the facts or statement of news, it is protected by copyright: Collins v. Metro-Goldwyn Pictures, 106 F. 2d 83 (C. C. A. 2d 1939) rev'g 25 F. Supp. 781 (D. C. N. Y. 1938) ; Chicago Record-Herald Co. v. Tribune Ass'n, 275 Fed. 797 (C. C. A. 7th 1921) ; Oliver v. Saint Germain Foundation, 41 F. Supp. 296 (D. C. Cal. 1941).

But even naked news may under certain circumstances be "quasi-property": International News Service v. Associated Press, 248 U. S. 215, 39 S. Ct. 68, 63 L. Ed. 211, 2 A. L. R. 293 (1918), aff'g 245 Fed. 244 (C. C. A. 2d 1917). As to property rights in news generally, see 18 Columbia L. Rev. 257 (1918).

If an idea can be expressed in a number of different ways, a number of different copyrights may result; and no infringement will exist: Dymow v. Bolton, 11 F. 2d 690 (C. C. A. 2d 1926) ; Solomon v. RKO Radio Pictures, 44 F. Supp. 780 (D. C. N. Y. 1942).

Material copied from a Government publication cannot be copyrighted: Andrews v. Guenther Pub. Co., 60 F. 2d 555 (D. C. N. Y. 1932). Nor can the opinions of judges. But a reporter of judicial decisions may take out a copyright to his headnotes, statement of facts, arguments and notations: Wheaton v. Peters, 33 U. S. 591, 8 Pet. 591, 8 L. Ed. 1055 (1834).

Neither the United States shield nor the portrait of George Washington can be monopolized via copyright: Carr v. National Capital Press, 71 F. 2d 220 (C. A. D. C. 1934).

To be entitled to copyright, material cannot be a copy of a prior work on which a copyright was obtained: Andrews v. Guenther Pub. Co., 60 F. 2d 555 (D. C. N. Y. 1932).

Where a portion of copyrighted material is original, and a portion is in the public domain, the copyright protects only what is original: Kipling v. G. P. Putnam's Sons, 120 Fed. 631 (C. C. A. 2d 1903), 65 L. R. A. 873; Andrews v. Guenther Pub. Co., *supra.*

Literary property in a book cannot be protected by a trademark, nor otherwise than by copyright: Atlas Mfg. Co. v. Street & Smith, 204 Fed. 398 (C. C. A. 8th 1913), 47 L. R. A. (N. S.) 1002, app. dism. 231 U. S. 348, 34 S. Ct. 73, 58 L. Ed. 262.

A British copyright protects authors in England, but affords no protection in this country against anyone who brings out a pirated edition. However, the pirate is not entitled to an American copyright. Ferris v. Frohman, 233 U. S. 424, 32 S. Ct. 263, 56 L. Ed. 492 (1912); American Code Co. v. Bensinger, 282 Fed. 829 (C. C. A. 2d 1922); Scribner v. Stodart, 21 Fed. Cas. 876.

The law will not lend itself to the protection of immoral material: Broder v. Zeno, 88 Fed. 74 (C. C. Cal. 1904); Martinetti v. Maguire, 16 Fed. Cas. 920 (C. C. Cal. 1867); Glyn v. Western Feature Film Co., W. N. Pt. 5 (Ch. Div., Eng., 1916). But see Cain v. Universal Pictures Corp., 47 F. Supp. 1013 (D. C. Cal. 1942); and Simonton v. Gordon, 12 F. 2d 116 (D. C. N. Y. 1925).

Edward S. Rogers, "Morals and Copyright," 18 Mich. L. Rev. (1920). Matters not protected by copyright: Leon L. Lancester, Jr., 15 Notre Dame Law, 331-44 (1940).

### Priority in Copyright

Priority in time does not confer copyright monopoly. Successor works are entitled to copyright if independently produced: Twentieth Century-Fox Film Corporation v. Dieckhaus, 153 F. 2d 893 (C. C. A. 8th 1946), rev'g. 54 F. Supp. 425 (D. C. Mo. 1944), cert. den. 329 U. S. 716, 67 S. Ct. 46, 91 L. Ed. 621; Harold Lloyd Corp. v. Witwer, 65 F. 2d 1 (C. C. A. 9th 1933), rev'g. 46 F. 2d 792 (D. C. Cal. 1930), cert. dism. 54 S. Ct. 94, 78 L. Ed. 1507.

### No Copyright in a Title

The copyright of a work does not give the copyright owner the exclusive right to the use of the title of the work: Becker v. Loew's, Inc., 133 F. 2d 889 (C. C. A. 7th 1943); cert. den. 319 U. S. 772, 63 S. Ct. 1438, 87 L. Ed. 1720; reh. den. 320 U. S. 811, 64 S. Ct. 30, 88 L. Ed. 490. Atlas Mfg. Co. v. Street & Smith, 204 Fed. 398 (C. C. A. 8th 1913), 47 L. R. A. (N. S.) 1002, app. dism. 231 U. S. 348, 34 S. Ct. 73, 58 L. Ed. 262;

Warner Bros. Pictures v. Majestic Pictures Corporation, 70 F. 2d 310 (C. C. A. 2d 1934); Weissman v. Radio Corporation of America, 80 F. Supp. 612 (D. C. N. Y. 1948); Affiliated Enterprises v. Rock-Ola Mfg. Corporation, 23 F. Supp. 3 (D. C. Ill. 1937); Glaser v. St. Elmo Co., 175 Fed. 276 (C. C. N. Y. 1909).

### Unfair Competition

While copyright does not protect the name or title of copyrighted material, under appropriate circumstances a name may be protected under other theories of law, including the doctrine of unfair competition: Atlas Mfg. Co. v. Street & Smith, *supra*.

Titles litigated: "Varga Girl": Esquire v. Varga Enterprises, 185 F. 2d 14 (C. C. A. 7th 1950). *Lone Ranger*: Lone Ranger v. Cox, 124 F. 2d 650 (C. C. A. 4th 1942), rev'g 39 F. Supp. 487 (D. C. Cal. 1941); Lone Ranger v. Currey, 79 F. Supp. 190 (D. C. Pa. 1948). *Webster's Dictionary*: G. & C. Merriam Co. v. Saalfield, 198 Fed. 369 (C. C. A. 6th 1912). *Tom, Dick and Harry:* Van Dover v. RKO Radio Pictures, 50 U. S. P. Q. 348, 31 T. M. Rep. 251 (D. C. Ill. 1941). *Amos and Andy*: Feldman v. Amos and Andy, 68 F. 2d 746 (Ct. of Cust. and Pat. App. 1934). *March of Time*: Time, Incorporated v. Barshay, 27 F. Supp. 870 (D. C. N. Y. 1939). *Stella Dallas*: Prouty v. National Broadcasting Company, 26 F. Supp. 265 (D. C. Mass. 1939). *The Queen of the Flat Tops*: Johnston v. Twentieth Century-Fox Film Corp., 82 C. A. 2d 796, 187 P. 2d 474 (1947). "Mutt and Jeff": Fisher v. Star Publishing Co., 231 N. Y. 414, 132 N. E. 133 (1921). *Information Please*: Golenpaul v. Rossett, 18 N. Y. S. 2d 889, 174 Misc. 114 (1940). *The Rosary:* Selig Polyscope Co. v. Unicorn Films Corp., 163 N. Y. S. 62 (1917). See also Chaplin v. Amador, 93 Cal. App. 358 (1928).

*Contra*: N. Y. Herald v. Star Co., 146 Fed. 204 (C. C. N. Y. 1906), aff'd 146 Fed. 1023 (C. C. A. 2d 1906); Outcault v. N. Y. Herald, 146 Fed. 205 (C. C. N. Y. 1906); Hene v. Samstag, 198 Fed. 359 (D. C. N. Y. 1912).

For full discussion of the doctrine of unfair competition as applied to the appropriation of titles, see Warner Bros. Pictures v. Majestic Pictures Corporation, 70 F. 2d 310 (C. C. A. 2d 1934). See also 39 Trade Mark Review 75-93.

Use of the doctrine of unfair competition to supplement copyright in the protection of literary and musical property: P. Oberst, 29 Ky. L. J. 271-85 (1941).

Where the substance, not the title, of literary property is wrongfully copied, remedy can be had only under the copyright law, not under the theory of unfair competition: Field v. True Comics, 89 N. Y. S. 2d 35 (1949).

## Copyright Infringement

Copyright infringement consists of (a) the copying of (b) all or a material or substantial part of (c) copyrighted and copyrightable material: Perris v. Hexamer, 99 U. S. 674, 25 L. Ed. 308 (1879); Shurr v. Warner Bros. Pictures, 144 F. 2d 200 (C. C. A. 2d 1944); Twentieth Century-Fox v. Stonesifer, 140 F. 2d 579 (C. C. A. 9th 1944), aff'g 48 F. Supp. 196 (D. C. Cal. 1942); Arnstein v. Edward B. Marks Music Corporation, 82 F. 2d 275 (C. C. A. 2d 1936); Ansehl v. Puritan Pharmaceutical, 61 F. 2d 131 (C. C. A. 8th 1932); Dymow v. Bolton, 11 F. 2d 690 (C. C. A. 2d 1926); Marks v. Leo Feist, 290 Fed. 959 (C. C. A. 2d 1923); Eggers v. Sun Sales Corp., 263 Fed. 373 (C. C. A. 2d 1920); Wilson v. Haber Bros., 275 Fed. 346 (C. C. A. 2d 1921); Carr v. National Capital Press, 71 F. 2d. 220 (C. A. D. C. 1934); Hirsch v. Paramount Pictures, 17 F. Supp. 816 (D. C. Cal. 1937); Lowenfels v. Nathan, 2 F. Supp. 73 (D. C. N. Y. 1932); Rush v. Oursler, 39 F. 2d 468 (D. C. N. Y. 1930); Roe-Lawton v. Hal. E. Roach Studios, 18 F. 2d 126 (D. C. Cal. 1927); Frankel v. Irwin, 34 F. 2d 142 (D. C. N. Y. 1918).

Justice Story stated the rule for determining piracy in Emerson v. Davies, Fed. Cas. No. 4, 436, 3 Story, 768 (C. C. Mass. 1845), as follows: "The true test of piracy is to ascertain whether the defendant has, in fact, used the plan, arrangements, and illustrations of the plaintiff, as the model of his own book, with colorable alterations and variations only to disguise the use thereof; or whether his work is the result of his own labor, skill, and use of common materials, and common sources of knowledge, open to all men, and the resemblances are either accidental or arising from the nature of the subject. In other words, whether the defendant's book is, quo ad hoc, a servile or evasive imitation of the plaintiff's work, or a bona fide original compilation from other common or independent sources."

The test of infringement in books dealing with stock incidents and characters is whether the association and grouping of the incidents and characters are such as to make a new conception or novel arrangement, or whether the conception of the author seeking protection has in fact been appropriated. Simonton v. Gordon, 297 F. 625 (D. C. N. Y. 1924). See also 12 F. 2d 116 (D. C. N. Y. 1925).

Infringement by abridgment: G. Ricordi & Co. v. Mason, 201 Fed. 182 (C. C. N. Y. 1911).

Infringement by parody: Hill v. Whalen & Martell, 220 Fed. 359 (D.

C. N. Y. 1914); R. Ricordi & Co. v. Mason, 201 Fed. 184 (D. C. N. Y. 1912); Green v. Minzensheimer, 177 Fed. 286 (C. C. N. Y. 1909); Bloom & Hamlin v. Nixon, 125 Fed. 977 (D. C. Pa. 1903), 2 Mich. L. Rev. 480 (1904). See Philip Wittenberg, "Parody as Plagiary," *Authors' League Bulletin,* Vol. 33, No. 2, Nov. 1945.

Infringement generally: A. F. Driscoll, "Copyright Infringement," 11 Fordham L. Rev. 63-70 (1942); and T. M. Ryan, "Infringement," 20 Notre Dame Law 172-3 (1944).

## *Similarity*

Similarity—even close similarity—is not enough. To constitute plagiarism, there must be copying: Twentieth Century-Fox v. Stonesifer, 140 F. 2d 579 (C. C. A. 9th 1944), aff'g 48 F. Supp. 196 (D. C. Cal. 1942); Wilkie v. Santly Bros., 91 F. 2d 978 (C. C. A. 2d 1937) aff'g 13 F. Supp. 136 (D. C. N. Y. 1935); Harold Lloyd Corporation v. Witwer, 65 F. 2d 1 (C. C. A. 9th 1933), cert. dism. 54 S. Ct. 94, 78 L. Ed. 1507; Pinci v. Twentieth Century-Fox Film Corp., 95 F. Supp. 844 (D. C. N. Y. 1951); Gingg v. Twentieth Century-Fox, 56 F. Supp. 701 (D. C. Cal. 1944); Cain v. Universal Pictures Co., 47 F. Supp. 1013 (D. C. Cal. 1942); O'Rourke v. RKO Radio Pictures, 44 F. Supp. 480 (D. C. Mass. 1942); Seltzer v. Sunbrock, 22 F. Supp. 621 (D. C. Cal. 1938).

In a passage cited with approval in Chautauqua School v. National School, 238 Fed. 151 (C. C. A. 2d 1916), and in Fred Fisher v. Dillingham, 298 Fed. 145 (D. C. N. Y. 1924), Drone says in his well-known work on Copyright (p. 205): "Works alike may be original. It is not essential that any production, to be original or new within the meaning of the law of copyright, shall be different from another. Whether the composition for which copyright is claimed is the same as or different from, or whether it is like or unlike, an existing one, are matters of which the law takes no cognizance, except to determine whether the production is the result of independent labor or of copying. Two or more authors may write on the same subject, treat it similarly, and use the same common materials in like manner or for one purpose. Their productions may contain the same thoughts, sentiments, ideas; they may be identical. Such resemblance or identity is material only as showing whether there has been unlawful copying. In many cases the natural or necessary resemblance between two productions which are the result of independent labor will amount to substantial identity . . . But, notwithstanding their likeness to one another, any number of productions of the same kind may be original within the meaning of the law, and no conditions as to originality are imposed upon the makers, except that each shall be the producer of that for which he claims protection."

"To sustain it [an infringement suit], however, more must appear than the mere similarity or even identity, of the supposed infringement with the part in question. In this lies one distinction between a patent and a copyright. One may infringe a patent by the innocent reproduction of the machines patented, but the law imposes no prohibition upon those who, without copying, independently arrive at the precise combination of words or notes which have been copyrighted." Fred Fisher v. Dillingham, 298 Fed. 145 (D. C. N. Y. 1924).

## Copying

There may be similarity without copying, but there can't be copying without similarity: Arnstein v. Edward B. Marks Music Corporation, 11 F. Supp. 535 (D. C. N. Y. 1935), aff'd 82 F. 2d 275 (C. C. A. 2d 1936); Chautauqua School v. National School, 238 Fed. 151 (C. C. A. 2d 1916); West Publishing Co. v. Edward Thompson Co., 169 Fed. 833 (C. C. N. Y. 1909), mod. 176 Fed. 833 (C. C. A. 2d 1910); Hirsch v. Paramount Pictures, 17 F. Supp. 816 (D. C. Cal. 1937); Fred Fisher v. Dillingham, 298 Fed. 145 (D. C. N. Y. 1924).

There can be no copyright infringement without copying: Ricker v. General Electric Co., 162 F. 2d 141 (C. C. A. 2d 1947); Ansehl v. Puritan Pharmaceutical, 61 F. 2d 131 (C. C. A. 8th 1932); Kirke La Shelle Co. v. Armstrong, 159 N. Y. S. 363, 173 App. Div. 232 (1916).

"Copying the whole or a substantial part of a copyrighted work constitutes and is an essential element of infringement. It is not confined to literal repetition or reproduction but includes also the various modes in which the matter of any work may be adopted, imitated, transferred, or reproduced with more or less colorable alteration to disguise the piracy. But, on the principle of *de minimis non curat lex,* it is necessary that a substantial part of the copyrighted work be taken." 9 Cyc. 939, 940. Quoted in Hoffman v. Le Traunik, 209 Fed. 375 (D. C. N. Y. 1913), at p. 379

Copying need not be *in ipsissima verba.* Copying "by evasion" is sufficient to constitute infringement: Fleischer Studios v. Ralph A. Freundlich, 5 F. Supp. 808 (D. C. N. Y. 1934), aff'd 73 F. 2d 276 (C. C. A. 2d 1934), cert. den. 294 U. S. 717, 55 S. Ct. 516, 79 L. Ed. 1250; Ansehl v. Puritan Pharmaceutical, *supra;* Nutt v. National Institute, 31 F. 2d 236 (C. C. A. 2d 1929), aff'g 28 F. 2d 132 (D. C. Conn. 1928); King Features Syndicate v. Fleischer, 299 Fed. 533 (C. C. A. 2d 1924); Gingg v. Twentieth Century-Fox, 56 F. Supp. 701 (D. C. Cal. 1944); Triangle

Publications v. N. E. Publishing Co., 46 F. Supp. 198 (D. C. Mass. 1942) ;
Bobrecker v. Denebeim, 28 F. Supp. 383 (D. C. Mo. 1939) ; Borden v.
General Motors, 28 F. Supp. 330 (D. C. N. Y. 1939).

To constitute copyright infringement, the whole or even a large portion
of a copyrighted book need not be copied. It is enough if a material part
is copied, even though a small part of the whole. Perkins Marine Lamp &
Hardware Co. v. Goodwin Stanley Co., 86 F. Supp. 630 (D. C. N. Y.
1949).

Copying must be established with reasonable certainty: Pinci v. Twentieth Century-Fox Film Corp., 95 F. Supp. 884 (D. C. N. Y. 1951).

## What Is a Copy?

"A copy is that which comes so near to the original as to give to every
person seeing it the idea created by the original": West v. Francis, 5 B. &
Ald. 737, 106 Full Reprint 1361 (1822). Quoted with approval, White-
Smith Music Co. v. Apollo Co., 209 U. S. 1, 28 S. Ct. 319, 52 L. Ed. 655,
14 Ann. Cas. 628. See also Harold Lloyd Corporation v. Witwer, 65 F.
2d 1 (C. C. A. 9th 1933), rev'g 46 F. 2d 792 (D. C. Cal. 1930), cert.
dism. 54 S. Ct. 94, 78 L. Ed. 1507; Gingg v. Twentieth Century-Fox,
56 F. Supp. 701 (D. C. Cal. 1944) ; Barbadillo v. Goldwyn, 42 F. 2d 881
(D. C. Cal. 1930) ; Carr v. National Capital Press, 71 F. 2d 220 (C. A.
D. C. 1934) ; King Features Syndicate v. Fleischer, 299 Fed. 533 (C. C. A.
2d 1924).

*Abie's Irish Rose* case: Nichols v. Universal Pictures Corporation, 45 F.
2d 119 (C. C. A. 2d 1930), aff'g 34 F. 2d 145 (D. C. N. Y. 1929), cert.
den. 282 U. S. 902, 51 S. Ct. 216, 75 L. Ed. 795.

## Access and Similarity

Where access is shown, the defendant must adduce strong proof of independent conception. "With access admitted, similarity of incident rests
upon a high degree of probability of copying, and a low degree of probability of independent creation." Shipman v. RKO Radio Pictures, 100 F.
2d 533 (C. C. A. 2d 1938), aff'g 20 F. Supp. 249 (D. C. N. Y. 1938).
Also Kustoff v. Chaplin, 120 F. 2d 551 (C. C. A. 9th 1941) ; Cain v.
Universal Pictures Co., 47 F. Supp. 1013 (D. C. Cal. 1942) ; O'Rourke
v. RKO Radio Pictures, 44 F. Supp. 480 (D. C. Mass. 1942) ; Hirsch v.
Paramount Pictures, 17 F. Supp. 816 (D. C. Cal. 1937) ; Golding v. RKO
Pictures, 35 Cal. 2d 690, 221 P. 2d 95 (1950).

Direct access need not be proved. It may be inferred from (a) the circumstances, and (b) the similarity of the two works: Wilkie v. Santly
Bros., 13 F. Supp. 136 (D. C. N. Y. 1935), aff'd 91 F. 2d 978 (C. C. A.

2d 1937) ; Jewel Music Pub. Co. v. Leo Feist, 62 F. Supp. 596 (D. C.
N. Y. 1945) ; Allen v. Walt Disney Productions, 41 F. Supp. 134 (D. C.
N. Y. 1941).

Duplication of errors is highly significant evidence of infringement:
Callaghan v. Myers, 128 U. S. 617, 662, 9 S. Ct. 177, 190, 32 L. Ed. 547
(1888).

Evidence of plagiarism: H. G. Fox, 6 U. Toronto L. J. 414-60 (1945-6).

### The "Ordinary Observer" Test

Twentieth Century-Fox v. Stonesifer, 140 F. 2d 579 (C. C. A. 9th
1944), aff'g 48 F. Supp. 196 (D. C. Cal. 1942) ; Kustoff v. Chaplin,
120 F. 2d 551 (C. C. A. 9th 1941) ; Harold Lloyd Corporation v. Witwer,
65 F. 2d 1 (C. C. A. 9th 1933), cert. dism. 54 S. Ct. 94, 78 L. Ed. 1507;
King Features Syndicate v. Fleischer, 299 Fed. 533 (C. C. A. 2d 1924) ;
Gingg v. Twentieth Century-Fox, 56 F. Supp. 701, 702 (D. C. Cal. 1944) ;
Cain v. Universal Pictures Co., 47 F. Supp. 1013 (D. C. Cal. 1942) ;
Hirsch v. Paramount Pictures, 17 F. Supp. 816 (D. C. Cal. 1937) ; Echeverria v. Warner Bros. Pictures, 12 F. Supp. 632 (D. C. Cal. 1935) ; Wiren v.
Shubert Theater Corporation, 5 F. Supp. 358 (D. C. N. Y. 1933) aff'd
70 F. 2d 1023 (C. C. A. 2d 1934) ; Roe-Lawton v. Hal. E. Roach Studios,
18 F. 2d 126, 128 (D. C. Cal. 1927) ; Dymow v. Bolton, 11 F. 2d 690,
692 (C. C. A. 2d 1926) ; Frankel v. Irwin, 34 F. 2d 142, 144 (D. C. N.
Y. 1918) ; Stanley v. C. B. S., 35 Cal. 2d 653, 221 P. 2d 73 (1950).

"Infringement of a work of imagination is determined by the result of
comparative reading on the imagination of the reader, not by a dissection
of sentences or incidents." Frankel v. Irwin, 34 F. 2d 142, 144 (D. C.
N. Y. 1918). Labored analyses and expert testimony are frowned on:
Nichols v. Universal Pictures Corporation, 45 F. 2d 119, 122 (C. C. A. 2d
1930), cert. den. 282 U. S. 902, 51 S. Ct. 216, 75 L. Ed. 795; Lowenfels
v. Nathan, 2 F. Supp. 73, 80 (D. C. N. Y. 1932).

### Intent to Infringe

Lack of intention to infringe is no defense. The result, not the inten-
tion, determines the question of infringement: Buck v. Jewell La Salle
Realty, 283 U. S. 191, 51 S. Ct. 410, L. Ed. 971 (1931) ; Harold Lloyd
Corporation v. Witwer, 65 F. 2d 1 (C. C. A. 9th 1933), rev'g 46 F. 2d
792 (D. C. Cal. 1930), cert. dism. 54 S Ct. 94, 78 L. Ed. 1507; Toksvig v.
Bruce Pub. Co., 181 F. 2d 664 (C. C. A. 7th 1950) ; Shipman v. RKO
Pictures, 100 F. 2d 533 (C. C. A. 2d 1938) ; Leigh v. Gerber, 86 F. Supp.
320 (D. C. N. Y. 1949) ; Alden-Rochelle v. ASCAP, 80 F. Supp. 888
(D. C. N. Y. 1948) ; Buck v. Russo, 25 F. Supp. 317 (D. C. Mass. 1938) ;

Witmark & Sons v. Calloway, 22 F. 2d 412 (D. C. Tenn. 1927); Haas v. Leo Feist, 234 Fed. 105 (D. C. N. Y. 1916). But see Fendler v. Morosco, 253 N. Y. 281 (1930), rev'g 217 App. Div. 791.

While intent to infringe is not essential to make the infringer liable, it has a bearing on the question of fair use: New York Tribune v. Otis & Co., 39 F. Supp. 67 (D. C. N. Y. 1941).

"Everything registers somewhere in our memories, and no one can tell what may evoke it. . . . Once it appears that another has in fact used the copyright as the source of his production, he has invaded the author's rights. It is no excuse that in so doing his memory has played him a trick." Fred Fisher v. Dillingham, 298 Fed. 145, 147, 148 (D. C. N. Y. 1924).

Innocent publisher of plagiarized material is liable: De Acosta v. Brown, 146 F. 2d 408 (C. C. A. 2d 1944), aff'g 50 F. Supp. 615 (D. C. N. Y. 1943), cert. den. 325 U. S. 862, 65 S. Ct. 1197, 89 L. Ed. 1982, and 325 U. S. 862, 65 S. Ct. 1198, 89 L. Ed. 1983. See 93 U. Pa. L. Rev. 459-60 (1945), and 19 So. Calif. L. Rev. 140-1 (1945).

### From One Medium into Another

Strip cartoon character held infringed by a doll: King Features Syndicate v. Fleischer, 299 Fed. 533 (C. C. A. 2d 1924).

*The Charge of the Cuirassiers*: G. Ricordi & Co. v. Mason, 201 Fed. 182 (C. C. N. Y. 1911).

*Tableaux Vivants*: Hanfstaengl v. Empire Palace, 2 Chancery 1 and 3 Chancery 109 (1894), aff'd A. C. 20 (L. R. 1895).

See also Turner v. Robinson, 10 Irish Chancery 121, 510 (1859, 1860). A two-dimensional design for a memorial held infringed by a memorial in three-dimensions: Jones Bros. Co. v. Underkoffler, 16 F. Supp. 729 (D. C. Pa. 1936).

A copyrighted illustration may not, without the owner's permission, be stamped on leather and applied to the seats and backs of chairs: Falk v. T. P. Howell & Co., 37 Fed. 202 (C. C. N. Y. 1888).

### Penalties

Penalties for infringement, civil: 17 U. S. Code, Section 101. Criminal: 17 U. S. Code, Section 104.

See J. H. Neu, "The Rights of a Copyright Owner," 17 Notre Dame Law 373-406 (June 1942).

### Fair Use

The Supreme Court quotation about the purpose of copyright is from Fox Film Corp. v. Doyal, 286 U. S. 123, 127, 52 S. Ct. 546, 76 L. Ed. 1010 (1932).

Fair use is the privilege in others than the copyright owner to use the copyrighted material in a reasonable manner without the owner's consent, notwithstanding the monopoly granted to the owner: Toksvig v. Bruce Pub. Co., 181 F. 2d 664 (C. C. A. 7th 1950).

As respects fair use, the basic distinction between a patent and a copyright is that the public may not use a patented invention, but may freely avail itself of any system, art or manufacture described in a copyrighted book: Aldrich v. Remington Rand, 52 F. Supp. 732 (D. C. Tex 1942).

Criteria of fair use: Folsom v. Marsh, 2 Story 100, Fed. Cas. No. 4901 (C. C. Mass. 1845); Lawrence v. Dana, Fed. Cas. No. 8136, 4 Cliff. 1 (C. C. Mass. 1869); Bradbury v. Hotten, L. R. 8 Excheq. 1 (1872); Toksvig v. Bruce Pub. Co., supra; Sampson & Murdock Co. v. Seaver Radford Co., 140 Fed. 539 (C. C. A. 1st 1905); Thompson v. Gernsback, 94 F. Supp. 453 (D. C. N. Y. 1950); New York Tribune v. Otis & Co., 39 F. Supp. 67 (D. C. N. Y. 1941); Carr v. National Capital Press, 71 F. 2d 220 (C. A. D. C. 1934); Yale University Press v. Row, Peterson & Co., 40 F. 2d 290 (D. C. N. Y. 1930); M. Witmark v. Pastime Amusement Co., 298 Fed. 470 (D. C. S. Car. 1924); Karll v. Curtis Publishing Co., 39 F. Supp. 836 (D. C. Wisc. 1941); Henry Holt & Co. v. Liggett & Myers Tobacco Co., 23 F. Supp. 302 (D. C. Pa. 1938).

Lord Cottenham: "When it comes to a question of quantity, it must be very vague. One writer might take all the vital part of another's book, though it might be but a small proportion of the book in quantity. It is not only quantity, but value, that is always looked to. It is useless to refer to any particular cases as to quantity." Bramwell v. Holcomb, 3 My. & Cr. 737 (1836). See also Saunders v. Smith, 3 My. & Cr. 711 (1838).

"It is always contemplated necessarily that the person who buys a copy of a protected work and reads it will get therefrom certain ideas, and possibly certain information and knowledge that may theretofore have been unknown to him. No one would argue that the individual thus acquiring information, knowledge, ideas or other elements from the protected work is not free to use those ideas, that information or that knowledge in any way he sees fit to use it. The copyright statute does not contemplate any such prohibition. The reader is free to use the ideas, the knowledge or the information. He is prohibited only from *copying* the protected work either in whole or in part, and the question of whether he has copied the protected work . . . remains at all times solely a question of fact." A. F. Driscoll: "Copyright infringement," 11 Fordham L. Rev. 63-70 (1942).

"A copyrighted work is subject to fair criticism, serious or humorous. So far as is necessary to that end, quotations may be made from it, and it may be described by words, representations, pictures, or suggestions. It is not always easy to say where the line should be drawn between the use which for such purposes is permitted and that which is forbidden." Hill v. Whalen, 220 Fed. 359 (D. C. N. Y. 1914).

Fair use: E. F. Miller, 15 So. Calif. L. Rev. 249-54 (1942).

Infringement by mimicry: Bloom & Hamlin v. Nixon, 125 Fed. 977 (D. C. Pa. 1903). See note, 2 Mich. L. Rev. 480 (1904). See also Green v. Minzensheimer, 177 Fed. 286 (C. C. N. Y. 1909), and Green v. Luby, 177 Fed. 287 (C. C. N. Y. 1909).

Acknowledgement of source by the infringer is no defense to a suit for infringement: Toksvig v. Bruce Pub. Co., 181 F. 2d 664 (C. C. A. 7th 1950).

Common law rights in literary property are generally limited to unpublished works, and are of a wider and more exclusive nature than statutory rights in published works. The common law prohibits *any kind of unauthorized interference* with or use of an unpublished work, while a statutory copyright permits fair use: Stanley v. C. B. S., 35 Cal. 2d 653, 221 P. 2d 73 (1950).

## CHAPTER 2

### NOTES

1. Ralph Waldo Emerson, *Quotation and Originality,* Complete Works, London: George Rutledge & Sons, Ltd., 1883, Vol. 8, pp. 170-172.
2. Wendell Phillips, Lecture, "The Lost Arts," *Warner's Library of the World's Best Literature,* Vol. 29, p. 11, 425.
3. "It has long been a commonplace of criticism that great poets seldom invent their myths; and it may in time become a commonplace of criticism that they seldom invent their forms. But in default of the lesser invention, they have the larger imagination; and there is no pedantry in seeking to emphasize the distinction between these two qualities, often carelessly confused. The poets, by the mere fact that they are poets, possess the power of imagination, which alone gives vitality and significance to the ready-made plots they are willing to run into ready-made molds. Invention can do no more than devise; imagination can interpret. The details of *Romeo and Juliet* may be more or less contained in the tale of the Italian novelist; but the inner meaning of that ideal tragedy of youthful love is seized and set forth only by the English dramatist." Brander Matthews, "Invention and Imagination," *Inquiries and Opinions,* New York: Charles Scribner's Sons, 1907, pp. 98-99.

4. Theodore Meyer Greene, *The Arts and the Art of Criticism,* Princeton: Princeton University Press, 1940, p. 406.

"And yet there remains a tendency to insist, when we praise a poet, upon those aspects of his work in which he least resembles any one else. In these aspects or parts of his work we pretend to find what is individual, what is the peculiar essence of the man. We dwell with satisfaction upon the poet's difference from his predecessors, especially his immediate predecessors; we endeavour to find something that can be isolated in order to be enjoyed. Whereas if we approach a poet without this prejudice we shall often find that not only the best, but the most individual parts of his work may be those in which the dead poets, his ancestors, assert their immortality most vigorously." T. S. Eliot, "Tradition and the Individual Talent," *Selected Essays,* 1917-1932, New York: Harcourt, Brace and Company, Inc., 1932. See also Irving Babbitt, "On Being Original," *Literature and the American College,* Boston: Houghton Mifflin Company, 1908, pp. 215-233; and Logan Pearsall Smith, "Four Romantic Words," *Words and Idioms,* London: Constable & Co., Ltd., 1925, pp. 66-134.

## LEGAL MATERIAL

To be copyrightable, a work must be "original." The test as to originality is whether the work is the result of independent labor or of copying: Higgins v. Keuffel, 140 U. S. 428, 11 S. Ct. 731, 35 L. Ed. 470 (1891); Burrow-Giles Lithographic v. Sarony, 111 U. S. 53, 59, 4 S. Ct. 279, 28 L. Ed. 349 (1884); Trade-Mark Cases: 100 U. S. 82, 94 (1879); Baker v. Selden, 101 U. S. 99, 102, 25 L. Ed. 841 (1880); Harold Lloyd Corporation v. Witwer, 65 F. 2d 1 (C. C. A. 9th 1933), cert. dism. 54 S. Ct. 94, 78 L. Ed. 1507; Dorsey v. Old Surety Life Ins. Co., 98 F. 2d 872 (C. C. A. 10th 1938); Deutsch v. Arnold, 22 F. Supp. 101 (D. C. N. Y. 1938), mod. 98 F. 2d 686 (C. C. A. 2d 1938); Gerlach-Barklow v. Morris & Bendien, 23 F. 2d 158, 161 (C. C. A. 2d 1927); Jewelers' Circular Pub. Co. v. Keystone Pub. Co., 281 Fed. 83, 87 (C. C. A. 2d 1922); Edwards & Deutsch v. Boorman, 15 F. 2d 35 (C. C. A. 7th 1926); American Code Co. v. Bensinger, 282 Fed. 829 (C. C. A. 2d 1922); Gross v. Seligman, 212 Fed. 930, 931 (C. C. A. 2d 1914); National Institute v. Nutt, 28 F. 2d 132, 135 (D. C. Conn. 1928); Aronson v. Fleckenstein, 28 Fed. 75 (C. C. Ill. 1896); Emerson v. Davies, Fed. Cas. No. 4436 (C. C. Mass. 1845); Andrews v. Guenther Pub. Co., 60 F. 2d 555 (D. C. N. Y. 1932); Yale University Press v. Row, Peterson & Co., 40 F. 2d 290 (D. C. N. Y. 1930); Hogue-Sprague v. Meyer, 31 F. 2d 583, 586 (D. C. N. Y. 1929); Fred Fisher v. Dillingham, 298 Fed. 145, 147 (D. C. N. Y. 1924); Stevenson v. Harris, 238 Fed. 432 (D. C. N. Y. 1917); Chautauqua School v. National School, 211 Fed. 1014, 1016 (D. C. N. Y. 1914); Hoffman v. Le Traunik, 209 Fed. 375 (D. C. N. Y. 1913); Jones Bros. Co. v. Underkoffler, 16 F. Supp. 729 (D. C. Pa. 1936); Brown v. Ferris, 204 N. Y. S. 190 (1924); Aronson v. Baker, 43 N. J. Eq. 365, 12 A. 177 (1888); Wood v. Boosey, 2 L. R. Q. B. 340 (1867).

The copyright case in which Justice Story discusses originality is *Emerson* v. *Davies, supra*. Here is what he says: "In truth, in literature, in science and in art, there are, and can be, few, if any, things, which, in an abstract sense, are strictly new and original throughout. Every book in literature, science, and art, borrows, and must necessarily borrow, and use much which was well known and used before. No man creates a new language for himself, at least if he be a wise man, in writing a book. He contents himself with the use of language already known and used and understood by others. No man writes exclusively from his own thoughts, unaided and uninstructed by the thoughts of others. The thoughts of every man are, more or less, a combination of what other men have thought and expressed, although they may be modified, exalted, or improved by his own genius or reflection. If no book could be the subject of copyright which was not new and original in the elements of which it is composed, there could be no ground for any copyright in modern times, and we should be obliged to ascend very high, even in antiquity, to find a work entitled to such eminence. . . ."

The originality which qualifies material for statutory copyright has to do with form of expression, not with novelty of subject matter. Chamberlin v. Uris Sales Corporation, 150 F. 2d 512 (C. C. A. 2d 1945), aff'g 56 F. Supp. 987 (D. C. N. Y. 1944); Whist Club v. Foster, 42 F. 2d 782 (D. C. N. Y. 1929).

Copyrights and patents distinguished: Wheaton v. Peters, 33 U. S. 591, 8 Pet. 591, 8 L. Ed. 1055 (1834); J. F. Oberlin, 26 J. Patent Office Soc. 203-6 (March 1944); and J. H. Neu, 17 Notre Dame Law 373-406 (June 1942). As to the degre of originality required of an invention to warrant the issuance of a patent, see Great A. & P. Tea Co. v. Supermarket Equip. Corp. 340 U. S. 147, 71 S. Ct. 127, 95 L. Ed. 118 (1950).

Artistic merit not essential to copyright: Atlas Mfg. Co. v. Street & Smith, 204 Fed. 398 (C. C. A. 8th 1913), 47 L. R. A. (N. S.) 1002, app. dism. 231 U. S. 348, 34 S. Ct. 73, 58 L. Ed. 262 (1913); Bleistein v. Donaldson Lithographing Co., 188 U. S. 239, 251, 23 S. Ct. 298, 47 L. Ed. 460 (1903); Allegrini v. De Angelis, 59 F. Supp. 248 (D. C. Pa. 1945), aff'd 149 F. 2d 815 (C. C. A. 3d 1945); Contemporary Arts v. F. W. Woolworth Co., 93 F. Supp. 739 (D. C. Mass. 1950); Henderson v.

Tompkins, 60 Fed. 758, 764 (C. C. Mass. 1894); Boucicault v. Fox, Fed. Cas. 1691, 5 Blatchf. 87 (C. C. N. Y. 1862).

In Bleistein v. Donaldson Lithographing Co., *supra,* Mr. Justice Holmes said: "Personality always contains something unique. It expresses its singularity even in handwriting, and a very modest grade of art has in it something irreducible, which is one man's alone. That something he may copyright. . . ."

"To be worthy of copyright, a thing must have some value as a composition, sufficiently material to lift it above utter insignificance and worthlessness." Henderson v. Tompkins, 60 Fed. 758 (C. C. Mass. 1894), quoting from Drone on Copyright.

Requisite amount of originality: Shapiro, Bernstein & Co. v. Miracle Record Co., 91 F. Supp. 473 (D. C. Ill. 1950); National Comics Publications v. Fawcett Publications, 93 F. Supp. 349 (D. C. N. Y. 1950); Amsterdam v. Triangle Publications, 93 F. Supp. 79 (D. C. Pa. 1950).

## CHAPTER 3

### NOTES

1. I don't say that this is universal practice in the theater. It is widespread enough to try the soul of any young playwright. Scripts have on occasion been kept for two or three years, and sometimes lost. The path of an unknown writer in any field is certainly not strewn with roses; but no book or magazine publisher would dream of treating him as callously as does the stage impresario.

2. "To anyone understanding the subtlety of mental processes, and especially the movements of the imagination," says Brander Matthews, "a similarity of situation is often not only not a proof of plagiarism, but a proof that there has been no plagiarism. This sounds like a paradox, but I think I can make my meaning clear and evident. When we find the same strikingly original idea differently handled by two authors, we may absolve the later from any charge of literary theft if we find that his treatment of the novel situation differs from his predecessor's. If the treatment is different, we may assume that the second writer was not aware of the existence of the first writer's work. And for this reason: if the later author were acquainted with the startlingly novel effect of the earlier author, he could not have treated the same subject without repeating certain of the minor peculiarities also. He must perforce have taken over with the theme in some measure treatment also. All literary workmen know how difficult it is to disentangle the minor

details from the main idea and to strip the idea naked, discarding the mere detail. Had the second writer known of the first writer's work, he could not help being influenced by it. Thus it is that a similarity of subject may be evidence of originality." *Pen and Ink,* New York: Charles Scribner's Sons, 1902, p. 46.

3. See "How Writers Perpetuate Stereotypes," *The Writer's War Board,* 1945; and "Negro Stereotypes on the Screen," *Hollywood Quarterly,* Vol. 1, No 2 (Jan. 1946).

4. John Crosby has described this type in the New York *Herald Tribune.* "A Woman of Growing Awareness," he says, "is one who is charmed by a strange man in a subway station (he retrieves her purse) or a saloon where she goes to the telephone (he rescues her from a drunk) or a midtown street corner (he gives her directions) and then marries him a week later after a whirlwind courtship mostly conducted on the roller coaster at Coney Island. Gradually, she Grows Aware. There is something awfully fishy about her husband. He spends all his time in the cellar, digging. He disappears for weeks at a time, visiting his mother, he says. When he returns, he carries a lead box bearing the words hydrochloric acid in which, he explains, are his dirty shirts which he plans to wash personally in the cellar. After twenty minutes if this is radio, at the end of the second act if it's a play, page 212 if it's a book, she says: 'Why are you staring at me that way?' That is a Woman of Growing Awareness. So widespread is this role it's become almost a separate branch of the acting profession."

5. "Courtroom procedure never changes in the movies. The judge always looks like Lewis Stone; or, if it's a rural courthouse, like Edgar Kennedy. He's either patient and dignified, or irascible and prejudiced. No middling nonsense. Every character, major or minor, is a type. The testifying policeman is a dolt, the false witnesses are shifty-eyed, the housewife-juror all but wears her apron, and the lawyers are a class unto themselves. The whole entourage resembles an actual courtroom about as much as Lana Turner resembles the average working-girl she occasionally portrays." Milton Lewis, "Film Court Trials Stranger than Truth," New York *Herald Tribune,* December 11, 1949.

6. "To Make Boxing Films, Follow the Formula," New York *Herald Tribune,* April 17, 1949. See Victor P. Hass' recipe for swashbuckling romantic fiction in *The Saturday Review of Literature,* August 20, 1949. And here is Archer Winsten speaking of the Cagney movie *White Heat:* "If you look at the synopsis of this picture, you'll think you've seen it a thousand times. Here's the train robbery by the gang, the pursuit by the Treasury Agents, and the contention between Gang

Leader Cagney and the jealous underling who covets Cagney's pretty moll. . . . And here are the prison sequences, the crash-out, and the finale where everyone opposing the law gets killed." *The New York Post Home News,* Sept. 4, 1949. It's only fair to say that Winsten thought the picture fine despite its trite outlines.

7. Sidney Skolsky, "Clichés and Cucumongas," *The New York Post,* September 25, 1947. Also his columns of December 8, 1943, and December 13, 1944, in the same paper.

8. See Pierre Sichel, "Film Clichés Still Make Beautiful Music," New York *Herald Tribune,* Nov. 13, 1949; John Crosby's columns in the New York *Herald Tribune,* Nov. 12, 1948, Sept. 15, 1949, and Jan. 21, 1951. See also Frank Sullivan's numerous cliché-expert pieces in *The New Yorker.*

9. "The modern poets, in their search for epic material, have laid under tribute the history of the world and the mythologies of all races. Yet the limited number of really epic subjects thus discovered testifies either to the weakness of literary invention or to the narrow bounds of heroic possibilities. A few old themes, already used in the twelfth and thirteenth centuries, have served again for most of the ambitious narrative compositions of the nineteenth. Tennyson, Browning, William Morris, and Swinburne, in English, and Richard Wagner in German have been the chief narrative poets of our time, and their work has been largely to infuse modern poetical sentiments and modern philosophy into medieval stories. Except Browning, who is a son of the Renaissance, these poets have all found a great part of their epic material in the early traditions of the Celtic and Germanic races." George McLean Harper, "The Legend of the Holy Grail," *Warner's Library of the World's Best Literature,* Vol. 19, p. 7515.

Dr. Richard Chase insists that myth is the backbone of literature, and that the writers of today, confronted with the spiritual bankruptcy of the naturalistic and symbolistic schools, must turn to mankind's myths if they are to produce books that will survive. See *Quest for Myth,* Louisiana State University Press, 1949.

10. "It is easy to see that what is best written or done by genius, in the world, was no man's work, but came by wide social labor, when a thousand wrought like one, sharing the same impulse. Our English Bible is a wonderful specimen of the strength and music of the English language. But it was not made by one man, or at one time; but centuries and churches brought it to perfection. There never was a time when there was not some translation existing. The Liturgy, admired for its energy and pathos, is an anthology of the piety of ages and

nations, a translation of the prayers and forms of the Catholic Church —these collected, too, in long periods, from the prayers and meditations of every saint and sacred writer, all over the world. Grotius makes the like remark in respect to the Lord's Prayer, that the single clauses of which it is composed were already in use, in the time of Christ, in the rabbinical forms. He picked out the grains of gold." Ralph Waldo Emerson, *Representative Men,* Boston: Houghton Mifflin Company, 1883.

### LEGAL MATERIAL

Access, even when coupled with similarity, is not conclusive as to copying. It merely shows opportunity to copy: See Legal Material, Chapter I.

"Similarity or identity is merely evidence of copying, and it is only where the similarity or identity is due to copying from the copyrighted work that the later work may be deemed an infringement." Gingg v. Twentieth-Century-Fox, 56 F. Supp. 701 (D. C. Cal. 1944).

Stock characters: "Maids and cooks . . . are part and parcel of almost every household comedy." Detectives are "dramatic props that are as old as American play writing." West v. Hatch, 49 F. Supp. 307 (D. C. N. Y. 1943).

Jack London's *Just Meat*: London v. Biograph Co., 231 Fed. 696 (C. C. A. 2d 1916).

The broad outlines of an old plot may be freely appropriated; a particular treatment of it may not: Dymow v. Bolton, 11 F. 2d 690 (C. C. A. 2d 1926) ; Dam v. Kirke La Shelle Co., 166 Fed. 589 (C. C. N. Y. 1908), aff'd 175 Fed. 902 (C. C. A. 2d 1910) ; Stephens v. Howells Sales Co., 16 F. 2d 805 (D. C. N. Y. 1926) ; Frankel v. Irwin, 34 F. 2d 142 (D. C. N. Y. 1918) ; Underhill v. Belasco, 254 Fed. 838 (D. C. N. Y. 1918) ; Eichel v. Marcin, 241 Fed. 404 (D. C. N. Y. 1917).

The *Vendetta* case: Stephens v. Howells Sales Co., 16 F. 2d 805 (D. C. N. Y. 1926).

Gozzi's estimate is mentioned in International Film Service Co. v. Affiliated Distributors, 283 Fed. 229 (D. C. N. Y. 1922).

"The dramatic situations which form the stuff of drama are few. The entire dramatic literature of the world can be reduced to some three dozen situations. In fact, an ingenious Frenchman has written a book in which, after analyzing the entire dramatic literature from the time of the Greek and Hindu dramas to the present time, he concludes that all these dramatic works present, in variant form, the few situations which he has analyzed. A rule, therefore, which would place originality not in the manner of treatment of a theme, but in the theme, would place the hack writer upon the same footing with the genius." Echeverria v. Warner Bros. Pictures, 12 F. Supp. 632, 634 (D. C. Cal. 1935).

There is no property right in hackneyed incident: Stowing away to escape pursuit: Tamas v. Twentieth Century-Fox Film Corporation, 25 N. Y. S. 2d 899 (1941). The unexpected discovery of the heroine in a place where she should not be ("That is an old device. It was common property of all playwrights when Sheridan used it in *The School for Scandal.*"): Hubges v. Belasco, 130 Fed. 388 (C. C. N. Y. 1904). Dummy used to cast shadow on window shade, creating impression shadow is that of real person: Stevenson v. Harris, 238 Fed. 432 (D. C. N. Y. 1917). Heroine held a prisoner in a Chinese den: Curwood v. Affiliated Distributors, 283 Fed. 223 (D. C. N. Y. 1922). Injury to the bridegroom on his wedding day: Alexander v. Theater Guild, 26 F. 2d 741 (D. C. N. Y. 1927), aff'd 26 F. 2d 742 (C. C. A. 2d 1928). Interruption of a stage performance by the supposed murder of a member of the audience: Rush v. Oursler, 39 F. 2d 468 (D. C. N. Y. 1930).

But a *new* combination of old materials is protectible by copyright: Daly v. Brady, 39 F. 265 (C. C. N. Y. 1889), rev'd 56 F. 482 (C. C. A. 2d 1892), app. dism. 163 U. S. 155, 16 S. Ct. 961, 41 L. Ed. 111; Boucicault v. Fox. Fed. Cas. No. 1691, 5 Blatchf. 87 (C. C. N. Y. 1862).

No exclusive property rights can be had in a locale, notwithstanding the prior use of it in copyrighted works. The Canadian Northwest: International Film Service v. Affiliated Distributors, 283 Fed. 229, 234 (D. C. N. Y. 1922). Theatrical boardinghouse: Christie v. Harris, 47 F. Supp. 39 (D. C. N. Y. 1943), aff'd 154 F. 2d 827 (C. C. A. 2d 1946), cert. den. 329 U. S. 734, 67 S. Ct. 97, 91 L. Ed. 634. Reform school: Bein v. Warner Bros. Pictures, 105 F. 2d 969 (C. C. A. 2d 1939). Tropical island: Fendler v. Morosco, 253 N. Y. 281 (1930). The Hollywood Bowl: Echeverria v. Warner Bros. Pictures, 12 F. Supp. 632 (D. C. Cal. 1935). Convent: Underhill v. Belasco, 254 Fed. 838 (D. C. N. Y. 1918). Congressional circles in Washington: Maxwell v. Goodwin, 93 Fed. 665 (C. C. Ill. 1899).

## CHAPTER 4

### NOTES

1. See Morris L. Ernst and Alexander Lindey, *The Censor Marches On,* New York: Doubleday & Company, Inc., 1940.
2. See A. D. F. Hamlin, *A History of Ornament, Ancient and Medieval,* New York: Appleton-Century-Crofts, Inc., 1916, p. 10.

3. Alexander F. B. Clark, *Jean Racine*, Cambridge, Mass.: Harvard University Press, 1945, p. 42.

4. " 'Where do you get all your ideas? Do they just come to you?' people ask. The last thing they do is 'just come.' My ideas are produced with blood, sweat, brain-racking toil, the help of *The New Yorker* art staff, and the collaboration of keen-eyed undercover operatives. For the first few years I did think up most of my own situations. I had to. I was developing a style and a new kind of format, and there was no way anyone else could do it for me. But as time went on, and a distinct pattern for my work was set, it became easier for others to make a contribution. By 'others,' I mean the scant handful of gifted idea-men (there are hordes of the other kind) who have grown up in the field the past few years. This system, I think, is as it should be. No man, after he has evolved several hundred variations on the few basic human themes, can be expected to keep it up indefinitely. Not entirely by himself, at any rate. He has a large job, alone, in continuing to improve and vary the style he has developed; the struggle to avoid easy stagnation (if he wants to avoid it) is endless. For ideas for the pictures, new minds and fresh slants become a necessity." Peter Arno, *Ladies & Gentlemen*, New York: Simon & Schuster, 1951.

5. Channing Pollock, "The Plagiarism Racket," *The American Mercury*, May, 1945.

### LEGAL MATERIAL

Parody and burlesque: Hill v. Whalen & Martell, 220 Fed. 359 (D. C. N. Y. 1914).

Mimicry: Held, no infringement: Green v. Minzensheimer, 177 Fed. 286 (C. C. N. Y. 1909). Held, infringement: Green v. Luby, 177 Fed. 287 (C. C. N. Y. 1909). Held, no infringement: Bloom & Hamlin v. Nixon, 125 Fed. 977 (D. C. Pa. 1903), 2 Mich. L. Rev. 480 (1904).

Although common sources are open to all, an author who takes something from the public domain and treats it in his own way is protected against anyone who copies his work and not the earlier source: Wilkie v. Santly Bros., 91 F. 2d 978 (C. C. A. 2d 1937), aff'g 13 F. Supp. 136 (D. C. N. Y. 1935); Fred Fisher v. Dillingham, 298 Fed. 145 (D. C. N. Y. 1924). See also Heim v. Universal Pictures Co., 51 F. Supp. 233 (D. C. N. Y. 1943), aff'd 154 F. 2d 480 (C. C. A. 2d 1946).

For the application of the common-source rule to compilations, digests, directories, lists and charts, tabulations, and trade catalogues, see Legal Material, Chapter 9.

*The Case of Becky:* Bachman v. Belasco, 224 Fed. 817 (C. C. A. 2d 1915), aff'g 224 Fed. 815 (D. C. N. Y. 1913).

For Dr. Johnson's views on coincidence, see Lewys v. O'Neill, 49 F. 2d 603, 606 (D. C. N. Y. 1931), and Gingg v. Twentieth Century-Fox, 56 F. Supp. 701, 710 (D. C. Cal. 1944).

## CHAPTER 5

### NOTES

1. Letter to Mrs. S. E. Dawson, Nov. 24, 1882. See Sir Edward Cook, *More Literary Recreations,* London: The Macmillan Company, 1919, pp. 177-184; and *The Spectator* (London), Aug. 28, 1926.

2. John H. Wigmore, "Did Poe Plagiarize the Murders in the Rue Morgue?" 13 Cornell Law Quarterly 219 (1927). This is an outstanding job of literary sleuthing. It shows a first-class legal mind at work. When Professor Wigmore first tackled the problem, everything pointed to Poe's guilt. But Professor Wigmore wanted facts. He ran down every clue, assayed every bit of evidence. When he finally absolved Poe, the verdict was unassailable.

3. For examples of parallels in literary research, see Harold Jenkins, "Benlowes and Milton," *Modern Language Review,* Cambridge, April, 1948; H. J. Oliver, "The Composition and Revisions of *The Compleat Angler,*" *Modern Language Review,* July, 1947; Calvin S. Brown, Jr., "More Swinburne-D'Annunzio Parallels," *Publications of the Modern Language Association of America,* 1940; H. Arlin Turner, "Hawthorne's Literary Borrowings," *Publications of the Modern Language Association of America,* 1936; A. C. Bradley, *A Commentary on Tennyson's "In Memoriam,"* New York: The Macmillan Company, 1907; Ernst Dick, *Plagiats de Chateaubriand,* University of Bonn, 1905 (a doctoral thesis); John Churton Collins, *Illustrations of Tennyson,* London: Chatto & Windus, 1902; and R. D. Haven, *The Influence of Milton on English Poetry,* Cambridge, Mass.: Harvard University Press.

4. See, for example, unsigned editorial, *The Saturday Review of Literature,* June 20, 1936, which excoriates literary boondogglers. "Of these boondogglers," says the editorial, "the source hunters are the worst because they are usually the most honest, the most successful in earning their pay for work accomplished, and the most shortsighted." A writer's sources, the editorial insists, are at the most the clay from which he made his bricks. What he builds lies as far from the research of the boondogglers as the cathedral from the brickyard.

5. See Chapters 3 and 4 for a discussion of the other causes.

## LEGAL MATERIAL

Judge Hough's comment: Frankel v. Irwin, 34 F. 2d 142, 144 (D. C. N. Y. 1918).

The *Abie's Irish Rose* case: Nichols v. Universal Pictures Corporation, 45 F. 2d 119 (C. C. A. 2d. 1930), cert. den. 282 U. S. 902, 51 S. Ct. 216, 75 L. Ed. 795.

The *Strange Interlude* case: Lewys v. O'Neill, 49 F. 2d 603 (D. C. N. Y. 1931).

The *Of Thee I Sing* case: Lowenfels v. Nathan, 2 F. Supp. 73, 80 (D. C. N. Y. 1932).

The *Death Takes a Holiday* case: Wiren v. Shubert Theater Corporation, 5 F. Supp. 358 (D. C. N. Y. 1933), aff'd 70 F. 2d 1023 (C. C. A. 2d 1934).

The *Gone with the Wind* case: Davis v. The Macmillan Company, unreported (D. C. N. Y. 1937).

The *Stage Door* case: Christie v. Harris, 47 F. Supp. 39 (D. C. N. Y. 1943), aff'd 154 F. 2d 827 (C. C. A. 2d 1946), cert. den. 329 U. S. 734, 67 S. Ct. 97, 91 L. Ed. 634.

Parallel columns used in court decisions: Ansehl v. Puritan Pharmaceutical, 61 F. 2d 131 (C. C. A. 8th 1932); West Pub. Co. v. Lawyers Co-operative Pub. Co., 79 Fed. 756 (C. C. A. 2d 1897).

## CHAPTER 6

### NOTES

1. In this chapter and the next, the history of borrowing and plagiarism is briefly considered. The survey is limited to literature for the most part, and covers the period from antiquity to, roughly, the end of the nineteenth century. The evolution of the concept of literary property and the rise of statutory copyright are dealt with in Chapter 8. Plagiarism cases involving recent books are discussed in Chapter 9; those involving recent plays, in Chapters 10 and 11; those involving motion pictures, in Chapter 12. The history of borrowing and theft in art and music, as well as recent plagiarism cases having to do with those media, will be found in Chapters 13 and 14.

2. "You must be a big man to plagiarize with impunity. Shakespeare can take his 'borrowed plumes' from whatever humble bird he likes, and, in spite of poor Greene's carping, his splendour is undimmed, for we know that he can do without them. Burns could pick up a lilt in any

chapbook and turn it to pure gold without a 'by your leave.' These
gods are beyond the range of our pettifogging *meums* and *tuums*.
Their pockets are so rich that a few coins that do not belong to them
are no matter either way. But if you are a small man of exiguous
talents and endeavour to eke out your poverty from the property of
others you will discover that plagiarism is a capital offense, and that
the punishment is for life. In literature—whatever the case may be in
life—there is one law for the rich and another for the poor, and
'that in the captain's but a choleric word which in the soldier is
flat blasphemy.' " Alfred George Gardiner, *Many Furrows,* New York:
E. P. Dutton & Co., Inc., 1925, p. 74.

3. John T. Winterich, Introduction to Homer's *Odyssey,* New York: The
   Heritage Press, 1942. The literature on Homer is tremendous. See Rhys
   Carpenter, *Folk Tale, Fiction and Saga in the Homeric Epics,* Berke-
   ley: The University of California Press, 1946.

4. Harold Ogden White, *Plagiarism and Imitation during the English
   Renaissance,* Cambridge, Mass.: Harvard University Press, 1935. John
   F. Dalton, *Roman Literary Theory and Criticism,* New York: Long-
   mans, Green and Co., Inc., 1931.

5. Ralph Waldo Emerson, *Representative Men,* Boston: Houghton Mifflin
   Company, 1883, pp. 159-160.

6. Sir Sidney Lee, "The Elizabethan Sonnet," Cambridge: *The Cambridge
   History of English Literature,* 1918, Vol. III, p. 248. As to borrowing generally during the Elizabethan age, see Harold Ogden White,
   *op. cit.;* H. M. Paull, *Literary Ethics,* London: T. Thornton Butterworth, Ltd., 1928; and Phoebe Sheavyn, *The Literary Profession in the
   Elizabethan Age,* London: Manchester University Press, 1909.

7. Works on Shakespeare's sources run into thousands. For a recent example, see Thomas Marc Parrott, *Shakespearean Comedy,* New York:
   Oxford University Press, 1949. See also Barrett Wendell, *The Traditions of European Literature,* New York: Charles Scribner's Sons,
   1920; and Paul Barnett, "Cleopatra Was Plutarch's Girl, but
   Shakespeare Made Her His," New York *Herald Tribune,* March 7,
   1948.

8. J. C. Hadden, "Plagiarism and Coincidence," *The Scottish Review,*
   April, 1896.

9. See George Saintsbury, "Milton," *The Cambridge History of English
   Literature,* 1920, Vol. VII, pp. 118-119.

10. Voltaire, *Philosophical Dictionary* (trans. by H. I. Woolf), New York:
    Alfred A. Knopf, Inc., 1924, pp. 217-218.

For a discussion of the derivation of Milton's minor poems, includ-

ing "L'Allegro," "Il Penseroso," "Comus," and "Lycidas," see Thomas
Warton's preface to *Milton's Poems upon Several Occasions,* London.
J. G. G. and J. Robinson, 1791.

For specific examples of Milton's borrowings, see Richard Hurd, *A
Letter to Mr. Mason,* Cambridge: W. Thurlburn & J. Woodyer, 1757.

## CHAPTER 7

### NOTES

1. H. J. Oliver, "The Composition and Revisions of *The Compleat
Angler,*" *Modern Language Review,* London, July, 1947, p. 295. Oliver
points out that *The Compleat Angler* itself became a sort of recognized textbook, and that others stole from it.
2. In the preface to his *Holy War,* Bunyan thus replied to the attacks
on him:

> Some say Pilgrim's Progress is not mine,
> Insinuating as if I would shine
> In name and fame by the worth of another,
> Like some made rich by robbing of their brother.
>
> Or that so fond I am of being sire,
> I'll father bastards, or, if need require,
> I'll tell a lie in print to get applause.
> I scorn it; John such dirt-heap never was
> Since God converted him. Let this suffice
> To show why I my Pilgrim patronize.
>
> It came from my own heart, so to my head,
> And thence into my fingers trickled;
> Then to my pen, from whence immediately
> On paper I did dripple it daintily.
>
> Manner and matter too was all mine own;
> Nor was it unto any mortal known,
> Till I had done it. Nor did any then,
> By books, by wit, by tongue, or hand, or pen,
> Add five words to it, or wrote half a line
> Thereof; the whole and every whit is mine.

See "Plagiarism and John Bunyan," *The Catholic World,* October,
1867.

3. *The Adventurer,* No. 95, quoted by Judge Woolsey in Lewys v. O'Neill, 49 F. 2d 603 (D. C. N. Y. 1931).

4. The English Opium Eater (Thomas De Quincey), "Samuel Taylor Coleridge," Tait's *Edinburgh Magazine,* Vol. I (N. S.), September, 1834.

5. John Livingston Lowes, *The Road to Xanadu,* Boston: Houghton Mifflin Company, 1927.

6. A. G. Gardiner, *Many Furrows,* New York: E. P. Dutton Company, 1925. Also Lowes, op. cit., p. 427.

7. H. H. Kidd, "Is Dickens Still a Hero?" Durham, N. C.: *South Atlantic Quarterly* (Purdue University), July, 1927, pp. 280-281.

8. A. C. Bradley, *A Commentary on Tennyson's "In Memoriam,"* New York: The Macmillan Company, 1907, p. 71.

9. See Raoul Deberdt "Les Grands Plagiats du Siècle," *La Revue des Revues,* Vol. 88, pp. 276-285 (1899).

10. Ernst Dick, *Plagiats de Chateaubriand,* University of Bonn (1905).

11. Edward Wright, "The Art of Plagiarism," London: *Contemporary Review,* April, 1904; Christine M. McLean, "Victor Hugo's Use of Chamberlayne's *L'Etat Present de L'Angleterre* in *L'Homme Qui Rit,*" London: *Modern Language Review,* 1913, Vol. 8; and Olin H. Moore, "Further Sources of Victor Hugo's *Quatrevingt-Treize,*" *Publications of the Modern Language Association of America,* 1926, Vol. 41.

12. Matthew Josephson, *Zola and His Time,* New York: The Macaulay Company, 1928, p. 347. See also p. 239.

13. Paul Hazard, "Les Plagiats de Stendhal," Paris: *Revue des Deux Mondes,* 1921, Per. 6, Tome 65, pp. 344-364.

14. *Benjamin Franklin,* New York: The Viking Press, 1938, pp. 112-113.

15. Nelson F. Adkins, "Chapter on American Cribbage: Poe and Plagiarism," New York: *The Papers of the Bibliographical Society of America,* Vol. 42, Third Quarter, 1948, pp. 169-210.

## CHAPTER 8

### NOTES

1. George H. Putnam, *Books and Their Makers during the Middle Ages,* New York: G. P. Putnam's Sons, 1896, Vol. I, p. 46.

2. Frank Luther Mott, *A History of American Magazines,* Cambridge: Harvard University Press, 1939, p. 39.

## LEGAL MATERIAL

The nature of literary property: American Tobacco Co. v. Werckmeister, 207 U. S. 284, 28 S. Ct. 72, 52 L. Ed. 208 (1907); Holmes v. Hurst, 174 U. S. 82, 19 S. Ct. 606, 43 L. Ed. 904 (1898); Aronson v. Baker, 43 N. J. Eq. 365, 12 A. 177 (1887); Baker v. Libbie, 210 Mass. 599, 97 N. E. 109 (1912); Esquire v. Varga Enterprises, 185 F. 2d 14 (C. C. A. 7th 1950), and same parties, 164 F. 2d 522 (C. C. A. 7th 1947), and 166 F. 2d 651 (C. C. A. 7th 1948); White v. Kimmell, 94 F. Supp. 502 (D. C. Cal. 1950). Frank Thayer, *Legal Control of the Press*, Chicago: The Foundation Press, 1944, pp. 467-8.

Common law copyright and early phases of statutory copyright: Caliga v. Inter-Ocean Newspaper Co., 215 U. S. 182, 30 S. Ct. 38, 54 L. Ed. 150 (1909); Holmes v. Hurst, 174 U. S. 82, 19 S. Ct. 606, 43 L. Ed. 904 (1898); Wheaton v. Peters, 33 U. S. (8 Pet.) 591, 8 L. Ed. 1055 (1834); Little v. Hall, 59 U. S. 165, 18 How. 165, 15 L. Ed. 328 (1855); Atlas Mfg. Co. v. Street & Smith, 204 Fed. 398 (C. C. A. 8th 1913), 47 L. R. A. (N. S.) 1002, app. dism. 231 U. S. 348, 34 S. Ct. 73, 58 L. Ed. 262 (1913); Cheney Bros. v. Doris Silk Corp., 35 F. 2d 279 (C. C. A. 2d 1929); Bobbs-Merrill Co. v. Straus, 147 Fed. 15, 77 C. C. A. 607, 15 L. R. A. (N. S.) 766 (C. C. A. 2d 1906), aff'd 210 U. S. 339, 28 S. Ct. 772, 52 L. Ed. 1086 (1908); Press Pub. Co. v. Monroe, 73 Fed. 196 (C. C. A. 2d 1896), err. dism. 164 U. S. 105, 17 S. Ct. 40, 41 L. Ed. 367; Carew v. Melrose Music, 92 F. Supp. 971 (D. C. N. Y. 1950); Baker v. Libbie, 210 Mass. 599, 97 N. E. 109 (1912); Jewelers' Agency v. Jewelers' Pub. Co., 155 N. Y. 241, 49 N. E. 872 (1898); Palmer v. De Witt, 47 N. Y. 532 (1872).

The judicial policy with respect to the protection of common-law copyright was well stated by Judge Yankwich in White v. Kimmell, 94 F. Supp. 502 (D. C. Cal. 1950): "The consistency with which the courts for over a century and a half have upheld an author's common-law right to his manuscript and the ardor which they have shown to protect his rights, despite limited publication, is one more indication of the healthfulness of the common-law system and the determination of the courts to use their powers, aided by equitable principles, to protect intellectual products against piracy. No reason exists why we should depart from these strict standards. In these days of quick communication of ideas, a rule which would make a limited disclosure, such as occurred in this case, synonymous with publication would deny to the creator in the intellectual field the right to the product of his creative imagination. This would be harmful to the development of ideas. For, if we encourage piracy, we discourage creative minds from sharing, in a restricted manner, their ideas before their full fruition. The policy of the law, in protecting intellectual products, is to encourage productivity. A protected limited sharing may enhance it by giving additional time for a fuller development. A weakening of this right might result either in premature publication or a total withholding of ideas, under fear of injury to the author's ownership in them. Either would be a loss to the creative spirit, which the courts should not consciously encourage."

See also Harry P. Warner, "Protection of the Content of Radio and Tele-vision Programs by Common-Law Copyright," 3 Van. L. Rev. 209-40 (1950); "A Modern Conception of Common-Law Copyright," 15 Temple U. L. Q. 531-41 (1941); S. C. Masterson, "History and Development of Copyright," 28 Calif. L. Rev. 620-32 (1940); Howard B. Pickard, "Com-mon-Law Rights before Publication," 11 Okla. B. A. J. 679-99 (1940); Edward S. Rogers, "Literary Property," 7 Mich. L. Rev. 101 (1908); Sir Frederick Pollock, "Expansion of the Common Law," 4 Columbia L. Rev. 96, 100, 101 (1904).

Queen Victoria and Prince Albert: Prince Albert v. Strange, 1 Mac. & G. 25, 41 Full Reprint 1171 (1849).

The Mark Twain manuscript: Chamberlain v. Feldman, 84 N. Y. S. 2d 713, 80 U. S. P. Q. 85 (1948). See 37 Geo. L. J. 448-9 (1949), and 62 Harv. L. Rev. 1406-7 (1949).

But the sale of an unpublished manuscript under *ordinary* circumstances raises the inference that literary property is transferred at the same time, since in such a transaction the publication of the work is usually contem-plated. Pushman v. New York Graphic Society, 287 N. Y. 302, 39 N. E. 2d 249 (1942); 35 Harv. L. Rev. 600 (1922).

"Birds in a cage": Millar v. Taylor, 4 Burr. 2303, 2378, 98 Reprint 201 (1769).

*The Autocrat of the Breakfast Table* case: Holmes v. Hurst, 174 U. S. 82, 19 S. Ct. 606, 43 L. Ed. 904 (1898).

General publication means unrestricted public use. The presentation of a play on the stage or the performance of a musical composition or the delivery of a lecture does not constitute general publication. Ferris v. Frohman, 223 U. S. 424, 32 S. Ct. 263, 56 L. Ed. 492 (1912); Nutt v. National Institute, 31 F. 2d 236 (C. C. A. 2d 1929); Uproar Co. v. National Broadcasting Co., 8 F. Supp. 358 (D. C. Mass. 1934); McCarthy & Fischer v. White, 259 Fed. 364 (D. C. N. Y. 1919); 35 Ill. L. Rev. 546, 550 (1941).

The circulation of information among students does not destroy the common-law copyright of the author. A lecturer permitting students to take notes of his lecture and to take the notes with them does not thereby lose his right to copyright his material afterward. White v. Kimmell, 94 F. Supp. 502 (D. C. Cal. 1950).

Nor does the lending of manuscript copies of a musical composition to musicians and orchestra leaders constitute general publication: Allen v. Walt Disney Productions, 41 F. Supp. 134 (D. C. N. Y. 1941).

But the public sale of phonograph records is a dedication to the public, and ends common-law copyright: Shapiro, Bernstein & Co. v. Miracle Record Co., 91 F. Supp. 473 (D. C. Ill. 1950). See RCA Mfg. Co. v. Whiteman, 114 F. 2d 86, 88 (C. C. A. 2d 1940), cert. den. 311 U. S. 712; White v. Kimmell, 94 F. Supp. 502 (D. C. Cal. 1950) ; and Jewelers' Agency v. Jewelers' Pub. Co., 155 N. Y. 241, 49 N. E. 872 (1898).

The erection of a building constitutes "publication" of the architectural plans for it: Kurfiss v. Cowherd, 233 Mo. App. 397 (1938).

Failure of author to secure copyright protection is conclusive evidence of his abandonment of his common-law rights, and makes his work public property: Tamas v. Twentieth Century-Fox Film Corporation, 25 N. Y. S. 2d 899 (1941).

As to general and limited publication, see also Bobbs-Merrill Co. v. Straus, 210 U. S. 339, 28 S. Ct. 722, 52 L. Ed. 1086 (1908) ; American Tobacco Co. v. Werckmeister, 207 U. S. 284, 28 S. Ct. 72, 52 L. Ed. 208 (1907) ; Banks v. Manchester, 128 U. S. 244, 9 S. Ct. 36, 32 L. Ed. 425 (1888) ; Atlas Mfg. Co. v. Street & Smith, 204 Fed. 398 (C. C. A. 8th 1913), 47 L. R. A. (N. S.) 1002, app. dism. 231 U. S. 348, 34 S. Ct. 73, 58 L. Ed. 262 (1913).

"As a result of the decisions of this court, certain general propositions may be affirmed. Statutory copyright is not to be confounded with the common-law right. At common law, the exclusive right to copy existed in the author until he permitted a general publication. Thus, when a book was published in print, the owner's common-law right was lost. At common law an author had a property in his manuscript, and might have an action against anyone who undertook to publish it without authority. The statute created a new property right, giving to the author, after publication, the exclusive right to multiply copies for a limited period. This statutory right is obtained in a certain way and by the performance of certain acts which the statute points out. That is, the author, having complied with the statute, and given up his common-law right of exclusive duplication prior to general publication, obtained by the method pointed out in the statute an exclusive right to multiply copies and publish the same for the term of years named in the statute. Congress did not sanction an existing right; it created a new one. Wheaton v. Peters, 33 U. S. (8 Pet.) 591, 661, 8 L.

Ed. 1055, 1080 (1834). Those violating the statutory rights of the author or proprietor are subject to certain penalties, and to the payment of certain damages, as is provided in the statute." Caliga v. Inter-Ocean Newspaper Co., 215 U. S. 182, 30 S. Ct. 38, 54 L. Ed. 150 (1909).

The measure of damages for the infringement of common-law copyright is the value of the defendant's work to the plaintiff, or the reasonable value of the plaintiff's work. Nash v. Alaska Airlines, 94 F. Supp. 428 (D. C. N. Y. 1950).

## Statutory Copyright

Definition of: Fox Film Corp. v. Doyal, 286 U. S. 123, 52 S. Ct. 546, 76 L. Ed. 1010 (1932).

A statutory copyright operates to divest the author of his common-law right of literary property; and he cannot have at the same time the benefit of the copyright statute and also retain his common-law right: Bobbs-Merrill Co. v. Straus, 147 Fed. 15, 77 C. C. A. 607, 15 L. R. A. (N. S.) 766 (C. C. A. 2d 1906), aff'd 210 U. S. 339, 28 S. Ct. 772, 52 L. Ed. 1086 (1908) ; Savage v. Hoffmann, 159 Fed. 584 (C. C. N. Y. 1908) ; Jeweler's Agency v. Jeweler's Pub. Co., 155 N. Y. 241, 49 N. E. 872 (1898).

On the expiration of the copyright of a novel, any person may use the plot for a play, copy or publish it, or make any other use of it he sees fit: Atlas Mfg. Co. v. Street & Smith, 204 Fed. 398 (C. C. A. 8th 1913), 47 L. R. A. (N. S.) 1002, app. dism. 231 U. S. 348, 34 S. Ct. 73, 58 L. Ed. 262 (1913) ; Glaser v. St. Elmo Co., 175 Fed. 276 (C. C. N. Y. 1909).

Acquisition of statutory copyright: See J. H. Neu, "The Rights of a Copyright Owner," 17 Notre Dame Law 373-406 (June 1942).

Classes of matter eligible for copyright: 17 U. S. C. Sec. 5. See Edward S. Rogers, "The Subject Matter of Copyright," 68 U. Pa. L. Rev. 215 (1920).

Exclusive rights in copyrighted works specified: 17 U. S. C. Sec. 1.

What copyright does and does not protect: See Legal Material, Chapter I.

One secures a copyright on published material by accompanying its publication with a copyright notice at the place and in the form required by statute. Subsequent registration under the provisions of the law does not create the copyright but only records it. It is sufficient if registration is completed before commencing an action for infringement. Washingtonian Publishing Co. v. Pearson, 306 U. S. 30, 37, 59 S. Ct. 397, 83 L. Ed. 470; reh. den. 306 U. S. 668, 59 S. Ct. 588, 83 L. Ed. 1063 (1939); Krafft v. Cohen, 117 F. 2d 579 (C. C. A. 3d 1941) rev'g 32 F. Supp. 821 (D. C. Pa. 1940).

The first English copyright statute: 8 Anne, Ch. 19. The two historic cases construing the Statute of Anne are Millar v. Taylor, 4 Burr. 2303, 98 Reprint 201 (1769) ; and Donaldson v. Becket, 4 Burr. 2408 2 Bro. P. C. 129 (1774).

The constitutional basis of copyright: U. S. Constitution, Article 1, Section 8.

The Act of 1909 was accompanied by Report No. 2222, 60th Congress, Second Session, February 22, 1909.

## CHAPTER 9

### NOTES

1. Frances R. Grant, *The New York Times Book Review,* November 16, 1941. But see "Was Rebecca Plagiarized?" *The Saturday Review of Literature,* November 29, 1941, and February 7, 1948.
2. Hervey Allen, "The Sources of Anthony Adverse," *The Saturday Review of Literature,* January 13, 1934.
3. Homer A. Watt, "Plagiarism in College Texts," *Educational Review,* September, 1921.
4. George Jean Nathan, "Twice Told Tales of the Magazines," *The Bookman,* January, 1912. Nathan may have concocted some of the episodes cited, but they ring true enough.

### LEGAL MATERIAL

*The Outline of History* case: Deeks v. Wells, 1 D. L. R. 353 (1933).

*The Thundering Herd* case: Maddux v. Grey, 43 F. 2d 441 (D. C. Cal. 1930).

The *Gone with the Wind* case: Susan Lawrence Davis v. The Macmillan Company, (unreported), United States District Court for the Southern District of New York, opinion dated July 30, 1937, judgment entered in favor of defendant November 8, 1937.

The *Clara Barton* case: De Acosta v. Brown, 50 F. Supp. 615 (D. C. N. Y. 1943), aff'd 146 F. 2d 408 (C. C. A. 2d 1944), cert. den. 325 U .S. 862, 65 S. Ct. 1197, 89 L. Ed. 1893 (1945). See note 93 U. PA. L. REV. 459-60 (1945).

The *Rebecca* case: Judge Bondy's opinion was not separately reported. The Circuit Court of Appeals therefore prefixed it to its own opinion: MacDonald v. Du Maurier, 144 F. 2d 696 (C. C. A. 2d 1943). Judge Bright's opinion: MacDonald v. Du Maurier, 75 F. Supp. 655 (D. C. N. Y. 1948).

Fair use generally: See Legal Material in Chapter I. See also Sampson & Murdock Co. v. Seaver-Radford Co., 140 Fed. 539 (C. C. A. 1st 1905); and Hill v. Whalen & Martell, 220 Fed. 359 (D. C. N. Y. 1914).

The "Go! You Packers, Go!" case: Karll v. Curtis Pub. Co., 39 F. Supp. 836 (D. C. Wis. 1941).

The "Poor Pauline" case: Broadway Music Corporation v. F-R Pub. Corporation, 31 F. Supp. 817 (D. C. N. Y. 1940). See also Shapiro, Bernstein & Co. v. P. F. Collier (unreported, D. C. N. Y. 1934).

On the subject of permissions generally, see Melville Cane, "Why Ask for Permission," *The Saturday Review of Literature,* July 1, 1950; Jacques Barzun, "Quote 'Em Is Taboo," *The Saturday Review of Literature,* September 22, 1945; and Silas Bent, "Bugaboo or Bluff," *The Authors' League Bulletin,* April, 1941.

In interpreting the Copyright Law, care must be taken not to allow it to be made an instrument of oppression and extortion: Hanfstaengl v. Empire Palace, 3 Chancery 109 (1894).

The utterance of Mr. Justice Story is from Emerson v. Davies, Fed. Cas. No. 4436, 3 Story 768 (C. C. Mass. 1845).

As to the use of materials in the public domain generally, see Fred Fisher v. Dillingham, 298 Fed. 145 (D. C. N. Y. 1924); Stanley v. C. B. S., 35 Cal. 2d 653, 221 P. 2d 73 (1950); Aronson v. Baker, 43 N. J. Eq. 365, 12 A. 177 (1887).

Where a later writer presents the same information that an earlier one has, the question is not whether the later writer could have obtained the same data by going to the same sources the earlier one did, but rather, did he go to the same sources and did he do his independent research? Toksvig v. Bruce Pub. Co., 181 F. 2d 664 (C. C. A. 7th 1950); Nutt v. National Institute, 31 F. 2d 236, 237 (C. C. A. 2d 1929).

Although biographical facts are in the public domain and may be freely availed of by anyone, a particular treatment of those facts is protectible by copyright. Plaintiff's copyrighted biography *The Life of Hans Christian Andersen* held infringed by the defendant's *Flight of the Swan*; Toksvig v. Bruce Pub. Co., 181 F. 2d 664 (C. C. A. 7th 1950).

Compilations are protectible by copyright:

Directories: Bleistein v. Donaldson Lithographing Co., 188 U. S. 239, 23 S. Ct. 298, 47 L. Ed. 460 (1903); Adventures in Good Eating v. Best Places to Eat, 131 F. 2d 809 (C. C. A. 7th 1942); Leon v. Pacific Tel. & Tel. Co., 91 F. 2d 484 (C. C. A. 9th 1937); Jewelers' Circular Pub. v. Keystone Pub., 281 Fed. 83 (C. C. A. 2d 1922); Sampson & Murdock Co. v. Seaver-Radford Co., 140 Fed. 539 (C. C. A. 1st 1905); Hartford Printing Co. v. Hartford Directory, 146 Fed. 332 (C. C. Conn. 1906);

Chain Store Business Guide v. Wexler, 79 F. Supp. 726 (D. C. N. Y. 1948); American Travel & Hotel Directory v. Gehring, 4 F. 2d 415 (D. C. N. Y. 1925); Trow Directory v. United States Directory, 122 Fed. 191 (C. C. N. Y. 1903); Chicago Directory v. United States Directory, 122 Fed. 189 (C. C. N. Y. 1902); Trow Directory etc. v. Boyd, 97 Fed. 586 (C. C. N. Y. 1899); List Pub. Co. v. Keller, 30 Fed. 772 (C. C. N. Y. 1887); Williams v. Smythe, 110 Fed. 961 (C. C. Pa. 1901).

Trade catalogues: Ansehl v. Puritan Pharmaceutical, 61 F. 2d 131 (C. C. A. 8th 1932); No-Leak-O Piston Ring v. Norris, 277 Fed. 951 (C. C. A. 4th 1921); Campbell v. Wireback, 269 Fed. 372 (C. C. A. 4th 1920); Da Prato Statuary Co. v. Giuliani Statuary Co., 189 Fed. 90 (C. C. Minn. 1911).

Interest tables: Edwards & Deutsch Litho. Co. v. Boorman, 15 F. 2d 35 (C. C. A. 7th 1926), cert. den. 273 U. S. 738, 47 S. Ct. 247, 71 L. Ed. 867.

Code books: American Code Co. v. Bensinger, 282 Fed. 829 (C. C. A. 2d 1922).

Lists: New Jersey Motor List Co. v. Barton Business Service, 57 F. 2d 353 (D. C. N. J. 1931).

School examination review book: College Entrance Book Co. v. Amsco Book Co., 119 F. 2d 874 (C. C. A. 2d 1941).

Handwriting chart: Deutsch v. Arnold, 98 F. 2d 686 (C. C. A. 2d 1938).

List of jewelers and their trade-marks: Jewelers' Circular Pub. Co. v. Keystone Pub. Co., 281 Fed. 83, 26 A. L. R. 571 (C. C. A. 2d 1922), cert. den. 259 U. S. 581 42 S. Ct. 464, 66 L. Ed. 1074.

Dictionary: United Dictionary Co. v. G. & C. Merriam Co., 208 U. S. 260, 28 S. Ct. 290, 52 L. Ed. 478 (1908).

Law books: Myers v. Callaghan, 128 U. S. 617, 9 S. Ct. 177 (1888); West Pub. Co. v. Edward Thompson Co., 169 Fed. 833 (C. C. N. Y. 1909), mod. 176 Fed. 833 (C. C. A. 2d 1910); West Pub. Co. v. Lawyers Co-op. Pub. Co. 79 Fed. 756 (C. C. A. 2d 1897).

Case annotations to statutes: W. H. Anderson Co. v. Baldwin Law. Pub. Co., 27 F. 2d 82 (C. C. A. 6th 1928).

But judicial decisions are not, in themselves, copyrightable: Banks v. Manchester, 128 U. S. 244, 9 S. Ct. 36, 32 L. Ed. 425 (1888).

## CHAPTER 10

### NOTES

1. Maxwell Anderson, *The Essence of Tragedy, and Other Footnotes And Papers,* Washington, D. C.: Anderson House, 1939. See also Allardyce

Nicoll, *World Drama from Aeschylus to Anouilh*, New York: Harcourt, Brace and Company, Inc., 1950.

2. Moses L. Malevinsky, *The Science of Playwriting*, New York: Brentano's, 1925. See M. Glushien, "Literary Property," 15 Cornell L. Q. 633 (1930).

3. Carl J. Weber, "Plagiarism and Thomas Hardy," *The Colophon*, New Series, No. 3, 1937.

4. Richard H. Rovere, "Profile: 89 Centre Street," *The New Yorker*, December 7, 1946.

5. Belasco took the last part of *Hearts of Oak* from Leslie's *The Mariner's Compass*; based *La Belle Russe* on situations lifted from *Forget Me Not* and *The New Magdalen*; modeled the exciting episode in the third act of *The Girl I Left Behind Me* after a similar one in Boucicault's *Jessie Brown* (here was a bit of poetic justice!); and rifled Sardou's *La Tosca* for the dramatic scene in the third act of *The Darling of the Gods*, in which a military despot extorts information from a woman by compelling her to gaze on her lover subjected to torture. William Winter, *The Life of David Belasco*, New York: Moffat, Yard and Company, 1918.

### LEGAL MATERIAL

No property rights in themes, ideas and topics: See Legal Material, Chapter I.

In Chatterton v. Cave, L. R. 3 App. Cas. 483 (1878), Lord Blackburn said: "An idea may be taken from a drama and used in forming another, without the representation of the second being a representation of any part of the first. For example, I have no doubt that Sheridan, in composing *The Critic*, took the idea from *The Rehearsal*; but I think it would be an abuse of language to say that those who represent *The Critic* represent *The Rehearsal* or any part thereof; and if it were left to me to find the fact, I should, without hesitation, find that they did not."

The *Abie's Irish Rose* case: Nichols v. Universal Pictures Corporation, 34 F. 2d 145 (D. C. N. Y. 1929), aff'd 45 F. 2d 119 (C. C. A. 2d 1930), cert. den. 282 U. S. 902, 51 S. Ct. 216, 75 L. Ed. 795.

Facts and history are not copyrightable: Caruthers v. RKO Radio Pictures, 20 F. Supp. 906 (D. C. N. Y. 1937); Davies v. Bowes, 209 Fed. 53 (D. C. N. Y. 1913).

Piracy may consist in appropriating the action of a play without the words: Daly v. Palmer, Fed. Cas. 3552, 6 Blatchf. 256 (C. C. N. Y. 1892); Sheldon v. Metro-Goldwyn Pictures Corp., 106 F. 2d 45 (C. C. A. 2d 1939), aff'd 309 U. S. 390, 60 S. Ct. 861, 84 L. Ed. 825; Wiren v. Shubert,

5 F. Supp. 358 (D. C. N. Y. 1933), aff'd 70 F. 2d 1023 (C. C. A. 2d 1934); Frankel v. Irwin, 34 F. 2d 142 (D. C. N. Y. 1918); Casino Productions v. Vitaphone Corporation, 295 N. Y. S. 501, 163 Misc. 403 (1937).

Copyright does not protect old plots: Dymow v. Bolton, 11 F. 2d 690 (C. C. A. 2d 1926); London v. Biograph Co., 231 Fed. 696, 145 C. C. A. 582 (C. C. A. 2d 1916); Stephens v. Howells Sales Co., 16 F. 2d 805 (D. C. N. Y. 1926); Fred Fisher v. Dillingham, 298 Fed. 145 (D. C. N. Y. 1924); Stodart v. Mutual Film Corp., 249 Fed. 507 (D. C. N. Y. 1917); Eichel v. Marcin, 241 Fed. 404 (D. C. N. Y. 1913).

The *Spider* case: Rush v. Oursler, 39 F. 2d 468 (D. C. N .Y. 1930).

Protectible combination of incidents: Frankel v. Irwin, *supra.*

The copyright of a play does not carry with it the exclusive right to the use of the title: Warner Bros. Pictures v. Majestic Pictures Corporation, 70 F. 2d 310 (C. C. A. 2d 1934); and cases cited in Legal Material, Chapter I.

Dramatization of novel in public domain: Glaser v. St. Elmo Co., 175 Fed. 276 (C. C. N. Y. 1909).

The *Polly Preferred* case: Dymow v. Bolton, *supra.*

The *Strange Interlude* case: Lewys v. O'Neill, 49 F. 2d 603 (D. C. N. Y. 1931).

The real-water river: Serrana v. Jefferson, 33 Fed. 347 (C. C. N. Y. 1888).

The *Under the Gaslight* case: Daly v. Palmer, 6 Blatchf. 256, Fed. Cas. No. 3552 (C. C. N. Y. 1868); Daly v. Brady, 56 Fed. 482 (C. C. A. 2d 1892), rev'g 39 Fed. 265 (C. C. N. Y. 1889), app. dism. 163 U. S. 155, 16 S. Ct. 961, 41 L. Ed. 111. See also 69 Fed. 285 (C. C. N. Y. 1895), and 75 Fed. 1022 (C. C. A. 2d 1896).

The *Wizard of Oz* case: Bloom & Hamlin v. Nixon, 125 Fed. 977 (D. C. Pa. 1903); 2 Mich. L. Rev. 480 (1904).

In Green v. Minzensheimer, 177 Fed. 286 (C. C. N. Y. 1909), the singing of a single verse and chorus of a copyrighted song, *without* musical accompaniment, by way of mimicry, was held permissible; but in Green v. Luby, 177 Fed. 287 (C. C. N. Y. 1909), the singing of the same song in its *entirety, with* accompaniment, was held to constitute infringement.

The *Merry Widow* case: Savage v. Hoffman, 159 Fed. 584 (C. C. N. Y. 1908). But where one operetta, *Robert Macaire,* was found substantially identical with another, *Erminie,* an injunction was granted against the infringer. Aronson v. Baker, 43 N. J. Eq. 365, 12 A. 177 (1887).

The *Sweet Kitty Bellairs* case: Hubges v. Belasco, 130 Fed. 388 (C. C. N. Y. 1904).

*The Case of Becky* case: Bachman v. Belasco, 224 Fed. 817 (C. C. A. 2d 1915), aff'g 224 Fed. 815 (D. C. N. Y. 1913).

*The Boomerang* case: Longson v. Belasco, 254 Fed. 990 (D. C. N. Y. 1918), aff'd 38 F. 2d 1015 (C. C. A. 2d 1930), cert. den. 282 U. S. 845, 51 S. Ct. 24, 75 L. Ed. 750.

The *Marie Odile* case: Underhill v. Belasco, 254 Fed. 838 (D. C. N. Y. 1918).

## CHAPTER II

### NOTES

1. *They Knew What They Wanted,* New York: Doubleday & Company, Inc., 1925, p. xii. A portion of the preface is worth quoting: "Of the story of this play, I have this to say. It has been generously related to the legend of Paolo and Francesca, to the dirtiest anecdotes of the Gallic pornographica, and to its superb contemporary of the New York theatre, Eugene O'Neill's *Desire under the Elms.* On that last score, Mr. O'Neill and I can readily, as they say, 'get together' and agree that no two plays could possibly bear less resemblance to each other than this simple comedy of mine and his glorious tragedy of New England farmers and their Puritan philosophy. Of the second alleged source and kinship I cannot speak with authority because I am not sure that I know all the dirtiest French anecdotes. The first relationship I hotly deny. The story of this play, in its noblest form, served Richard Wagner as the libretto for the greatest of all romantic operas. It is shamelessly, consciously, and even proudly derived from the legend of Tristram and Yseult, and the difference between the legend of Tristram and Yseult and that of Paolo and Francesca is simply that the Italian wronged husband killed everybody in sight while his northern counterpart forgave everybody—which amounts to the monumental difference between a bad temper and tolerance."

2. Frank Harris, *Shakespeare and His Love,* London: Frank Palmer, 1910.

3. Standard Edition of the Works of Bernard Shaw, Vol. 21 (*Pen Portraits and Reviews*), Edinburgh: P. & T. Clark, Ltd., 1932.

4. "The Skin of Whose Teeth?" *The Saturday Review of Literature,* December 19, 1942.

5. "Finnegan's Teeth," *The New Yorker,* December 26, 1942.

### LEGAL MATERIAL

The *Cheating Cheaters* case: Eichel v. Marcin, 241 Fed. 404 (D. C. N. Y. 1913).

The *At Bay* case: Vernon v. Shubert, 220 Fed. 694 (D. C. N. Y. 1915).

The *Arms and the Girl* case: Stevenson v. Harris, 238 Fed. 432 (D. C. N. Y. 1917).

The *No. 13 Washington Square* case: Frankel v. Irwin, 34 F. 2d 142 (D. C. N. Y. 1918).

The *White Cargo* case: Simonton v. Gordon, 12 F. 2d 116 (D. C. N. Y. 1925).

The *Polly Preferred* case: Dymow v. Bolton, 11 F. 2d 690 (C. C. A. 2d 1926).

*The Fool* case: Waxman v. Pollock, 24 F. 2d 1023 (C. C. A. 2d 1928), cert. den. 278 U. S. 604, 49 S. Ct. 11, 73 L. Ed. 532.

The *They Knew What They Wanted* case: Alexander v. Theatre Guild, 26 F. 2d 741 (D. C. N. Y. 1927), aff'd 26 F. 2d 742 (C. C. A. 2d, 1928).

*The Spider* case: Rush v. Oursler, Fayder v. Lewis, 39 F. 2d 468 (D. C. N. Y. 1930).

The *Of Thee I Sing* case: Lowenfels v. Nathan, 2 F. Supp. 73 (D. C. N. Y. 1932).

The *Death Takes a Holiday* case: Wiren v. Shubert, 5 F. Supp. 358 (D. C. N. Y. 1933), aff'd 70 Fed. 2d 1023 (C. C. A. 2d 1934).

The *Stage Door* case: Christie v. Harris, 47 F. Supp. 39 (D. C. N. Y. 1943), aff'd 154 F. 2d 827 (C. C. A. 2d 1946), cert. den. 329 U. S. 734, 67 S. Ct. 97, 91 L. Ed. 634.

The *Blithe Spirit* case: Hewitt v. Coward, 41 N. Y. S. 2d 498, 180 Misc. 1065, aff'd 266 App. Div. 992, 45 N. Y. S. 2d 118 (1943).

The *Dear Ruth* case: Columbia Pictures v. Krasna, 65 N. Y. S. 2d 67 (1946), aff'd 69 N. Y. S. 2d 796, 271 App. Div. 1008, app. den. 73 N. Y. S. 2d 486, 272 App. Div. 794.

The *Deep Are the Roots* case: Heywood v. Jericho Co., 85 N. Y. S. 2d 464, 193 Misc. 905 (1948).

The *Bird of Paradise* case: Fendler v. Morosco, 253 N. Y. 281 (1930), rev'g. 217 App. Div. 791.

The *Strange Interlude* case: Lewys v. O'Neill, 49 F. 2d 603 (D. C. N. Y. 1931).

The *Oscar Wilde* case: Harris v. Miller, 50 U. S. P. Q. 306, also 50 U. S. P. Q. 625 (D. C. N. Y. 1941).

*The Man Who Came to Dinner* case: McConnor v. Kaufman, 49 F. Supp. 738 (D. C. N. Y. 1943), aff'd 139 F. 2d 116 (C. C. A. 2d 1943).

CHAPTER 12

LEGAL MATERIAL

Rosen v. Loew's, 162 F. 2d 785 (C. C. A. 2d 1947).

The *Roman Scandals* case: Eisman v. Samuel Goldwyn, 23 F. Supp. 519 (D. C. N. Y. 1938), rev'd 104 F. 2d 661 (C. C. A. 2d 1939). Same case: Dellar v. Samuel Goldwyn, 40 F. Supp. 534 (D. C. N. Y. 1941), aff'd 150 F. 2d 612 (C. C. A. 2d 1945), cert. den. 327 U. S. 790, 66 S. Ct. 802, 90 L. Ed. 1646; reh. den. 328 U. S. 878, 66 S. Ct. 1020, 90 L. Ed. 1016.

The *A Circus Romance* case: Bobbs-Merrill Co. v. Equitable Motion Pictures Corp., 232 Fed. 791 (D. C. N. Y. 1916).

The *I Dream Too Much* case: Shipman v. RKO Radio Pictures, 100 F. 2d 533 (C. C. A. 2d 1938), aff'g 20 F. Supp. 249 (D. C. N. Y. 1938).

The *I Married an Angel* case: Sarkadi v. Wiman, 43 F. Supp. 778 (D. C. N. Y. 1942), aff'd 135 F. 2d 1002 (C. C. A. 2d 1943).

The *My Man Godfrey* case: West v. Hatch, 49 F. Supp. 307 (D. C. N. Y. 1943).

The *Show Business* case: O'Brien v. RKO Radio Pictures, 68 F. Supp. 13 (D. C. N. Y. 1946).

The Borden case: Borden v. General Motors Corporation, 28 F. Supp. 330 (D. C. N. Y. 1939).

The *Test Pilot* case: Collins v. Metro-Goldwn Pictures, 106 F. 2d 83 (C. C. A. 2d 1939) rev'g 25 F. Supp. 781 (D. C. N. Y. 1938).

The *Alcatraz Prison* case: Gropper v. Warner Bros. Pictures, 38 F. Supp. 329 (D. C. N. Y. 1941).

The *Night of Love* case: Barbadillo v. Goldwyn, 42 F. 2d 881 (D. C. Cal. 1930).

The *Cimarron* case: Caruthers v. RKO Radio Pictures, 20 F. Supp. 906 (D. C. N. Y. 1937).

The *I Am the Law* case: Curwood v. Affiliated Distributors, 283 Fed. 223 (D. C. N. Y. 1922).

The *Alexander's Ragtime Band* case: Twentieth Century-Fox Film Corp. v. Dieckhaus, 153 F. 2d 893, at pp. 898-899 (C. C. A. 8th 1946), rev'g 54 F. Supp. 425 (D. C. Mo. 1944), cert. den. 329 U. S. 716, 67 S. Ct. 46, 91 L. Ed. 621.

The *Across the Pacific* case: Echeverria v. Warner Bros. Pictures, 12 F. Supp. 632 (D. C. Cal. 1935). "The writer [the plaintiff] really thought," said Judge Yankwich, "that because she had conceived the idea of using the Hollywood Bowl as locale, she was entitled, in *saecula saeculorum,* as the catechism says, to the exclusive use of that idea."

The *Hell's Angels* case: Barry v. Hughes, 103 F. 2d 427 (C. C. A. 2d 1939), cert. den. 308 U. S. 604, 60 S. Ct. 141, 84 L. Ed. 505. One of the questions raised in this case was the extent to which a picture company might become liable for innocently purchasing and using a narrative possibly pilfered from someone else. The Circuit Court of Appeals said: "It has been held that one who copies from a plagiarist is himself necessarily a plagiarist, however innocent he may be, but that would be a harsh result, and contrary to the general doctrine of torts. The wrong is copying; that is using the author's work as a source. A copy of a copy does indeed do just that, but one is ordinarily liable for only those consequences of one's acts which a reasonable person would anticipate. Laying aside a possible action for unjust enrichment, or for an injunction after discovery, we should hesitate a long while before holding that the use of material apparently in the public domain, subjected the user to damages, unless something put him actually on notice."

The *Modern Times* case: Kustoff v. Chaplin, 120 F. 2d 551 (C. C. A. 9th 1941).

The *Meet John Doe* case: Shurr v. Warner Bros. Pictures, 144 F. 2d 200 (C. C. A. 2d 1944).

The *Condemned Women* case: O'Rourke v. RKO Radio Pictures, 44 F. Supp. 480 (D. C. Mass. 1942).

*The Mortal Storm* case: Rosen v. Loew's, 162 F. 2d 785 (C. C. A. 2d 1947).

The *Miracle on Thirty-fourth Street* case: Burns v. Twentieth Century-Fox Film Corp., 75 F. Supp. 986 (D. C. Mass. 1948).

The *Wilson* case: Pinci v. Twentieth Century-Fox Film Corp., 95 F. Supp. 884 (D. C. N. Y. 1951).

See also Dezendorf v. Twentieth Century-Fox Film Corporation, 32 F. Sup. 359 (D. C. Cal. 1940); and Brody v. Columbia Pictures Corp., 90 F. Supp. 711 (D. C. Mass. 1950).

The *When Tomorrow Comes* case: Cain v. Universal Pictures Co., 47 F. Supp. 1013 (D. C. Cal. 1942).

*The Road to Glory* case: Sheets v. Twentieth Century-Fox Film Corporation, 33 F. Supp. 389 (D. C. Cal. 1940).

The *Ben Hur* case: Harper & Brothers v. Kalem Co., 169 Fed. 61 (C. C. A. 2d 1909), aff'd 222 U. S. 55, 32 S. Ct. 20, 56 L. Ed. 92, Ann. Cas. 1913 A, 1285.

*The Strength of Donald MacKenzie* case: Stodart v. Mutual Film Corp., 249 Fed. 507 (D. C. N. Y. 1917).

The *Hotel for Women* case: Twentieth Century-Fox v. Stonesifer, 140 F. 2d 579 (C. C. A. 9th 1944) aff'g 48 F. Supp. 196 (D. C. Cal. 1942).

The *So's Your Uncle* case: Universal Pictures v. Harold Lloyd, 162 F. 2d 354 (C. C. A. 9th 1947).

The *Ghost Ship* case: Golding v. RKO Pictures, 35 Cal. 2d 690, 221 P. 2d 95 (1950).

The *Abie's Irish Rose* case: Nichols v. Universal Pictures Corporation, 45 F. 2d 119 (C. C. A. 2d 1930), aff'g 34 F. 2d 145 (D. C. N. Y. 1929), cert. den. 282 U. S. 902, 51 S. Ct. 216, 75 L. Ed. 795.

*The Freshman* case: Harold Lloyd Corporation v. Witwer, 65 F. 2d 1 (C. C. A. 9th 1933), rev'g 46 F. 2d 792 (D. C. Cal. 1930), cert. dism. 54 S. Ct. 94, 78 L. Ed. 1507.

The *Letty Lynton* case: Sheldon v. Metro-Goldwyn Pictures Corporation, case tried and complaint dismissed, Judge Woolsey: 7 F. Supp. 837 (D. C. N. Y. 1934), rev'd 81 F. 2d 49 (C. C. A. 2d 1936). Damages found, Judge Leibell: 26 F. Supp. 134 (D. C. N. Y. 1938), mod. 106 F. 2d 45 (C. C. A. 2d 1939), aff'd 309 U. S. 390, 60 S. Ct. 681, 84 L. Ed. 825 (1940). See R. G. Berry, 13 So. Calif. L. Rev. 505 (1940).

Apportionment of damages: Mawman v. Tegg, 2 Russ. 385 (1826; Lord Eldon), cited with approval in Callaghan v. Myers, 128 U. S. 617, 9 S. Ct. 177, 32 L. Ed. 547 (1888).

On the general copyright aspects of the screen, see M. H. Aronson, Motion Picture Copyright, 25 Wash. U. L. Q. 554 (1940).

## CHAPTER 13

### NOTES

1. See Jean Lipman, "Print to Primitive," *Antiques,* July, 1946.
2. W. R. Valentiner, "Leonardo as Verrocchio's Co-worker," *The Art Bulletin,* Vol. XII, No. 1 (1930).
3. *Frank Lloyd Wright on Architecture,* ed. by Frederick Gutheim, New York: Duell, Sloan & Pearce, Inc., 1941, pp. 4 and 63. See also Le Corbusier, *Towards a New Architecture,* trans. by Frederick Etchells, London: John Rodker, 1927; Lewis Mumford, *Architecture,* Chicago: American Library Association, 1926, p. 29; *Building for Modern Man,* ed. by Thomas H. Creighton, Princeton: Princeton University Press, 1949; and Sheldon Cheney, *A Primer of Modern Art,* New York: Liveright Publishing Corp., 1924, pp. 313-317.

### LEGAL MATERIAL

The "Superman" case: Detective Comics, Inc. v. Bruns Publications, Inc. 28 F. Supp. 399 (D. C. N. Y. 1939), mod. 111 F. 2d 432 (C. C. A. 2d

(1940). See also National Comics Publications v. Fawcett Publications, 93 F. Supp. 349 (D. C. N. Y. 1950).

The Circus Posters case: Bleistein v. Donaldson Lithographing Co., 188 U. S. 239, 23 S. Ct. 298, 47 L. Ed. 460 (1903).

The Chromos of Vegetables case: Stecker Lithographic Co. v. Dunston Lithographic Co., 233 Fed. 601 (D. C. N. Y. 1916).

Copyright protection of advertising: Bleistein v. Donaldson Lithographing Co., 188 U. S. 239, 23 S. Ct. 298, 47 L. Ed. 460 (1903). See M. G. Borden, 35 Ky. L. J. 205-11 (1947); and Note, 17 Minn. L. Rev. 327-8 (1933).

Common-law copyright in advertising design held infringed: Nash. v. Alaska Airlines, 94 F. Supp. 428 (D. C. N. Y. 1950).

A trade catalogue is protectible by copyright. When the plaintiff's copyrighted catalogue contained 2,813 illustrations of statuary and 18 of these were reproduced in the defendant's catalogue, which contained 393 illustrations, the copying was held sufficient to justify the granting of an injunction limited to the illustrations copied. Da Prato Statuary Co. v. Giuliani, 189 Fed. 90 (C. C. Minn. 1911). See also Perkins Marine Lamp & Hardware Co. v. Goodwin Stanley Co., 86 F. Supp. 630 (D. C. N. Y. 1949).

The copyright of a drawing illustrating an article does not give the copyright owner an exclusive right in the article illustrated. For example, the drawing of a toy, if copyrighted, protects the drawing, not the toy: Seip v. Commonwealth Plastics, 85 F. Supp. 741 (D. C. Mass. 1943).

The "Alphonse and Gaston" case: Empire City Amusement Co. v. Wilton, 134 Fed. 132 (C. C. Mass. 1903).

The "Mutt and Jeff" case: Hill v. Whalen & Martell, 220 Fed. 359 (D. C. N. Y. 1914).

The "Barney Google and Spark Plug" case: King Features Syndicate v. Fleischer, 299 Fed. 533 (C. C. A. 2d 1924).

The "Popeye the Sailor" case: King Features Syndicate v. Kleeman Ltd., Ch. 523 (1940) Vol. 1.

The "Betty Boop" case: Fleischer Studios v. Ralph A. Freundlich, 5 F. Supp. 808 (D. C. N. Y. 1934), aff'd 73 F. 2d 276 (C. C. A. 2d 1934), cert. den. 294 U. S. 717, 55 S. Ct. 516, 79 L. Ed. 1250.

The Miniature Shrine case: Allegrini v. De Angelis, 59 F. Supp. 248 (D. C. Pa. 1945). But see Contemporary Arts v. F. W. Woolworth Co., 93 F. Supp. 739 (D. C. Mass. 1950), where a copyrighted sculpture of a cocker spaniel was held infringed by ceramic copies.

The "Grace of Youth" case: Gross v. Seligman, 212 F. 930 (C. C. A. 2d 1914).

Where a photographer so combines the pose, costume, and expression of his subject as to produce an individual interpretation, the picture is entitled to the benefit of copyright law: Burrow-Giles Lithographic Co. v. Sarony, 111 U. S. 53, 4 S. Ct. 279, 28 L. Ed. 349 (1883); Falk v. Gast Lithograph & Engraving Co., 48 Fed. 262 (C. C. N. Y. 1891), aff'd 54 Fed. 890 (C. C. A. 2d 1893).

The Scarves case: Home Art v. Glensder Textile Corporation, 81 F. Supp. 551 (D. C. N. Y. 1948).

The Mezzotints case: Alfred Bell & Co. v. Catalda Fine Arts, 74 F. Supp. 973 (D. C. N. Y. 1947), 86 F. Supp. 399 (D. C. N. Y. 1949), aff'd 191 F. 2d 99 (C. C. A. 2d 1951).

Infringement of copyright in painting: Leigh v. Gerber, 86 F. Supp. 320 (D. C. N. Y. 1949).

As to unfair competition in art, see Esquire v. Varga Enterprises, 185 F. 2d 14 (C. C. A. 7th 1950).

Copyrighting works of art: A. C. Hugin, 31 J. Pat. Off. Soc. 710-13 (1949).

## CHAPTER 14

### NOTES

1. See Ernest Newman, *The Elastic Language* (Borzoi Reader), New York: Alfred A. Knopf, Inc., 1936, p. 640; and Deems Taylor, *The Well Tempered Listener,* New York: Simon and Schuster, Inc., 1940, p. 97.
2. For much of the material in this section I am indebted to Dr. Paul Nettl's excellent article "Musical Kleptomaniacs" in *The Etude,* February, 1947.
3. See Herbert Weinstock, *Handel,* New York: Alfred A. Knopf, Inc., 1946. Also Eric Blom, *Stepchildren of Music,* London: G. T. Fowles & Co., Ltd., 1925; "Literary and Musical Plagiarism," *The Nation,* November 6, 1902; and Dr. Paul Nettl, *op. cit.*
4. See Jacques Barzun, *Berlioz and the Romantic Century,* Boston: Little, Brown, & Company, 1950. Also Ernest Newman, "On the Alleged Stealing of Great Composers," *The American Mercury,* September, 1932.
5. Deems Taylor, *op. cit.* p. 94.
6. See Constantin von Sternberg, "On Plagiarism," *Musical Quarterly,* Vol. V, July, 1919.
7. See Dr. Paul Nettl, *op. cit.* Also Clittenden Turner, "Plagiarism and Original Sin," *Arts and Decoration,* February, 1923.

8. Rose Heylbut, "Pirating Parnassus," *The Etude,* February, 1941.
9. Clittenden Turner, *op. cit.*
10. See William K. Zinsser, "Stravinsky Adapts Theme of His Firebird Suite to Profit from Juke-Box Trade," New York *Herald Tribune,* October 26, 1947.
11. See for example Dr. Sigmund Spaeth, "Musical Plagiarism," *Harper's Magazine,* August, 1936.
12. Deems Taylor, *op. cit.* p. 95.

## LEGAL MATERIAL

The courts have commented on the limited alphabet of music, and the handicap imposed on the composer by the conventional structure of the popular song: Darrell v. Joe Morris Music Co., 113 F. 2d 80 (C. C. A. 2d 1940); Marks v. Leo Feist, 290 Fed. 959 (C. C. A. 2d 1923); Fred Fisher, Inc. v. Dillingham, 298 Fed. 145 (D. C. N. Y. 1924); Carew v. RKO Pictures, 43 F. Supp. 199 (D. C. Cal. 1942); and Jewel Music Pub. Co. v. Leo Feist, 62 F. Supp. 596 (D. C. N. Y. 1945).

The rights conferred by the law on the copyright owner of a musical composition: Copyright Act, Section 1(a), (b) and (d).

Infringement generally: Arnstein v. Porter, 154 F. 2d 464 (C. C. A. 2d 1946), modifying in part and otherwise reversing and remanding 66 U. S. P. Q. 281 (D. C. N. Y. 1945); judgment dismissing complaint, 71 U. S. P. Q. 235 (D. C. N. Y. 1946), aff'd 158 F. 2d 795 (C. C. A. 2d 1946), cert. den. 330 U. S. 851, 67 S. Ct. 1096, 91 L. Ed. 1294; reh. den. 331 U. S. 867, 67 S. Ct. 1529, 91 L. Ed. 1871. Also Marks v. Leo Feist, Inc. 290 Fed. 959 (C. C. A. 2d 1923); Gingg v. Twentieth Century-Fox, 56 F. Supp. 701 (D. C. Cal. 1944); Hirsch v. Paramount, 17 F. Supp. 816 (D. C. Cal. 1937); Boosey v. Empire Music Co., 224 Fed. 646 (D. C. N. Y. 1915).

What is a copy: West v. Francis, 5 Barn. & Ald. 737, quoted with approval Boosey v. Whight, 80 L. T. R. 561; Gingg v. Twentieth Century-Fox, *supra.*

What constitutes similarity: Arnstein v. Broadcast Music, 137 F. 2d 410 (C. C. A. 2d 1943), aff'g 46 F. Supp. 379 (D. C. N. Y. 1942); Marks v. Leo Feist, Inc., *supra*; Gingg v. Twentieth Century-Fox, *supra*; Newcomb v. Young, 43 F. Supp. 744 (D. C. N. Y. 1942); Davilla v. Harms, 36 F. Supp. 843 (D. C. N. Y. 1940).

In Baron v. Leo Feist, 173 F. 2d 288 (C. C. A. 2d 1949), where the similarities were held to be sufficient to establish infringement, the Circuit Court of Appeals said: "The extraordinarily great similarities—which approximate identity—between plaintiff's copyrighted song "L'Année Passée" and defendants' infringing song, "Rum and Coca-Cola," in melody, un-interrupted sequence of identical notes, rhythm, construction, harmony, identity of unusual dissonant chords, and other respects, are so great as to preclude the inference of coincidence, and they constitute sufficient internal evidence of copying, even in the absence of the direct extrinsic proof of copying."

The average-listener test: Arnstein v. Edward B. Marks Music Corpora-tion, 11 F. Supp. 535 (D. C. N. Y. 1935), aff'd 82 F. 2d 275 (C. C. A. 2d 1936); Arnstein v. Broadcast Music, *supra*; Gingg v. Twentieth Century-Fox, *supra*; Davilla v. Harms, *supra*; Hirsch v. Paramount, *supra*.

The "Chatterbox" case: Carew v. RKO Pictures, 56 F. Supp. 701 (D.C. Cal. 1944). See also Blume v. Spear, 30 Fed. 629 (C. C. N. Y. 1887).

The "Some Day My Prince Will Come" case: Allen v. Walt Disney Productions, 41 F. Supp. 134 (D. C. N. Y. 1941).

The most startling similarity—even identity—is not enough. The law recognizes that similarity may occur without copying. If two composers in-dependently arrive at the same combination of notes, both are entitled to copyright, and priority is of no consequence. To be actionable, similarity must be due to copying. Arnstein v. Edward B. Marks Music Corporation, *supra*; Newcomb v. Young, *supra*; Arnstein v. ASCAP, 29 F. Supp. 388 (D. C. N. Y. 1939).

The "On the Beach at Bali-Bali" case: Darrell v. Joe Morris Music Co., 113 F. 2d 80 (C. C. A. 2d 1940).

The "Hubba Hubba" case: Weissman v. Radio Corporation of America, 80 F. Supp. 612 (D. C. N. Y. 1948).

The "I Didn't Raise My Boy to Be a Soldier" case: Haas v. Leo Feist, 234 Fed. 105 (D. C. N. Y. 1916).

There must be access: Heim v. Universal Pictures Co., 51 F. Supp. 233 (D. C. N. Y. 1943), aff'd 154 F. 2d 480 (C. C. A. 2d 1946), and cases cited *supra* and *infra*.

Burden of proof as to access: Jewel Music Pub. Co. v. Leo Feist, 62 F. Supp. 596 (D. C. N. Y. 1945).

Inference of access: Arnstein v. Edward B. Marks Music Corporation, *supra*; Wilkie v. Santly Bros., 13 F. Supp. 136 (D. C. N. Y. 1935), aff'd 91 F. 2d. 978 (C. C. A. 2d 1937); Allen v. Walt Disney Productions, *supra*.

Access to other material: Sheldon v. Metro-Goldwyn Pictures Corp., 106 F. 2d 45 (C. C. A. 2d 1939), aff'd 309 U. S. 390, 60 S. Ct. 861, 84 L. Ed. 825.

Copying must be substantial or material: Arnstein v. Broadcast Music, *supra*; Marks v. Leo Feist, Inc., *supra*; Gingg v. Twentieth Century-Fox, *supra*; Davila v. Harms, *supra*; Hirsch v. Paramount, *supra*; Boosey v. Empire Music Co., *supra*.

The "Starlight" case: Music: Wilkie v. Santly Bros., 13 F. Supp. 136 (D. C. N. Y. 1935), aff'd 91 F. 2d 978 (C. C. A. 2d 1937). Title and lyrics of same song: Newcomb v. Young, 43 F. Supp. 744 (D. C. N. Y. 1942). In the "Starlight" lyrics case, this was the chorus of the plaintiff's song:

> Starlight, Starbright,
> First star I see tonight.
> Starlight, Starbright,
> I wish I might have the wish I wish tonight.
> Will the years just bring tears?
> Happiness seems so far;
> Send me the love I'm dreaming of, oh!
> Star, bright star.

And this the chorus of the defendants':

> Starlight, Starlight,
> First star I've seen tonight,
> Help me find the one I love.
> Starlight, Starlight.
> Who knows, you might
> Know the one I'm thinking of.
> Can't you hear me sighing,
> In a lonely pray'r.
> Can't you see me crying,
> From a-way up there,
> Come closer Starlight, Starlight,
> First star I've seen tonight.
> Help me find the one I love.

The old rhyme runs:

> Starlight—Starbright,
> First star I've seen tonight;
> I wish I may, I wish I might
> Get the wish I wish tonight.

The "Dardanella" case: Fred Fisher v. Dillingham, 298 Fed. 145 (D. C. N. Y. 1924).

Slight changes made in the original by the infringer in order to cover up his tracks will not purchase immunity: Francis Day & Hunter v. Feldman & Co., 111 L. T. 521 (1914).

"The most unlettered in music can distinguish one song from another, and the mere adaptation of the air, either by changing it to a dance or by transferring it from one instrument to another, does not, even to common apprehensions, alter the original subject. The ear tells you that it is the same. The original air requires the aid of genius for its construction, but a mere mechanic in music can make the adaptation or accompaniment. Substantially, the piracy is when the appropriated music, though adapted to a different purpose from that of the original, may still be recognized by the ear. The adding of variations makes no difference in the principle." Boosey v. Fairlie, 7 Ch. D. 301 (1877), 4 A. C. 711 (1879).

Originality generally: Fred Fisher v. Dillingham, *supra*; and Chapter 2. Requisite amount of originality: Shapiro, Bernstein & Co. v. Miracle Record Co., 91 F. Supp. 473 (D. C. Ill. 1950). Words and Music: Standard Music Roll Co. v. Mills, 241 Fed. 360 (C. C. A. 3d 1917). Originality of lyrics: Newcomb v. Young, *supra*.

In an action for the infringement of a copyrighted song, proof that other songs are similar to it is immaterial unless it casts doubt upon the originality of the copyrighted song or upon the allegation that defendant copied it: Baron v. Leo Feist, 78 F. Supp. 686 (D. C. N. Y. 1948).

The "Without a Word of Warning" case: Hirsch v. Paramount, *supra*.

The "Perhaps" case: Heim v. Universal Pictures Co., *supra*.

Protection of title under doctrine of unfair competition: Jollie v. Jacques, Fed. Cas. No. 7437, 1 Blatchf. 618 (C. C. N. Y. 1852); Von Tilzer v. Jerry Vogel Music Co., 53 F. Supp. 191 (D. C. N. Y. 1943); International Film Service v. Association Producers, 273 Fed. 585 (D. C. N. Y. 1921). See cases cited in next chapter.

"The Man Who Broke the Bank at Monte Carlo" case: Francis Day & Hunter v. Twentieth Century-Fox, 56 Times Law Reports 9 (1939).

Arrangements of a copyrighted piece of music are in themselves copyrightable, if authorized by the owner of the original copyright. Orchestral score arranged for piano: Carte v. Evans, 27 Fed. 861 (C. C. Mass. 1886), and Baron v. Leo Feist, 173 F. 2d 288 (C. C. A. 2d 1949). But see *The Mikado* case, 25 Fed. 183 (C. C. N. Y. 1885). See also Wood v. Boosey, L. R. 3 Q. B. 223, 18 ERC 578. Piano score arranged for orchestra: Chappell v. Columbia Graphophone Co., 2 Ch. 124 (1914). Song arranged for orchestra: Edmonds v. Stern, 248 Fed. 897 (D. C. N. Y. 1918).

Material which is taken bodily from the public domain and incorporated in a new copyrighted composition remains in the public domain and does not gain protection under the copyright. In such case the copyright extends only to the new and original portion. On the other hand, a composer who *creatively*—that is to say, with the exercise of his own skill, labor and judgment—utilizes a public domain theme is protected against anyone who copies his treatment instead of going to the source. Fred Fisher v. Dillingham, *supra.*

Lack of intent to infringe is no excuse: Fred Fisher v. Dillingham, *supra*; Shapiro, Bernstein v. Veltin, 47 F. Supp. 648 (D. C. La. 1942), and cases there cited.

Defense of laches: Davilla v. Harms, 36 F. Supp. 843 (D. C. N. Y. 1940).

The "Rum and Coca-Cola" case: Khan v. Leo Feist, 165 F. 2d 188 (C. C. A. 2d 1947), aff'g 70 F. Supp. 450 (D. C. N. Y. 1947). See also Baron v. Leo Feist, 173 F. 2d 288 (C. C. A. 2d 1949).

The Arnstein cases: Arnstein v. Shilkret, U. S. D. C., S. D. N. Y., E. 65, p. 83, Op. No. 8152 (1933); Arnstein v. Edward B. Marks Music Corporation, 11 F. Supp. 535 (D. C. N. Y. 1935), aff'd 82 F. 2d 275 (C. C. A. 2d 1936); Arnstein v. ASCAP, 29 F. Supp. 388 (D. C. N. Y. 1939); Arnstein v. Broadcast Music, 137 F. 2d 410 (C. C. A. 2d 1943), aff'g 46 F. Supp. 379 (D. C. N. Y. 1942); Arnstein v. Twentieth Century-Fox, 52 F. Supp. 114 (D. C. N. Y. 1943); and Arnstein v. Porter, 154 F. 2d 464 (C. C. A. 2d 1946), modifying in part and otherwise reversing and remanding 66 U. S. P. Q. 281 (D. C. N. Y. 1945); judgment dismissing complaint, 71 U. S. P. Q. 235 (D. C. N. Y. 1946), aff'd 158 F. 2d 795 (C. C. A. 2d 1946), cert. den. 330 U. S. 851, 67 S. Ct. 1096, 91 L. Ed. 1294; reh. den. 331 U. S. 867, 67 S. Ct. 1529, 91 L. Ed. 1871.

Musical copyright generally, see Alfred M. Shafter, *Musical Copyright,* 2d Ed., Chicago: Callaghan and Company, 1939; and E. De Matt Henderson, "The Law of Copyright, Especially Musical," *Copyright Law Symposium,* New York: ASCAP, 1939.

## CHAPTER 15

### NOTES

1. Dr. Maurice Davies, *Fun, Ancient and Modern,* London: Tinsley Brothers, 1878, p. 198. See also Albert Rapp, *The Origins of Wit and Humor,* New York: E. P. Dutton & Co., Inc., 1951

2. Irene Nye, "Humor Repeats Itself," *The Classical Journal,* University of Chicago, Vol. IX, 1913-1914.

3. Even pronouncements which issue from the halls of justice are not devoid of parallels. Judges do, of course, openly quote from one another's opinions; the process is at once the foundation of the system of precedents, and the jurist's badge of erudition. But judges also repeat, without ascription, utterances which they deem facetious or

pungent or gnomic. Nearly a century and a half ago, Lord Stowell remarked in an English divorce case that people do not go to houses of ill fame to say their paternoster. It is not at all unlikely that he had culled the observation from Burton's *Anatomy of Melancholy* (Loveden v. Loveden, 2 Hag. Cons. 1, 4 Eng. Ecc. 461, Consistory Court of London, 1810). Decades later a Missouri judge ventured the guess, in a rape case, that a man wearing nothing but his shirt does not get into the bed of a married woman who is not his wife at two o'clock in the morning to say his paternoster (Slate v. Smith, 80 Mo. 516, 1883). Again, no acknowledgment. It remained for Judge (later Mayor) Gaynor, in a subsequent case, to give Burton his due (Kerr v. Kerr, 134 App. Div. 141, New York 1909).

4. *Joe Miller's Complete Jest Book* (reprint), New York: William T. Henderson, 1903. Richard Tarlton, *Tarlton's Jests,* 1611 (reprint), London: Willis and Southern, 1866, edited by W. Carew Hazlitt. John Taylor, *Wit and Mirth,* 1630 (reprint), same publisher and same editor. Archie Armstrong, *Banquet of Jests,* 1630 (reprint), Edinburgh, 1872. See Robert O. Foote, "Who Was Joe Miller?" *A Treasury of Laughter,* ed. by Louis Untermeyer, New York: Simon and Schuster, 1946, pp. 246-251.

5. For these two anecdotes I am indebted to Thornton Delehanty, from whom I've taken them practically verbatim. See New York *Herald Tribune,* January 28, 1945.

6. New York *Herald Tribune,* May 19, 1947. I have borrowed freely from Crosby in this section. See his columns in the New York *Herald Tribune* August 6, 1948, October 27, 1947, April 24, 1947, November 11, 1946, and September 20, 1946. See also Paul Denis in *The New York Post,* July 7, 1948 and September 19, 1947.

7. Julian P. Boyd, *The Declaration of Independence,* Princeton University Press, 1945. See also Joseph Lewis, *Thomas Paine: Author of the Declaration of Independence,* New York: Freethought Press Association, 1947; and Maurice S. Sullivan, "The Grand Army of Plagiarists," *The Catholic World,* November, 1923.

8. "Theft of Thunder," *New School Bulletin,* Vol. II, No. 6, October 9, 1944.

9. Jhan and June Robbins, "Piracy on Fifth Avenue," *This Week Magazine,* New York *Herald Tribune,* June 5, 1949.

10. Rev. R. M. Sargent, "Plagiarism," *The Congregational Quarterly,* October, 1867. See "Plagiarism" (Anon.), *Leisure Hour,* London, April, 1874; and Augustus C. Thompson, "Ministerial Plagiarism," *Hartford Seminary Record,* October, 1894.

### LEGAL MATERIAL

No property right in radio ideas as such: See Bowen v. Yankee Network, 46 F. Supp. 62 (D. C. Mass. 1942); also Chapter I.

Use of radio idea: Cole v. Lord, 28 N. Y. S. 2d 404, 262 App. Div. 116 (1941).

For a discussion of the protection of ideas in radio programs, see H. P. Warner, "Protection of the Content of Radio and Television Programs by Common Law Copyright," 3 Vand. L. Rev. 209-40 (1950); Note, "Protection of Ideas in Radio Programs," 12 Air L. Rev. 231 (1941); C. A. Greco, "Copyright Protection and Radio Broadcasting," 3 La. L. Rev. 200-11 (1940); Louis G. Caldwell, "Piracy of Broadcast Programs," 30 Columbia L. Rev. 1087 (1930).

The *Hollywood Preview* case: Stanley v. C.B.S., 35 Cal. 2d 653, 221 P. 2d 73 (Cal. 1950).

The title of a radio program is subject to ownership, and is protectible by law. *Information Please:* Golenpaul v. Rossett, 18 N. Y. S. 2d 889, 174 Misc. 114 (1940). *March of Time:* Time, Inc. v. Barshay, 27 F. Supp. 870 (D. C. N. Y. 1939). *Old Maestro:* Premier-Pabst Brewing Corp. v. Elm City Brewing Co., 9 F. Supp. 754 (D. C. Conn. 1935).

The *Woody Woodpecker* case: Blanc v. Lantz, 83 U. S. P. Q. 137 (Cal. Super. Ct. 1949). See 3 Van. L. Rev. at pp. 216-7.

Copyright of a book does not make the author the exclusive owner of the art described in it: Baker v. Selden, 101 U. S. 99, 25 L. Ed. 841 (1880); Bauer v. O'Donnell, 229 U. S. 1, 33 S. Ct. 616, 57 L. Ed. 1041, 50 L. R. A. (N. S.) 1185, Ann. Cas. 1915-A 150 (1913).

The Copyright Law does not protect business ideas. Bank Night: Affiliated Enterprises v. Gruber, 86 F. 2d 958 (C. C. A. 1st 1936). Roller Skating Derby: Seltzer v. Corem, 107 F. 2d 75 (C. C. A. 7th 1939), rev'g 26 F. Supp. 892 (D. C. Ind. 1939); and Seltzer v. Sunbrock, 22 F. Supp. 621 (D. C. Cal. 1938). Plan for consolidating a complicated system of freight tariff schedules: Guthrie v. Curlett, 36 F. 2d 694 (C. C. A. 2d 1929). System of letter file indexes: Amberg File & Index Co. v. Shea Smith & Co., 82 Fed. 314 (C. C. A. 7th 1897). Shorthand system: Brief English Systems v. Owen, 48 F. 2d 555 (C. C. A. 2d 1931). Sales method: Kaeser & Blair v. Merchants' Ass'n, 64 F. 2d 575 (C. C. A. 6th 1933). Culbertson bridge system: Downes v. Culbertson, 275 N. Y. Supp. 233, 153 Misc. 14 (Sup. Ct. 1934). Plan for installment buying: Moore v. Ford Co., 28 F. 2d 529 (D. C. N. Y. 1928).

The copyright in a life insurance policy does not bar others from using policy forms embodying the same ideas and some of the same language: Dorsey v. Old Surety Life Ins. Co., 98 F. 2d 872 (C. C. A. 10th 1938).

An old game like backgammon cannot be removed from the public domain and converted into private property by the expedient of copyrighting its rules and layout: Chamberlin v. Uris Sales Corporation, 150 F. 2d 512 (C. C. A. 2d 1945), aff'g 56 F. Supp. 987 (D. C. N. Y. 1944).

There are two interesting cases involving the use of architectural ideas. In one case, the subject matter was covered by statutory copyright, and in the other, by common law copyright. I. J. Muller designed a novel bridge approach calculated to streamline traffic. He copyrighted it. He later claimed that his scheme had been used in the construction of the Triborough Bridge in New York. Howard Ketcham prepared a color chart for the New York World's Fair, and submitted it to the Fair with detailed instructions. He did not copyright his material. The Fair turned him down. When the Trylon and Perisphere became a reality, he too felt that he had been victimized. Both men sued. Both of them lost. Judge Leibell found no evidence of copying in the one case, and Judge Moscowitz found none in the other. Judge Leibell indicated that even if copying had been proved, under the rule laid down by the Supreme Court in Baker v. Selden, *supra*, the plaintiff would have had no remedy. Muller v. Triborough, 43 F. Supp. 298 (D. C. N. Y. 1942); Ketcham v. N. Y. World's Fair, 34 F. Supp. 657 (D. C. N. Y. 1940). See Palmer v. Dewitt, 47 N. Y. 532 (1872), 7 Am. Rep. 480. There is an apparent conflict in the dicta in the Muller and Ketcham cases. The conflict can probably be reconciled on the ground that the one case turned on statutory copyright (with its inseparable doctrine of fair use), and the other on common law copyright.

Architects' copyright: 202 Law Times 328-9 (1946). Architectural plagiarism: Kurfiss v. Cowherd, 233 Mo. App. 397 (1938).

See also "Non-Patentable and Non-Copyrightable Business Ideas," 97 U. Pa. L. Rev. 94-9 (1948).

Protection of legal rights in ideas, see Booth v. Stutz Motor Car Co., 56 F. 2d 962 (C. C. A. 7th 1932); Moore v. Ford Motor Co., 43 F. 2d 685 (C. C. A. 2d 1930); Hampton v. La Salle Hat Co., 88 F. Supp. 153 (D. C. N. Y. 1949), noted 3 Okla. L. Rev. 314-17 (1950); Plus Promotions v. RCA Mfg. Co., 49 F. Supp. 116 (D. C. N. Y. 1943); American Mint Corp. v. Ex-Lax, 31 N. Y. S. 2d 708, 263 App. Div. 89 (1941); Stone v. Liggett & Myers Tobacco Co., 23 N. Y. S. 2d 210, 260 App. Div. 450 (1940); Alberts v. Remington Rand, 23 N. Y. S. 2d 892, 175 Misc. 486 (1940); Williamson v. N. Y. C. R. R. Co., 16 N. Y. S. 2d 217, 258 App. Div. 226 (1939); Healey v. R. H. Macy & Co., 297 N. Y. S. 165, 251 App. Div. 440 (1937), aff'd 277 N. Y. 681, 14 N. E. 2d 388

(1938); Larkin v. Pennsylvania R. R. Co., 210 N. Y. S. 374, 125 Misc. 238 (1925), aff'd 215 N. Y. S. 875, 216 App. Div. 832; Schonwald v. F. Burkart Mfg. Co., 356 Mo. 435, 202 S. W. 2d 7 (1947), 170 A. L. R. 459n, noted 13 Mo. L. Rev. 91-2 (1948), 27 Ore. L. Rev. 166-7 (1948), and 22 St. John's L. Rev. 165-7 (1947).

See also 97 U. Pa. L. Rev. 94-9 (1948); 29 J. Pat. Off. Soc. 895 (1947); 4 La. L. Rev. 118-27 (1941); 4 Missouri L. Rev. 239-267 (1939); 47 Harv. L. Rev. 1419 (1934).

Copyright does not extend to gadgets, whether alone or affixed to printed material. A greeting card in the shape of a traveling bag which, when opened, disclosed a pair of doll's rubber pants, held not copyrightable: Jackson v. Quickslip Co., 110 F. 2d 731 (C. C. A. 2d 1940), aff'g 27 F. Supp. 338 (D. C. N. Y. 1939).

The Oneida silverware case: Oneida, Ltd. v. National Silver Co., 25 N. Y. S. 2d 271 (1940). "Where a person gifted with genius and imagination," said Judge Davis, "has by industry produced something attractive and interesting to the general public, which has a commercial or monetary value, there is always a temptation to persons of lesser qualities to imitate and exploit it to their own profit. In books or plays such imitative acts are called plagiarism; in commercial art or design it is called piracy; in general it is given the colloquial term, 'chiseling.'"

The character of the Lone Ranger was made famous on the radio. The owners of the program made a grant of film rights. A picture was produced, and Lee Powell played the rôle of the hero. Some time later he joined the Wallace Brothers Circus and made personal appearances. He rode a white horse and gave the cry "Hi Yo Silver." The posters claimed him to be the Lone Ranger in the flesh. The owners of the radio serial sued. The Court felt that the circus act was the "fraudulent attempt of someone to reap where he has not sown," and forbade it. Lone Ranger v. Cox, 124 F. 2d 650 (C. C. A. 4th 1942), rev'g 39 F. Supp. 487 (D. C. Cal. 1941).

Copyright protection of jewelry: S. B. Warner, 31 J. Pat. Off. Soc. 487-90 (1949).

The legal difficulties inherent in any attempt to protect fashion designs or fabric patterns are discussed in Fashion Originators' Guild v. Federal Trade Commission, 114 F. 2d 80 (C. C. A. 2d 1940), aff'd 312 U. S. 457, 61 S. Ct. 703, 85 L. Ed. 949 (1941); Cheney Bros. v. Doris Silk Corporation, 35 F. 2d 279 (C. C. A. 2d 1929); Margolis v. National Bellas Hess Co., 249 N. Y. S. 175, 139 Misc. 738 (1931); and Verney Corp. v. Rose Fabric Converters Corp., 87 F. Supp. 802 (D. C. N. Y.

1950). See also 35 Ill. L. Rev. 546-65 (1941); and 22 J. Pat. Off. Soc. 557-62 (1940).

The Judge Shientag quote is from Margolis v. National Bellas Hess, *supra*.

The Fashion Originators' Guild case: See *supra*.

## CHAPTER 16

### NOTES

1. "Self-Plagiarism" (Anon.), *The Atlantic Monthly*, September, 1893. See also Brander Matthews, *Rip Van Winkle Goes to the Plays*, New York: Charles Scribner's Sons, 1926, particularly chapter "On the Right of an Author to Repeat Himself."

2. See Frances Winwar, *Oscar Wilde and the Yellow Nineties*, New York: Harper & Brothers, 1940.

3. See Ernest Newman, "On the Alleged Stealing of Great Composers," *The American Mercury*, September, 1932; also Eudora Ramsay Richardson, "The Ubiquitous Plagiarist," *Readings in Present Day Writers* (Raymond W. Pence, Ed.), New York: The Macmillan Company, 1933.

4. See Brander Matthews, *op. cit.* Also "Plagiarizing One's Own" (Anon.), *The Bookman*, February, 1904.

5. Dr. Paul Nettl, "Musical Kleptomaniacs," *The Etude*, February, 1947.

6. Leonard Lyons, "Lyons Den," *The New York Post*, April 8, 1947.

7. For a discussion of present-day pen names and the reasons for their use, see John K. Hutchens, "On the Books," New York *Herald Tribune Book Review*, April 17, 1949.

8. Charles Nodier, "Des Artifices Que Certains Auteurs Ont Employés Pour Déguiser Leurs Noms," *Bulletin du Bibliophile et du Bibliothécaire*, Paris, 1835, July, pp. 1-10.

9. Literature is full of hoaxes. See H. M. Paull, *Literary Ethics*, London: T. Thornton Butterworth, Ltd., 1928.

10. A great deal has been written about the forgery of works of art. The best brief summary I know of is the symposium in the May, 1948, issue of the *Magazine of Art*. See also James Henry Duveen, *Art Treasures and Intrigue*, New York: Doubleday & Company, Inc., 1935. Concerning Han Van Meegeren, see John Godley, *The Master Art Forger*, New York: Wilfred Funk, 1951. As to literary forgeries, see Richard D. Altick, *The Scholar Adventurers*, New York: The Macmillan Company, 1950.

11. Hippolyte Cérès, *Un Maître Mal Connu de Provençe,* Paris: Imprimerie Douillard, 1821.

### LEGAL MATERIAL

As to the legal aspects of unconscious plagiarism, see Chapter 18.

The Frankfurter quote is from Kingsley v. Dorsey, 388 U. S. 939, 70 S. Ct. 341, 94 L. Ed. 258 (1949).

### CHAPTER 17

#### NOTES

1. *The Works of E. A. Poe (Marginalia),* Vol. VI, London: J. Shiels & Co., 1895, p. 186. See also Nelson F. Adkins, "Chapter on American Cribbage," *The Papers of the Bibliographical Society of America,* Vol. 42, Third Quarter, 1948.
2. See Chapter 18.
3. A. G. Gardiner, *Many Furrows,* New York: E. P. Dutton & Co., Inc., 1925, p. 69. See also Edward Wright, "The Art of Plagiarism," London: *Contemporary Review,* April, 1904.

#### LEGAL MATERIAL

Legal definition of infringement: See Chapter I.

Intent to infringe immaterial: Cases cited under Intent to Infringe, Legal Material, Chapter I; also Pathé Exchange v. Local No. 306, 3 F. Supp. 63 (D. C. N. Y. 1932); Stern v. Jerome H. Remick & Co., 175 Fed. 282 (C. C. N. Y. 1910); Fishel v. Lueckel, 53 Fed. 499 (C. C. N. Y. 1892) and cases cited in Chapter 18.

While theoretically every wrong requires both act and intent, the paramount element is the act. The trend of the law has been to establish liability regardless of the existence of wrongful intent, or at least to presume intent from the act. See Peo. v. Fernow, 286 Ill. 627, 122 N. E. 155 (1919); 24 Michigan Law Review 304 (1926); and 4 American Law Review 1538 (1919).

Compilations: See Legal Material, Chapter 9. In the text I've discussed only the question of borrowing from various protected sources—not in themselves compilations—to prepare a compendium. There remains, of course, the problem of one compiler looting the work of another compiler.

The legal rule on this was well stated in the old English case of Jarrold v. Houlston, 3 K. & J. 708 (1857). There the publishers of Dr. Brewer's *Guide to Science* obtained an injunction against the publication of the

*Reason Why*. Both books embodied the same plan and dealt with popular information on scientific subjects. The earlier book had been used to a large extent in the preparation of the later one, although copying was denied. The judge said: "If, knowing that a person whose work is protected by copyright has, with considerable labour, compiled from various sources a work in itself not original, but which he has digested and arranged, you, being minded to compile a work of a like description, instead of taking the pains of searching into all the common sources, and obtaining your subject-matter from them, avail yourself of the labour of your predecessor, adopt his arrangements, adopt, moreover, the very questions he has asked, or adopt them with but a slight degree of colourable variation, and thus save yourself pains and labour by availing yourself of the pains and labour which he has employed, that I take to be an illegitimate use."

Acknowledgment of source is no defense in a copyright infringement suit: Toksvig v. Bruce Pub. Co., 181 F. 2d 664 (C. C. A. 7th 1950).

Property rights in news: See Legal Material, Chapter I.

## Chapter 18

### NOTES

1. June E. Downey, *Creative Imagination*, New York: Harcourt, Brace and Company. Inc., 1929, p. 158. See also Herbert Read, *Art Now*, London: Faber and Faber, Ltd., 1948, pp. 48-52; and Editorial, "Unsung," *The Saturday Review of Literature*, August 27, 1949.

2. W. L. Northridge, *Theories of the Unconscious*, London: Routledge and Kegan Paul, Ltd., 1924, pp. 18 and 19. See also note 2.

3. See John Livingstone Lowes, *The Road to Xanadu*, Boston: Houghton Mifflin Company, 1927, p. 427.

4. Joseph Jastrow, *The Subconscious*, Boston: Houghton Mifflin Company, 1906. See George Stephen Painter, *Fundamental Psychology*, New York: Liveright Publishing Corp., 1938; and Charles Edward Spearman, *Creative Mind*, New York: D. Appleton-Century-Crofts Company, 1931.

5. *Broadway Journal*, Vol. 1, p. 212, April 5, 1845. See Nelson F. Adkins, "Chapter on American Cribbage," *The Papers of the Bibliographical Society of America*, Vol. 42, Third Quarter, 1948, pp. 169-210.

### LEGAL MATERIAL

Intention to infringe is not essential under the Copyright Act: Buck v. Jewell-La Salle Realty Co., 283 U. S. 191, 198, 51 S. Ct. 410, 411, 75 L. Ed.

971, 76 A. L. R. 1266 (1931); Douglas v. Cunningham, 294 U. S. 207,
55 S. Ct. 365, 79 L. Ed. 862 (1935); Twentieth Century-Fox Film Corp.
v. Dieckhaus, 153 F. 2d 893 (C. C. A. 8th 1946), rev'g 54 F. Supp.
425 (D. C. Mo. 1944), cert. den. 329 U. S. 716, 67 S. Ct. 46, 91 L. Ed.
621; De Acosta v. Brown, 146 F. 2d 408, 411 (C. C. A. 2d 1944), aff'g
50 F. Supp. 615 (D. C. N. Y. 1943), cert. den. 325 U. S. 862, 65 S. Ct.
1197, 89 L. Ed. 1982 and 325 U. S. 862, 65 S. Ct. 1198, 89 L. Ed. 1983;
and Edwards & Deutsch Lithographing Co. v. Boorman, 15 F. 2d 35 (C.
C. A. 7th 1926). See also Legal Material, Chapters 1 and 17.

The "Dardanella" case: Fred Fisher v. Dillingham, 298 Fed. 145, 147
(D. C. N. Y. 1924).

The *Letty Lynton* case: Sheldon v. Metro-Goldwyn Pictures Corp., 106
F. 2d 45 (C. C. A. 2d 1939), aff'd 309 U. S. 390, 60 S. Ct. 681, 84 L.
Ed. 825.

## CHAPTER 19

### NOTES

1. "One grieves when the character of good men is taken away; but who
grieves when solicitors are told they have no character to be taken away?
Often I wonder why our profession is so much abused. There are black
sheep to be found in every flock. But what of the ninety and nine that
went not astray? I may be a prejudiced party, but I have known hundreds
of practitioners who were large-hearted, open-handed, fair-minded men:
tolerant, perhaps too tolerant, of human frailty; quickened in their own
sympathies by being called upon to advise all sorts and conditions of
men in all sorts and conditions of trouble; devoting some of their office
time and much of their leisure to philanthropic, intellectual, and social
work." Reginald L. Hine, *Confessions of an Un-Common Attorney,*
New York: The Macmillan Company, 1947, pp. 37-38.

2. As to the administration of law, see Jerome Frank, *Courts on Trial,*
Princeton: Princeton University Press, 1949. As to "justice," see Edmond N. Cahn, *The Sense of Injustice,* New York: New York University Press, 1949; and Roscoe Pound, *Justice According to Law,*
New Haven: Yale University Press, 1951. As to the judicial process
generally, see extensive bibliography, *The Record* of the Association of
the Bar of the City of New York, Vol. 7, No. 2 (Feb., 1952).

3. "The law student today recognizes that many of the most beautifully
intricate and subtle of legal theories are merely a particular form of
legal rationalization or fiction designed to make the circle of the assump-

tion of an immutable body of law square with the necessity that the administration of law must accomplish what are recognized as desirable social ends. Theories are now recognized as often a means of justifying decisions rather than as reasons for making them." Francis H. Bohlen, "The Reality of What the Courts Are Doing," *Legal Essays,* Berkeley: University of California Press, 1935, p. 44.

4. Edwin W. Patterson, "John Dewey and the Law," *American Bar Association Journal,* Vol. 36, No. 8, August, 1950, p. 619 *et seq.*

5. See Channing Pollock, "The Plagiarism Racket," *The American Mercury,* May, 1945; Howard Barnes, "The Plagiarism Racket," *Theater Guild Magazine,* Oct.-Nov., 1929; "The Plagiarism Racket" (unsigned editorial), *The Nation,* October 23, 1929; Arthur Garfield Hays, "The Plagiarism Plague," *Vanity Fair,* July, 1930; and Sigmund Spaeth, "Musical Plagiarism," *Harper's Magazine,* August, 1936.

### LEGAL MATERIAL

*The Great Dictator* case: New York *Times,* May 2, 1947.

The *Citizen Kane* case: *Variety,* February 21, 1950.

The *Letty Lynton* case: Sheldon v. Metro-Goldwyn Pictures Corporation, 81 F. 2d 49 (C. C. A. 2d 1936), rev'g 7 F. Supp. 837 (D. C. N. Y. 1934). Judge Woolsey found no infringement but the decree was reversed, and an injunction and accounting were ordered. Decree on accounting: 26 F. Supp. 134 (D. C. N. Y. 1938). Decree modified: 106 F. 2d 45 (C. C. A. 2d 1939), aff'd 309 U. S. 390, 60 S. Ct. 861, 84 L. Ed. 825.

*The Road to Glory* case: Sheets v. Twentieth Century-Fox Film Corporation, 33 F. Supp. 389 (D. C. Cal. 1940).

*The Bird of Paradise* case: Fendler v. Morosco, 253 N. Y. 281 (1930), rev'g 217 App. Div. 791.

The *Abie's Irish Rose* case: Nichols v. Universal Pictures Corporation, 45 F. 2d 119 (C. C. A. 2d 1930), aff'g 34 F. 2d 145 (D. C. N. Y. 1929), cert. den. 282 U. S. 902, 51 S. Ct. 216, 75 L. Ed. 795.

If there is evidence of access and similarities do exist, the testimony of experts may be received on the question whether the similarities are sufficient to prove copying: Arnstein v. Porter, 154 F. 2d 464 (C. C. A. 2d 1946), modifying in part and otherwise reversing and remanding 66 U. S. P. Q. 281 (D. C. N. Y. 1945); judgment dismissing complaint, 71 U. S. P. Q. 235 (D. C. N. Y. 1946), aff'd 158 F. 2d 795 (C. C. A. 2d 1946), cert. den. 330 U. S. 851, 67 S. Ct. 1096, 91 L. Ed. 1294; reh. den. 331 U. S. 867, 67 S. Ct. 1529, 91 L. Ed. 1871.

The *Outline of History* case: Deeks v. Wells, 1 D. L. R. 353 (1933).

*The Freshman* case: Harold Lloyd Corporation v. Witwer, 65 F. 2d 1

(C. C. A. 9th 1933), rev'g 46 F. 2d 792 (D. C. Cal. 1930), cert. dism. 54 S. Ct. 94, 78 L. Ed. 1507.

For lengthy descriptions of the plots of the works at bar, see the *Letty Lynton, The Bird of Paradise,* and the *Abie's Irish Rose* cases, *supra*; the *Modern Times* case, Kustoff v. Chaplin, 120 F. 2d 551 (C. C. A. 9th 1941); the *My Man Godfrey* case, West v. Hatch, 49 F. Supp. 307 (D. C. N. Y. 1943); the *Blonde Venus* case, Ornstein v. Paramount Productions, 9 F. Supp. 896 (D. C. N. Y. 1935); and the *Death Takes a Holiday* case, Wiren v. Shubert, 5 F. Supp. 358 (D. C. N. Y. 1933), aff'd 70 F. 2d 1023 (C. C. A. 2d 1934).

There have, of course, been some opinions of exemplary terseness. See for example Dymow v. Bolton, 11 F. 2d 690 (C. C. A. 2d 1926), two pages; Bachman v. Belasco, 224 Fed. 817 (C. C. A. 2d 1915), page and a half; Dezendorf v. Twentieth Century-Fox, 32 F. Supp. 359 (D. C. Cal. 1940), one page; and—a model of brevity—Hubges v. Belasco, 130 Fed. 388 (C. C. N. Y. 1904), fifteen lines. The prize probably goes to the opinion of the Circuit Court of Appeals in the kewpie doll case: "It would serve no useful purpose to compare in detail the so-called statuette which plaintiff copyrighted [i.e., the kewpie doll] and the doll that defendant sold; it is sufficient to say that the doll at the very least is a plain copy of a substantial and material part thereof. Consequently it is an infringement." Wilson v. Haber Bros., 275 Fed. 346 (C. C. A. 2d 1921).

As to the helpfulness of precedents, see Fendler v. Morosco, *supra.* Judge Lehman said in that case: "We can derive little aid from a restatement of the decisions arrived at by the courts in the reported cases, for each case was decided upon its own facts. All use similar tests, though exact formulation of the test is as difficult as its application when the question is close."

The *Of Thee I Sing* case: Lowenfels v. Nathan, 2 F. Supp. 73 (D. C. N. Y. 1932).

The *Death Takes a Holiday* case: Wiren v. Shubert Theatre Corporation, 5 F. Supp. 358 (D. C. N. Y. 1933), aff'd 70 F. 2d 1023 (C. C. A. 2d 1934).

The *Blonde Venus* case: Ornstein v. Paramount Productions, 9 F. Supp. 896 (D. C. N. Y. 1935).

The *Cimarron* case: Caruthers v. RKO Pictures, 20 F. Supp. 906 (D. C. N. Y. 1937).

The *I Dream Too Much* case: Shipman v. RKO Radio Pictures, 20 F. Supp. 249 (D. C. N. Y. 1937), aff'd 100 F. 2d 533 (C. C. A. 2d 1938).

The *Roman Scandals* case: Motion to dismiss complaint granted, Eisman v. Samuel Goldwyn, 23 F. Supp. 519 (D. C. N. Y. 1938); reversed and trial ordered, Dellar v. Samuel Goldwyn, 104 F. 2d 661 (C. C. A. 2d 1939). Judgment for defendant, 40 F. Supp. 534 (D. C. N. Y. 1941), aff'd 150 F. 2d 612 (C. C. A. 2d 1945), cert. den. 327 U. S. 790, 66 S. Ct. 802, 90 L. Ed. 1646; reh. den. 328 U. S. 878, 66 S. Ct. 1020, 90 L. Ed. 1016.

The Cole Porter case: Arnstein v. Porter, 154 F. 2d 464 (C. C. A. 2d 1946), modifying in part and otherwise reversing and remanding 66 U. S. P. Q. 281 (D. C. N. Y. 1945); complaint dismissed, 71 U. S. P. Q. 235 (D. C. N. Y. 1946), aff'd 158 F. 2d 795 (C. C. A. 2d 1946), cert. den. 330 U. S. 851, 67 S. Ct. 1096, 91 L. Ed. 1294; reh. den. 331 U. S. 867, 67 S. Ct. 1529, 91 L. Ed. 1871. See Chapter 14 for a discussion of this case. See also Note, 20 So. Calif. L. Rev. 215 (1947).

The *Dear Ruth* case: Columbia Pictures v. Krasna, 65 N. Y. S. 2d 67 (1946), aff'd 69 N. Y. S. 2d 796, 271 App. Div. 1008, app. den. 73 N. Y. S. 2d 486, 272 App. Div. 794.

The *Deep Are the Roots* case: Heywood v. Jericho, 85 N. Y. S. 2d 464, 193 Misc. 905 (1948).

The *State of the Union* case: Millstein v. Leland Hayward, 10 F. R. D. 198 (D. C. N. Y. 1950).

Summary judgment affirmed: Ricker v. General Electric Co., 162 F. 2d 141 (C. C. A. 2d 1947).

Complaint dismissed on *plaintiff's* motion for interlocutory decree and preliminary injunction: Park v. Warner Brothers, 8 F. Supp. 37 (D. C. N. Y. 1934).

Motion for summary judgment denied because of existence of triable issues: Thompson v. Gernsback, 94 F. Supp. 453 (D. C. N. Y. 1950).

Decree reversed and case remanded for trial, on the ground that the parties never agreed that the "cutting continuity" of the movie *Test Pilot,* alleged to infringe a book by the same name, was a fair representation of the film: Collins v. Metro-Goldwyn Pictures, 106 F. 2d 83 (C. C. A. 2d 1939), rev'g 25 F. Supp. 781 (D. C. N. Y. 1938).

Other circuits have evinced no disaffection with the practice of disposition by motion. See for example Christianson v. West. Pub. Co., 149 F. 2d 202 (C. C. A. 9th 1945).

For summary judgment in plagiarism cases, see 20 So. Calif. L. Rev. 2156 (1947); and 55 Yale L. J., 810 (1946).

## CHAPTER 20

### NOTES

1. See Jerome Frank, *Courts on Trial,* Princeton: Princeton University Press, 1949.
2. Zechariah Chafee, Jr., "Reflections on the Law of Copyright," *Columbia Law Review,* Vol. 45, pp. 503-29, 719-38, July and Sept. 1945. See also "Report of the Committee on Copyrights," *American Bar Association,* Section of Patent, Trade-Mark and Copyright Law, 1951.
3. Serjeant Talfourd, a leading English barrister of the nineteenth century, found it peculiarly unjust to bound the term of the author's exclusive property—as the law of Britain then did—by his natural life or twenty-eight years, whichever was longer. "It denies to age and experience," he said, "the probable reward it permits to youth—to youth, sufficiently full of hope and joys to slight its promises. It gives a bounty to haste, and informs the laborious student, who would wear away his strength to complete some work which 'the world will not willingly let die,' that the more of his life he devotes to its perfection, the more limited shall be his interests in its fruits. It stops the progress of remuneration at the moment it is most needed; and when the benignity of nature would extract from her last calamity a means of support and comfort to the survivors—at the moment when his name is invested with the solemn interest of the grave—when his eccentricities or frailties excite a smile or a shrug no longer—when the last seal is set upon his earthly course, and his works assume their place among the classics of his country—your law declares that his works shall become your property, and you requite him by seizing the patrimony of his children." The law in question was St. 54 Geo. III, c. 156. See "Fifty Years Ago: Mark Twain on Copyright," London: The Author, Vol. LX, No. 4, Summer, 1950.
4. U. S. Constitution, Article I, Section 8.
5. "It would be a wise move on the part of the American Society of Composers and Publishers to appoint an unprejudiced referee to pass on all accusations of musical plagiarism. . . . Of course, the amateurs who are outside the Society would probably go right on suing or threatening to sue, but even they might eventually discover the error of their ways, and abide by the decision of a fair-minded intermediary. Meanwhile thousands of dollars and many hours of valuable time would be saved, and our courts would be spared the absurd spectacle of musically ignorant lawyers wrangling before an equally ignorant judge as to whose brain should be credited with inventing such lyric masterpieces

as 'You Nasty Man,' 'Eeeny, Meeny, Miny, Moe,' and 'The Music Goes Round and Round.' " Sigmund Spaeth, "Musical Plagiarism," *Harper's Magazine*, August, 1936.

### LEGAL MATERIAL

As to the charge against Lord Campbell, see 12 Can. B. Rev. 93 (1934). "General propositions do not decide concrete cases. The decision will depend on a judgment or intuition more subtle than any articulate major premise." Justice Holmes, in Lochner v. New York, 198 U. S. 45, 74, 25 S. Ct. 539, 49 L. Ed. 937 (1905).

Precedents can be found for either side of any question: Cowell v. Gregory, 130 N. Car. 80, 40 S. E. Rep. 849 (1902).

Where a copyrighted poem is set to music and incorporated in a phonograph record for public use, there's no infringement under Section 1(d) of the Copyright Act because a poem is not a "dramatic work" but a "book" within the meaning of the statute. Corcoran v. Montgomery Ward & Co., 121 F. 2d 575 (C. C. A. 9th 1941).

Held, no infringement if copyrighted poem is recited on the radio: Kreymborg v. Durante, 21 U. S. P. Q. 557, 22 U. S. P. Q. 248 (D. C. N. Y. 1934).

Manufacturing provisions of the Copyright Act: 17 U. S. C. Sec. 16.

The Copyright Act, like the patent statute, makes the public benefit the primary consideration, to which the interests of the owner are secondary: U. S. v. Paramount Pictures, 334 U. S. 131, 68 S. Ct. 915, 92 L. Ed. 1260 (1948).

"The primary object of conferring the monopoly lies in the general benefits derived by the public from the labors of others. A copyright, like a patent, is at once the equivalent given by the public for benefits bestowed by the genius and meditations and skill of individuals, and the incentive to further efforts." Fox Film Corp. v. Doyal, 286 U. S. 123 (p. 127-8), 52 S. Ct. 546, 76 L. Ed. 1010 (1932). See also the dictum of Lord Mansfield in 1 East 361n (1801); and R. P. Rejent, "Promoting the Progress of Science and the Useful Arts," 16 Notre Dame Law, 344 (1941).

"As so often happens, the problem is to find a passable compromise between opposing interests, whose relative importance, like that of all social or personal values, is incommensurable." Learned Hand, in U. S. v. Levine, 83 F. 2d 156, 157 (C. C. A. 2d 1936).

On the subject of the balancing of opposing interests in general, see James Willard Hurst, "Law and the Balance of Power," *The Record* of the Association of the Bar of the City of New York, Vol. 6, No. 4, April 1951. Also 52 Yale Law Journal 1 (1942).

"Kant's conception of the legal order," Dean Pound writes, "as a reconciling or harmonizing of wills in action by means of universal rules becomes in the hands of the social utilitarian a compromise or adjustment of advantages, a balance of interests. In the hands of economic realists it becomes a reconciliation or harmonizing of wants—'the satisfaction of every one's wants so far as they are not outweighed by other wants.' In the hands of the positive sociologists it becomes an adjustment of social functions. In the hands of psychological sociologists it becomes a reconciling or harmonizing or adjusting of claims or demands or desires."

In the *Marie Odile* case, Judge Mayer commented on the nine-month delay in the return of the plaintiff's manuscript as a possible cause of the suit; Underhill v. Belasco, 254 Fed. 838, 839 (D. C. N. Y. 1918).

In Ornstein v. Paramount Productions, 9 F. Supp. 896 (D. C. N. Y. 1935), the copyrighted play *Woman,* which Paramount's picture *Blonde Venus* was alleged to infringe, had been submitted to the company in 1931; it had never been returned. It was still in Paramount's possession in 1935, when the suit arose.

As to treatment of authors likely to engender suspicion, see Vernon v. Shubert, 220 Fed. 694, 695 (D. C. N. Y. 1915).

The *White Cargo* case: Simonton v. Gordon, 12 F. 2d 116 (D. C. N. Y. 1925).

The *Letty Lynton* case: Sheldon v. Metro-Goldwyn Pictures Corporation, 81 F. 2d 49 (C. C. A. 2d 1936), rev'g 7 F. Supp. 837 (D. C. N. Y. 1934). Judge Woolsey found no infringement but the decree was reversed, and an injunction and accounting were ordered. Decree on accounting 26 F. Supp. 134 (D. C. N. Y. 1938). Decree modified: 106 F. 2d 45 (C. C. A. 2d 1939), aff'd 309 U. S. 390, 60 S. Ct. 861, 84 L. Ed. 825.

The *Ghost Ship* case: Golding v. RKO Pictures, 35 Cal. 2d 690, 221 P. 2d 95 (1950). Golding and Faulkner wrote a play called *The Man and His Shadow,* dealing with a homicidal captain on a cruise ship. They submitted it to Val Lewton, one of the producers at RKO. Lewton was looking for a story with action on board a ship, in order to utilize an old set. According to Golding, Lewton told him: "I don't have to buy my stories. I don't have to lay out money for originals; I get my idea and I call in a couple of writers on the lot, and I make my stories that way." The play was rejected. Some time later RKO released *Ghost Ship.* It too was laid aboard a vessel and had as its central figure an obsessed captain. A jury gave Golding and Faulkner twenty-five thousand dollars in damages for infringement of their common law copyright.

# Bibliography

As I've indicated in the foreword, this bibliography does not purport to be exhaustive. It does not include all the texts I've consulted, but only those that were found to be either broadly useful or illuminating on some special point. The titles have been grouped under three headings: general books, general periodicals, and legal texts. Legal periodicals are not listed; they may be found in the Notes.

## Books: General

ALTICK, RICHARD D., *The Scholar Adventurers,* New York: The Macmillan Company, 1950.

ALTROCCHI, RUDOLPH, *Sleuthing in the Stacks,* Cambridge, Mass.: Harvard University Press, 1944.

ANDERSON, MAXWELL, *The Essence of Tragedy, and other Footnotes and Papers,* Washington, D.C.: Anderson House, 1939.

BABBITT, IRVING, "Genius and Taste," in *Criticism in America,* ed. by H. L. Mencken, New York: Harcourt, Brace and Company, Inc., 1924.

BABBITT, IRVING, *Literature and the American College,* Boston: Houghton Mifflin Company, 1908.

BARZUN, JACQUES, *Berlioz and the Romantic Century,* Boston: Little, Brown & Company, 1950.

BLOM, ERIC, *Stepchildren of Music,* London: G. T. Fowles & Co., Ltd., 1925.

BOYD, JULIAN P., *The Declaration of Independence,* Princeton: Princeton University Press, 1945.

BRADLEY, A. C., *A Commentary on Tennyson's "In Memoriam,"* New York: The Macmillan Company, 1907.

BREEN, HENRY H., *Modern English Literature, Its Blemishes and Defects,* London: Longman, Brown, Green & Longman, 1857.

BURTON, ROBERT, *Anatomy of Melancholy,* Oxford: Henry Cripps, 1624.

BUTLER, SAMUEL, *Unconscious Memory,* New York: E. P. Dutton & Co., Inc., 1920.

CARPENTER, RHYS, *Folk Tale, Fiction and Saga in the Homeric Epics,* Berkeley: The University of California Press, 1946.

CÉRÈS, HIPPOLYTE, *Un Maître Mal Connu de Provençe,* Paris: Imprimerie Douillard, 1821.

CERF, BENNETT, *Try and Stop Me,* New York: Simon and Schuster, Inc., 1944.

CLARK, ALEXANDER F. B., *Jean Racine,* Cambridge, Mass.: Harvard University Press, 1945.

COLBY, F. M., *Imaginary Obligations,* New York: Dodd, Mead & Company, 1905.

COLBY, F. M., *The Colby Essays,* ed. by Clarence Day, New York: Harper & Brothers, 1926.

COLLINS, JOHN CHURTON, *Illustrations of Tennyson,* London: Chatto & Windus, 1902.

COOK, SIR EDWARD, *More Literary Recreations,* London: Macmillan & Co., Ltd., 1919.

CREIGHTON, THOMAS, *Building for Modern Man,* Princeton: Princeton University Press, 1949.

CROSS, WILBUR L., *The Life and Times of Laurence Sterne,* New York: The Macmillan Company, 1909.

DALTON, JOHN F., *Roman Literary Theory and Criticism,* New York: Longmans, Green & Co., Inc., 1931.

DAVIDSON, ARTHUR F., *Alexandre Dumas, Père,* Philadelphia: J. B. Lippincott Company, 1902.

DAVIES, DR. MAURICE, *Fun, Ancient and Modern,* London: Tinsley Brothers, 1878.

DES HONS, GABRIEL, *Anatole France et Jean Racine,* Paris: A. Colin, 1927.

DICK, ERNST, *Plagiats de Chateaubriand,* Bonn: University of Bonn, 1905.

DOWNEY, JUNE ETTA, *Creative Imagination,* New York: Harcourt, Brace and Company, Inc., 1929.

DRINKWATER, JOHN, *The Muse in Council,* London: Sidgwick & Jackson, Ltd., 1925.

DRYDEN, JOHN, Preface to *An Evening's Love (The Mock Astrologer),* London: William Miller, 1808.

DRYDEN, JOHN, "An Essay of Dramatic Poesy," *Critical Essays and Dramatic Fragments,* ed. by Thomas Seccombe, New York: E. P. Dutton & Co., Inc., 1903.

DUHAMEL, GEORGES, *In Defence of Letters,* London: J. M. Dent & Sons, Ltd., 1930.

DUVEEN, JAMES HENRY, *Art Treasures and Intrigue,* New York: Doubleday & Company, Inc., 1935.

EDWARDS, W. A., *Plagiarism,* Cambridge, England: G. Fraser, 1933.

ELIOT, T. S., "Tradition and the Individual Talent," *Selected Essays, 1917-1932,* New York: Harcourt, Brace and Company, Inc., 1932.

EMERSON, RALPH WALDO, *Quotation and Originality,* Complete Works, Vol. 8, London: George Rutledge & Sons, Ltd., 1883.

EMERSON, RALPH WALDO, *Representative Men,* Boston: Houghton Mifflin Company, 1883.

ERNST, MORRIS L., AND ALEXANDER LINDEY, *The Censor Marches On,* Doubleday & Company, Inc., 1940.

ERSKINE, JOHN, "Originality in Literature," *American Character and other Essays,* Chautauqua: 'The Chautauqua Press, 1927.

FOOTE, ROBERT O., "Who Was Joe Miller?" *A Treasury of Laughter,* ed. by Louis Untermeyer, New York: Simon and Schuster, Inc., 1946.

FORD, FORD MADOX, *The March of Literature,* London: George Allen & Unwin, Ltd., 1931.

FRANCE, ANATOLE, "Apology for Plagiarism," *On Life and Letters,* Fourth Series, trans. by Bernard Miall, London: John Lane, The Bodley Head, Ltd., 1924.

FRANK, JEROME, *Courts on Trial,* Princeton: Princeton University Press, 1949.

GARDINER, A. G., *Many Furrows,* New York: E. P. Dutton & Co., Inc., 1925.

GEROULD, G. H., *The Patterns of English and American Fiction,* Boston: Little, Brown & Company, 1942.

GODLEY, JOHN, *The Master Art Forger,* New York: Wilfred Funk, 1951.

GOTSHAL, S., AND LIEF, A., *Pirates Will Get You,* New York: Columbia University Press, 1945.

GRANDGENT, C. H., *Prunes and Prisms,* Cambridge: Harvard University Press, 1928.

GREENE, THEODORE MEYER, *The Arts and the Art of Criticism,* Princeton: Princeton University Press, 1940.

HAMLIN, A. D. F., *A History of Ornament, Ancient and Medieval,* New York: Appleton-Century-Crofts, Inc., 1916.

HARPER, GEORGE MCLEAN, "The Legend of the Holy Grail," in *Warner's Library of the World's Best Literature,* New York: The International Society, 1897, Vol. 19.

HAZLITT, WILLIAM, *Criticisms on Art,* London: J. Templeman, 1843.

HOLMES, ELIZABETH, *Aspects of Elizabethan Imagery,* Oxford: Basil Blackwell & Mott, 1929.

HOLT, ELIZABETH GILMORE, *Literary Sources of Art History,* Princeton: Princeton University Press, 1947.

HOWELLS, WILLIAM DEAN, *Literature and Life,* New York: Harper & Brothers, 1902.

INGE, W. R., *Labels & Libels,* New York: Harper & Brothers, 1929.

JOHNSON, DR. SAMUEL, *The Rambler* (No. 143), London: Jones & Co., 1825.

JOSEPHSON, MATTHEW, *Zola and His Time,* New York: The Macaulay Company, 1928.

JUDGE, C. B., *Elizabethan Book Pirates,* Cambridge, Mass.: Harvard University Press, 1934.

KEITH, ALEXANDER, *Burns and Folk-Songs,* Aberdeen: D. Wyllie and Son, 1922.

LANG, ANDREW, "Alexandre Dumas, Senior," *Warner's Library of the World's Best Literature,* Vol. 12, New York: The International Society, 1896.

LEAHY, W. H., *How to Protect Business Ideas,* New York: Harper & Brothers, 1936.

LE CORBUSIER, *Towards a New Architecture,* trans. by Frederick Etchells, London: John Rodker, 1927.

LEE, SIR SIDNEY, "The Elizabethan Sonnet," *The Cambridge History of English Literature,* Vol. III, Cambridge: The University Press, 1918.

LEWIS, JOSEPH, *Thomas Paine: Author of the Declaration of Independence,* New York: Freethought Press Association, 1947.

LOWES, JOHN LIVINGSTON, *The Road to Xanadu,* Boston: Houghton Mifflin Company, 1927.

MALEVINSKY, MOSES L., *The Science of Playwriting,* New York: Brentano's, 1925.

MATTHEWS, BRANDER, *Gateways to Literature,* New York: Charles Scribner's Sons, 1912.

MATTHEWS, BRANDER, *Inquiries and Opinions,* New York: Charles Scribner's Sons, 1907.

MATTHEWS, BRANDER, *Pen and Ink,* New York: Charles Scribner's Sons, 1902.

MATTHEWS, BRANDER, *Rip Van Winkle Goes to the Plays,* New York: Charles Scribner's Sons, 1926.

MAUREVERT, GEORGES, *Le Livre des Plagiats,* Paris: Arthème Fayard et Cie., 1923.

MOTT, FRANK LUTHER, *A History of American Magazines,* Cambridge: Harvard University Press, 1939.

MUMFORD, LEWIS, *Architecture*, Chicago: American Library Association, 1926.

NICHOLSON, MARGARET, *A Manual of Copyright Practice*, New York: Oxford University Press, 1945.

NICOLL, ALLARDYCE, *World Drama from Aeschylus to Anouilh*, New York: Harcourt, Brace and Company, Inc., 1950.

NORTHBRIDGE, W. L., *Theories of the Unconscious*, London: Routledge and Kegan Paul, Ltd., 1924.

PAINTER, GEORGE STEPHEN, *Fundamental Psychology*, New York: Liveright Publishing Corp., 1938.

PARROTT, THOMAS MARC, *Shakespearean Comedy*, New York: Oxford University Press, 1949.

PAULL, H. M., *Literary Ethics*, London: T. Thornton Butterworth, Ltd., 1928.

PHILLIPS, WENDELL, "The Lost Arts," *Warner's Library of the World's Best Literature*, Vol. 29, New York: The International Society, 1897.

POE, EDGAR ALLAN, *The Works of E. A. Poe (Marginalia)*, Vol. VI, London: J. Shiels & Co., 1895.

POUND, EZRA, *Make It New*, London: Faber & Faber, Ltd., 1934.

PUTNAM, GEORGE H., *Books and Their Makers during the Middle Ages*, Vol. I, New York: G. P. Putnam's Sons, 1896-1897.

QUILLER-COUCH, SIR ARTHUR, *Adventures in Criticism*, London: Cambridge University Press, 1924.

QUILLER-COUCH, SIR ARTHUR, *Studies in Literature*, Second Series, London: Cambridge University Press, 1923.

RAPP, ALBERT, *The Origins of Wit and Humor*, New York: E. P. Dutton & Co., Inc., 1951.

READ, HERBERT, *Art Now*, London: Faber and Faber, Ltd., 1948.

REES, HELEN EVANGELINE, *The Psychology of Artistic Creation*, New York: Columbia University Press, 1942.

RICHARDS, IVOR A., *Coleridge on Imagination*, New York: Harcourt, Brace and Company, Inc., 1935.

RICHARDSON, EUDORA RAMSAY, "The Ubiquitous Plagiarist," in *Readings in Present Day Writers*, New York: The Macmillan Company, 1933.

SAINTSBURY, GEORGE, "Milton," *The Cambridge History of English Literature*, Vol. VII, Cambridge: The University Press, 1920.

SHAW, BERNARD, *Pen Portraits and Reviews*, Standard Edition of the Works of Bernard Shaw, Vol. 21, Edinburgh: P. & T. Clark, Ltd., 1932.

SHEAVYN, PHOEBE, *The Literary Profession in the Elizabethan Age*, London: Manchester University Press, 1909.

SHERIDAN, RICHARD BRINSLEY, *The Critic*, London: J. M. Dent & Sons, Ltd., 1897.

SHERMAN, STUART PRATT, "Tradition," in *Essays by Present Day Writers*, ed. by R. W. Pence, New York: The Macmillan Company, 1924.

SMITH, LOGAN PEARSALL, *Words and Idioms*, London: Constable & Co., Ltd., 1925.

SPEARMAN, CHARLES EDWARD, *Creative Mind*, New York: Appleton-Century-Crofts, Inc., 1931.

STARRETT, VINCENT, *Books Alive*, New York: Random House, 1940.

TAYLOR, DEEMS, *The Well Tempered Listener*, New York: Simon and Schuster, Inc., 1940.

VAN DOREN, CARL, *Benjamin Franklin*, New York: The Viking Press, Inc., 1938.

VASARI, GIORGIO, *Lives of the Artists*, ed. by Betty Burroughs, New York: Simon and Schuster, Inc., 1946.

VOLTAIRE, FRANÇOIS, "Milton, on the Reproach of Plagiarism Against," in *Philosophical Dictionary*, trans. by H. I. Woolf, New York: Alfred A. Knopf, Inc., 1924.

WALSH, WILLIAM S., *Handy-Book of Literary Curiosities*, Philadelphia: J. B. Lippincott Company, 1925.

WEINSTOCK, HERBERT, *Handel*, New York: Alfred A. Knopf, Inc., 1946.

WENDELL, BARRETT, *The Traditions of European Literature*, New York: Charles Scribner's Sons, 1920.

WHITE, HAROLD OGDEN, *Plagiarism and Imitation during the English Renaissance*, Cambridge, Mass.: Harvard University Press, 1935.

WINTER, WILLIAM, *The Life of David Belasco*, New York: Moffat, Yard and Company, 1918.

WINWAR, FRANCES, *Oscar Wilde and the Yellow Nineties*, New York: Harper & Brothers, 1940.

WITTENBERG, PHILIP, *Protection and Marketing of Literary Property*, Boston: The Writer, Inc., 1937.

WRIGHT, FRANK LLOYD, *Frank Lloyd Wright on Architecture*, ed. by Frederick Gutheim, New York: Duell, Sloane & Pearce, Inc., 1941.

### Periodicals: General

ADAMS, W. H. D., "Imitators and Plagiarists," *Gentlemen's Magazine*, New Series, London, May, 1892.

ADKINS, NELSON F., "Chapter on American Cribbage: Poe and Plagiarism," *The Papers of the Bibliographical Society of America*, Vol. 42, Third Quarter, 1948.

ALLEN, HERVEY, "The Sources of Anthony Adverse," *The Saturday Review of Literature*, January 13, 1934.

ANDERSON, R. G., "Other Men's Thunder," *The Saturday Evening Post*, January 2, 1926.

BAILEY, J. O., "Poe's Stonehenge Drawn from Cyclopedia," *Studies in Philology*, North Carolina University, October, 1941.

BARNES, HOWARD, "The Plagiarism Racket," *Theatre Guild Magazine*, October and November, 1929.

BENSON, E. F., "Plagiarism," *Nineteenth Century*, London, 1899.

CLEATON, I. & A., "Vogue for Vogues," *The Saturday Review of Literature*, March 6, 1937.

COOKE, ALICE LOVELACE, "Some Evidence of Hawthorne's Indebtedness to Swift," Texas University, *Studies in English*, No. 18, 1938.

DEBERDT, RAOUL, "Les Grands Plagiats du Siècle," *La Revue des Revues*, Vol. 88, 1899.

DE QUINCEY, THOMAS, "Samuel Taylor Coleridge," *Tait's Edinburgh Magazine*, Vol. I, New Series, September, 1834.

DE VOTO, BERNARD, "Always Different, Always the Same," *The Saturday Review of Literature*, May 29, 1937.

FELLOWS, OTIS, "Maupassant's Apparition," *The Romanic Review*, Columbia University, February, 1942.

FITZGERALD, ROBERT, "Aeneas and Augustine," *The Nation*, December 11, 1943.

FORD, F., "Bugbear of Plagiarism," *The Writer*, January, 1888.

GILBERT, HENRY F., "Originality," *Musical Quarterly*, January, 1919.

GOSSE, SIR EDMUND, "Plagiarism," *The Living Age*, March 13, 1926.

GRAHAM, JOE, "Plagiaristic Plays," *The Cornhill Magazine*, London, June, 1932.

HADDEN, J. C., "Plagiarism and Coincidence," *The Scottish Review*, Paisley, Scotland, April, 1896.

HARPER, HILDRETH, "A Pageant of Plagiarists," *Book Notes Illustrated*, December, 1923–January, 1924.

HAYS, ARTHUR GARFIELD, "The Plagiarism Plague," *Vanity Fair*, July, 1930.

HAZARD, PAUL, "Les Plagiats de Stendhal," Paris, *Revue des Deux Mondes*, Per. 6, Tome 65, 1921.

HEYLBUT, ROSE, "Pirating Parnassus," *The Etude*, February, 1941.

HOLLIS, D., "In Defense of Plagiarism," *The Spectator*, London, August 20, 1927.

HUDDLESTON, F. J., "A Few Plagiarisms," *Tinsley's Magazine*, London, 1889.

IRELAND, BARON, "Plagiarism," *Harper's Magazine*, February, 1924.

KERNOCHAN, MARSHALL, "Musical Reminiscence-Hunting," *Outlook*, March 11, 1931.

KIDD, H. H., "Is Dickens Still a Hero?" *South Atlantic Quarterly*, July, 1927.

LANG, A., "Plagiarism," *Contemporary Review*, London, June, 1887.

LEVY, NEWMAN, "They've Stolen My Plot!" *The Atlantic Monthly*, July, 1949.

LIPMAN, JEAN, "Print to Primitive," *Antiques*, July, 1946.

McLEAN, CHRISTINE M., "Victor Hugo's Use of Chamberlayne's *L'Etat Present de L'Angleterre* in *L'Homme Qui Rit*," *Modern Language Review*, London, Vol. 8, 1913.

McNAUGHT, W., "On Influence and Borrowing," *The Musical Times*, London, February, 1949.

MEAGHER, MARGARET C., "These Plagiarists!" *The Catholic World*, February, 1938.

MITCHELL, A., "Plagiarism," *The Knickerbocker*, April, 1854.

MIZENER, ARTHUR, "Fitzgerald in the Twenties," *Partisan Review*, January, 1950.

MOORE, OLIN H., "Further Sources of Victor Hugo's *Quatrevingt-Treize*," *Publications of the Modern Language Association of America*, Vol. 41, 1926.

MORLEY, S. GRISWOLD, "Notes on Spanish Sources of Molière," *Publications of the Modern Language Association of America*, Vol. 19, 1904.

NATHAN, GEORGE JEAN, "Twice Told Tales of the Magazines," *The Bookman*, January, 1912.

NETTL, DR. PAUL, "Musical Kleptomaniacs," *The Etude*, February, 1947.

NEWMAN, ERNEST, "On the Alleged Stealing of Great Composers," *The American Mercury*, September, 1932.

NODIER, CHARLES, "Des Artifices Que Certains Auteurs Ont Employée Pour Déguiser Leurs Noms," *Bulletin du Bibliophile et du Bibliothécaire*, Paris, July, 1835.

NYE, IRENE, "Humor Repeats Itself," *The Classical Journal*, University of Chicago, Vol. IX, 1913-1914.

OLIVER, H. J., "The Composition and Revisions of *The Compleat Angler*," *Modern Language Review*, London, July, 1947.

POE, EDGAR ALLAN, "Pinakidia," *Southern Literary Messenger*, Vol. II, August, 1836.

POLLOCK, CHANNING, "The Plagiarism Racket," *The American Mercury*, May, 1945.

ROBINSON, CHARLES, "Plagiarism," *The Writer*, August, 1895.

ROBINSON, HENRY MORTON, AND JOSEPH CAMPBELL, "The Skin of Whose Teeth?" *The Saturday Review of Literature*, December 19, 1942.

SAMUEL, BUNFORD, "Plagiarism, Real and Apparent," *The Bookman*, April, 1909.

SARGENT, REV. R. M., "Plagiarism," *The Congregational Quarterly*, October, 1867.

SCHNEIDER, HANS, "Psychology of Unconscious Plagiarism," *Music Teachers' National Association Proceedings*, Series 17, 1922.

SMITH, HARRISON, "Was Rebecca Plagiarized?" *The Saturday Review of Literature*, November 29, 1941, and February 7, 1948.

SPAETH, SIGMUND, "Dixie, Harlem and Tin Pan Alley," *Scribner's Magazine*, January, 1936.

SPAETH, SIGMUND, "Musical Plagiarism," *Harper's Magazine*, August, 1936.

STEPHENSON, ROBERT C., "The English Sources of Pushkin's Spanish Themes," *Studies in English*, No. 18, University of Texas, 1938.

SULLIVAN, MAURICE S., "The Grand Army of Plagiarists," *The Catholic World*, November, 1923.

THOMPSON, A. C., "Ministerial Plagiarism," *Hartford Seminary Record*, October, 1894.

TOWNE, CHARLES HANSON, "Wanted, A Black List Bureau," *The Bookman*, February, 1907.

TURNER, CLITTENDEN, "Plagiarism and Original Sin," *Arts and Decoration*, February, 1923.

UNSIGNED, "Architectural Piracy," *Architectural Record*, January, 1914.

UNSIGNED, "Biography and Plagiarism," *The Saturday Review of Literature*, January 4, 1936.

UNSIGNED, "Boondoggling in Literature," *The Saturday Review of Literature*, June 20, July 4, and July 25, 1936.

UNSIGNED, "Catching the Plagiarist," *The Publishers' Weekly*, November 6, 1937.

UNSIGNED, "Did Dumas Steal the Three Musketeers?" *The Literary Digest*, January 19, 1929.

UNSIGNED, "Has Plagiarism Become a First Aid to the Artist?" *Current Opinion*, October, 1915.

UNSIGNED, "If Charlie Plagiarized, What Then?" *The Literary Digest*, September 12, 1931.

UNSIGNED, "Literary and Clerical Cutpurses," *The Literary Digest*, July 27, 1929.

UNSIGNED, "Literary and Musical Plagiarism," *The Nation*, November 6, 1902.

UNSIGNED, "Plagiarism," *Leisure Hour*, London, April, 1874.

UNSIGNED, "Plagiarism and John Bunyan," *The Catholic World*, October, 1867.

UNSIGNED, "Plagiarizing One's Own," *The Bookman*, February, 1904.

UNSIGNED, "Second Storey Work or Inspiration," *The Spectator*, London, September 24, 1927.

UNSIGNED, "Self-Plagiarism," *The Atlantic Monthly*, September, 1893.

UNSIGNED, "The Musical Sleuth in Action," *The Literary Digest*, August 25, 1928.

UNSIGNED, "The Plagiarism Racket," *The Nation*, October 23, 1929.

UNSIGNED, "The Rights of Plagiarism," *The New Statesman*, London, April 17, 1920.

VALENTINER, R. W., "Leonardo as Verocchio's Co-worker," *The Art Bulletin*, Vol. XII, No. 1 (1930).

VON STERNBERG, CONSTANTIN, "On Plagiarism," *Musical Quarterly*, Vol. V, July, 1919.

WATT, HOMER A., "Plagiarism in College Texts," *Educational Review*, September, 1921.

WEBER, C. J., "Plagiarism and Thomas Hardy," *The Colophon*, New Series, No. 3, 1937.

WILSON, EDMUND, "Poe as a Literary Critic," *The Nation*, October 31, 1942.

WILSON, EDMUND, "Dr. Johnson," *The New Yorker*, November 18, 1944.

WOLSELEY, R. E., "Who Wrote That?" *The Etude*, October, 1940.

WRIGHT, EDWARD, "The Art of Plagiarism," *Contemporary Review*, London, April, 1904.

ZABEL, MORTON DAUWEN, "Dickens: The Reputation Revised," *The Nation*, September 17, 1949.

## Books: Legal

AMDUR, L. H., *Copyright Law and Practice*, New York: Clark Boardman Company, Ltd., 1936.

AMERICAN SOCIETY OF COMPOSERS, AUTHORS AND PUBLISHERS, *Second Copyright Law Symposium*, New York: The Society, 1940.

AMERICAN SOCIETY OF COMPOSERS, AUTHORS AND PUBLISHERS, *Third Copyright Law Symposium*, New York: The Society, 1940.

BALL, HORACE G., *Law of Copyright and Literary Property*, New York and Albany: Banks and Company, Matthew Bender and Company, 1944.

CALLMANN, R., *Law of Unfair Competition and Trade Marks*, Chicago: Callaghan & Co., Inc., 1945.

COPINGER, W. A., *Law of Copyright in Works of Literature, Art, Architecture, Photography, Music and the Drama*, London: Sweet & Maxwell, Ltd., 1936.

DERENBERG, W. J., *Trade Mark Protection and Unfair Trading*, New York and Albany: Matthew Bender and Company, 1936.

DE WOLF, R. C., *An Outline of Copyright Law*, Boston: John W. Luce Company, 1925.

DRONE, EATON S., *A Treatise on the Law of Property in Intellectual Productions in Great Britain and the United States*, Boston: Little, Brown & Company, 1879.

HOWELL, HERBERT A., *The Copyright Law*, Washington: The Bureau of National Affairs, Inc., 1948.

LADAS, S. P., *International Protection of Literary and Artistic Property*, New York: The Macmillan Company, 1938.

RUSSELL-CLARKE, A. D., *Copyright in Industrial Designs*, New York: Pitman Publishing Corp., 1930.

SHAFTER, ALFRED M., *Musical Copyright*, Chicago: Callaghan and Company, 1939.

SHAW, RALPH R., *Literary Property in the United States*, Scarecrow Press, 1950.

For comprehensive bibliography of books and magazine articles dealing with copyright matters, see Henriette Mertz, *Copyright Bibliography*, Washington, Copyright Office, Library of Congress, 1950.

# Index